INVADING THE PRIVATE

To our colleague who will be sadly missed

Wanda Kerver-Poldervaart

Invading the Private

State accountability and new investigative methods in Europe

Edited by
STEWART FIELD
CAROLINE PELSER

Ashgate

Dartmouth

Aldershot • Brookfield USA • Singapore • Sydney

Published by
Ashgate Publishing Ltd
Gower House
Croft Road
Aldershot
Hants GU11 3HR
England

Ashgate Publishing Company
Old Post Road
Brookfield
Vermont 05036
USA

British Library Cataloguing in Publication Data
Invading the private : state accountability and new
   investigative methods in Europe
   1.Police - Methodology - Europe 2.Criminal investigation -
   Methodology - Europe
   I. Field, Stewart II.Pelser, Caroline
   363.2'52'094

Library of Congress Cataloging-in-Publication Data
Invading the private : state accountability and new investigative
   methods in Europe / edited by Stewart Field, Caroline Pelser.
         p.   cm.
      ISBN 1-85521-942-5 (hardcover)
         1. Undercover operations--Europe, Western. 2. Electronic
surveillance--Europe, Western. 3. Criminal investigation--Europe.
Western. I. Field, Stewart. II. Pelser, Caroline.
HV8080.U5.I58 1998   98-34290
363.25'2--dc21   CIP

ISBN 1 85521 942 5

Printed and bound by Athenaeum Press, Ltd.,
Gateshead, Tyne & Wear.

The editors would like to thank Wieneke Matthijsse for her work in making the text camera-ready

Contents

List of contributors   ix

1   Introduction
    Stewart Field and Caroline Pelser   1

Part I
The new intelligence gathering: covert and proactive policing

2   The criminal informant: police management, supervision
    and control
    Steven Greer and Nigel South   31

3   Police surveillance and its regulation in England and Wales
    Timothy John and Mike Maguire   47

4   The legal framework of covert and proactive policing in France
    Stewart Field   67

5   Proactive policing in France
    Claude Journès   83

6   Special police methods of investigation: new legislation
    in the Netherlands
    Theo de Roos   95

7   Proactive investigation: a Belgian perspective
    Cyrille Fijnaut and Frank Verbruggen   111

8   Intelligence services and undercover operations:
    the case of Euromac
    Nikos Passas and Jack A. Blum   143

Part II
The new information gathering: some new sources

9   Sun Tzu goes electronic. The changing nature of proactive
    methods in (criminal) intelligence
    Bob Hoogenboom   163

10 Data bases – positive policing or civil liberties nightmare?
    Fiona Donson   181

11 Financial investigation and privacy in Britain and the Netherlands
    Roan Lamp, Michael Levi and Wanda Kerver-Poldervaart   197

12 Police intelligence gathering and access to journalists' materials
    Chrisje Brants   221

13 Journalists and the protection of sources of information
    in the Netherlands
    Chrisje Brants   225

14 Journalistic material in the UK criminal process
    Ruth Costigan   239

15 The privilege against self-incrimination in proactive policing
    Peter Alldridge and Bert Swart   253

Part III
Accountability and control: some potential strategies

16 Controlling cross border undercover operations
    Jack A. Blum and Nikos Passas   275

17 Proactive policing: limiting the role of the defence lawyer
    Ed Cape and Taru Spronken   291

18 Judicial regulation of covert and proactive policing in
    the Netherlands and England and Wales
    Stewart Field and Nico Jörg   323

19 Proactive policing and the principles of immediacy and orality
    John R. Spencer   353

20 Invading the private? Towards conclusions
    Stewart Field   371

List of contributors

PETER ALLDRIDGE, LL.B. (London) (1978), LL.M. (Wales) (1985) is Senior Lecturer at Cardiff Law School. He publishes in the areas of criminal law, criminal justice, computers and law and evidence.

JACK A. BLUM is a graduate of Bard College (B.A. 1962), and the Columbia University Law School (J.D. 1965). He is a partner in the Washington DC law firm of Lobel, Novins & Lamont, a member of the adjunct faculty of George Mason University and a senior editor of the journal Crime, Law & Social Change. He works on problems of financial fraud, tax evasion and international criminal law.

CHRISJE BRANTS is Professor of Criminal Law and Criminal Procedure at the Willem Pompe Institute, University of Utrecht. She first trained and worked as a journalist, before studying law and criminology at the University of Amsterdam and obtaining a doctorate there in 1990 with a study of the social construction of fraud in the Netherlands. Her main fields of interest are criminal law and the media, criminal policy, comparative criminal law and procedure and the influence of the European Union on national systems of criminal law.

ED CAPE is an experienced criminal solicitor and Principal Lecturer in Law at the University of the West of England, Bristol. He has written regularly both for the profession and academic press on issues relating to criminal law, evidence and procedure, and is the author of *Defending Suspects at Police Stations*. In addition to presenting courses for practitioners in the area of criminal litigation, he is currently conducting research on criminal lawyers and legal aid, and on victims of crime.

RUTH COSTIGAN, Lecturer in Law at the University of Wales Swansea since 1993, has taught at the University of Glamorgan, Cardiff Law School and Queen's University Belfast. She has published in the areas of law and sexuality, prisons and press freedom. Current research projects concern the use of journalists' material in the criminal process, photographic and video evidence and the law and sexuality.

FIONA DONSON is Lecturer in Law at Cardiff Law School at the University of Wales, Cardiff. In 1997 she received her doctorate from King's College, London with research into the use of public law as a method of participation in environmentally sensitive decision-making. Her main research interests include civil liberties in the UK, public law, strategic litigation by, and against, protesters and environmental law and protest.

STEWART FIELD studied law at Oxford and Criminology at Cambridge. His doctoral thesis, on the history of the Factory Inspectorate, was researched while a student at the Centre for Socio-Legal Studies (1981-4). A lecturer at Cardiff Law School since 1984, his research interests are in criminal justice process, regulatory crime and criminal law.

CYRILLE FIJNAUT studied in the sixties and seventies at the Dutch Police Academy and the Catholic University of Leuven (degrees in criminology and philosophy). Currently he is Professor of Criminology and Criminal Law at the Catholic University of Leuven and the Erasmus University Rotterdam, and visiting Professor of Law at the New York University School of Law. His main research is related to organized crime, comparative criminal procedure, international policing and general criminology.

STEVEN GREER, B.A. (Oxon), M.Sc., Ph.D. is Reader in Law at the University of Bristol. He has written extensively in the fields of criminal justice and human rights. His most recent book, *Supergrasses*, came runner up in the 1996 Socio-Legal Book prize.

BOB HOOGENBOOM has published on the history of policing, organized crime, white collar crime, private policing, industrial espionage, regulatory bodies and financial integrity. For eight years he was a lecturer of the Dutch Police Academy. He has worked for the Home Office, the Ministry of Justice, Leyden University and the Erasmus University Rotterdam. Dr Hoogenboom is employed by Moret, Ernst & Young in the Caribbean and works in the field of forensic accounting.

TIMOTHY JOHN is a lecturer in the Institute of Police and Criminological Studies at the University of Portsmouth. He has collaborated with Mike Maguire on research into aspects of proactive policing for the Police Research Group. He is currently examining the continued development of the use of these techniques and of the means by which they are regulated.

NICO JÖRG has been Advocate-General at the Supreme Court of the Netherlands since 1 February 1998. He studied law at Groningen University (1968); Ph.D. in 1979. He was formerly a lecturer and senior lecturer in criminal law and criminal procedure at the University of Utrecht (1969-1993) and visiting scholar at Yale Law School (1983/4) and Berkeley School of Law (1987). Since 1993 he has been a full time judge and since 1996 a vice-president of the Court of Appeals, Arnhem.

CLAUDE JOURNÈS studied law, history and political science at the University of Lyon where he received his doctorate for a thesis on Marxism in Britain (1975). He has been a Professor since 1996. His major book deals with the British state. He specializes in policing in western democracies and the connection between literature and law.

WANDA KERVER-POLDERVAART first worked in insurance before studying law at the University of Utrecht (1992) and becoming a lecturer at the Willem Pompe Institute, University of Utrecht. She also taught courses for practitioners in the area of criminal litigation in cooperation with the Dutch Bar Association. Her main fields of interest were economic law, financial fraud, tax evasion and environmental law. Sadly, Wanda Kerver passed away in the spring of 1997.

ROAN LAMP studied political science at the University of California at Davis and received a bachelor's degree from that university in 1990. From 1990 to 1995 he studied law at the University of Utrecht. Currently he is a doctoral candidate at the Willem Pompe Institute, University of Utrecht and is working on a thesis on the international confiscation of proceeds of crime and the struggle against money laundering.

MICHAEL LEVI is Professor of Criminology at the University of Wales, Cardiff. Among other specialist interests such as violent crime, he has written several books on fraud, the impact of money-laundering reporting and proceeds of crime investigation and confiscation. He is currently editing a special issue of the Howard Journal of Criminal Justice on organized crime. He has recently been appointed as 'scientific expert' to a Council of Europe initiative on organized crime.

MIKE MAGUIRE is Professor of Criminology and Criminal Justice at the University of Wales, Cardiff. He has conducted research and published in a variety of fields, including policing, prisons, parole, victims, burglary, street crime and criminal statistics. He is co-editor of the influential *Oxford Handbook of Criminology* (Oxford University Press 1994 and 1997). He has particular interest in proactive crime investigation, having undertaken a major study of its organization and effectiveness (*Intelligence, Surveillance, Informants: Integrated Approaches*, Home Office, 1995, with Timothy John) and having written on several aspects of its regulation. He was also a member of a JUSTICE working group on this topic.

NIKOS PASSAS (LL.B. Univ. of Athens; M.A.-Criminology, Univ. of Paris-II; Ph.D., Univ. of Edinburgh) is Associate Professor at Temple University, Philadelphia. He teaches theories of crime, international criminal law, white-collar and organized crime, and cross-border crime. His research focuses on international misconduct and its control. His books include *Organized Crime* and *The Future of Anomie Theory*. He is series editor at Northeastern University Press for books on transnational crime.

CAROLINE PELSER studied law at Leyden University (1989). In 1995 she received her doctorate from Leyden University with a study on the underlying decision-making structure of the final judgement in criminal cases, in particular the issue of categorization and the requirements which the court must meet in complying with the law's demands for a reasoned decision. Since 1994 she has been a lecturer at the Willem Pompe Institute, University of Utrecht. She publishes in the areas of criminal law and procedure.

THEO DE ROOS studied law at the Free University of Amsterdam (1972). He worked in legal teaching and legal aid up to 1975. Since 1977 he has been a lawyer in Amsterdam, specializing in criminal law. From 1980 to 1984 he was a research assistant at the Willem Pompe Institute, University of Utrecht. In 1987 he received his doctorate from Utrecht University (Penalization of Economic Offences: a study on Criminal Policy). From 1990 to 1997 he was part time Professor of Criminal Law at Maastricht University. Since September 1997 he has been full time Professor of Criminal law at Leyden University. His main research topics are the rights of the accused and defence lawyers in criminal cases, ethics and codes of conduct for (defence) lawyers and environmental criminal law.

NIGEL SOUTH is Reader in Sociology and a member of the Management Committee of the Human Rights Centre at the University of Essex, Colchester, England. He has previously published on several aspects of policing, including the history and use of informants. Recent books include: V. Ruggiero, N. South and I. Taylor (eds.), *European Criminology: Crime and Social Order in Europe* (Routledge, 1998); and R. Weiss and N. South (eds.), *Comparing Prison Systems* (Gordon and Breach, 1998).

JOHN R. SPENCER read law at Selwyn College, Cambridge from 1965-1969, and then made his career in the Law Faculty, being appointed a Professor there in 1995. His main area of interest is criminal procedure and evidence. Within this area he has written extensively on children's evidence, and more recently on comparative criminal procedure.

TARU SPRONKEN studied law at the University of Utrecht. She graduated in 1979 and became an advocate and defence counsel in private practice in Maastricht. Since 1987 she has been a lecturer in criminal law and criminal procedure at the University of Maastricht and defence counsel at the Advocatenpraktijk Universiteit Maastricht. She is also a teacher for the Dutch Bar Association and member of its Advisory Board on Criminal Justice and the Dutch Association of Defence Counsel. She has published on anonymous testimony, proactive policing and the position of defence counsel and is writing a thesis on the role and professional responsibility of the defence counsel in the Netherlands.

BERT SWART studied law at the Universities of Nijmegen and Poitiers. He was a Research Associate and then Associate Professor at the University of Amsterdam. From 1980 to 1996 he was Professor of Criminal Law and Criminal Procedure at the University of Utrecht. He is now a member of the Amsterdam Court of Appeal and holds the Van Hamel Chair of International Criminal Law at the University of Amsterdam. He has published extensively on the international and European aspects of criminal law and procedure.

FRANK VERBRUGGEN obtained his law degree from the Catholic University of Leuven (1992), where he became an associate at the Institute of Criminal Law. He spent a year at Yale Law School (1994) studying federalism and criminal and international law. Currently he is researching the difficulties of translating criminal policy targeting organized crime and terrorism into legal doctrine. His publications focus on international and Belgian criminal law, with a particular interest in the role of the police. He also works for the Parliamentary Committee of Inquiry on Organized Crime in Belgium.

1 Introduction

STEWART FIELD AND CAROLINE PELSER

Introduction

In this book we seek to examine a range of policing techniques which are new, if not in their conception, then at least in their importance to the form of police inquiries in the late 20th century. Some of them are beginning to be discussed under the categories of 'proactive' or 'covert' policing; others are termed 'technological' because they depend intimately on the development of the new information technologies. To indicate what is at stake, we start with a story from the Netherlands which, despite its obviously dramatic ingredients – secrecy, deceit, organized crime and policing – remains little known in the United Kingdom. It concerns what became known as the 'IRT' affair: its relevance to any consideration of new policing techniques in Europe will become obvious.

Scandal in the Netherlands: the 'IRT' affair

On 7 December 1993 the Chief Commissioner of Police, the Chief Public Prosecutor and the Mayor of Amsterdam announced the disbanding of the Interregional Police Team Noord-Holland/Utrecht (IRT). The three officials refused to take responsibility for the apparent use of certain methods of investigation by the special task force (which was composed of both Amsterdam and Utrecht police officers and was targeting organized crime). The press-release that was issued remained silent as to the methods supposedly used and didn't specify which investigation was concerned. However, it was to lead to the resignation of two Cabinet Ministers in 1994, and to a full-blown parliamentary inquiry in 1995 into all investigative methods adopted by the police in its battle against organized crime in the previous decade.

1

The members of Parliament concluded that Dutch criminal investigation was confronted by a threefold crisis: it was not regulated, it was not controlled and it was badly organized.

The establishment of the IRT

The stage for disaster was set in 1987, when a specialist police agency (the Central Criminal Information Office, CRI) found that no less than 200 criminal organizations operated on Dutch territory.[1] The Cabinet decided that the different police forces in the Netherlands had to join forces. Inter-regional police teams were supposed to become operational in all juris-dictions. The IRT Noord-Holland/Utrecht nevertheless remained a pioneer. Although interregional, the supervision of the team was in the hands of the Utrecht police.

The team's strategy was to operate proactively. No longer were com-mitted offences the objective of the criminal investigation; rather the team targeted criminal organizations. The IRT necessarily relied heavily upon intelligence work and special methods of investigation which were dubious and sometimes new (at least new on such a scale). Nonetheless, organiz-ational problems prevented the IRT Noord-Holland/Utrecht from becoming successful. An ecstasy gang was rounded up, but any regular police force could have accomplished this (Middelburg and Van Es 1994, p. 50). Its most important target, 'mafia leader' Klaas Bruinsma (alias The Reverend), was liquidated in June 1991. It has been suggested that his death came as a salvation for the team, which had still not succeeded in penetrating Bruinsma's organization after two and a half years (Middelburg and Van Es 1994, p. 24; Haenen and Meeuws 1996, p. 31). After Bruinsma's untimely death, police attention shifted to his former underboss Urka. This inves-tigation, *Operation Delta*[2], eventually led to the dismantling of the IRT, rather than the dismantling of its target, the Delta organization.

Operation Delta

A reconstruction of the IRT scandal is an arduous task, not least because, during the affair, false information was deliberately given out to check whether the Amsterdam police force was corrupt, as the Chief Commissioner of the Utrecht police suspected. An investigation by the *Rijksrecherche*[3] found no proof of corruption. It did find unwillingness to cooperate, rivalry and disputes about competency between the Amsterdam and the Utrecht police forces.

Clashes about its supervision and strategy had plagued the IRT from the start and led to malfunctioning. In order to work as efficiently as possible and to prevent leaks to the outside world and the underworld, utmost secrecy was observed (the team adhered to the need to know principle). Within the Amsterdam police force this attitude led to dissatisfaction and irritation about the close internal solidarity of the team. In Utrecht, on the other hand, the team was shown off and seen as a source of prestige. The team's much too complicated organizational structure, with its obscure communication lines within the team and with the responsible Chief Public Prosecutor, added to an unpleasant atmosphere. Were these organizational problems the reason for the disbanding of the IRT?

According to the so-called Wieringa commission they were. This commission of wise men had been set up by the Minister of Justice to deal with the storm of protest in Parliament following the announcement by the three Amsterdam officials that the team had been disbanded. The Wieringa commission was asked to examine the origin and the daily functioning of the IRT and to assess the grounds on which it was decided to disband the IRT and the consequences of this decision. It concluded that the IRT's disbanding had been incorrect and totally unnecessary. The disputed special methods of investigation had been a project of infiltration employed 'in a well-considered and careful way' (Commissie-Wieringa 1994). Yet, the commission failed to explain why this was so and what precisely had been done. The details about the investigative operation were classed as top secret and were only set out in a confidential addendum to the report, the so-called *red book*, which was made available only to the Ministers of Justice and Internal Affairs. The Wieringa commission was of the opinion that the methods of investigation could not have been the reason for the disbanding of the IRT. Rather, the commission spoke highly of an innovative and successful team. Tensions within the Public Prosecution Service and the Amsterdam police force were identified as the true reason. The Wieringa commission went so far as to blame Amsterdam officials for disbanding the IRT in such a thoughtless way, frustrating an important investigation and endangering lives of informers and policemen.

The belief that the special methods of investigation were 'well-considered', was immediately debated in the learned journals. De Roos (1994), for example, criticized the report in *Nederlands Juristenblad* for being one-sided, incomplete and unfair. How could a team be using investigative tools in a well-considered and careful way if it was operating in a power vacuum as the Wieringa commission had found? To experiment with special methods of investigation that are on the very edge of permissibility in such a situation is risky, to say the least. Indeed, when details about the controversial methods of investigation became clear, the conclusions of the Wieringa commission were shown as inadequate.

The Cabinet did not endorse the conclusions of the Wieringa commission and brushed the report aside. It supported the police force and the judicial authorities in Amsterdam, with good reason, for shortly after the publication of the Wieringa report, more information became public about the special methods of investigation used by the police. On 25 March 1994 *NRC Handelsblad* revealed the existence of so-called 'looking-in' operations (*inkijkoperaties*). This is a euphemism for burglaries by policemen in houses, sheds and companies of possible suspects of serious offences. These burglaries, which are not reported in the written file, serve to establish whether an official search will be worthwhile. The method is clearly illegal. Shortly after, *Het Parool* (30 March 1994) published details about the so-called Delta-method: a police informer was allowed by officials of the Public Prosecution Service to import, over a one year period, more than 40,000 kilograms of hashish. What's more, this infiltrator was actually persuaded by the police to move over from trafficking hash to importing cocaine. Preparations were made to import into the Netherlands 2000 kilograms of cocaine. In this way the infiltrator was supposed to win the trust of the infiltrated group. The criminal profits of the infiltrator, which were substantial, were furthermore not handed over to the judicial authorities.

The Dutch Opium Act distinguishes between soft drugs (i.e. drugs with 'acceptable risks' such as marihuana, cannabis, hashish) and hard drugs (i.e. drugs with 'unacceptable risks' such as heroin, cocaine, LSD, amphetamines). As a result of a historic compromise between proponents of legalization and governments fearful of international disapproval of legalization, the sanctions imposed on possession, trade, cultivation, importation and exportation of soft drugs are relatively mild (Silvis 1994, pp. 44-46; Silvis and Williams 1995, pp. 151-152). The Delta organization exclusively traded soft drugs. Since it was the IRT's objective to round up the complete organization and to take its leaders out of circulation, it was plain that the organization had to commit more serious offences: they needed to be trafficking hard drugs. The infiltrator had to induce the bosses to move over from hashish to cocaine.

Following this stream of details about the IRT's methods of investigation, there were parliamentary debates on 7 April and 25 May 1994. Following a motion prohibiting the Ministers of Justice and Internal Affairs from themselves engaging in organized crime, both Ministers resigned.

Parliamentary inquiry

During the so-called IRT-debate on 7 April 1994 Parliament decided that it needed to know which methods of investigation were used in the Netherlands with regard to organized crime, who was controlling who and finally, whether these methods were acceptable in a constitutional state.[4] The Parliament decided to start a parliamentary investigation on the methods used by the IRT, most importantly so-called deep infiltration.[5] A preliminary parliamentary working group presented a report on 21 October 1994: 'Investigation wanted' (*Opsporing gezocht*). It recommended a full parliamentary inquiry into the methods of investigation used by the police and the judicial authorities. The primary target of the parliamentary inquiry was to be the regulation of the methods used by police and judicial authorities, in the proactive as well as in the reactive phase. The working group believed that a gap in statute law had to be closed. The Parliamentary Committee of Inquiry on methods of investigation used by the police and judicial authorities, under the chairmanship of Labour MP, the late Maarten van Traa, was set up on 6 December 1994.

During the parliamentary inquiry the extent to which the government had lost their grip on police investigations became painfully clear. The IRT and the Criminal Intelligence Unit of Kennemerland appeared to be involved in importing or transporting drugs, infiltrators were allowed to keep their criminal profits and an informer became a millionaire thanks to the financing of the Ministry of Justice. In February 1996 the Parliamentary Committee of Inquiry presented its final report *Inzake Opsporing* ('Concerning Investigation'), in which it concluded that three crises dominated Dutch criminal investigation: its regulation, its organization and its control. Based on this report a Bill was introduced into Parliament in June 1997.[6]

Scandal in the United Kingdom: the Colin Stagg affair and others

In the United Kingdom the most publicised instance of covert policing in recent years led to a very much more ambivalent reaction. In 1992 Rachel Nickell was murdered on Wimbledon Common in London. The circumstances – she was stabbed repeatedly and sexually assaulted and was found with her two year old son clinging to her body and covered in her blood – were horrific in the extreme. Media and public alarm made the investigation front page news. A man named Colin Stagg (Harding 1997; Ames 1994; Doherty 1994) was targeted for largely circumstantial reasons. His home was nearby, he had no alibi, he showed physical similarities to somebody seen near the scene, he had a previous conviction for indecent exposure and he fitted the character profile of the killer drawn up by a psychologist. A female undercover officer befriended him and sent him a series of letters including episodes of sexual fantasy as she tried to persuade him to confess. She suggested that she would like him to have been the killer; Stagg said later he went along with her because he thought he might thereby obtain sexual favours. He repeatedly denied involvement in the murder to the undercover officer but the police alleged that certain comments made to her demonstrated a knowledge of the circumstances of the killing that went beyond what had been released to the press.

In 1993 the trial judge ruled Stagg's alleged comments inadmissible, condemning the use of a policewoman as 'bait' and calling the undercover operation 'deception of the grossest kind'. But the subsequent media debate has shown great ambivalence: while the operation drew a great deal of condemnation from legal groups, some sections of the tabloid press – notably the *Mail on Sunday* – apparently encouraged by nods and winks from police contacts (Harding 1997), ran the story in terms of a guilty man acquitted on a technicality and released 'evidence' not heard at trial that allegedly implicated Stagg. Thus, while in some quarters the episode indicated the need for greater control over covert operations by the police, for others the episode demonstrated excessive legal control over effective pursuit of the truth. Not surprisingly, in a climate in which both major parties were seeking to outdo each other in sometimes simple-minded crime control rhetoric, no parliamentary or judicial inquiry followed and the general terms of covert policing were not put in question.

But gradually other stories on covert policing methods have begun to emerge in the British media. The use of informers, their incitement of offences, and the price paid in human and monetary terms for their services; that dangerous combination, rivalry between policing organizations and secrecy with its concomitant: the cock-up; the belatedly charged debate over surveillance powers in the Police Act 1997: in varying ways a basis is developing for a more balanced appraisal than was evident in the initial press enthusiasm for a policing 'fix' that was apparently new, dramatic and glossed with high-tech glamour. In recent years major drugs cases have been compromised by police and Customs attempts to turn some of those involved into informants and their subsequent attempts to conceal this. It appears that officers may have been aware of threats made by other criminals to their would-be informer to pressure him to participate but had done nothing to reveal this to the authorities (Rose 1997a). Stories have emerged of payments made to Brazilian drug barons to act as informants for Customs (Rose 1997b). There is evidence that organized crime figures from the Jamaican 'Yardies' have been allowed to remain illegally in Britain in order to persuade them to act as informants. They have gone on to commit serious criminal offences, including rape, murder and robbery (Davies 1997). Drug dealers have claimed an 'umbrella of protection' because they operate as informants (Connett 1997). In addition there has been the more familiar scandal of undercover operatives investigating football violence 'improving' evidence by falsely registering it as recorded much closer to events than was actually the case. When these cases come to light there is always the suspicion that similar practices may be going on with greater subtlety or precision and not being discovered (Armstrong and Hobbs 1995, pp. 181-182).

But only in 1997, in rather precise political circumstances, did the issues raised by police covert surveillance begin to become front-page worries. The then Conservative Government in 1996 introduced a Bill giving the police powers to enter covertly and plant electronic surveillance devices on any kind of premises – subject only to prior authorization by a senior police officer. It had became apparent that this was a widespread practice which had no lawful basis in that entry under such circumstances involved at least a civil trespass and very likely criminal damage. The lack of a statutory basis attracted adverse comment from the Law Lords in *R v Khan*,[7] from the judge charged with monitoring surveillance by MI5 under the Security Service Act (Norton-Taylor 1995; Ford 1996), and a challenge before the European Court of Human Rights seemed inevitable.[8] The Government's attempt in the Police Bill[9] to legalize the practice without any mechanism for prior judicial authorization seemed at first likely to succeed: only the small Liberal Democrat group in the House of Commons was arguing for prior approval by a circuit judge. But there followed a belated revival of what the social historian E.P. Thompson once described as the 'very ancient cultural tradition in Britain of bloody-mindedness towards the intrusion of authority' (Thompson 1980, p. 178). An unlikely alliance developed of liberal forces with right-wing newspapers such as the *Daily Mail, Daily Telegraph, The Times*, and *The Economist*, along with senior Conservative Peers, Law Lords, the Lord Chief Justice and lawyers' organizations.[10] Yet what was striking was the tardiness with which the issue was taken up on the left of the political mainstream, especially by the Labour Party: a critique of crime control measures based on the constitutional need to control intrusive state powers seems to have been perceived as politically dangerous (for comment see Young 1997). After a damaging defeat in the Lords the Government worked out a compromise with the then Labour Shadow Home

Secretary. It involved requiring permission for bugging to be given by 'surveillance commissioners' for operations involving entry into or inter-ference with premises without the consent of the occupier.[11] These commis-sioners[12] will have to approve the surveillance after initial authorization by the Chief Constable unless the case is urgent.[13] Thus at least some signs of concern over state accountability surfaced.

A further bringing of issues to public attention has been the debate over the Security Services. This seems likely to have far-reaching implications in expanding use of proactive methods (*The Guardian*, 26 March 1995). In March 1993, the then Home Secretary Kenneth Clarke said that MI5 would probably never become involved in work against 'drug trafficking or organ-ized crime' as such activities were 'most unlikely' to constitute a threat to national security. Two years later, it became apparent that MI5 was engaged in policing work and the new Home Secretary declared that the police and MI5 should be seen as 'complementary and ... operating in a broadly similar field.' It became apparent that MI6 cooperates with the Metropolitan Police, the National Criminal Intelligence Service (NCIS), MI5, HM Customs and the Immigration Department. The Security Services Act 1996 however gave MI5 an overt role in the policing of 'serious crime', prompting both a little anxiety about the compatibility of their methods with traditional notions of criminal process, and a certain excitement about elite 'spooks' chasing serious criminals.[14]

Definitions of covert, proactive policing

All these aspects of recent actuality relate to techniques of policing that may variously be termed covert, proactive, 'intelligence-led'[15] or technological policing.[16] These new forms of investigation are not easy to define because they involve a number of interrelated concepts which may nevertheless be analytically differentiated. As yet, there is no apparent agreement amongst researchers as to terminology. We start by considering the concepts of 'proactive' and 'covert' policing.

The development which these terms seek to capture is a trend that can be seen through much of Western Europe (and indeed North America), in which, rather than starting inquiries into specific offences after they have been committed, police forces begin to target particular 'known' offenders expected to commit future crimes (hence 'proactive' policing). Information-gathering techniques – such as the use of informers, undercover police operations and electronic surveillance – are then used which have as their common denominator secrecy (hence 'covert' policing). The object of investigation is usually unaware of its existence. Partly a response to developing concern over drugs, terrorism and organized crime more generally, proactive and covert policing is nevertheless an increasingly common practice for addressing other serious offences as diverse as commercial fraud and burglary.

Thus 'covert' policing denotes a range of investigation techniques which embrace:

a. Observation and surveillance either directly (by tailing or the use of observation posts) or through electronic means (including bugging and interception of communications);
b. Police infiltration of criminal gangs/networks by use of
   (i) informers,
   (ii) undercover police officers;[17]
c. Other kinds of undercover work, such as
   (i) controlled delivery of illegal goods and services,
   (ii) front store operations.

What unites these methods is their covert nature: investigation proceeds often before the target is aware of its existence. This means that they are almost exclusively used prior to arrest. After arrest the defendant sees them coming.

In terms of criminal procedure, 'proactive' refers to the opposite of reactive. The police do not react to the offence being committed but anticipate this by targeting likely prospects. Thus proactive policing is the gathering of information about individuals, groups and the links between them, usually by the secret methods outlined above, not just before arrest, but before a criminal offence has occurred or at least before a reasonable suspicion against the target has arisen.[18]

The distinction between covert and genuinely proactive policing is important because where the investigation is covert *and* proactive in the sense that the offence has not yet occurred, the evidence that the prosecution will seek to advance will be largely the evidence accumulated at the time of the offence because the police will be waiting for the defendant. Usually this results in such probative evidence that the police do not want to use the evidence actually generated during the proactive investigating. However the secret methods associated with proactive investigation may well be employed to investigate crimes already committed – investigations that are technically reactive. But where the investigation is covert but subsequent to the offence the police may want to actually use the evidence generated during the secret investigation (as in the Colin Stagg affair).

In this book we will also consider other important developments in policing techniques that go beyond the covert and/or proactive: these are broader policing developments that represent a step away from traditional reactive policing but bear an uncertain relationship to covert or proactive policing in the two senses outlined above. In different ways, these have the potential to penetrate the private sphere just as much as the stereotypical undercover police 'sting'operation. On the one hand they simply exploit new capacities generated by broader technological and social change: the development of the 'information society' or the 'surveillance society'. Examples include the rise of closed circuit television and developing technologies for storing and accessing data (which lead to police computerized data bases of fingerprint, DNA or general intelligence systems). Alongside this, there is the growth of new powers to demand information about citizens within but also outside the conventional criminal justice system (including information originally obtained by the state for purposes other than criminal investigation and information obtained by private institutions). This reflects changes in the way the 'crime problem' has been socially constructed and the perceived need to penetrate private spheres (private organizations like crime syndicates or quasi-legitimate businesses or the family itself). Increasingly powers exist to demand financial records and other information from banks and other financial institutions about apparently routine transactions which may conceal illegality or traces of illegality: the classic example is the new legislation in Europe imposing a duty on banks to report unusual transactions. New powers in Britain also permit the police to seek information and photographs from journalists and information from newspapers without the suspect becoming aware that they are under investigation and that information is being demanded. Furthermore, increasingly citizens may be required to provide ultimately incriminating information (whether samples or financial records) before they attain the status (and protection) of the 'suspect'.

We do not seek to bring all these policing techniques together because they are all necessarily covert or proactive. True, they may sometimes be 'covert' in the sense that the target may not be aware of them – which makes possible their proactive use, thus enabling effective penetration of private spheres. But one is perhaps stretching the meaning of 'covert' too much to use it for routine scanning of data bases or financial records. Furthermore, sometimes the information gathered will be used proactively, perhaps to develop and define targets, but in large part the information will be used in a reactive context: an offence is committed and the police will search intelligence data bases for similar descriptions or modes of operation or matching prints/samples; an offence is committed and is revealed to the police as a result of the monitoring by financial institutions. There is a proactive element: the police develop the data bases and financial institutions set in place the routine information-gathering systems before the relevant offence has been committed. In England and Wales DNA samples are not primarily taken to investigate the offence for which the person has already been arrested – he or she may have made a full confession leading to other overwhelming evidence. The objective is to develop a data base to aid the investigation of future (unconnected) offences. However the proactive acts are not *investigative* in the sense that a particular investigation has been started targeting a particular potential offender or offending group (as will often be the case with surveillance on organized crime). Such acts are analogous to the general cultivation of informers or setting up of front store operations: they prepare for subsequent criminal acts by unknown persons. If one tries to force all these developments under the description proactive one risks developing a term so broad as to be unhelpful: proactive might then embrace traditional non-committed patrolling of the streets or the creation of neighbourhood watch schemes or any kind of preparatory activity (setting up forensic labs for example). This may be proactive policing but it is not proactive *investigation*. Proactive and covert investigation (in the two narrower senses above) is best viewed as merely a sub-category of a broader trend toward new techniques for extracting information from private spheres. What all these developing police techniques have in common is that they raise questions about privacy and the possibility of holding a criminal investigation accountable though the traditional processes of criminal procedure (the intervention of defence lawyer, judge, the questioning of witnesses).

An addendum on purpose

A further characteristic commonly found, especially in Dutch proactive policing, is that the purpose of investigation is not to prosecute particular individuals but to disrupt criminal networks and organizations and deter crime.[19] This has been much less apparent in the United Kingdom, where proactive methods are still regarded primarily as a means of evidence-gathering preparatory to criminal prosecutions. This is even true of the use of sophisticated proactive methods against drug-related crime. Only in relation to football hooliganism, where tactics have included deep-cover infiltration, the 'turning' of informers and international cooperation, have some steps been made beyond that. An element of the strategy has been deterrence and disruption: not just prosecutions but also measures such as refusing passes and passports to known agitators and passing on information to police forces abroad.

This question of purpose should not then be seen as a defining – because necessary – feature of covert or proactive policing: it may be better seen as a related development which brings the potential of such policing into sharper focus. In particular it draws in the problem of intelligence services work in the crime domain in that they have traditionally conducted covert operations without any thoughts of prosecution.

Some recent context: the 'rise' of covert and proactive policing

Proactive and/or covert policing cannot be described as a new phenomenon in Europe. However, both the extent of its use and the social construction of the crime problem against which it has been targeted have been highly variable between jurisdictions and over time. Nadelmann has argued that the use of covert means in a criminal context (as opposed to the political) has been more characteristic of Germany, Austria, the Netherlands and Belgium and that there has been greater cultural resistance in Italy, France and Spain. He links this to cultural differences in Mediterranean and North European states and differences in the perceived seriousness of drugs problems (Nadelmann 1995, pp. 272, 280 *et seq*).[20] Of the French policing system, Fijnaut and Marx argue that undercover policing – far from being marginal – has been from the beginning an essential feature. It has also had a particular focus: the combatting of political dissidence and subversion (Fijnaut and Marx 1995, p. 2). Under French influence undercover policing became an accepted police strategy in several Northern European countries. The 19th century German states used covert and proactive policing in both political and criminal contexts (Fijnaut and Marx 1995, pp. 6-7). In Belgium the influence of French models meant that such techniques were used more in the field of 'political' policing than in that of 'ordinary' crime. Undercover work was not much used in the latter context before the late 1960s. By then it was American concerns that shaped the agenda: the Drugs Enforcement Agency (DEA) with its technical support and training was vital to the importation of undercover methods to be used against drugs and organized crime (Van Outrive and Cappelle 1995, p. 141).[21] In the Netherlands DEA influence seems to have even more profoundly shaped policing strategy in the 1970s – something to which we will return. In the next section we chart in detail the very different social conditions and definitions of the crime problem that prompted the rise of proactive and covert methods in two of the countries examined in this book: Britain and the Netherlands.[22]

The rise of proactive and covert policing in Britain

In Britain, traditional attitudes towards covert policing have to be understood in the light of political and ideological controversies surrounding the introduction in the middle-third of the 19th century, of a more organized state policing in the face of extensive middle-class and working-class opposition. The early police forces had to be presented as a uniformed presence exactly to make them politically acceptable to those opposed to Continental 'spy systems'.[23] Admittedly some forms of covert work went on: paid informers were the prime investigative and enforcement technique in Britain even prior to the development of an organized police force (Greer 1995, pp. 13-15). Furthermore, after its development, surveillance work and even some undercover work went on (Fijnaut and Marx 1995, pp. 8-9). But cultural and political sensibilities about policing seem to have led to historically less use in Britain of 'covert' methods against crime than either on the Continent or in the US.[24] The detective branch in the 19th century was small and low-key and expected to avoid a number of practices necessary to covert policing (Armstrong and Hobbs 1995, p. 178).

These long established traditions of cultural hostility to certain forms of policing penetration of private spheres seem to have been rather rapidly abandoned in the mid 1980s. After the use of covert and proactive policing against the apparently dramatic threat posed by football hooliganism in that decade, by the early 1990s street crime and (to a lesser extent) the potential threat of organized crime became the next targets. From 1992 the law and order temperature was especially high. Michael Howard – with political ambitions of his own and an openly populist style – became Home Secretary in 1993, the same year as the furore caused by the murder of 2 year-old Jamie Bulger by two pre-teenage boys. Tony Blair had become Home Secretary in 1992 and Leader of the Opposition in 1993 and with him arrived 'New Labour' with its absolute conviction that a tough crime stance was vital to win the next election. Sensitivities about civil liberties and state accountability were politically less potent than sometimes over-dramatized crime threats.[25] Along with this came a cooler relationship between Conservative Government and senior police officers as demands on the latter to demonstrate efficiency by hitting performance-related targets grew in the wake of the Sheehy report. Not surprisingly scepticism about the potential of covert and proactive policing was little in evidence.

For years proactive investigation had been the guiding principle behind certain specialist squads (in particular Drugs Squads and Regional Crime Squads). The predominant targets were drugs and, to a lesser extent, armed robbery.[26] Only in 1985 was football hooliganism added as a further major target (Armstrong and Hobbs 1995). Noticeably the National Football Intelligence Unit, charged with national and international coordination of intelligence dates only from 1990. It was in the 1990s that renewed emphasis on 'getting tough on crime' (defined in 'traditional' terms) and Government concerns about efficient use of policing resources and police desire to demonstrate efficiency, prompted an important policy shift towards proactive targeting of prolific street offenders. The officially endorsed argument was that small numbers of offenders committed a high proportion of offences and that selective targeting made proactive methods both viable and necessary.[27] The Audit Commission (1993) urged police to 'target the criminal not the crime'.[28]

Another potent factor in the rise of new policing methods was police anxiety about the requirements of the 1984 Police and Criminal Evidence Act (PACE) and its Codes of Practice which made it more difficult to assert prolonged psychological pressure on suspects to confess. Accumulating evidence before arrest removes some of the pressure of time-limits and to a certain extent neutralizes some of the obstacles to obtaining confession evidence. Another factor may be the profound shift in criminological assumptions charted in a recent article by David Garland. He has argued that, amongst a range of attempts to redefine success and failure, the police are now holding out low expectations that they can control what they refer to as 'random' or 'opportunist' crime. Instead their self-legitimation is founded on an ability to deal with serious crime and in apprehending serious criminals (Garland 1996, p. 458). Further, Armstrong and Hobbs have suggested that the expansion to the policing of football hooliganism in the mid-80s was not happenstance. It was a relatively non-contentious target which, by enabling the media to present undercover police as unambiguous heroes in the war against crime, may have played a part in legitimizing similar practices in other areas (Armstrong and Hobbs 1995, pp. 190-191).

Proactive methods have since been widely used as an evidence-gathering preliminary to strategies of high-profile, mass, coordinated dawn arrests and criminal prosecutions for burglary and car-crime. The most high-profile activities have been Operations Bumblebee, Gemini and Eagle-Eye. 'Operation Bumblebee' in London used some limited undercover operations in setting up fake 'fencing' stores, but mainly involved informers and surveil-lance to target known burglars: the Metropolitan Police Commissioner said that as burglary was a priority for policing in London, it was logical to use the same technical resources against it as were used against other priorities such as terrorism and armed crime' (Condon 1994). 'Operation Gemini' in Gloucestershire, has directed similar methods at both burglary and car-related crime.[29] Operation Eagle Eye' has used enhanced intelligence, closed circuit television, other surveillance techniques and information from the public in an operation against street robbery.[30]

Alongside this there has been the development of official police and Government concern over organized crime. This was late emerging (at least by Dutch standards)[31] and remains relatively low-key. It was not until the beginning of 1995 that a House of Commons Select Committee on Home Affairs decided to examine organized crime as a serious problem, in the context of regular policing and crime control.[32] The comparatively tardy emergence of concern is reflected in relatively slow moves to develop a specialised police service to deal with organized crime. The National Crime Intelligence Service (NCIS) coordinating separate police units dealing with such matters as football hooliganism, drugs and international crime, was not set up until 1993 and suffered from a lack of resources, an uneasy relation-ship with local forces and regional crime squads, and squabbles about whether it should have an operational arm (*The Guardian*, 26 March 1995, p. 6). However, the Police Act 1997 puts NCIS on a statutory footing and introduces for the first time a National Crime Squad with a remit 'to prevent and detect serious crime of relevance to more than one police area in England and Wales'.[33] This seems likely to reinforce the tendency towards the new methods.

Underlying realities

That is the 'headline' impact of proactive policing. But work by Maguire and John in 1994-1995 suggested that, outside these much publicised examples, much proactive policing was still at developmental stage in local CID units (Maguire and John 1995). For many forces, especially in medium-sized towns, proactivity was the coming thing rather than something that had actually arrived. For the most part identifying suspects was still performed by traditional means: identification by victims or witnesses at the scene, catching offenders 'in the act' or through 'secondary' clear-ups. Maguire and John analysed 832 cases in detail in a particular sub-division that had produced 321 detected suspects. Officers in the cases estimated surveillance as a key factor in only 3 per cent, crime intelligence in 1 per cent and informers in 7 per cent. Proactive or covert techniques had been used in under 15 per cent of cases and regarded as useful in under 4 per cent. CID cases and the more serious offences showed a somewhat different profile but even so, of 150 CID cases detected, officers saw proactive methods as a key factor in detection in only twelve. Nevertheless, around 60 per cent of police forces already had at least one full-time specialist mobile surveillance team. Specialist proactive squads were developed in the 1980s in local CID desks – usually burglary squads or force drugs squads. The difficulties of integrating these experiments organizationally had led some forces to experiment more radically with predominantly proactive use of CID time. Such developments, as yet relatively unchallenged, may well change the nature and purpose of proactive policing in Britain and trigger a move towards the sort of situation that already existed in the Netherlands by the 1980s and early 1990s.

The rise of proactive and covert policing in the Netherlands[34]

Dutch recent history of proactive policing is more substantial, stretches back to the 1970s and has a rather different social focus. Since the 1990s organized crime has been central to Dutch official debate rather than opportunist street crime. This changes both the details of policing methods and the nature of problems of accountability. Proactive policing developed in the 1970s as a response to drugs offences and it became increasingly clear that the use of undercover agents, informers and surveillance teams had become an integral part of Dutch police work. This was recognized in the setting up of a separate national Criminal Intelligence Department (CID) at the end of the decade. Twenty years later the fear was of sophisticated organizations reaching across crime definitions, involved in traditional 'mafia' type work (drugs, gambling, prostitution enforced by violence) but also environmental crime (such as highly lucrative trade in illegal waste dumping) and white-collar crime (fraud, corruption, money-laundering). In 1991 a survey of all the regional CIDs produced a police estimate of 599 criminal groups connected to serious or organized crime with 10 per cent being assessed as 'highly organized' (Klerks 1995, pp. 135-136). Initial 1970s style strategies – the use of surveillance and informers to facilitate arrest and conviction first of individual suppliers but then organizers of the drug trade – gave way in the 1990s to tactics of disruption of criminal networks and organizations in which prosecution often played a marginal role. Intelligence gathering became part of a strategy of state disinformation and disruption. By the beginning of the 1990s, bugging, the use of long distance microphones and homing devices, so-called 'looking-in operations',[35] deals with criminal informers, and active participation in criminal activities after infiltration (usually controlled delivery) were all in widespread use in police investigations. The full consequences of this only became clear with the discovery of the prevalence of illegal 'looking in' operations and the shift from controlled delivery to permitting large-scale release of drugs into the marketplace itself in order to cement the status and reputation of an informer within an organization. The IRT scandal was also partly sparked off by a case where the team concerned had deliberately withheld information about the investigation from defence, prosecution and court. It became evident that the police had somehow been allowed to get 'out of control'.

On the one hand, at the level of social ideology, one might not have expected the Netherlands to be a country where obsessions with crime fighting might be allowed to get out of hand and undermine systems of police accountability. A semi-institutionalized politics of accommodation and a restrained media tradition – product of the absence of a tabloid press comparable to that of the United Kingdom – seems to produce lower levels of public anxiety about street crime. The rapid extension of covert and proactive policing may thus reflect the logic of Garland's argument on the criminology of adapting to high crime levels (Garland 1996). Given that there has been greater stress on living with ordinary street crime in the Netherlands, the need may have been all the greater – for legitimizing purposes – demonstrably to deal with 'new or 'exceptional' forms of crime – and indeed to exaggerate the significance of these targets. Certainly it was concern at a political level over new forms of crime, especially fraud and organized crime, that seems to have been the backdrop to the polices breaking free of supervisory mechanisms. Another historical and cultural element may have been the strong public confidence in the police (and one might add the monitoring role of the Dutch public prosecutor)[36] because, until recently, there had been an absence of public scandal. This may have produced complacency amongst judges to accepting of police assurances and practices.

One might add to this the key influence of the DEA from the 1970s onwards, in the context of American definition of the Netherlands as the key European point of drugs distribution.[37]

The book: structure and themes

The emergence of these tactics in Britain and the Netherlands and the scandals that have resulted are the backdrop to this book.[38] It represents an attempt to address these developments with a focus on their implications for state accountability, particularly through the traditional mechanisms of criminal procedure. Some of the chapters in the book are directly comparative contributions in which Dutch and British authors have come together to produce joint papers on particular questions. Other chapters provide the resources for further comparative work, deepening our knowledge of the practice of the new policing methods in particular countries and the mechanisms of accountability that regulate them. These are based on experience in England and Wales, the Netherlands, Belgium, France and the United States. The preponderance of British/Dutch comparative work is largely the product of the fact that the book emerges out of a long-term research link between the law departments of the University of Wales at Cardiff and Aberystwyth on the one hand, and the University of Utrecht's Willem Pompe Institute for Criminal Law and Criminology, on the other.[39] But this is not an inappropriate choice given British initial but now abandoned reluctance to use such methods against conventional crime and Fijnaut and Marx's comment 'the new surveillance seems to have been taken further [in the Netherlands] than in the rest of Europe' (Fijnaut and Marx 1995, p. 19).

The other countries are also well-chosen for contrasts and significance. France has perhaps the longest tradition of covert political policing. The United States has played a prime role in the 'reintroduction' of such methods into Europe in the second half of the 20th century (Fijnaut and Marx 1995, ch. 1). Belgium (because of its size and position) and the USA have especially rich experience of cross-border policing and the latter's experience of cross-jurisdictional work within its federal structure reinforces this. A projected chapter on Germany did not materialize, which is less unfortunate than it would otherwise have been, because there are now three significant recent papers in English which discuss the situation there. Busch and Funk (1995) have outlined the development of proactive policing from 70s onwards in Germany, with increasing sophistication in its direction at organized crime. Gropp (1993) and Joubert (1994) give extensive accounts of important new legislation in Germany placing such methods on a detailed statutory footing. We did not attempt to broaden the scope of the book to southern Europe: cultural assumptions about such policing seem very different to attitudes in Northern Europe and North America and we sacrificed diversity in comparison for depth.

The focus of the book is essentially complementary to that of Fijnaut and Marx. They direct attention more to the sociology of policing and the general question of the societal effects and causes of the emergence of 'surveillance societies'.[40] Written predominantly by lawyers or those based in Law Schools, this book is directed at more concrete issues of accountability (often directly or indirectly legal). Though this is not treated as purely a question of criminal process the key question posed revolves around the problems provoked for traditional notions of accountability within policing and criminal justice.

The issues here can be simply stated in outline. It has long been a truism of criminal justice research in jurisdictions within both adversarial and inquisitorial traditions that what happens at trial – what witnesses are called, what questions are posed, what forensic evidence is presented – is substantially determined by pre-trial decisions, especially those made during the police investigation.[41] Given the lower visibility of these decisions, each procedural tradition has developed means which are supposed to ensure that the evidence produced at trial will enable legal truth to be found by procedural means considered fair by prevailing social standards.[42] For the adversarial tradition this is the autonomous responsibility of the defence – under presumed conditions of rough equality of bargaining power – to seek out and present evidence which supports its contentions. For the inquisitorial tradition it is the monitoring and supervising of the investigation by prosecuting and examining magistrates. Their professional responsibility – as members of the magistracy – is to ensure that both inculpatory and exculpatory evidence is investigated and presented in the official dossier which will be the starting point for decision-making at trial.

The timing and secrecy of covert and/or proactive policing has profound implications for both these traditional mechanisms for checking and rendering the police investigation accountable at trial. The timing of proactive investigation is important because it worsens a problem traditional to defence participation in reactive investigations, namely that they arrive too late on the scene. Rights of access to legal advice accrue at best on arrest, and in many countries within the inquisitorial tradition, only after 24 or 48 hours.[43] If most of the investigation has by then been completed defence capacity to participate is inevitably limited. The best that one can then do is to assert a right to information about the case (what Brants and Field (1995a) describe as the key defence participation right: the right to know). From this effective rights to assert one's case and challenge adverse decisions may flow. The problem then is that the covert nature of the policing may mean not just that defence access to information about the policing methods is postponed. The police usually argue that the needs of covert operations demand that the defence should *never* be given the identity, for example, of those who have informed or the location of surveillance posts or told how undercover operations were conducted. Thus the timing and secrecy necessary to such investigations render problematic the exercise of defence rights to participate in the pre-trial and trial process. This in turn has profound implications for the equality of bargaining power that is the basis of adversarial claims to find truth and to fairness of procedure. Less obviously it may threaten judicial monitoring and supervising systems within the inquisitorial tradition: overloaded prosecutors and examining magistrates find it hard to look below the surface of apparently straightforward dossiers without the promptings of defence intervention. Without knowledge of the police investigation the defence participation in this process becomes problematic.[44] This may be less important if judges or prosecutors know what is going on but the evidence is that sometimes the police do not think they need to know (and the judges and prosecutors themselves sometimes do not appear to want to know).

The other challenge to criminal process discussed in this book is more broadly from the diverse range of new information gathering techniques. Some simply involve derogations from traditional notions of due process such as the privilege against self-incrimination; others involve challenges to rights of privacy or freedom of expression. There are expanded technological mechanisms for accumulating and sorting information gathered outside the criminal process and that information is increasingly made available later to the criminal justice authorities. Thus information is gathered at a moment when the suspect is not yet suspect and thus has none of the protections that go along with that status. The penetration of private domains in pursuit of new crime targets (commercial fraud, organized crime) seems to prompt these measures to sidestep traditional criminal process protections.

The book is divided into three parts. The first 'the new intelligence gathering: covert and proactive policing' outlines covert and proactive policing practice in England and Wales (Greer and South, John and Maguire), France (Field and Journès), the Netherlands (De Roos), Belgium (Fijnaut and Verbruggen) and the United States (Passas and Blum). They consider the 'stereotypical' covert and proactive techniques such as surveillance (both physical and electronic), undercover operations and the use of informers, examining existing legal and administrative constraints and the challenges that such policing represents to them. The second part 'the new information gathering: some new sources' broadens the scope beyond these various stereotypical types of secretive detective work to other methods.

Much 'penetration' of the private world may simply involve the bringing together of diverse elements of intelligence so as to 'know' a life in a way that may constitute an invasion of the private. Hoogenboom, in a chapter on the possibilities that the new information technology is opening up with sophisticated electronic and open-source[45] intelligence systems, stresses that, once one starts to talk data bases, one of the key resources is this ability to reanalyse openly available information and, by making new connections, transform its significance. As Donson asks in relation to state data bases: what happens to the information, who has access to it and for what purpose? Are the controls real? How easy are 'leaks'? The need for external accountability, external auditing by other organizations, and a sceptical culture to animate internal regulation seem essential.

In some respects this kind of work is an extension of some forms of journalism and hence twinned chapters are presented by Brants and Costigan on the way that policing in the Netherlands and Britain can simply follow the tracks of investigative and photo journalism. Their chapters examine the different legal powers that exist in the two countries to force journalists to give up materials and their increasing use by the police. They contrast the thinking about human rights such as freedom of expression in the two countries: the Netherlands, with the European Convention on Human Rights directly applicable is more explicit in its reasoning. Whether its solutions protect journalists more or less effectively is less clear from the chapters.

These new powers to compel journalists to produce information can also be regarded as one example of a more general trend to new policing powers which compel cooperation from citizens and private agencies. Lamp, Levi and Kerver compare Dutch and British rules compelling banks to disclose unusual transactions which may represent money-laundering and their attempts to reconcile this with rights to privacy. Again Dutch concern for dealing explicitly with the rights concerned is evident; though again the results are quite similar (because the policy imperatives are the same).

Another step towards 'cooperation' involves the compelling of *suspects* to give up materials or information (whether inside or outside the criminal justice system) that may subsequently be used in evidence against them. This is the erosion of the privilege against self-incrimination which has been such a marked trend in the 1980s and which is discussed by Alldridge and Swart. In some ways we are then a long way away from covert or proactive policing. The privilege against self-incrimination inevitably starts to bite where proactive policing ends: it is something one asserts against somebody who is (and is known to be) acting on behalf of the state. But the erosion of the privilege stems from similar concerns about the failure of traditional methods in areas of crime perceived as particularly problematic (in terms of the difficulties of penetrating into private domains) and which have been defined as new crime threats. This is seen to justify a form of 'inquisitorial procedure' conferring on state officials greater powers than elsewhere to require answers and to reach into private spheres, to limit suspect's control over their body, bank accounts and business affairs.

Hoogenboom's chapter also broadens the discussion on intelligence-gathering in another direction by introducing the 'cross-over effect' by which techniques developed by defence ministries and business corporations can be later exploited by law enforcement agencies. The transfer of techniques and procedures initially used in terrorist contexts has been well documented (Hillyard 1987). But cross-over from intelligence work is perhaps even more problematic: here the aims of national defence are exactly to sidestep the mechanisms of accountability developed by another state. This poses questions of accountability for the future that are even more intractable than those posed by (almost traditional by comparison) national covert and proactive investigation by the conventional police. Passas and Blum address this theme, arguing that the aims and methods of intelligence services and law enforcement agencies are simply incompatible: principles of legality and state accountability are simply laid aside in the latter and the two must be kept separate. This is an argument all the more germane in Britain given the role given to MI5 by the Security Services Act 1996 to investigate 'serious crime'.

Passas and Blum illustrate another key issue by their discussion of the Euromac/Operation Quarry affair: the possible effects of spectacular lack of accountability and competence in selecting targets in undercover operations. Like other authors they question the 'rationality' of the process and the selection of investigative methods, stressing the dangers of what are in effect mechanisms of social discrimination. Such techniques become even more elusive when applied domestically against private individuals whose capacity to develop private intelligence services are normally quite limited.

Part 3 – Accountability and control: some potential strategies – starts to try to analyse possible responses. The four chapters interrogate four points of traditional control over the techniques discussed in Parts 2 and 3: the defence lawyer, the judge, the trial and the nation-state. To take the last first, Blum and Passas pick up on the difficulties posed by cross-border operations discussed by Fijnaut and Verbruggen in Part 1 when discussing the experience of Belgium. Contrasting evidential and substantive criteria for intervention and competing political and agency priorities create a need for coordination and cooperation between agencies that is even more pronounced than in covert policing within national boundaries. But this in turn poses problems because the structures of accountability that have been created have typically been built around the nation-state. To step clear of the borders as limitations to operations is to step clear of the regulatory framework. Facing this problem they call for an international tribunal to provide both control and coordination.

Cape and Spronken, examining the situation in England and Wales and the Netherlands, outline the difficulties posed for defence lawyers in their attempts to participate meaningfully in debates about guilt and innocence. They see defence lawyers as very often left in the dark by the concealment of the detail of such operations. Field and Jörg consider the way in which these limits to defence participation might be compensated for by a more active pre-trial role for judges in those two respective countries. This is a trend that can be seen in the Netherlands as a response to the IRT scandal and which might develop in England and Wales if some serious institutional obstructions could be overcome. Spencer looks at the implications for the principles of orality and immediacy in trial procedure of an acceptance of the needs of covert and proactive policing.

Notes

1 That is 200 organizations met one or more of the applied criteria. The figure was to rise spectacularly in the following year. Professional criminologists nevertheless found that the figures were little more than a hoax.
2 This triangular character was chosen because the syndicate was supposed to be leaded by a strong triumvirate.
3 I.e. an independent agency which, by order of the Public Prosecution Service, is responsible for the investigation of (probable) crimes committed by public officers.
4 TK 1994-1995, 23 945, nr. 2, p. 3.
5 Motion Dijkstal, Kohnstamm and Brouwer, TK 1993-1994, 23 593, nr. 9; TK 1994-1995, 23 945, nr. 2, p. 7.
6 TK 1996-1997, 25 403, nrs. 1-3. See De Roos in this volume.
7 [1996] 3 WLR 162.
8 See now *Govell v UK*, European Commission.
9 Announced July 1996: Campbell, 1996.
10 See editorial, *The Guardian* 17 and 21 January, and also Wadham and Colvin 1997 and Travis 1997a.
11 There is also special protection in respect of lawyers, doctors, journalists and others who hold confidential records.

12 They are to be current or retired High Court judges. There will be one chief commissioner and five or six others: Travis 1997b.

13 For detailed consideration see John and Maguire in this volume.

14 Contrast M. Evans, Elite MI5 'watchers' would be used in supporting role, *The Times*, 6 June 1996 with his 'Spies in quandary over legal niceties', *The Times*, same date, Gibb 1996 and Norton-Taylor and Davies 1996.

15 The term used at a recent conference: see *New Law Journal News* (1997) 147 (6789), pp. 591, 609.

16 Fijnaut and Marx (1995, p. 1) have talked about the 'increased salience of covert and technological policing'.

17 In either case they will often be participating to some degree in the criminal activity.

18 An example of the genuinely proactive operation is the practice of parking expensive cars with quality sound systems and mobile phones on seats in high car crime areas while the vehicle is kept under video surveillance and officers are hidden nearby. This represents covert and proactive policing but hardly qualifies as 'intelligence-led' (Baily 1995).

19 Busch and Funk (1995, p. 63) note the same preoccupation in Germany on targeting networks not individual crimes.

20 For some suggestive rather than extensively documented ideas on the way national differences may be ascribed in part to different traditions of citizen/state relations see also Marx 1995, p. 326.

21 For American influence see generally Nadelmann 1995, pp. 280 and passim.

22 Here we build on the analysis of Brants and Field 1995a.

23 On fear of French republican influence see Armstrong and Hobbs 1995, pp. 177-178.

24 Marx 1995, p. 325. In the political sphere one must remember the 19th century use of the Special Branch against Irish nationalists.

25 For a detailed and sober assessment of the key period after the arrival of Michael Howard at the Home Office in 1993, see Lord Windlesham 1996, especially Part II.

26 Nine Regional Crime Squads were created in 1965. Now around 1200 detectives work within them targeting serious criminal offences that transcend force boundaries. On the use of covert policing against drugs see Dorn, Murji and South 1992.

27 According to the Home Office 7 per cent males convicted of six or more offences account for 65 per cent of recorded offences (Home Office 1991).

28 Audit Commission 1993.

29 *The Guardian*, 30 July 1995; for an assessment of these and one other such initiative see Stockdale and Gresham 1995.

30 *The Guardian*, 30 July 1995; for an assessment of these and one other such initiative see Stockdale and Gresham 1995.

31 See below.

32 Even then the Committee concluded that the problem was not as acute as in the rest of Europe – though they saw several potential sources of expansion, especially through connections with East/Central Europe (House of Commons Select Committee on Home Affairs 1995).

33 Police Act 1997, Parts 1 and 2.

34 This section draws on Brants and Field 1995a.

35 Entering premises without a warrant in order to obtain information on the presence of possibly incriminating evidence in anticipation of a legal search and seizure operation later.

36 On this see Brants and Field 1995b and Field, Alldridge and Jörg 1995.

37 For discussion of DEA encouragement, training and provision of equipment for the Dutch police to develop infiltration techniques see Klerks 1995, p. 116 and Nadelmann 1995.

38 And one could cite scandals in Sweden, France, Belgium, the United States or Mexico. See Fijnaut and Marx 1995, p. 25 for discussion of high-ranking Swedish police accused of illegal listening and planting of bugs and of leading Belgian figures in covert policing being arrested on corruption charges (at p. 20). Special covert policing sections in the Belgian Gendarmerie have been disbanded for concealing information from the Public Prosecutor. See Van Outrive and Cappelle 1995, p. 150. For United States and France see contributions by Passas and Blum and Field in this volume.

39 Fennell et al. 1995, and Harding and Swart 1996 are two previous volumes that have come out of this relationship.

40 For an interesting review of possible explanations see Marx 1995, pp. 323-4.

41 Amongst a host of possible references, we mention one relating to criminal process in England and Wales, and one concerning the Netherlands: McConville, Sanders and Leng 1991 and Wagenaar, Van Koppen and Crombag 1993.

42 On the centrality of these two goals see Jörg, Field and Brants 1995 and Brants and Field 1995a.

43 For an overview of such rules in Europe see Van den Wyngaert 1993.

44 For a stress on the importance of defence prompting in Dutch pre-trial criminal process, see Field, Alldridge and Jörg 1995.

45 I.e. sources that are publicly available.

References

Ames, J. (1994), Nickel case acquittal 'good news for justice', 91 (34) *Law Society Gazette* 4.

Armstrong, G. and D. Hobbs (1995), High Tackles and Professional Fouls: The Policing of Soccer Hooliganism, in: C. Fijnaut and G.T. Marx (eds.), *Under-*

cover: Police Surveillance in Comparative Perspective, The Hague: Kluwer, pp. 175-193.

Audit Commission (1993), *Tackling Crime Effectively,* London: Audit Commission.

Baily, E. (1995), Police are baiting cars with stereos and mobile phones to trap thieves, *Daily Telegraph* 18 February.

Brants, C. and S. Field (1995a), *Participation Rights and Proactive Policing: Convergence and Drift in European Criminal Process*, Deventer: Kluwer.

Brants, C. and S. Field (1995b), Discretion and Accountability in Prosecution: A Comparative Perspective on Keeping Crime out of Court, in: P. Fennell, C. Harding, N. Jörg and B. Swart (eds.), *Criminal Justice in Europe*, Oxford: Clarendon Press, pp. 127-148.

Busch, H. and A. Funk (1995), Undercover Tactics as an Element of Preventive Crime Fighting in the Federal Republic of Germany, in: C. Fijnaut and G.T. Marx (eds.), *Undercover: Police Surveillance in Comparative Perspective*, The Hague: Kluwer, pp. 55-69.

Campbell, D. (1996), Howard sets statutory code for police bugs, *The Guardian*, 3 July.

Commissie-Wieringa (1994), *Rapport van de bijzondere onderzoekscommissie IRT*, 's-Gravenhage: Ministerie van Binnenlandse Zaken.

Condon, Sir Paul, *The Guardian*, 17 June 1994.

Connett, D. (1997), Tactics under fire as police use more informants, *The Observer* 30 March.

Davies, N. (1997), Police Yardie scandal, and, Second Front: How the Yardies duped the Yard, *The Guardian,* 3 February.

Doherty, M. (1994), Watching the Detectives, 144 (6670) *New Law Journal* 1525-6.

Dorn, N., K. Murji and N. South (1992), *Traffickers: Drug Markets and Law Enforcement*, London: Routledge.

Field, S., P. Alldridge and N. Jörg (1995), Prosecutors, Examining Judges and Control of Police Investigations, in: P. Fennell, C. Harding, N. Jörg and B. Swart (eds.), *Criminal Justice in Europe*, Oxford: Clarendon Press, pp. 227-249.

Fijnaut, C. and G.T. Marx (1995), The Normalization of Undercover Policing in the West: Historical and Contemporary Perspectives, in: C. Fijnaut and G.T. Marx (eds.), *Undercover: Police Surveillance in Comparative Perspective,* The Hague: Kluwer, pp. 1-27.

Ford, R. (1996), Judge backs bugging of criminals' homes, *The Times* 7 June.

Garland, D. (1996), The Limits of the Sovereign State – Strategies of Crime Control in Contemporary Society, 36 (1) *British Journal of Criminology* 445.

Gibb, F. (1996), MI5's police role could undermine open justice, *The Times* 7 May.

Greer, S. (1995), *Supergrasses, A Study in Anti-Terrorist Law Enforcement in Northern Ireland*, Oxford: Clarendon Press.

Gropp, W. (1993), Special Methods of Investigation for Combatting Organized Crime, 1 *European Journal of Crime, Criminal Law and Criminal Justice*, pp. 20-36.

Haenen, M., T.-J. Meeuws (1996), *Het IRT moeras; Grote ego's en hun vuile oorlog*, Amsterdam: Uitgeverij Balans.

Harding, C. and B. Swart (eds.) (1996), *Enforcing European Community Rules*, Aldershot: Dartmouth.

Harding, L. (1997), Stagg at bay, *The Guardian*, 15 January.

Hillyard, P. (1987), The Normalization of Special Powers: from Northern Ireland to Britain, in: P. Scraton (ed.), *Law, Order and the Authoritarian State*, Milton Keynes: Open University Press.

Home Office (1991), *Digest of Information on Criminal Justice System*, London: Home Office.

House of Commons Select Committee on Home Affairs (1995), *House of Commons papers session 1994-5, 3rd report: organised crime, volume 1*, London: HMSO.

Inzake opsporing (1996), Enquêtecommissie opsporingsmethoden, 's-Gravenhage: Sdu Uitgevers.

Jörg, N., S. Field and C. Brants (1995), Are Inquisitorial and Adversarial Systems Converging, in: P. Fennell, C. Harding, N. Jörg and B. Swart (eds.), *Criminal Justice in Europe*, Oxford: Clarendon Press, pp. 41-56.

Joubert, C. (1994), Undercover Policing – A Comparative Study, 2 *European Journal of Crime, Criminal Law and Criminal Justice*, pp. 18-38.

Klerks, P. (1995), Covert Policing in the Netherlands, in: C. Fijnaut and G.T. Marx (eds.), *Undercover: Police Surveillance in Comparative Perspective*, The Hague: Kluwer, pp. 103-140.

Lord Windlesham (1996), *Responses to Crime: Legislating with the Tide*.

Maguire, M. and T. John (1995), *Intelligence, Surveillance and Informants: Integrated Approaches*, Home Office Police Research Group Crime Detection and Prevention Series: Paper 64, London: Home Office.

Marx, G.T. (1995), Undercover in Comparative Perspective: Some Implications for Knowledge and Social Research, in: C. Fijnaut and G.T. Marx (eds.), *Undercover: Police Surveillance in Comparative Perspective*, The Hague: Kluwer, pp. 323-337.

McConville, M., A. Sanders and R. Leng (1991), *The Case for the Prosecution*, London: Routledge.

Middelburg, B., K. van Es (1994), *Operatie Delta; Hoe de drugsmafia het IRT opblies*, Amsterdam/Antwerpen: Uitgeverij L.J. Veen.

Nadelmann, E. (1995), The DEA in Europe, in: C. Fijnaut and G.T. Marx (eds.), *Undercover: Police Surveillance in Comparative Perspective*, The Hague: Kluwer, pp. 269-289.

Norton-Taylor, R. (1995), No check on police bugs, *The Guardian*, 21 April.

Norton-Taylor, R. and N. Davies (1996), On Her Majesty's Secret Service, *The Guardian*, 29 January.

Outrive, L. van, and J. Cappelle (1995), Twenty Years of Undercover Policing in Belgium: The Regulation of a Risky Police Practice, in: C. Fijnaut and G.T.

Marx (eds.), *Undercover: Police Surveillance in Comparative Perspective*, The Hague: Kluwer, pp. 141-153.

Roos, Th. de (1994), Rapportage Commissie Wieringa: unfair, eenzijdig, onvolledig, *Nederlands Juristenblad,* pp. 438-439.

Rose, D. (1997a), Drugs catch sunk by crime squad, *The Observer,* 26 January.

Rose, D. (1997b), Drugs informer 'set up' jailed businessman, *The Observer,* 9 February.

Silvis, J. (1994), Enforcing Drug Laws in the Netherlands, in: Ed. Leuw, I. Haen Marshall (ed.), *Between prohibition and legalization; The Dutch experiment in drug policy,* Amsterdam/New York: Kugler Publications, pp. 41-58.

Silvis, J. and K.S. Williams (1995), Managing the Drug Problem: Tolerance or Prohibition, in: P. Fennell, C. Harding, N. Jörg and B. Swart (eds.), *Criminal Justice in Europe, A Comparative Study,* Oxford: Clarendon Press, pp. 149-170.

Stockdale, J. and P. Gresham (1995), *Combatting Burglary: An evaluation of three strategies. Crime Detection and Prevention Series Paper 59,* London: Home Office Police Research Group.

Thompson, E.P. (1980), *Writing by Candlelight,* London: Merlin.

Travis, A. (1997b), Safeguards on police bugging welcomed, *The Guardian,* 13 August.

Travis, A. (1997a), Straw U-turn on 'spy bill', *The Guardian,* 17 January.

Wadham, J. and M. Colvin (1997), Good as far as it goes, *The Guardian,* 17 January.

Wagenaar, W., P. van Koppen and H. Crombag (1993), *Anchored Narratives: the Psychology of Criminal Evidence,* Hemel Hempstead: Harvester Wheatsheaf.

Wyngaert, C. van den (ed.) (1993), *Criminal Procedure Systems in the European Community,* London: Butterworth.

Young, H. (1997), Wake up and defend our basic freedoms, *The Guardian,* 4 March.

Part I
The new intelligence gathering: covert and proactive policing

2 The criminal informant: police management, supervision and control

STEVEN GREER AND NIGEL SOUTH

Introduction

Police informants create a range of opportunities and dilemmas for law enforcement which have been publicly debated for centuries (Radzinowicz 1956; Beresford 1958; Harney and Cross 1960/1968; Oscapella 1980). A number of empirical studies following Skolnick's ground-breaking account in the 1960s (Skolnick 1966) have documented the role of one particularly important type in liberal democracy – the 'underworld' or 'criminal' inform-ant likely to be involved in crime associated in some way with the offences which constitute the substance of his or her information. The insights provided by this research have not necessarily, however, led to better pro-cessing of either these informants or of the intelligence they offer. The need for such improvements could hardly be more urgent. In the contemporary UK, and elsewhere, significant sectors of policing are increasingly proactive, intelligence-driven, and informant-dependent. The Audit Commission (1993 and 1996), amongst others, has sought to promote this trend, and section 1 (1) of the Security Service Act 1996 extends the responsibilities of MI5 to include supporting the police and other agencies in the prevention and detection of serious crime. This chapter considers one of the central issues in intelligence-led policing. It attempts to describe and assess the recruit-ment, cultivation, management, supervision, and control of criminal inform-ants by the police in the context of the familiar relationship between formal legal rules, administrative guidelines, management processes, operational discretion, and the daily working practices of police officers.

Recruitment

Most criminal informants are recruited while detained as suspects at police stations during the course of police investigations (Laurie 1972; McConville et al. 1991; Dunnighan and Norris 1996). Recruitment and subsequent 'handling' by the police are intertwined since the suspect is likely to be motivated to inform by the expectation of what the police can offer in return (ibid.). The recruitment of suspects as informants is largely unregulated by legal rules. In a recent survey of informant handlers and other key respondents, South (1995) found that some police officers thought that the Police and Criminal Evidence Act 1984 (PACE) – which formalizes a wide range of police powers – made this more difficult by, for example, limiting the scope for 'casual' contact when 'off-the-record' deals could be struck, and by requiring interviews to be documented and tape recorded. However, for several reasons these obstacles are more apparent than real. First, the pressures upon suspects to answer questions in interviews are considerable, especially since the curtailment of their right to silence by the Criminal Justice and Public Order Act 1994. Secondly, embarking upon a discourse with the police almost invariably commits the suspect to a police-dominated bargaining process where each side seeks to arrive at an agreement by exchanging something of value (Sanders and Young 1994, p. 159). Thirdly, in spite of the provisions of PACE, there are still plenty of opportunities for the police to establish negotiating positions 'off the record', for example in discussions with suspects after formal interview or while giving those released on police bail a lift home (Maguire and John 1995, p. 27).

Confirming the insights of earlier studies, Dunnighan and Norris (1996, p. 402) state that 'very few potential informers volunteer for their role'. Their survey found that 84 per cent were either under arrest or subject to police inquiry when they were recruited and that in 85 per cent of cases detectives reported that it was they, and not the suspect, who had raised the prospect of informing. What precisely the police may be prepared to offer will depend both upon the offence with which the suspect is accused, and upon what the suspect him, or herself, can provide (Ericson 1981). If the offence is relatively minor and a 'one off', there is little scope for recruitment as an informant. Police interest will, therefore, tend to centre upon the eliciting of an admission preferably leading to a guilty plea. In his or her turn the suspect will typically be motivated by the hope of being charged with the least serious offence possible, and/or a sentence discount as a reward for having cooperated. A suspect's confession can be used to identify other participants (if any), and to increase the pressure upon them to confess.

In certain cases an accused may even be persuaded to 'turn Queens evidence' against his accomplices by testifying against them at trial. However, the scope for suspects to inform on an on-going basis as part of their deal with the police is greatest in relation to more 'regularized' crime involving more than one participant. The most attractive recruit is the 'bit player' guilty of a relatively minor offence who has access to much bigger fish and who may be deemed more valuable on the streets supplying information about others than behind bars himself (Dorn et al. 1992).

Dunnighan and Norris (1996) distinguish four strategies used by the police to recruit and motivate suspects to become informants: financial, instrumental, informational, and affective. Although financial rewards provided an inducement for some two thirds of informants in this study, they were rarely the dominant motive. More influential were the 'instrumental strategies' at the disposal of the police, for example dropping charges, the promise of future help, bail, or assistance in securing a sentence concession either through the preparation of a letter (or 'text') to the trial judge or less formally by offering to testify at trial on the defendant's behalf. In the recruitment negotiations information can, and will, be manipulated by the police to the suspect's disadvantage. Dunnighan and Norris found that using these 'informational strategies' the police will encourage mistaken beliefs, for example, that bail or cautioning are conditional upon cooperation. 'Affective strategies' include pretending to befriend suspects and exploiting the influence the police may have with other official agencies, for example the Department of Social Security and local authority housing departments. According to South (1995) other recruitment factors include the gravity of the offence and the urgency of the investigation. More pressure to turn informant may be exerted upon suspects where the offence is serious and the police have very little other information or evidence to work from. However, more routinely, the principal concern of the police is to ensure that the informant feels well disposed toward their prospective 'handler' and, therefore, a low-key bargaining style will generally be preferred (McConville et al. 1991, pp. 62-63).

Handling and cultivation

Several studies show that informal rules of thumb, learned on the job or imbibed with occupational culture, are much more instrumental in determining how informants are handled and cultivated by the police than either legal rules or administrative guidelines provided by the Home Office, the

Association of Chief Police Officers (ACPO), or specific forces (South 1995; Maguire and John 1995, p. 27; Dunnighan and Norris 1996). Although the various administrative guidelines have no formal legal status, their central principles tend largely to coincide with the courts' own view of what is lawful, particularly over the distinction between the activities of informants and those of *agents provocateurs* (see below). There are two principal legal risks for the police in using informants. One is the prospect that a subsequent prosecution may have to be abandoned if a court were to insist upon disclosure of the fact that an informant had been involved, especially if he or she also had to be named. Disclosure will only be required, however, if the trial judge is convinced that the informant's role is a critical factor in determining the defendant's guilt or innocence (see Tapper 1995, pp. 527-8). The other legal constraint is the possibility that evidence provided by an informant may be ruled inadmissible on the grounds of unfairness under section 78 of PACE. This provides for the exclusion of prosecution evidence where the trial judge considers that its admission would 'have such an adverse effect on the fairness of the proceedings that the court ought not to admit it'. However, in a series of cases involving the activities of alleged *agents provocateurs* participating in 'sting' operations, the courts have exercised their discretion against exclusion where they have been satisfied, for example, that the defendant had a previous disposition towards the kind of offence charged, that, in conformity with Home Office guidelines, the informant played a relatively minor and passive role, that the 'sting' was not an attempt to by-pass the PACE Codes of Conduct on interviews with suspects, and that the evidence obtained could be considered reliable (Sharpe 1994; Robertson 1994). Needless to say the risks of both compulsory disclosure and the exclusion of vital evidence are likely to be difficult to predict, particularly in the early stages of the police-informant relationship. Overseas enforcement agencies – the US DEA and FBI, the Royal Canadian Mounted Police (RCMP) and the Australian Federal Police – regard the uncertainties associated with disclosure as a significant problem for the British police (South 1995). However, Dunnighan and Norris (1996, p. 456) claim that handlers and supervisors can easily side-step it by simply concealing from the Crown Prosecution Service the fact that an informant has been used.

The indeterminacy of the legal risks may explain their remoteness from every day informant-handling. Two further reasons may account for the primacy of rules of thumb over Home Office and police guidelines. First, official guidelines tend to lack the kind of detail which the handler may most require. Secondly, the absence of adequate training means that such bureaucratic norms are unlikely to be internalized by the officers concerned. Dunnighan and Norris (1996, p. 404), for example, state that only one third of handlers in their study had received any formal training in informant handling and half of those had considered it useless. Half of all detectives surveyed said they had learned to run informants by talking informally to other officers, and a further third indicated that they were self taught (ibid.).

Researchers have identified several particularly important rules of thumb (although, of course, handlers will by no means always adhere to these anymore than they will always adhere to formal rules). First, and most important of all, is the need to sustain informants' confidence that their new-found role will not be compromised. Danger is an occupational hazard for nearly all criminal informants and the risks can include death or serious injury according to the kind of activity being informed upon. Being seen to act upon information received, or at least attempting to explain why this has not happened, are also vital to the nurturing of the police-informant relationship. Secondly, the promises made in the recruitment negotiations must either be honoured, or reasons given to explain why they have not. This implies that the police should only make promises in the first place which they are confident can be kept. Thirdly, the police officer(s) assigned as informant handler(s) must be in control at all times, remaining constantly alert to the varied subtle risks of this relationship being inverted. This not only maximizes effectiveness but (combined with adequate supervision and accountability) is also a safeguard against officers succumbing to corruption (Darbyshire and Hilliard 1993). Fourthly, handlers should keep regular records of their meetings with informants documenting in particular if payments were made, and if so how much. Some overseas agencies, such as the FBI and RCMP, employ formal 'contracts' with informants detailing permissible and prohibited conduct and setting out expectations plus payment and other arrangements. Fifthly, regular consultation with police superiors is vital particularly when difficulties in the relationship or in the informant's role arise. Finally, there are various rules of thumb about where, and where not, to meet. The ideal place is 'off-plot' where the informant is not known. The venue should be checked before the rendezvous and both parties should have agreed a plausible story in advance in case they encounter anyone who knows them.

Interpersonal skills are the key to success in the informant-handler relationship. Many officers in South's interviews observed that in 'developing' informants, it is worthwhile to know as much as possible about their background and circumstances, for example family and social life, and financial situation. This information not only serves to check informants' bona fides, and to suggest ways the police can assist with problems, but it can strengthen the relationship by offering topics of conversation apart from those relating to informing. However, family names may need to be changed and code names provided in order to reduce the risk of exposing the informant to danger. Although vital, South (1995) notes that 'affective strategies' can also create problems. A well recognized risk is over-familiarity between handler and informant, particularly between a male officer and a female source (Graef 1990). This may follow from naivety, foolishness or manipulative intent on the part of the officer, a degree of hero worship by the informant, or the natural outcome of mutual attraction. Informants may also attempt to 'overperform' believing that their own interests – be they higher rewards, improved security and protection, or merely reflected glory – will be better served the more the career of their handler flourishes.

Supervision and control

South (1995) suggests that a bureaucratized, multi-tiered structure of informant supervision and control is emerging, though unevenly, in police forces in England and Wales. As with recruitment and handling, this structure is built upon administrative guidelines, occupational culture, and working practices rather than upon formal law or professional training. The most developed structures will typically involve the sharing of day-to-day responsibility for a given informant with a co-handler, the careful documentation by handlers of transactions with informants, managerial supervision by an Informant Controller, and the maintenance of a centralized informant register by a Registrar at force level (Maguire and John 1995, pp. 28-30).

Co-handlers and controllers

The merits of co-handling are varied and include: protection (albeit not entirely watertight) against corruption; continuity over holiday periods or when a handler transfers to another area or to other duties; another perspective on day-to-day management issues; maximizing the chance of action being taken on information received; and 'in-service' training with a more experienced officer acting as 'mentor' to a less experienced colleague (South 1995). Some European countries, for example the Netherlands, favour an even stronger version of shared responsibility – the designation of specialist informant-handling teams. However, in spite of all this, South (1995) found a wide divergence of both practice and opinion on co-handling between police forces and amongst individual officers in south east England.

Responsibility for supervising the handling of informants, including ensuring that relevant guidelines are observed, dealing with court applications for disclosure, and analysing informant-derived intelligence, lies with the Informant Controller for a division, area, or region, usually a Detective Inspector or Chief Inspector. The relationship between handlers and controllers is confidential and codenames are employed to protect the identity of informants. Controllers create a file for each informant using a code number supplied by the force Registrar (see below). Contact and information forms completed by handlers are then filed providing a full record of handler-informant interactions. Records in police pocket books, and on contact forms, are expected to include dates, times and places of meetings and full accounts of the content of discussions. The handler may convey to the Controller recommendations about how action may be taken on the information supplied. Having analysed these the Controller is expected to pass the information and advice they contain directly, or via the Registrar, to other forces or teams, or to local or force intelligence desks (see Maguire and John 1995, pp. 16-19). The importance of systematizing and formalizing informant handling was heavily emphasized by many police respondents in South's study (see also Maguire and John 1995, p. 27), as a means both of protecting police officers and informants, and of reducing the scope for misunderstanding, malpractice and the risk of miscarriages of justice resulting from misinformation. However, although standardized forms have now been introduced, complaints from lower rank officers about the increased paperwork associated with informant handling are still common.

Some police forces recognize that it is desirable that Controllers should meet both handlers and regular informants in order to gain some working knowledge of their activities and relationships (South 1995). It is also increasingly accepted that supervision is particularly important where rewards are involved, for these are transactions which can otherwise provide easy opportunities to compromise, embarrass, or corrupt officers. Many forces require the payment of rewards to be approved by a superior officer, and for these to be made in the presence of a superior officer (or at least co-handler), and with the completion of a receipt. Institutionalized supervision also enables Controllers to meet informants on a routine, non-threatening basis. In the past, some officers have been critical of the systems for approving payment of rewards and 'running expenses' on the grounds of their inflexibility and parsimony, with superiors almost invariably reducing the proposed amount. The calculation of rewards has always been a disputed matter and the availability of funds for expenses and rewards differs from force to force. The Audit Commission report (1993, para. 86) notes that 'the amounts of money available for payments are relatively very small; the total amount disbursed to registered informants in 1992 averaged £19,000 per force, with an average payment of £100'. A uniform scale, possibly related to local earnings levels and cost-of-living indicators, may be more appropriate. However, the police service has apparently concluded that no set formula for informant rewards is feasible and that each transaction must be judged on its own merits. The criteria for making such a judgment, and the payment procedure, are given in the new ACPO guidelines (1995).

The responsibilities and skills of the Informant Controller are governed, in common with other areas of the informant process, by administrative guidelines and craft knowledge rather than by formal rules and proper training. Typically Controllers receive no formal training at all. The result is a wide divergence of practice and opinion as to what is appropriate in both handling and supervision. Dunnighan and Norris (1996, p. 404) found, for example, that one third of supervisory officers considered it acceptable for officers to lie to colleagues about how they ran an informant. Supervisors were also evenly split over whether or not handlers should disclose their home telephone numbers to their sources (ibid.). In his interviews South (1995) found a common perception amongst police respondents that some Controllers lacked sufficient interest in their role, perhaps because of their lack of relevant experience, because they regard the matter as a low priority, or because they actively dislike this potentially troublesome type of police work (see also Maguire and John 1995, pp. 13 and 29).

The lack of shared standards and objectives between handlers and Controllers, and the absence of adequate guidance and training for Controllers, has tended to undermine effective supervision and to encourage rather than dispel the secrecy inherent in the police use of informants. Only one in three detectives in Dunnighan and Norris's study (1996) said they would seek advice from their Controller if they had an informant-related problem and 57 per cent of detectives thought Controllers were 'out of touch'. A further three quarters believed that 'you could not be sure of supervisory support when things went wrong' (Dunninghan and Norris 1996, p. 404).

Registration

All police forces in England and Wales now possess a central Informant Register containing informants' particulars. However, procedures are not uniform. Some forces require registration of all informants, whether 'criminal' or otherwise, paid or unpaid, while others insist upon a 'review period' when candidates are logged but are not fully registered until it is clear that they are to become regular contacts (see also Maguire and John 1995, p. 28). Registrars are likely to be centrally based Detective Chief Superintendents, although again arrangements vary. Having issued informants with a code number, the Registrar's function is to supervise the management of the force's informant process and to coordinate the intelligence resource which it represents.

Information technology has dramatically transformed the operation and efficiency of registration systems. South reports that some forces have already developed a sophisticated conception of what the technology might achieve. For example, where Registrars communicate with each other and exchange information within and between force data bases, dangerous and problematic informants can be more easily identified and weeded out. From a strategic, operational point of view, centralized recording of the particular fields of criminal knowledge that an informant possesses is an obvious way of maximising their utility and of turning them into a long term resource. This is a significant step away from past practices, when informants were seen as the handler's 'personal property'. Although all forces are now required to adopt nationally agreed ACPO guidelines, which envisage a standardized system, it is possible, indeed likely, that specific local conditions and needs will continue to result in some differences in practice.

Strategic management

The criminal informant's principal function is to provide intelligence about organized or recurrent crime rather than evidence capable of standing up in court (Ericson 1981, p. 129). Whether or not this is cost efficient has been hotly disputed. On the basis of a narrow test correlating ratio of reward money paid to rates of arrest, crimes cleared up and property recovered, the Audit Commission (1993) has argued that it is. Using a broader alternative which includes operational expenses, including those related to recruitment, contact and supervision, Dunnighan and Norris (1996) argue that the real costs are considerably higher. Somewhere in between, Maguire and John (1995, pp. 50-52) note the difficulties in assessing the value of information from informants. We would agree with this and also observe that the measures employed by the Audit Commission and Dunnighan and Norris, both ignore the fact that the utility of criminal informants varies greatly according to the type of offence, and that they may have an important intelligence function with only indirect crime control benefits.

Of course, informants can, and have been, used as courtroom witnesses, most notably in the supergrass cases in England in the 1970s (Campbell 1991 and 1994) and in Northern Ireland in the early 1980s (Greer 1995a). But pre- and post-trial protection arrangements make this expensive, and testifying at trial effectively ends an informant's active career. Moreover, the scope for the use of supergrasses in Britain has declined since the 1980s for three main reasons (Campbell 1994). First, in order to facilitate the move from armed robbery to illegal drugs, professional criminals formed more closely knit organizations less penetrable by informants than before (see also Dorn et al. 1992). Secondly, the penalties meted out to those who dared to betray became much more severe – death or serious injury (ibid.). Thirdly, juries became more distrustful of informant evidence (Campbell 1994).

The central strategic management issue concerns how the intelligence potential of the criminal informant can be maximized. This needs to be addressed by the police at two levels: the 'tasking', or proactive deployment, of informants by police handlers under supervision from Controllers; and the coordination and dissemination of the information this yields through registration and other organizational systems.

'Tasking' and the 'participating informant'

The 'tasking' of informants is as old as professional policing and was recently endorsed by the Audit Commission (1993, para. 130). While this may simply, and uncontroversially, mean that an informant is asked to 'keep an ear open' in relation to a particular offence or offences (Darbyshire and Hillyard 1993), much more tempting to the police, and much more problematic, are those cases where an informant is tasked to participate in a crime. In many situations it can be relatively easy for an informant to gain sufficient trust, or to occupy a peripheral position in a criminal enterprise, with a view to providing useful general information to the police. However, the highly specific, and even technical, nature of certain offences may make it difficult for tasked informants to gather much intelligence unless they are suitably skilled themselves and play an active role. Such 'fully' participating informants (PIs) are the mainstay of the strategy of Regional Crime Squads and their Drugs Wings (Maguire and Norris 1992, pp. 91-93; Dorn et al. 1992). RCS members and other specialist officers also believe that participating informants can be a 'cost effective' option in dealing with 'white collar' crimes such as fraud and tax evasion (South 1995). Tasked informants often complain that the mediocre 'one-off' payments they receive are no substitute for a proper 'salary' or retainer (South 1995) – this is a criticism also made recently by some senior Metropolitan police officers (Darbyshire 1993, p. 19). Maguire and John (1996, p. 29) found that one force is indeed now 'contemplating paying regular "retainers" to its best informants, rather than simply paying by results'.

Since any active participation in crime, even by a tasked PI is prima facie illegal, albeit subject to a legally recognized defence (see *R v Clarke* (1984) Cr App R 344), Home Office and police guidelines are more strict here than with respect to other criminal informants. Although authorization must, in principle, be sought from an officer of ACPO rank in advance, Dunnighan and Norris (1996, p. 456) found that this had only been obtained in respect of 10 per cent of PIs. The guidelines restrict the use of PIs to those cases where they are clearly necessary in order to enable the police to intercept and arrest the perpetrators. But PIs themselves must only play minor roles which should not involve planning or committing the offences in question. Nor should they become *agents provocateurs* by contributing to the intention to commit a crime which might otherwise not have been attempted (ICAC 1993; Marx 1988; Maguire and John 1995, p. 27). However, the reality is that, once let loose in a criminal organization, it is difficult for the police to retain any real control over a PI. Some clearly exploit this as a licence for wrongdoing. But it would be naive not to realize that even a bona fide PI might have to act in a manner consistent with wholehearted commitment to the joint criminal endeavour in order to remain credible and thus avoid the risks to life and limb which are likely to ensue should they be exposed. Although apparently demanding, South (1995) also reports inconsistency in the interpretation of the guidelines in practice. Recent clarifications following consultation with the Home Office have been welcomed by the police and current procedures are now set out in the new 1995 ACPO guidelines. However the Home Office has no plans to revise its 1969 guidelines to bring them into line with their ACPO counterpart.

Coordination and dissemination

The creation of a 'national data base of informants' by the National Criminal Intelligence Service in 1995, mirroring a similar data base on undercover officers, affords one strategy for the careful targeting of particular participating informants with specific 'skills' to particular jobs. In addition to coordinated tasking, however, the second crucial element in maximizing an informant's role involves ensuring that informant-derived information gets to the right place at the right time (Maguire and John 1995, pp. 27-28). Two separate issues can be distinguished here. One concerns the rapid dissemination of high grade 'hot tips' facilitating a swift police response, while the other relates to the more painstaking analysis of diverse strands of low-grade informant intelligence. In addition to offering a safeguard against abuses, handlers' records can also serve as an intelligence resource capable of being re-analysed to yield further information in the light of other material which the police may since have acquired. However, poor liaison, pressure of work, and inadequate police sick leave and holiday cover, can result in even high grade information failing to prompt the most appropriate police action. Failure to disseminate all types of potentially useful information to others at all levels of informant management is noted by a number of respondents in South's (1995) study. This failure reflects a long standing, more general, and much debated, organizational difficulty in sharing and disseminating information within the police service (see e.g. Baldwin and Kinsey 1982, p. 72; Maguire and Norris 1992, pp. 93-94; Maguire and John 1995).

The model adopted by the police in some other European countries provides an alternative to the experience in England and Wales. In the Netherlands for example, informants are handled and controlled by specialist police intelligence officers who are also responsible for the collation and analysis of the information and intelligence gathered and for its dissemination to appropriate operational units. Such an approach could be considered in England and Wales. Building upon existing local and force intelligence teams – particularly in those forces or areas with a high number of informants – it might offer both a lever of control while also maximising effectiveness (Maguire and John 1995, p. 29). Undeniably however, such a system itself poses dangers by, e.g. concentrating expertise and power in relatively few hands, removing the scrutiny often provided by the overlap of operations and investigations, and by creating the need for new specialized mechanisms of supervision.

Conclusion

We have each argued elsewhere that the use of criminal informants should be more accountable to institutions external to policing agencies (Greer 1995a & b; South 1995; see also ICAC 1993). However, the narrower remit of this paper leads us to suggest that the management of informants by the police also needs to be improved in both a functional and normative sense.

Notwithstanding familiar complaints about over-bureaucratization, it is difficult for the police to argue that current regulation is effective given the substantial and serious gulf between self-professed conceptions of best practice – as evidenced for example by the ACPO guidelines – and the contemporary operational reality. But, whatever its other merits, further elaboration of legal and administrative rules cannot, of itself, succeed in closing this gap. The solution must, therefore, be sought through better management structures and improved police training on both technical and ethical matters. Shared objectives and common conceptions of efficient and ethically-sensitive practice need to be hammered out first between handlers, Controllers and Registrars within the framework of evolving national guidelines. The recruitment of suspects as informants should only be on the basis of voluntary cooperation without reliance upon undue pressure or misleading information. Ideally this process should be mediated by defence lawyers and formalized in a written contract between handlers and suspects. The key to successful and ethical handling lies in adherence to three central principles: the relationship between informant and police should be professionally managed by teams of at least two handlers; accurate and detailed records should be kept and; consultations with superiors must be regular and open. Supervision will be improved if Controllers and Registrars have gained relevant experience and insight through having been handlers themselves, if they are properly trained and motivated, and if they also maintain regular contact with officers on the ground. However, while the current multi-tiered structure may be effective for supervision, there are serious queries over its effectiveness in the dissemination of informant-derived intelligence. There is much to be said, therefore, for the strengthening of local and force-based intelligence teams regularly briefed by informant handlers, especially when tasking and other targeted operations are being planned and executed.

References

ACPO (1978), *Third Report of the Working Party on a Structure of Criminal Intelligence Offices above Force Level (the Pearce Report)*, London: Association of Chief Police Officers.

ACPO (1994/1995), *National Guidelines on the Use and Management of Informants*, Association of Chief Police Officers, unpublished.

Audit Commission (1993), *Helping with Enquiries: Tackling Crime Effectively*, London: HMSO.

Audit Commission (1996), *Detecting a Change: Progress in Tackling Crime*, London: HMSO.

Baldwin, R. and R. Kinsey (1982), *Police Powers and Politics*, London: Quartet Books.

Beresford, M. (1958), The common informer, the penal statutes and economic regulation, *Economic History Review*, 2 (2), pp. 221-238.

Campbell, D. (1991), *That Was Business, This Is Personal*, London: Mandarin.

Campbell, D. (1994), *The Underworld*, London: BBC Books.

Darbyshire, N. (1993), Save this threatened species, *Daily Telegraph*, September 20th, p. 19.

Darbyshire, N. and B. Hillyard (1993), *The Flying Squad*, London: Headline.

Dorn, N., K. Murji and N. South (1992), *Traffickers: Drug Markets and Law Enforcement*, London: Routledge.

Dunnighan, C. and C. Norris (1996), The Nark's Game, *New Law Journal*, 22 March.

Ericson, R. (1981), *Making Crime: A Study of Detective Work*, Toronto: Butterworths.

Graef, R. (1990), *Talking Blues: The Police in their Own Words*, London: Fontana.

Greer, S. (1995a), *Supergrasses: A Study in Anti-Terrorist Law Enforcement in Northern Ireland*, Oxford: Clarendon Press.

Greer, S. (1995b), Towards a sociological model of the police informant, 46, 3, *British Journal of Sociology*, pp. 509-527.

Harney, M. and J. Cross (1960; 1968, 2nd edn), *The Informer in Law Enforcement*, Springfield, Ill.: Charles Thomas.

ICAC (1993), *Discussion Paper on Police Informants*, New South Wales: Independent Commission Against Corruption.

Laurie, P. (1972), *Scotland Yard*, London: Penguin books.

Maguire, M. and C. Norris (1992), *The Conduct and Supervision of Criminal Investigations*, Royal Commission on Criminal Justice, Research Study 5, London: HMSO.

Maguire, M. and T. John (1995), *Intelligence, Surveillance and Informants: Integrated Approaches*, (Crime Detection and Prevention Paper 64), Police Research Group, London: Home Office.

Marx, G.T. (1988), *Undercover: Police Surveillance in America*, Berkeley: University of California Press.

McConville, M., A. Sanders and R. Leng (1991), *The Case for the Prosecution: Police Suspects and the Construction of Criminality*, London: Routledge.

Oscapella, E. (1980), A study of informers in England, *Criminal Law Review*, pp. 136-146.

Radzinowicz, L. (1956), *A History of English Criminal Law and its Administration since 1750*, volume 2, London: Stevens.

Robertson, G. (1994), Entrapment Evidence: Manna from Heaven or Fruit of the Poisoned Tree?, *Criminal Law Review*, pp. 805-816.

Sanders, A. and R. Young (1994), *Criminal Justice*, London: Butterworths.

Sharpe, S. (1994), Covert Police Operations and the Discretionary Exclusion of Evidence, *Criminal Law Review*, pp. 793-804.

Skolnick, J. (1966), *Justice Without Trial: Law Enforcement in Democratic Society*, New York: Wiley.

South, N. (1995), *The Police Use of Informants: Some Key Issues and Recommendations*, unpublished report to the Police Research Group, London: Home Office.

Tapper, C. (1995, 8th edn), *Cross on Evidence*, London: Butterworths.

3 Police surveillance and its regulation in England and Wales

TIMOTHY JOHN AND MIKE MAGUIRE[1]

Introduction

'There is the tension within the organs of state, between those which look for the maximum use of intercepts for the common good, to forestall treason, spying and crime, and those whose functions and culture incline towards protection of the individual, and specifically to the protection of the individual's right of privacy.' (Lord Mustill in *R v Preston*).

As several other contributors to this volume have emphasized, there has been over recent years a widespread growth in the use of electronic and other forms of surveillance, fuelled partly by technological advances which have made it a much more powerful, cheaper and more convenient tool for police forces, state agencies and private organizations alike. In Britain, especially, the development of surveillance has greatly outstripped efforts to regulate it, most of which have taken place in an ad hoc fashion with little or no consideration of the principles involved or of the long-term implications for civil liberties. Government has been slow to legislate, and has typically done so only in response to an actual or anticipated defeat in the European Court of Human Rights. This vacuum in strategy and overview has resulted in a patchwork of regulation covering surveillance that does little to safeguard the privacy of those targeted or, indeed, of the public as a whole.

The main focus of this chapter will be upon the use of surveillance by the police, although it should not be forgotten that similar issues arise in many other contexts, including covert operations by secret services, customs, tax authorities, and private agencies. Many more questions, too, are raised by the more 'passive' and generalized (and sometimes fully overt) use of surveillance, notably in the rapid spread of closed circuit television (CCTV) systems in public as well as private spaces. Again, there is room only for a few general comments on this topic.

Where policing in England and Wales is concerned, decisions about whose behaviour is to be monitored, by what means, in what depth, and for how long, have traditionally been treated as operational matters and therefore left to the police with little or no external oversight – the argument being that the courts are the final arbiter of the admission of any evidence so gathered. With some important exceptions, police discretion has been tempered only by Home Office guidelines or internal standing orders that do not carry the force of law and are typically concerned more with administrative process than with broader issues such as the appropriateness of particular forms of surveillance in different kinds of situation. Furthermore, such guidelines can over time create a veneer of legitimacy for practices which the police have themselves initiated and gradually established as routine, with little public awareness or serious debate.

From the police perspective, the advantage of the vacuum in legislation has been considerable freedom of action, especially in cases where the purpose of surveillance is the gathering of intelligence rather than of evidence for a prosecution. The main disadvantage for the police has been uncertainty about whether evidence will be admitted at trial, as well as the prospect of challenges in the appeal courts. Even so, there are very few instances in which surveillance evidence has been ruled inadmissible, and generally only if there was some other impropriety in the operation in which it was obtained.[2]

In this chapter, we first point out some of the difficulties involved in regulating the use of surveillance, not least the sheer range of activities it encompasses and the problems of definition this creates.[3] We then provide an overview of the current position in England and Wales, examining relevant administrative rules, court decisions and legislation. Particular attention is paid to the two main forms of surveillance now covered by law: the interception of communications (chiefly 'telephone tapping') and the entry on to, or interference with, property in connection with the use of covert listening devices. We also make a few comments on a rather different form of surveillance which is as yet scarcely regulated at all: the use of closed circuit television in public places.

General approaches to definition and regulation

In the policing context, the term 'surveillance' is usually understood to embrace a wide range of methods of monitoring the behaviour, lifestyles or property of suspected or potential offenders – not just visual and optical, but aural, olfactory,[4] and electronic. At one extreme, it involves no more than use of the human eye or ear, and at the other the use of state-of-the-art technology which can 'see' or 'hear' through solid barriers from a great distance. Other important dimensions, from the point of view of threats to civil liberties, are whether the persons under surveillance are specific 'suspect' individuals or anybody who, for example, visits a particular location or uses a particular telephone line; whether they are in private or public space (and, if the former, whether private property has been entered or interfered with in order to listen in to their conversations); and whether they are being observed in order to gather evidence about specific criminal acts which they are suspected to have committed or planned, or simply to acquire general information about their lifestyles and associates. The term can also refer to the monitoring or searching of computer records, such as data bases of financial transactions or telephone calls, or to the interception of communications, including those made via the postal service, telephone, radio, fax, electronic mail, cellular phones and pagers.

This huge (and increasing) diversity immediately raises the thorny problem of defining the kinds of circumstances in which the law should intervene in the interests of protecting privacy. In many other countries, decisions in this area are guided by basic principles enshrined in Constitutions, Conventions or legislation. For example, the Fourth Amendment of the United States Constitution guarantees all citizens 'security from unreasonable search and seizure': this has been used by the Supreme Court to develop the concept of an individual's 'reasonable expectation of privacy',[5] which has been used as the key test of whether surveillance is or is not acceptable in particular sets of circumstances. Similarly, Article 8.1 of the European Convention on Human Rights, which is incorporated into the domestic law of many European countries, states that, 'Everyone has the right to respect for his private and family life, his home and his correspondence.'

Although the new Labour government elected in Britain in 1997 announced its intention to incorporate the European Convention into domestic law, what this will mean in practice is as yet unknown. At present, this country lacks any general law on privacy, and has always relied heavily for protection against excessive intrusion (by the police and other state agencies) upon a combination of self-regulation by the agencies concerned and the common law pronouncements of judges.

It has been the traditional view of the courts, as expressed by Lord Camden in 1765 in *Entick v Carrington*, that 'The eye cannot by the laws of England be guilty of a trespass'.[6] In other words, it has always been considered acceptable for the police, without any special authorization, not only to maintain surveillance on people in public places, but to observe people who are on private property from an external vantage point. However, it has increasingly widely been recognized that, once it is proposed to assist 'the eye' by means of some form of technical device which enhances its range or clarity of vision – and hence raises the level of intrusiveness upon privacy – issues of regulation demand serious consideration. Few would argue that *any* aid to vision (or, by analogy, to hearing) is a candidate for strict regulation: it would be absurd, for instance, to suggest that a short-sighted police officer should obtain authorization to wear glasses when observing a suspect. As the Younger Committee Report on Privacy noted in 1972, it is only some kinds of surveillance 'device' which tend to arouse public unease:

> 'It could include a motor car used to tail a suspect. It could include a ladder by which the window cleaner is enabled to peer at you in your bath ... We do not think that these are what the public mean when they express concern about "technical devices" for invading privacy. We are clear that the devices, or the associate devices that are essential to their operation, fall into two well-defined categories: electronic and optical extensions of the human senses'.[7]

Similarly, in 1979 in *Malone*, the case which eventually led to legislative controls on the interception of communications (see below), Sir Robert Megarry stated that, 'The question is not whether there ought to be a general prohibition of all surveillance, but in what circumstances, and subject to what conditions and restrictions, it ought to be permitted.'[8] Where, then, are the lines presently drawn in England and Wales?

Where Younger's 'optical extensions' are concerned, it has since become a standard element of standing orders in police forces across the country (echoing Home Office guidelines) that written authorization must be obtained from a senior officer for the use of equipment such as binoculars, cameras and video cameras. However, there is no *legal* requirement to do so, let alone any requirement for external involvement in, or oversight of, such decisions. While this currently arouses little concern, it may become a topic of more debate as the use increases of much more powerful optical devices such as aerial cameras with high magnification power, night vision equipment, infra-red heat sensors and even satellite photography.

By contrast, 'electronic' surveillance has attracted considerable attention over recent years, and has been subject to legal as well as administrative intervention. This falls into two main categories: the interception of communications and the 'bugging' of conversations. We shall discuss each in turn at some length.

Interception of communications

Despite a number of official reports from committees set up to consider how it might be regulated,[9] the interception of communications did not become subject to legislation until 1985, following the decision in *Malone* when it reached the European Court of Human Rights.[10] This decision made it clear that the Home Office guidelines which had until then constituted the only form of regulation of telephone tapping in England and Wales, did not conform to the 'in accordance with the law' requirements of Article 8.2 of the Convention.[11] The guidelines did not carry the force of law as they specified administrative process only, and were not available to the public even though a copy had been placed in the library of the House of Commons.[12] Furthermore, there was no means by which the domestic courts could review whether admission of such improperly obtained evidence would affect the fairness of the trial in the absence of a general right to privacy – consequently breaching Article 13.[13]

As a result of this decision, the Interception of Communications Act 1985 was introduced to bring the domestic law into line with Europe by providing a legislative basis for interception over the public telephone and postal systems. Under the Act, authority for interceptions is granted by the competent Secretary of State (generally the Home Secretary) rather than by the judiciary, as is the case in other European jurisdictions.[14] A Tribunal and a Commissioner appointed under the Act are responsible for overseeing the operation of the warrant procedure and providing appropriate remedies.[15]

Although the Act permits telephone tapping only in order to prevent or investigate 'serious crime', the definition of this term has been criticized for being too broad in scope. A crime is 'serious' if:

'(a) It involves the use of violence, results in substantial financial gain or is conducted by a large number of persons in pursuit of a common purpose; or
(b) The offence or one of the offences is an offence for which a person who has attained the age of twenty-one and has no previous convictions could reasonably be expected to be sentenced to imprisonment for three years or more.'[16]

This potentially allows the criteria to be satisfied even if the suspected criminal activity is relatively low level, especially if conducted by a group of people.[17] Indeed, the activities of some of the groups discussed by Fiona Donson in chapter 10 would fall within this definition even though they would not generally be considered to involve serious crime, and would fall outside the definition used in section 116 of the Police and Criminal Evidence Act 1984.[18]

A further perceived weakness of the legislation is the stipulation that 'No evidence shall be adduced and no question in cross-examination shall be asked which (in either case) tends to suggest that ... a warrant has been or is to be issued.'[19] As a result, defendants may never know that such a device has been used against them. The rule has also had the effect of making inadmissible evidence that might have been beneficial to the defence in a criminal trial. For example, in *R v Preston*, it became apparent to the defendant that a tap had been placed on his telephone. He wanted the transcripts to be admitted into evidence, as he claimed they would prove he had been forced to import drugs into the country by a gang which was holding his wife to ransom. However, the Court of Appeal confirmed their inadmissibility as evidence and upheld his conviction.[20]

The fact that (unlike in some other countries) there is no duty to inform a person, after the event, that his or her telephone has been tapped,[21] greatly restricts the ability of individuals to make complaints, and hence reduces the overall effectiveness of the Tribunal as a 'watchdog'. Moreover, in the few cases where individuals do find out that their telephone has been tapped, they have little chance of a remedy for any abuses of procedure which may have taken place. The Tribunal only has the power to conduct a review of the Secretary of State's decision to grant the warrant: at the time of writing, it has not yet found such a contravention. Its powers are greatly limited by the fact that it has no remit to investigate allegations of *illegal* taps taking place – that is in the absence of a warrant. As this is a criminal offence under the Act, such allegations are to be investigated by the police. There is a clear conflict of interest when it is the police themselves who might be suspected of using intercepts in this manner.

Although the regulation of telephone tapping is unsatisfactory, it does at least provide an open legislative basis and a degree of external regulation of the police through the authorization procedure and tribunal system. However, in many ways it is already 'out of date'. The significance of straightforward telephone taps has undoubtedly been reduced by advances in technology and in surveillance techniques which fall outside the remit of the Interception of Communications Act. For example, it does not cover telephone metering (the logging of calls made from a particular telephone), which can be a valuable tool for the police in building up a picture of the associates of a suspect. More importantly, the Act applies only to communications made over the 'public telecommunications system.' Consequently, private systems are deemed not to require a warrant for calls to be intercepted, neither do mobile telephones. The House of Lords in *R v Effick*[22] construed what constituted a 'public' system very narrowly. Effick had held a conversation on a domestic cordless telephone that had been recorded by the police. This was deemed to fall outside the Act as it in effect constituted a 'private' system. Consequently no warrant was required and the resultant conversation could be used as evidence. In *R v Governor of Belmarsh Prison and Another ex p Martin*[23] the same principle was applied to an inmate's conversation intercepted on a pay phone on a prison wing. In the similar case of *R v Ahmed and others,*[24] transcripts of calls made by the co-defendant from a police station pay-phone were held admissable as they also did not form part of the public system. On the other hand, the recent ECHR decision in *Halford v UK,*[25] in which the police were found to have breached Article 8 by intercepting a senior officer's calls on their own internal telephone system, may well lead to a reappraisal of the domestic law in this general area.

'Bugging'

The use of covert listening devices (commonly known as 'bugging'), which has increasingly replaced the interception of telephone calls as a means of monitoring conversations between suspected criminals, has remained unregulated by law in England and Wales until very recently. This can take place in public space, for example with the aid of long-range audio detectors capable of picking up specific conversations in crowds, but the main area of dispute has been the bugging of private property, which often involves prior entry and therefore, potentially, offences of trespass or burglary by the person placing the bug.

Until 1997, and the passing of the Police Act (see below), the use of covert listening devices was controlled only by internal Home Office guidelines,[26] with authority being granted by the Chief Constable, or in certain circumstances delegated to an Assistant Chief Constable.[27] Official figures indicate that such devices were used in a small but by no means insignificant number of police operations: for example, in 1995, 1300 authorizations were granted under this procedure (*The Times*, 21 January

1997, p. 11). There may also have been some unauthorized use, although informal conversations with police officers involved in proactive work suggest that this is rare, as special equipment has to be requisitioned and experts are often used to install it, making any disregard of official procedures difficult to conceal from the police organization.

The Home Office guidelines set out the criteria that should be met before the use of such devices was authorized. They are:

a. that the investigation concerned serious crime;
b. that normal methods of investigation had been tried and failed, or were unlikely to succeed if tried;
c. that there was good reason to believe that use of equipment would be likely to lead to an arrest and a conviction (or, where appropriate, to the prevention of acts of terrorism); and
d. that the use of the equipment was operationally feasible.[28]

In addition, the guidelines contained a requirement that the authorizing officer consider the correlation between the seriousness of the crime being investigated and the degree of intrusion that would take place:

'In judging how far the seriousness of the crime under investigation justifies the use of particular surveillance techniques, authorising officers should satisfy themselves that the degree of intrusion into the privacy of those affected by the surveillance is commensurate with the seriousness of the offence. Where the targets of the surveillance might reasonably assume a high degree of privacy, for instance in their homes, listening devices should be used only for the investigation of major organised conspiracies and of other particularly serious offences, especially crimes of violence.'[29]

Where authorization was granted, the guidelines stated that it had to be renewed by the authorizing officer after a month; and if surveillance was used more than once during the investigation, a record should have been kept of each occasion.[30] Unlike telephone tapping, as covered by the Interception of Communications Act, the product of such surveillance could be admitted into evidence.[31]

These guidelines reflected some important basic principles, such as proportionality and subsidiarity, which, in Europe and elsewhere, are integral to many pieces of legislation restricting the use of intrusive or deceptive methods of investigation. In this respect, they had few serious critics. However, they were heavily criticized on two scores: first, the fact that they did not have a legal basis; and second, that authorizations were granted by police officers rather than by a member of the judiciary. It was only in response to adverse comments by appeal court judges in the UK and another likely unfavourable decision in the European Court of Human Rights that legislation was eventually introduced, and even then it did not fully meet the second objection. The case of *Khan*[32] challenged the legality of the activities of police officers in gathering evidence, and in doing so raised many similar issues to those in *Malone*.

The appellant had been convicted of importing heroin into the United Kingdom. However, the only clear evidence of this was the recorded conversation between him and another man who, without either of their knowledge (though with the authorization of a Chief Constable, as laid down in the Home Office guidelines), had had a covert listening device attached to the outside wall of his home by the police. Khan was joined in his appeal to the House of Lords by a written submission from the human rights pressure group, Liberty. The appellant's main arguments were (a) that, as the police had no statutory right to install a listening device on private property, they were committing a civil trespass and hence the recording was inadmissible in evidence,[33] (b) that to admit it in evidence would breach Article 8, and (c) that, even if it was strictly admissible under law, the trial judge should have exercised his discretion under section 78 of PACE to exclude it on the grounds of 'unfairness'. The House of Lords dismissed the appeal, reaffirming that there was no general right to privacy under English law. Lord Nolan noted that it was well established that the fundamental test of the admissibility of evidence under English law was relevance.[34] Consequently, even if that evidence had been improperly and unlawfully obtained, it could still be admitted subject to the trial judges' discretion to exclude should it affect the fairness of the proceedings.[35] Article 8 of the Convention could be considered by the trial judge as a factor in this decision, but it was outside of his jurisdiction to decide on these grounds alone.

It was also argued that the police guidelines on the use of bugs were not sufficiently available to members of the public – another argument shared with *Malone*.[36] Although this did not affect the House of Lords decision in the case, it nevertheless prompted two of the Lords to comment on the lack of legislation in this area, echoing remarks of the Lord Chief Justice in an earlier hearing of the case that there was a clear need for clarity in the police use of bugging devices:

'The absence of such a [statutory] system seems astonishing, the more so in view of the statutory framework which has governed the use of such devices by the security service since 1989, and the interception of communications by the police as well as other agencies since 1985.'[37]

'Though I have no doubt in this case that the Chief Constable exercised his discretion fairly and *bona fide*, I consider that fairness both to accused persons and to those who have to exercise this discretion make it highly desirable that such interceptions should be covered by legislation.'[38]

The judges were assured by the government during the case that proposals to legislate in this area were imminent. The promise was kept by the publication of the Police Bill in November 1996. However, it immediately became clear that the proposal was essentially to retain the pre-existing system established by the guidelines, placing it on a statutory footing. In some respects, indeed, the government sought to extend police powers. It was proposed that authorization to enter and bug private premises would still be granted by the Chief Constable, even if the surveillance devices were to be used in solicitors' or journalists' offices and hence to impinge on legal privilege or confidential journalistic material. External oversight was to be exercised in a similar fashion to that established under the Interception of Communications Act 1985 – only after the event, through a review by independent Commissioners of the appropriateness of the authorizations granted. The wide definition of serious crime used in the 1985 Act was also adopted.

These proposals led to a heated debate in the House of Lords and in the media, primarily between those defending the maxim that an 'Englishman's home is his castle'[39] and those extolling the need to give the police greater powers to fight increasingly sophisticated criminals. The nature of the debate, and the polarisation of views it engendered, was encapsulated by Lord Thomas of Gresford:

'Since the 17th century everyone's home has been regarded as inviolate; since the 18th century it has been the rule of the common law that no executive warrant should allow an officer to invade someone's privacy, and here we are, because we face this terrible flood of terrorism, drugs and so on, throwing away basic constitutional freedoms.'[40]

After a number of amendments brought about by this opposition, the Bill was eventually passed as the Police Act 1997. The outcome was a number of somewhat curious and confusing compromises. Opponents to the original Bill had sought to ensure that all prior authorizations to enter or interfere with property were granted by circuit judges.[41] Under the Act, authority is still to be granted by a Chief, or Assistant Chief, Constable, but some authorizations will need prior approval from a Commissioner: this applies to the entry and bugging of private premises[42] and to cases in which bugging is likely to lead to knowledge being acquired of matters subject to legal privilege, confidential personal information or confidential journalistic material.[43] However, this requirement does not apply if the authorizing senior police officer 'believes the case is one of urgency.'[44] John Wadham, Director of Liberty, commenting on the House of Lords debate on this issue, noted that:

'The danger of this is that expediency may make such "urgent" applications too frequent and quashing authorisations once the surveillance is in progress is unlikely to happen. Liberty takes the view that surveillance is too important to allow such a loophole and that arrangements for urgent judicial authorisations are practicable' (*The Times*, 21 January 1997, p. 45).

The requirement for Commissioners to approve certain types of request also raises the question of the effectiveness of the complaints system. In such cases, there appears to be a clear conflict of interest in the event of a complaint, as it is another Commissioner who is responsible for investigating the decision.[45] Madeleine Colvin, legal officer at Justice, expressed this concern in *The Guardian* (17 January 1997, p. 19):

'We believe that it is mistaken to suppose that Commissioners can exercise independent control of operations that they themselves have authorised. At the same time, those making the complaint might well feel that their right to seek redress by way of an independent investigation is somewhat prejudiced for similar reasons.'

The criteria which the authorizing officer has to meet before granting the use of electronic devices is also somewhat broader than had been required under the guidelines. The requirement that 'there must be a good reason to believe that use of equipment would be likely to lead to arrest and conviction' has been replaced by the stipulation that it must be 'necessary for the action specified to be taken on the ground that it is likely to be of substantive value in the prevention or detection of serious crime.'[46] Similarly, the requirement that normal methods of investigation have been tried and failed, or would be unlikely to succeed if tried, has been replaced by 'what the action seeks to achieve cannot reasonably be achieved by other means.'[47] These subtle changes clearly give the authorizing officer far greater discretion to justify the use of these techniques solely on intelligence gathering grounds.

This leads to a situation where suspects, even at the court stage, might not be aware that covert surveillance has been used on their property or that of their associates, provided that the police can gain evidence from other sources as a result of the intelligence gained through the operation. It also offers little protection where the police have engaged in 'fishing expeditions' against individuals based on general suspicion alone, and no further evidence is forthcoming.

Finally, it should be emphasized that the new legislation covers only 'entry on or interference with property or with wireless telegraphy'. This leaves other forms of electronic surveillance regulated only by internal guidelines. Many alternative ways of listening in to conversations, in public and in private places, are already easily available, and others are being developed rapidly. Examples include long distance microphones (used from, say, a rented property near to someone's house) and laser technology (which can reconstruct conversations from the vibrations of windows caused by shockwaves from speech). Methods are also available for access to other forms of private communication, including those associated with computers.

Closed circuit television

Unlike the techniques discussed in the previous two sections, most surveillance by the use of closed circuit television (CCTV) is relatively overt: it is not difficult to know or find out that a particular building, road or street is permanently monitored by cameras (though a surprisingly high number of people remain unaware of street cameras) (Honess and Charman 1992). Indeed, there is often a clear general deterrent intention, with many cameras being easily visible and their presence advertised. (This deterrent intention is also demonstrated in the use of 'dummy' cameras containing no film, to deter motorists from speeding.)

In Britain, especially, there has been almost an exponential increase in the installation of CCTV cameras, and especially of interlinked systems of cameras covering large sections of city centres. Well over 200 towns and cities already have such systems, while – to take just a few examples from other settings – there are over 5000 cameras in the London Underground, cameras at all 30 junctions of the M25 motorway, and systems in rapidly increasing numbers of hospitals, schools, and even housing estates.[48] Where street cameras are concerned, the increase can be accounted for to a considerable degree by commercial considerations (attracting more people to city centres by making them safer places for ordinary people to use) (Norris et al., 1996) and has been fuelled by what have often been exaggerated claims about dramatic falls in crime after their installation.[49] On the whole, the public has been supportive of this trend, any concern about the threat to privacy being tempered by most people's perception that they are more protected than intruded upon (Honess and Charman 1992). Indeed, CCTV has quite often been touted as the panacea for a multitude of evils:

> 'Incidents such as the Bulger murder [where a young child was abducted from a shopping centre covered by CCTV and subsequently murdered] seem to fuel not a desire for better and more cohesive communities, but better and more effective surveillance ... [because] the initial pictures were so unclear' (*Sunday Times,* 28 August 1994).

Nevertheless, the sheer speed and scale of developments in this area has begun to raise some serious concerns.

First of all, there are few controls over the installation of CCTV cameras, either in terms of location or who can set them up. The range, quality and flexibility of the cameras are improving all the time, as are the capabilities for storage of images, especially in digital form, making them a much more powerful tool with high potential for intrusiveness (and indeed, if so desired, prurience). Secondly, there are few legal restrictions on how and by whom CCTV systems and their outputs may be used. Typically, they are financed and 'owned' either by the council, groups of local traders, or a combination of both, though it is becoming more common for police forces to act as full paying partners. Consequently, there are varying levels throughout the country of police involvement in their operation, and of police access to the screens and to recordings. In some areas, the police are fully involved in the monitoring of the system, including having screens located and manned within the local police station. In others, they are routinely informed by the council or private operators if a crime, public order incident or suspicious behaviour is observed, or are given access to the system when they wish to undertake a planned operation against, for example, shoplifters or drug dealers. In others, again, police involvement is rare, and access to recordings unusual except in serious cases. Similarly, there are differences in the extent to which other agencies are granted access. At the extreme, video tapes (of fights, accidents, copulating couples, and so on) have been sold to commercial distributors or to television companies, resulting in incidents being displayed for entertainment. One of the worst examples concerned a man filmed, without his knowledge, as he attempted to commit suicide: he later saw this without warning on a television programme.

Thirdly, the most worrying aspect for some commentators lies in the development of automated systems, which are already used to recognize car number plates and compare them with data bases (as in the 'ring of steel' around the City of London, designed to combat the threat of terrorist car bombs) and will in the near future become much more adept at recognizing specific kinds of movement or activity, and even individual faces in a crowd. The long term potential for the harassment or exclusion of people who are deemed 'undesirable' in any particular environment, not to mention for keeping track of individuals' movements around the country, is considerable, raising the spectre of 'Big Brother' (this argument is put forcefully by Norris et al., 1996).

In the absence of any central government interest in placing controls on CCTV, it is only recently that any systematic attempt at regulation has been made. This emerged from an initiative by a group representing local government authorities, the LGIU, which conducted a survey of interested parties' views and eventually produced a model code of practice, now recommended to all local councils. This draws heavily upon data protection principles, emphasizing the importance of the first principle of the Data Protection Act 1984, that 'The information to be contained in personal data shall be obtained, and personal data shall be processed, fairly and lawfully.'

The main requirements of the code of practice are that the owners of the system clearly and publicly define its purposes and objectives; that any recordings are used only in accordance with these objectives, and stored no longer than is necessary to achieve them; that there are protocols for the police use of the system; and that accountability is built in through audit, evaluation and independent inspection. Importance is also attached to the establishment of an effective complaints mechanism. However, laudable as this initiative is, adherence to the code is purely voluntary, and there are many systems which are not covered by it at all.

In sum, while CCTV has many obvious benefits, the potentially damaging implications of its unchecked expansion for personal privacy and other civil liberties have been largely ignored in the general euphoria. There is a strong case for a major government review of these issues and for the development of principled and effective forms of regulation. One avenue to consider might be the amendment of data protection laws to make them more directly applicable to the storage and analysis of images (this is of particular relevance to the growing use of digital cameras).

Concluding comments

The overall message of this chapter has been that, while the use of surveillance has expanded enormously in both degree and diversity, mechanisms for its regulation have remained weak, uncoordinated and unable to keep up with the pace of change. In illustrating a similar process over the last 50 years in the United States, Gary Marx describes a shift from a society in which a Secretary of War could simply state in response to demands for increased 'national security' that 'Gentlemen do not read each other's mail', to one in which monitoring of individuals' behaviour, communications, travels, financial transactions, and many other aspects of their lives, is easily carried out and far from a rare occurrence (Marx 1988, p. 2). An important feature of this change, in Britain as in the United States, is that it has been gradual and persistent, rather than sudden and dramatic: what Marx calls a process of 'surveillance creep'. It is partly this which explains the curiously low level of publicly expressed concern about the erosion of privacy and other civil liberties which has taken place, and which has allowed successive governments to do very little to prevent it. (Ironically, much more public vigilance on such issues has been in evidence in past eras when surveillance technology was unsophisticated.) Police surveillance forms only a small part of this overall picture, but is particularly important by dint of the special powers of the police and the scale of the technical and other resources available to them. An added dimension is recent legislation allowing the involvement of the largely unaccountable secret services in the collection of criminal intelligence.[50]

Of course, concern about police surveillance, like concern about the spread of CCTV, is greatly tempered by the belief that it is both necessary and effective in the 'fight against crime'. This is a particularly potent argument where operations against 'organized crime' are concerned, as electronic surveillance of private property may play an indispensable part in the eventual prosecution of key figures 'behind the scenes'. Consequently, there are few who would argue that its use should be forbidden altogether, and even in countries which have strict general laws on privacy, it is normally recognized that these may be breached by the police when there is an overriding reason to do so. Similarly, the European Court intimated in *Lüdi v Switzerland* (a judgement reminiscent of the American courts' approach) that a person who uses his home to engage in the planning of major drug trafficking offences, can no longer have a 'reasonable expectation of privacy' and hence has little cause for complaint when his room is bugged by the police.[51]

On the other hand, it is a long step from this position to acceptance of freedom for the police to undertake surveillance of any kind upon anyone at any time in the name of crime prevention. If any value at all is attached to the notion of personal privacy, there must be some relationship between the seriousness of the criminal activity suspected and the intrusiveness of methods used to investigate it. Equally, intrusive surveillance should not be used without a reasonable level of prior suspicion that criminal activity is taking place (as opposed to mere 'fishing expeditions'); without a demonstrable need to use, say, a 'bug' rather than some less intrusive method; and without a system of independent authorization in which the necessity of the action is probed and limits are placed upon the scope and time-scale of the proposed surveillance.

As we have shown, there are three main methods by which control can be exercised: internal guidelines or regulations (in combination with tight supervision to ensure they are followed); legislation; and decisions in the courts. All three are important in any effective system of regulation. In England and Wales, however, they as yet have failed to produce, individually or in combination, the kind of tight, principled and consistent regulation which gives one full confidence that powerful methods of surveillance will be used only where absolutely necessary and with due respect for civil liberties.

Notes

1   Professor Maguire wishes to extend grateful thanks to the Leverhulme Trust for the award of a research fellowship which allowed him to undertake background research for this and other related publications.
2   Typically where an undercover officer has befriended a suspect in order to induce them to 'confess' to a crime in a recorded conversation – see *R v Hall* (1994), *The Times*, 11 March and *R v Stagg* (1994), *The Times*, 15 September.
3   For a discussion of the regulation of other proactive policing methods, see Maguire and John 1996.
4   As in the use of 'sniffer dogs' to monitor luggage for drugs.
5   *Katz v United States*, 389 US 347. In subsequent cases, it has been declared that there is no infringement of a reasonable expectation of privacy in a number of surveillance situations, including the monitoring of 'public activity' (e.g. electronically tracking a vehicle) and of 'semi-private areas' (e.g. aerial surveillance of a back yard), and the recording of a conversation when one party has consented (e.g. by the use of a body bug). For further discussion of the position in the US, see Slobogin 1995.

6   St Tr 1029, 1066.

7   (1972 Ch19, para. 503). The report went on to opine that: 'The [public] fear of these devices is sharper when they are used surreptitiously ...' (para. 539).

8   *Malone v Metropolitan Police Commissioner* [1979] Ch 344.

9   Most importantly the Birkett Report (Cmnd. 283, 1957) and the Report of Lord Diplock, *The Interception of Communications in Great Britain* (Cmnd. 8191, 1981).

10 ECHR 2 August 1984, Series A, vol. 82 (*Malone v UK*). For detailed discussions of the case see Baxter, 1990, Andrews, 1985 and Pogany, 1984.

11 Article 8 states that:
    '1. Everyone has the right to respect for his private and family life, his home and his correspondence.
    2. There shall be no interference by a public authority with the exercise of this right except such as is in accordance with the law and is necessary in a democratic society in the interests of national security, public safety or the economic well-being of the country, for the prevention of disorder or crime, for the protection of health and morals, or for the protection of the rights and freedoms of others.'

12 The Court held that 'The law must be sufficiently clear in its terms to give citizens an adequate indication as to the circumstances in which and the conditions on which public authorities are empowered to resort to this secret and potentially dangerous interference with the right to respect for private life and correspondence.' (*Malone,* para. 67)

13 Such a requirement is now provided in section 78(1) of PACE 1984: 'In any proceedings the court may refuse to allow evidence on which the prosecution seeks to rely to be given if it appears to the court that, having regard to all the circumstances, *including the circumstances in which the evidence was obtained,* the admission of the evidence would have such an adverse affect on the fairness of the proceedings that the court ought not to admit it.' [Emphasis added]

14 Here legislators ignored the recommendation of the Royal Commission on Criminal Procedure, that magistrates' courts should be responsible for the granting of all warrants (Cmnd. 8092: 3.57). Later, in *Christie v UK*, this system of executive approval was held by the European Commission on Human Rights not to breach the Convention (Decision No. 21482/93 78-A DR 119).

15 Interception of Communications Act 1985, section 7 and section 8.

16 Interception of Communications Act 1985, section 10(3).

17 Discussing the adoption of this definition in the Police Act 1997, the playwright Harold Pinter noted that: 'The definition of possible criminality is quite extraordinarily broad; it could criminalise protestors against motorways or even a body of writers protesting for human rights in Turkey.' *The Guardian,* 13 January 1997, p. 5.

18 For an account of alleged covert intelligence operations against members of the Campaign for Nuclear Disarmament see Reeve and Smith 1986.

19 Interception of Communications Act 1985, section 9(1)(b).

20 *R v Preston* [1993] 4 All ER 638, [1994] 2 AC 130.

21 Such a duty exists, for example, in Denmark. It is also advocated in the Council of Europe Recommendation No. R(87)15 on the Use of Personal Data.

22 [1994] 3 WLR 583.

23 [1995] 2 All ER 231.

24 [1995] CrimLR 247.

25 ECHR 25 June 1997, 74/1996/692/884 (*Halford v UK*).

26 Guidelines on the Use of Equipment in Police Surveillance Operations 1984.

27 Guidelines, para. 7.

28 Guidelines, para. 4.

29 Guidelines, para. 5

30 Guidelines, para. 8.

31 Guidelines, para. 10

32 *R v Khan (Sultan)* [1996] 3 All ER 289. Other 'bugging' cases in which such challenges have failed include those in which listening devices were placed in police interview rooms and cells – *R v Ali* (1991), *The Times*, 19 February and *R v Bailey* (1993) *The Times*, 22 March. Also *R v Chief Constable of West Yorkshire Police ex p Govell* QBD, 23 May 1994 for judicial review of the police drilling a hole in the outside wall of his property in order to attach a listening device. The action was dismissed by the Divisional Court and is now going to Europe.

33 See also the judgement of Megarry V-C in *Malone v Metropolitan Police Commissioner* [1979] Ch 344: 'The reason why a search of premises which is not authorised by law is illegal is that it involves the tort of trespass to those premises: and any trespass, whether to land or goods or the person, that is made without legal authority is prima facie illegal. Telephone tapping by the Post Office, on the other hand, involves no act of trespass ... all that is done is done within the Post Office's own domain.' Clearly the situation in *Khan* could not be so distinguished.

34 *R v Sang* [1979] 2 All ER 1222, [1980] AC 402.

35 ECHR 15 June 1992, Series A, vol. 238 (*Lüdi v Switzerland*) where even though the surveillance evidence had been improperly obtained the conviction could still stand due to the existence of other corroborative evidence.

36 At *Khan* p. 295. The guidelines had been placed in the House of Commons library.

37 At p. 302 (Lord Nolan).

38 At p. 292 (Lord Slynn of Hadley).

39 Established in common law since the decision in *Entick v Carrington,* ibid.

40 *Hansard* 26 November 1996: Column 220.

41 Prior approval from the judiciary is a common feature of European and Commonwealth jurisdictions, as well as the United States.

42 Such property is defined in section 97(2)(a) of the Police Act if it (i) is used wholly or mainly as a dwelling or as a bedroom in a hotel, or (ii) constitutes office premises.

43 Police Act 1997, section 97(2)(b).

44 Police Act 1997, section 97(3).

45 Police Act 1997, section 102.

46 Police Act 1997, section 93(2)(a).

47 Police Act 1997, section 93(2)(b).

48 The figures given are taken from Norris, Moran and Armstrong 1996.

49 For example, 'Figures released last week showed that in the first full year of operation [in Airdrie], the cameras cut crime in the town by 75%; car crime was reduced by 94%, as were commercial break-ins; vandalism fell by 84%; public disorder offences were cut by 42%, and the number of serious assaults was halved.' *Sunday Times,* 17 April 1994.

50 Security Services Act 1996.

51 ECHR 15 June 1992, Series A, vol. 238 (*Lüdi v Switzerland*). Similar sentiments, though expressed more bluntly, can be identified in Lord Nolan's expression of 'relief' at being able to uphold the conviction in *Khan*: 'It would be a strange reflection of our law if a man who has admitted his participation in the illegal importation of a large quantity of heroin should have his conviction set aside on the grounds that his privacy had been invaded.' (at *Khan*, p. 302).

References

Andrews, J. (1985), Telephone Tapping in the UK, *10 European Law Review* 68.

Baxter, J. (1990), *State Security, Privacy and Information*, London: Harvester Wheatsheaf.

Honess, T. and E. Charman (1992), *Closed Circuit Television in Public Places: Its. Acceptability and Perceived Effectiveness*, Crime Prevention Unit Series, Paper 35, London: Home Office.

Maguire, M. and T. John (1996), Covert and Deceptive Policing in England and Wales: Issues in Regulation and Practice, 4 *European Journal of Crime, Criminal Law and Criminal Justice*, pp. 316-334.

Marx, G.T. (1988), *Undercover: Police Surveillance in America*, Berkeley: University of California Press.

Norris, C., J. Moran and G. Armstrong, *Algorythmic surveillance: the future of automated visual surveillance*, Paper to Conference on CCTV and Social Control, University of Hull, 9th July, 1996.

Pogany, I. (1984), Telephone Tapping and the European Convention on Human Rights, 134 *New Law Journal*.

Reeve, G. and J. Smith (1986), *Offences of the Realm: How Peace Campaigners Get Bugged,* London: CND.

Slobogin, C. (1995), *Technology and Law Enforcement Legislation*, Paper to First World Conference on New Trends in Criminal Investigation and Evidence.

4 The legal framework of covert and proactive policing in France

STEWART FIELD[1]

Introduction

Two distinctive features of covert policing in France are brought out in the literature. The first is its omnipresence in the political sphere (Monjardet and Lévy 1995; Brunet 1990). The second is that such policing tactics, at least in that political sphere, are of long standing: '[f]ar from being some modern invention, it is an age-old French tradition.' (Monjardet and Lévy 1995, p. 30). For these reasons Claude Journès' chapter (which follows this one) stresses exactly those historical and political dimensions of covert policing in France. But this leaves open questions as to the use of such methods in combating organized or ordinary street crime in contemporary France. This short chapter outlines the legal framework within which such policing takes place and uses both secondary literature and some preliminary findings from an empirical study of French defence lawyers to indicate something of contemporary practice.[2]

Monjardet and Lévy (1995, p. 30-31) have stressed that an understanding of the organizational separations of French policing is vital to an appreciation of the contexts of covert policing. They distinguish six main sections of the National Police: *Renseignements Généraux* and *Direction de la Surveillance du Territoire*, which are involved in the political policing discussed by Journès, the *Police Urbaine* and *CRS (Compagnies Républicaines de Sécurité)* which deal with public order policing,[3] and the *Police Judiciaire* and the Customs divisions. These last two sections, along with the investigative sections of the *Gendarmerie*, are the units that are most likely to use proactive or covert methods against ordinary street or organized crime because investigation of crime is the core of their mandate.

General framework

Certain covert methods have a special (if sometimes partial) regulatory framework[4] but most depend on general articles of the Code of Criminal Procedure (henceforth CCP) empowering police officers and investigating magistrates. Article 75 CCP gives the *police judiciaire* the right to proceed to preliminary inquiries, either on the instructions of the Prosecutor or on their own initiative.[5] Article 14 entrusts to them the task of detecting offences, looking for their authors and assembling evidence. Article 12 gives the *Procureur de la République* the duty of directing them in this task. These articles seem broad enough to include investigative work that anticipates a particular offence (i.e. proactive investigation).[6] Investigation into the most serious offences (*crimes* and complex *délits*) is controlled by the examining magistrate: investigative acts by the police may be done only under the authority of his or her *commissions rogatoires*.[7] It is these complex and important cases that one might expect to justify the use of covert methods in the eyes of the authorities but it must be remembered that the *juge d'instruction* can be given charge of a case only *after* an infraction has taken place (Chambon 1997, pp. 47-50). So the *juge d'instruction* can and does commission the use of covert methods but not *proactively* in the sense of investigation prior to the committing of the offence.

This is the legal framework for investigating specific infractions. As in other Continental jurisdictions, there is a different legal framework for policing aimed at the maintenance of public order and the prevention of offences on the one hand, and their investigation on the other. This is the distinction between the work of the *police administrative* and the *police judiciaire* but the divisions do not exactly correspond to the work of different sections of the police because in fact the same police officers can often exercise both functions (Stefani et al. 1996, pp. 286-288; West et al. 1992, pp. 173-174, 221-222). The difference is in the regulatory framework: it is administrative law which regulates the actions of the police in the domain of public order: criminal procedure only regulates police in the investigative sphere. If the administrative courts were to be regarded as having jurisdiction, they would determine not only the legality of the exercise of power but whether it was in the public interest: here notions of proportionality and subsidiarity of the measure are key criteria[8] (Carlier 1992). Because this part of the book is principally concerned with the covert *investigation* of offences, albeit sometimes before they have been committed, in what follows the emphasis will be on the legal framework for covert and proactive policing provided by criminal procedure.

Criminal procedure and covert techniques

Surveillance

One must distinguish between three systems of surveillance:
a. physical surveillance without complex technical means;
b. interception of telecommunications; and
c. surveillance by other technical means (bugs, video-cameras, directional etc.).

In our recent study of French defence lawyers we came across many instances of the use of telephone taps both in relation to drugs cases and those thought to involve 'organized criminality'.[9] The use of informers followed by telephone taps was regarded as almost routine in drugs cases by several criminal specialists.[10] We found evidence of surveillance and shadowing (sometimes with photography or video-recording) and informers being used against gypsies who were perceived to be often involved in professional crime, especially robbery and burglary, and who very rarely gave up admissions during police custody.[11] On the other hand the use of special technical equipment for covert recording of conversations (other than via telephone tapping) was something we did not come across: the magistrates with whom we discussed the legal position were clearly working from general principles. Neither they nor our avocats, when we raised the issue, seemed to have direct experience of such methods.[12] One Prosecutor said that this might be the kind of thing one might do in big terrorist cases around Paris but he had not come across it personally.[13] In part this may be because the technical assistance required for telephone taps is provided by France Telecom whereas other bugging systems require more expensive electronic equipment.[14] Furthermore, as we shall see, the legal framework specific to other forms of surveillance outside the realm of telecommunications is more problematic for the police.

Physical surveillance without technical devices

In France, as in most of Europe, observation or surveillance is regarded as a traditional and indispensable means of investigation in certain kinds of cases (Gropp 1993). It has no special legal framework and depends for its justification either on the general CCP articles (Articles 14, 75) empowering police officers (in the preliminary inquiry)[15] and investigating magistrates (where cases are judicially investigated). The CCP stresses the consensual nature of the preliminary inquiry but of course this does not exclude police presence in public places, even when observing a hunt meeting with binoculars.[16] Nor does it prevent the acceptance of evidence obtained by police by listening in a cupboard when they have been invited to enter by somebody with the authority to grant permission.[17] These general articles seem to be the only legal basis necessary for most physical surveillance from points to which the police have access by consensual means.[18] During police inquiries there is no formal need for the prior authority of the Prosecutor (but they would expect to be kept informed).[19] In the context of inquiries lead by investigating magistrates (*instructions*), the requirement that all investigative acts, which includes covert policing acts, be ordered by the *juge d'instruction* in the form of a *commission rogatoire* provides a judicial control. However, critics have suggested that the police retain a great deal of autonomy because the *commission rogatoire* might take the form of a direction to conduct 'all investigations useful to the search for the truth'. But within the context of a normal relationship it is extremely unlikely that the police would undertake surveillance without at least verbal consultation with the examining magistrate 'in charge' of the case.

Interception of telecommunications

As for technical surveillance devices, telephone tapping – and all interception of links by means of telecommunications – must be authorized by a *juge d'instruction* (unless they are so-called 'administrative taps' about which see below).[20] A 1991 Act inserted provisions into the CCP which restrict 'judicial taps' to investigations of *crimes* and *délits* punishable with more than two years imprisonment. They can last for up to four months and are renewable. The telecommunications of those who are not suspected of criminal involvement in the offence may be intercepted as well as those under suspicion. The recordings are transcribed in the form of a *procès-verbal* (written report) (Chambon 1997, pp. 126-127). The *juge d'instruction* must order the tap: the police may not listen to or record telephone conversations in preliminary inquiries (i.e. outside the context of *instruction*).[21] However there is a system of administrative taps which is described by Claude Journès in this volume in which the Secretary for Defence (who is in charge of the *Gendarmerie*) and the Secretary of the Interior (in control of the *Police Nationale*) can apply for administrative taps in order to combat – inter alia – organized crime. The number of taps ordered by examining magistrates (*écoutes judiciaires*) has increased dramatically in recent years (11 299 in 1995 as opposed to 5664 in 1991).[22] Furthermore the number of administrative taps – those most likely to be 'proactive' – permitted for the purpose of preventing organized crime had risen to 1321 by 1995.[23]

Two of the criminal specialists we observed stressed that they thought illegal tapping – *écoutes sauvages* – by investigators also went on.[24]

There is another situation in which the police may use recordings of telephone conversations outside the context (and controls) of a judicial investigation. Case law permits reliance on such recordings if they are made by third parties participating in the conversation, such as the *partie civile* or victim (for example by applying a listening device to the handset) – provided the police do not play an 'active' role in setting up the private recording.[25] It is not yet clear what the limits of 'active' participation are nor whether the *Cour de Cassation* would accept recordings made by informers or undercover agents recruited by the police. Furthermore, 'number tracing', whereby the numbers which are being called are identified but the conversations not monitored, can be authorized by the Prosecutor for police inquiries as well as by the *juge d'instruction*.[26]

Other technical means

In relation to 'bugging', the use of directional microphones or hidden cameras, the main substantive control is the offence under Article 226-1 *Nouveau Code Pénal* of 'violation of the intimacy of the private life of another'.[27] To be punishable this must be deliberate and done by:

a. listening in to, recording or transmitting private or confidential words without the consent of the speaker; or
b. capturing, recording or transmitting the image of somebody in a private place without their consent.[28]

This would seem to make criminal offences of a wide range of possible covert policing methods, for example the use of directional mikes or bugs to pick up conversations or zoom-lens cameras to photograph or video suspects. But, at least in the context of picking up conversations (as opposed to capturing images) the ambit of the offence was limited under its previous incarnation (Article 368 *Ancien Code Pénal*) by restrictive interpretation of what represented 'intimacy' of private life. Although the *Cour de Cassation* varied over time it often limited this part of the offence to conversations by members of the same family and even then excluded conversation which were financial.[29] Thus – though it remains to be seen how the new article will be interpreted – in some contexts it is not easy to define which conversations recorded by the police may fall foul of the legislation.

What would be the legal position if evidence was obtained by a breach of Article 226-1? The *Chambre Criminelle* has decided – in a case that clearly seemed to involve a violation of the intimacy of private life – that this need not necessarily lead to the evidence thereby obtained being excluded from the dossier.[30] But this was in a case where the recording had been made by the defendant's wife, not the police, and that was explicitly stated to be a factor in the decision to allow the evidence to be presented. The court refused to exclude the recording because, as it was made by a private party and not the police, it was not an official investigative act but merely a piece of evidence (and therefore not susceptible to nullification).[31] By implication, if the police or examining magistrate had made the recording the issues would be different (though the court does not explicitly decide that in that sort of case the evidence would definitely be excluded). The argument would be that it would be contrary to a general principle of criminal procedure, fairness in the search for evidence (*la loyauté de la preuve*) if the police were to be allowed to collect evidence using illegal means. Hence it might be argued that such evidence, and all other evidence that refers to it, should be excluded from the dossier. It is not absolutely certain that the *Cour de Cassation* would accept this: in recent years the Court has reiterated on several occasions the idea that it is not for criminal courts to exclude evidence simply on the grounds that it was obtained in an 'illicit or unfair' way.[32] However the cases have tended to involve questionable behaviour by the *victim* or *partie civile* and there is a significant difference between illicit and unfair on the one hand, and illegal on the other. What one can say is that the *Cour de Cassation* has never hitherto gone so far with covert methods *by the police* as to accept evidence obtained as the result of criminal offences by police officers.

If the court maintains this position it may lead to some fine distinctions: covert bugging by *private parties* in breach of Article 226-1 might lead to evidence being accepted whereas the same practice by the *police* (even under *commissions rogatoires*) would not. If that turns out to be the position one can expect cases involving recordings made by participating informers to raise some nice questions as to when the police are 'actively' involved. Only once they are would this become an investigative act and any illegal recording therefore liable to be nullified.

If an offence has not been committed by the police under Article 226-1, the legal position as to covert recordings is very uncertain. Procedurally the key question is whether the *Cour de Cassation* would accept reliance on evidence thus produced, whether ostensibly sanctioned by a *juge d'instruction* under the general powers of Articles 81 and 151 to conduct investigations useful to the search for the truth or by a prosecutor under his equivalent powers under Article 81 CCP. (In fact if such technical covert means were used 'reactively' they would probably involve a *juge d'instruction* because it would be likely to be the kind of case a prosecutor would regard as meriting an *instruction*.) The French courts tend to accept such evidence arguing that no legal provision prevents judges from making use of proof advanced by the parties on the ground that it has been obtained illicitly or unfairly (Stefani 1996, p. 35). Thus the courts have accepted written reports of police officers based on observations made while hidden in a cupboard of a Mayor when he tipped them off that he was going to be offered a bribe. The Court stressed that there was no interference with private life in the sense of a criminal offence, that the police officers were passive, just letting things happen and that they did not 'provoke' (i.e. cause) the offence. It would seem strange if the position were different had a tape-recorder been used to assist their memory in drawing up the *procès-verbal* (the technical term for an official report of investigative acts). And once that is admitted does it matter if the police are in the cupboard or just leave a microphone? This seems likely to put police in the clear – *provided* they avoid breaching Article 226 for most normal forms of evidence-gathering by covert surveillance (other than by intercepting telecommunications where they must get examining magistrate approval). Defence lawyers might argue for exclusion on the basis of Article 8 of the European Convention on Human Rights, given that the Convention is directly applicable in France. However the view expressed in *Lüdi* that what is protected is a 'legitimate expectation of privacy' tends to cut down the potential for such a defence.[33] If criminals can expect to meet undercover agents it is arguable they must expect to be the target of electronic surveillance. The only other substantive control of technical devices is the legislation discussed by Claude Journès on video-recording. This applies only to public places.

Infiltration or undercover operations by police

It has been claimed that the use of infiltration as a tactic in 'political' cases has reduced considerably since the arrival of the left in power and the unionization of the police (Brunet 1990, pp. 72-73). On the other hand, infiltration (and more widely the use of informers) is practically systematic in drugs cases, especially – but not exclusively – where the Customs are involved in the investigation.[34] Penetration is itself arguably lawful on the basis of the general investigative powers already cited provided it does not involve the commission of offences. But of course almost all serious long-term infiltration in organized crime does involve the commission of offences even if only as an accomplice in relatively minor crimes. It is here that infiltration has produced particular problems in the drugs context: in 1991 four Customs investigators were arrested in and around Lyon on drug trafficking charges by the *police nationale* after infiltrating a Moroccan cannabis ring. The subsequent scandal led to allegations that Customs investigators were out of control. This in turn led to more developed requirements of prior judicial authority for drugs undercover operations. A rapid legislative response was to legalize controlled deliveries of drugs provided they were submitted to the prior authorization of the *Procureur de la République*. Article 706-32 CCP now provides that 'in order to identify those responsible for drugs offences, officers and agents of the *police judiciaire* (including customs officers) may, after having informed the *Procureur de la République*, proceed to place drugs in transit under surveillance'. They are not criminally responsible when for a such purpose, with the authorization of the Prosecutor or the Examining Magistrate responsible for the case, they 'acquire, hold, transport or deliver such drugs or their product or put at the disposal of persons means of a legal nature, or means of transport or storage or conservation or communication'. However, authorization can only be given for such acts where they do not 'provoke' the commission of the offence.[35] The case law in this area is complex and contradictory.[36] The Prosecutor will have to decide whether what is proposed is legally acceptable or whether it goes too far. According to a French prosecutor such advance authorization is not granted by phone.[37] The officers will have to explain to the Prosecutor what they have found out about the network and how they are seeking to track its members. Apparently the more extensive the support the more the Prosecutor will want to know. Control would be detailed if, for example, it is being suggested that a boat be chartered by the authorities to transport the drugs so as to be able to arrest the traffickers on arrival in French territorial waters.[38]

This legislation deals with the criminality of the investigators. The question whether the evidence that they accumulate will be admissible is one that has caused difficulty because the reasoning of the courts does not always proceed from the same point of departure. Often the courts ask themselves whether the undercover operator provoked the offence in the sense of determining that it be committed. If so, the courts have tended to reason that the mens rea of the accused has been vitiated and he or she is acquitted. If there is evidence that the accused would have committed the offence anyway then he or she is convicted. Sometimes the courts decide this issue by looking at the intensity and extensiveness of the potentially 'entrapping' activity. Thus, restricted activity, such as simply not revealing one's identity, would not be regarded as provoking the infraction. However repeated exercise of pressure or persuasion might well be so regarded. Another factor sometimes stressed is whether the offence is simply part of a pre-existing course of criminality.[39]

Infiltration by non-police (participating informers)

Problems are still sometimes evident in Prosecutor/Customs relations in this sphere. Recently a court in Toulouse acquitted two defendants arrested by Customs while transporting large quantities of cocaine. The Customs denied that they had been involved in infiltrating the network, claiming to have received an anonymous tip-off. The defence lawyers claimed that the operation had been closely observed and even set up by Customs using two infiltrants (two traffickers who got away). The Prosecutor recognized that there had been infiltration and that he had approved it. Yet no written permission from Prosecutor or *juge d'instruction* could be found on the file (and remember the 1991 Act only authorizes *the police* to commit offences). There were also allegations that the Customs provided all the logistics for the operation.[40] Now one point to make is that in such situations the practical 'immunity' from prosecution accorded to the civilian infiltrants flows, not from the 1991 Act – which applies to police officers and customs officials – but from the general principle of *opportunité de poursuite*. Thus civilian undercover operatives run by the Customs remain vulnerable to prosecution by the Prosecutor – something which might suggest the need for close cooperation and information-sharing between the two. The problem has been the long-running tensions between police and customs, in part natural rivalry over their respective roles in the 'war against drugs' and in part a product of different institutional priorities. Customs, according to a prosecutor we met during our study of French lawyers, privilege large and thus valuable finds (which then receive wide publicity): the police and magistrates tend to target sophisticated distributors and think some customs operations are not run long enough to pick up these key targets.[41]

Another important point here is that the system of permissions for infiltration and surveillance in 'controlled delivery' operations only applies to drugs operations. Elsewhere judicial authority can make no difference if an undercover operation leads to the infiltrant (whether police officer or civilian) committing a criminal offence. He or she risks prosecution whether or not authority has been sought. The only recourse is to the principle of *opportunité de poursuite* (Levasseur 1996, pp. 464-465).

Informers[42]

For the purposes of this chapter informers will be defined – following Di Marino – as persons who provide information on a case without their identity being disclosed, who may or may not receive a particular advantage in exchange (Di Marino 1990, p. 64). The use of such informers – who of course may or may not be participating informers – does not require any kind of judicial prior authority: police reference to information received from an anonymous source is fairly frequent in French dossiers without such reference.[43] Its credibility is a matter for the appreciation of the judges (and jurors in the most serious cases).

In various ways French dossiers often effectively disguise the real role(s) of informers. Sometimes, a tip-off is presented as being anonymous when the identity of the informer is actually known. In one case the police themselves revealed in court that information presented in a police *procès-verbal* as having come from an anonymous source was actually a tip-off from a co-accused.[44] On another occasion, at another site, a researcher was observing the work of the Duty Prosecutor when a police officer came to report progress on investigating a hold-up. The officer said that two named persons were implicated but used a linguistic form that left the origins of the information as vague as possible.[45] The Prosecutor did not pursue the issue. The officer then said that the police had received an anonymous letter saying where one of the persons was to be found. The Prosecutor said later that one should not be fooled by this: it meant the information was from a known informer. But again it was not something pursued at the time or regarded as other than routine: the information was simply passed to a *juge d'instruction* for further investigation.[46] A researcher attended a meeting of Prosecutors and OPJs[47] at one site where the Prosecutor specifically told the police not to put the names of those who gave tip-offs in the file to avoid defence lawyers later asking for a confrontation with the witness. The Prosecutor explained that if the request is denied, lawyers would claim on the basis of Article 6.3.d of the European Convention that they had been denied the right to put questions to a witness against them and demand a nullity.[48] Hence withholding the name of the informer was a way of avoiding this: the judge could just say the informer was not known and so a confrontation was not possible. Once we followed a case where the file contained an apparently verbatim report of the anonymous phone call which suggested the call had been taped and may well have been genuinely anonymous. More usually such intelligence was reported in summary only – which might well allow the identity of a known informer to be hidden.[49] French defence lawyers said that stops by Customs of those carrying drugs were very rarely random but were often presented as if they were. The defence lawyer would often suspect that an informer was involved but could not be sure and there would be no trace in the file of the tip-off.[50] Avocats could certainly ask the President of the Tribunal or the *juge d'instruction* (if the case was being judicially investigated) for an anonymous witness to be sought and questioned but the judge or magistrate has a broad discretion to refuse in order to protect the identity of the informer.[51] We never saw a defence lawyer ask for this and an examining magistrate we interviewed said that he would be unlikely to accept such a request because the key information in the dossier was usually the evidence accumulated as a result of the tip-off not where tip-off came from.[52]

The Code of Criminal Procedure makes no reference to informers. The legality of using within the dossier anonymously given information is based on long-standing case law of the *Chambre Criminelle de la Cour de Cassation* that is unchallenged (Di Marino 1990, p. 66). Implicitly this is based on the fundamental starting point in French criminal procedure – freedom of proof – but the precise justification given is in terms of professional secrecy. The argument is that the protection of his or her sources is a necessary and honourable part of a police officer's professional duty and the court judging a case is completely free in its discussion and assessment of the information given (Di Marino 1990, pp. 70-73). But despite the system's fundamental premises on freedom of proof, there is jurisprudence of the *Cour de Cassation* which indicates that merely the word of an anonymous witness is not sufficient for a conviction. And if the informer is a co-accused the position is the same: the word of one accused against another cannot alone found a conviction.[53] It was rare in our sample for reports of anonymous informers to be the main basis of the evidence in a file.[54] The weight of such testimony is clearly less in the eyes of the courts than that of sworn testimony.[55] More frequently, especially in drugs cases, reference in the file to a phone-call giving an anonymous tip-off justified the opening of a judicial investigation or telephone taps or surveillance under *commissions rogatoires*.[56] A few years ago, we were told, the *Chambre d'Accusation*[57] would not have accepted telephone taps based on anonymous tip-offs but one effect of the law of 1991 has been to allow examining magistrates to order taps simply on that basis.[58] The criteria under Article 100 CCP are broad – the judge simply has to think the tap is necessary for the inquiry – and there is no appeal possible.

Conclusion

The French criminal justice system places a great deal of confidence in its tradition of judicial monitoring by prosecutors and examining magistrates to control police investigations. The system lacks detailed administrative guidelines for the use of covert policing or a general legal framework for it. It generally rejects the use of exclusion of evidence to regulate the police. Accordingly, where weaknesses in the system of regulation have been perceived in the context of covert or proactive policing the tendency has been to introduce a requirement of prior judicial authority to reinforce the monitoring process – for example that of the examining magistrate for telephone tapping or the prosecutor for infiltration by police in drugs cases. This is assumed to entrench the necessary values of legality and the rule of law. But where prosecutors or examining magistrates or judges do not want to get too close to police practice and allow it to stay outside the dossier, as in the case of the use of informers, a great deal of police discretion results, regulated only by the power of free discussion and assessment of evidence at trial. In relation to surveillance, Article 226 provides a substantive offence which places limits on police surveillance practice: if the police are penetrating private space other than by telephone tapping or metering[59] they will have to run along the edge of criminal action. To do so without consultation with prosecutors or *juges d'instruction* would be to take great risks with key working relationships. Nevertheless, the system depends primarily on the vigilance, assertiveness and competence of prosecutors and *juges d'instructions* and on the values that they bring to their work.

Notes

1   My thanks to Peter Alldridge and Pauline Roberts for helpful comments on an earlier draft.
2   This is a study based on interview, observation and case-file analysis done with Alan Bradshaw and Andrew West and funded by the Economic and Social Research Council ('Defence Lawyers in the French Criminal Justice System', ESRC Award No: R000236321). Reference will be made to interviews conducted with Prosecutors, Examining Magistrates and Defence lawyers as well as to individual case-files.
3   Here, covert work seems confined to highly dubious use of agents provocateurs amongst demonstrators, Monjardet and Lévy 1995, p. 32-34.
4   Telephone tapping and infiltration in drugs cases are the most important examples and will be discussed below.

5   See J.-Y. Lassalle, *Enquête Préliminaire, Juris Classeur, Procédure Pénale, arts. 75-78.* The *police judiciaire* is made up of police officers who have a status linked to their specialist task of investigating criminal offences.

6   Article 14 uses the phrase '*constater les infractions*'. Constater means 'to ascertain, to establish'. The head of the *Police Judiciaire* is charged with (inter alia) the 'discovery' of the most serious offences, Stefani et al. 1996, p. 293.

7   Article 14 CCP. Around 7 per cent of cases go to *instruction*. Note that there is not the concept of parallel investigation that exists in the Netherlands whereby the investigating magistrate can be charged with a case but the police may pursue their own separate inquiries into the same dossier.

8   See Carlier, C.E., 18.11.49, Rec., 490 or Ministre de l'Intérieur c. Epoux Leroy (C.E. 13.3.1968, Rec., 179, cited and excerpted in West 1992, pp. 174, 209.

9   Cases 22/26/50; intviews\av11\av16\proc9). The examples we found were all in a reactive context, ie a specific offence already committed was being investigated (though in an observation study of *defence* lawyers, since they intervene almost exclusively in prosecuted cases, one has less likelihood of coming across genuinely proactive policing. For that one needs to follow the police).

10   Intview\av16\av31\av37.

11   Intview\av16\proc9.

12   Intview\proc2\ji7.

13   Intview\proc9.

14   Though the telephone bill for systematic tapping is a significant constraint on its use.

15   Or the *enquête de flagrance,* which differs technically from the *enquête préliminaire* in ways that are not relevant here.

16   Crim. 23 août 1994, *Dr. pén* 1995 n° 49 obs. Marion, *Bull* n° 29[1].

17   Cass. crim., 22 avr. 1992:D. 1995, p. 59, note Matsopolou.

18   Public places or private places which they have legal permission to enter.

19   Intview\Proc9.

20   La Loi n° 91-646 du 10 juillet 1991. See Articles 100–100-7 CCP. Thus the Act covers not just telephones but also links via fax, minitel or telex.

21   Schuller-Maréchal case, Crim., 27 févr. 1996: Bull crim., n° 93; JCP, 1996,II. 22629, note M-L Rassat, D. 1996, p. 346, note C. Guéry.

22   *Le Monde* 29 March 1996. See also *Libération* 8 April 1997, 11 April 1997.

23   *Le Monde* 29 March 1996.

24   Intview\av16\av37.

25   Schuller-Maréchal case, note 21.

26   Cass. crim., 4 janv. 1974 Bull Crim N° 2, Stefani et al. 1996, p. 37.

27   Created by La Loi du 17 juillet 1970, formerly set out in Articles 368, 369 Ancien Code Pénal, now set out (after some modifications) in Article 226-1, Nouveau Code Pénal.

28 Punishable with between two months' and one year's imprisonment or a fine of between 2000F and 60 000F. Knowingly keeping, transporting or releasing recordings or documents produced by the offence under Article 368 to third parties or the public is punishable under Article 369.

29 Commentaire de M. Champenois on the Annual Report of the *Cour de Cassation*, by the private law section of the Law Faculty, University of Paris XII, *Juris Classeur Périodique* 1983, I, 3123 n. 97.

30 Cass. crim., 6 avr. 1993, 1993 JCP II N° 22144, note M.-L. Rassat.

31 Under Articles 170-172 CCP the Chambre d'Accusation can annul 'actes de procédure' or 'pièces de procédure' only. See however the fulminating riposte of Professor Rassat, note 30.

32 Cass. crim 15 juin 1993, Bull N° 210, Cass. crim., 6 avr. 1994, Bull N° 136.

33 ECHR 15 June 1992, Series A, vol. 238 (*Lüdi v Switzerland*).

34 For a journalist's account see Bordes 1992. This impression was confirmed by criminal lawyers in France during our ESRC study (intview\av16\av31).

35 It would probably be more natural in English to say 'entrapped the offender'.

36 For details on the case law see V. Maistre du Chambon, 'La régularité des provocations policières' J.C.P. 1989. I.3422; Crim.28 juin 1993, Bull N° 228.

37 Intview\Proc2.

38 One suspects of course that practice is variable.

39 See Maistre du Chambon, note 36. The author argues that the issue should revolve around procedural criteria, such as unfairness, rather than substantive ones, such as the abolition of the mens rea of the accused. Here criteria that read rather like proportionality are advocated, along with the question, 'was the defendant's intent already fixed before the intervention of the covert policing?'

40 'Le tribunal de Toulouse relaxe trois trafiquants de cocaïne', *Le Monde* 5 September 1996.

41 Intview\proc2.

42 See generally Di Marino 1990.

43 Based on analysis of over 80 Correctionel and Assises case-files under the ESRC research project previously cited. See also Di Marino 1990, p. 66.

44 Cases\saf26. We were also told that an apparent anonymous tip-off might disguise the existence of an adminstrative tap which had actually led to the subsequent judicial investigation being started (intview\av16)

45 'On parle de...' [There is talk of...].

46 Intview\proc9.

47 *Officiers de la police judiciaire:* police officers given responsibility for the investigation of offences.

48 Intview\proc6.

49 Cases\saf22/26.

50 Intview\av37, cases\saf50.

51 Articles 82-1 and 310 CCP.

52 Intview\ji7.

53 Intview\av11. This was a change in previous practice provoked by ECHR 19 December 1990, Series A, vol. 166 (*Delta v France*) and ECHR 20 November 1989, Series A, vol. 191-A (*Kostovski v Netherlands*).
54 For an exception see cases\saf26 where the result, following *Cour de Cassation* jurisprudence, was an acquittal.
55 The French system makes the distinction between sworn testimony and simple information (information *de titre de simples renseignements*).
56 Intview\av16.
57 Which is charged, inter alia, with the monitoring and supervision of the work of examining magistrates.
58 Intview\av16.
59 Monitoring the numbers to which calls have been made rather than the calls themselves.

References

Bordes, P., *Enquête aux frontières de la loi: les douaniers et le trafic de la drogue,* Paris: Robert Laffont, 1992.

Brunet, J.-P. (1990), *La police de l'ombre: indicateurs et provocateurs dans la France contemporaine*, Paris: Seuil.

Chambon, P. (1997), *Le Juge d'instruction,* Paris: Dalloz.

Di Marino, G. (1990), L'indicateur, in: J.M. Aussel, J. Borricand, G. Di Marino, A. Normandeau, J. Pradel (eds.), *Problèmes actuels de science criminelle III*, Aix-Marseille: Presses Universitaires d'Aix-Marseille.

Gropp, W. (1993), Special Methods of Investigation for Combatting Organized Crime, 1 *European Journal of Crime, Criminal Law and Criminal Justice*, pp. 20-36.

Monjardet, D. and R. Lévy (1995), Undercover Policing in France: Elements for Description and Analysis, in: C. Fijnaut and G.T. Marx (eds.), *Undercover: Police Surveillance in Comparative Perspective*, The Hague: Kluwer Law International, pp. 29-53.

Stefani, G., G. Levasseur and B. Bouloc (1996), *Procédure Pénale*, Paris: Dalloz, 16th ed.

West, A., Y. Desdevises, A. Fenet, D. Gaurier, M.-C. Heussaff (1992), *The French Legal System: an introduction*, London: Fourmat.

5 Proactive policing in France

CLAUDE JOURNÈS

Introduction

Proactive methods and engagement in politics represent one of the three important characteristics of the French police system which predate the Revolution, the others being centralization and the distinction between urban and rural forces, that is between the *gendarmerie* and the *police nationale*. (Journès 1993). Proactive political policing itself has very often been in the news. In February and March 1996 phone tapping hit the headlines as newspaper reports suggested it had been used between 1987 and 1993 against such figures as the unconventional barrister Jacques Vergès and the leader of an ultra-leftist group Alain Krivine. At the beginning of July the French Government admitted having bugged several advisers of former Defence Secretary François Léotard who was one of the leaders of the ruling coalition. This wire-tapping – done for reasons of security – was probably legal. But in fact it seems to have been done to find out whether secret money from arm sales to Saudi Arabia had been used with Léotard's support to help former Prime Minister Edouard Balladur in his unsuccessful presidential campaign against Jacques Chirac.

However it is important to define precisely the term 'proactive policing' as it has remained rather ambiguous – though it always entails some idea of prevention. In accordance with the definition generally adopted for this book, I shall not take it to suggest simply the opposite of reactive or fire-brigade policing, which might include visible patrolling designed to prevent crime or community involvement of the police in trying to build a partnership with social agencies and the public. I shall take it to indicate surveillance and especially undercover surveillance, use of informers, phone tapping, videosurveillance.

Proactive policing in the *Ancien Régime* was mainly done by the *mouches* (flies) – i.e. spies working for the Lieutenant of Police in Paris. They were used for criminal as well as political reasons and according to d'Argenson, the successor of La Reynie – the first Lieutenant of Police – were drawn from all parts of society from dukes to footmen (Buisson 1950, p. 125). They were said to be very numerous, to be everywhere and to keep the whole population in a kind of 'net' in the words of the writer Diderot (Journès 1988, pp. 20-21). Actually this was in part a myth as the *mouches* numbered probably no more than 340 (Emsley 1983, p. 12). We must also bear in mind that police functions at that time were wider than today. The police were in charge of everything from religion to trades, and the prevention of riots by regulation of the supply of corn to Paris was more important than fighting crime.

After the Revolution the main police functions were the maintenance of public order and fighting crime. Political policing was connected with Joseph Fouché (Buisson 1950, pp. 167 *et seq.*) who was Secretary of State for the Police four times between 1799 and 1815 and who set up a general surveillance system. One important part of his department was the division of general security and secret police which has been seen as the forerunner of *Renseignements Généraux* (the General Intelligence Service) which will be the main focus of this chapter. Fouché was mainly interested in prevention – in dissuading political offenders rather than punishing them – something that might be seen as proactive policing in a certain sense. His mainly undercover policing of politics used a variety of methods: mail surveillance in the 'black cabinet', the influencing of public opinion by censorship or the publishing of pro-government articles in newspapers, spies *(indicateurs)*, and spying on international diplomats working in France. Fouché kept files especially about royalists which led to a kind of map of Chouannerie.[1] Most of the information came from the *départements* through the *Préfets* (the local representatives of (central) Government). The flow of information to the centre allowed Fouché to get a general view and Napoléon could be updated by a daily letter.

After Fouché political policing continued. For instance, in Lyon after 1830 during the July Monarchy[2] it was used in several ways: bribery, undercover agents spying on political life, the tailing of suspects and surveillance of public places like theatres and cafés, and the investigation and infiltration of opposition movements as carlists,[3] republicans and working men's associations (Bollenot 1982).

In the 19th century, the rapid development of railways gave criminals and political opponents an opportunity for rapid escape and political policing became linked with the policing of railways. In the 20th century *Renseigne-*

ments Généraux were established before the second world war but took their true shape in 1941 under the Vichy Régime which was a decisive step in French police history. Like most of the reforms of this period, *Renseignements Généraux* were maintained after the war, coming to be seen more as part of a rationalising process than evidence of a policy of authoritarianism.

Although *Renseignements Généraux* have often been criticized, every Government has kept them. During the war in Algeria in 1961, some of its agents along with those of *Direction de la Surveillance du Territoire* (DST) – a police unit which performs the functions of a kind of MI5 – were brought together as a Liaison Bureau to fight against the extreme-right wing terrorist movement OAS (Organization of the Secret Army). Using intelligence gathering followed by arrests (Harstrich and Calvi 1991, pp. 19 *et seq.*), they were rather successful. After the events of May 1968, when Raymond Marcellin was Home Secretary, both central and regional operational brigades fought against ultra-leftism and this led in 1970 to the arrest of one of the leaders of the Maoist movement, Alain Geismar.

Until the eighties one can identify four trends in political policing in France. First, political policing has mainly used proactive methods but has never been limited to it. Intelligence gathering and political action have often worked together. Secondly, the information given to the public authorities has sometimes been of questionable accuracy. This was especially in the past and can be explained by limited capacities of the officers themselves. For instance, in the 19th century in Lyon the vagueness of reports by the political police was deplored (Bollenot 1982, p. 134). In some other cases there has been a kind of blindness especially about nationalist movements in the colonies as in the twenties and thirties when intelligence services thought that the rise of nationalism in Morocco was connected with Russian, German or even British influence (Oved 1988). Questionable accuracy may also be explained in part by a lack of motivation on the part of some officers at the end of the second world war. On 6 June 1944 the Head of *Renseignements Généraux* complained about the 'unimportant mail' (Buisson 1950, p. 342) he got from his men. At the time the Resistance movement was becoming popular in police ranks. However, there has been a tendency towards increased accuracy of information. Thirdly, the means used have always been partly legal and partly illegal. One of the oldest methods has been the use of informers. *Concièrges* were often said to be used in this capacity as well as ex-convicts, prostitutes and pimps. In most cases there was some kind of bargain: the police would be more lenient on petty crime committed by these people or help them if they were foreigners waiting, for instance, for a work permit. But some would give information to the police for money; some of these worked within the OAS and a few were killed by the organization after being discovered. In 1969 a mole – the only worker in the leadership – was also found in a maoist group and in the eighties members of the terrorist group *Action directe* were sold to the police.

Another technique has been to use undercover policemen. This was widely done during the sixties and seventies in Paris, one historian talking of dozens of officers being involved (Brunet 1990, p. 68). As the police knew nothing or very little about student and ultra leftist movements the best way was to send some young inspectors to Universities. Women inspectors seem to have been successful (Harstrich and Calvi 1991, p. 141).

Other techniques used have been mail opening, breaking into flats before asking for a search warrant, phone tapping, bugging. Illegality has often been a characteristic feature of such operations. The *Renseignements Généraux* did nothing to prevent a bomb attack by the OAS against an arab café in Paris because they wanted to evaluate the reliability of their informer. These illegal tactics sometimes become public and create scandal.

And this is precisely the final trend: the whiff of scandal. In October 1965 two inspectors of the Paris section of *Renseignements Généraux* played a part in the kidnapping of the Moroccan political opponent Mehdi Ben Barka who was shortly afterwards murdered in France by his country's Home Secretary. In 1973 members of the DST tried to put bugs in the offices of the satirical weekly *Le Canard Enchaîné*.

Although proactive policing in France has not only existed in the political field, it has always been more controversial in that context than in relation to criminal affairs. We may assume that the reason why the public debate has arisen about political proactive policing more than the activities of the judicial police (*police judiciaire*) stems from the French history of policing heavily engaged in politics. This distinctive French tradition – nowadays mainly embodied in *Renseignements Généraux* – does not have a close equivalent in other countries like Britain.

I shall try to outline the work that *Renseignements Généraux* now do, and then how proactive policing is undergoing a process of regulation and finally why this has not been entirely successful.

Police work in Renseignements Généraux

In 1996 3900 men out of 125 000 in the National Police were working in *Renseignements Généraux*. It is only one of the 'services' within the French police. The largest one with 65 000 officers deals with public security and ordinary uniformed policing. There is also a 'service' specializing in public order maintenance, the *Compagnies Républicaines de Sécurité* (CRS) with around 15,000 men. There is a 'service' responsible for the control of immigration and illegal employment which is a little bigger than *Renseignements Généraux* – as is the judicial police 'service'.[4] The *Direction de la Surveillance du Territoire* – which uses proactive methods and deals with counterespionage – the Inspectorate General, the Training and Logistical 'Service' and other administrative departments are less numerous. All of them are under the responsibility of the Director-General of the National Police, a civil servant of senior rank working directly with the Home Secretary. The central Directorates of these 'services' are in Paris but most of the other officers are scattered throughout the country. Thus most of the personnel of *Renseignements Généraux* – 2700 – work outside Paris. That means there are a few of them in every *département*, usually closely connected to the *Préfet*.

We must not forget that France has got two national police forces. The Police Nationale is responsible for towns of more than 10,000 inhabitants. The other force is the *Gendarmerie Nationale* which employs more than 95,000 people working openly in uniform. The *gendarmes* are part of the army. Most of them do ordinary police work but some of them have a public order remit similar to that of the CRS.

Since an executive order of 17 November 1951 *Renseignements Généraux* have been charged with the 'search for and central accumulation of political social and economic intelligence necessary for the information of Government'. They are plain-clothed policemen but a distinction is normally made between their open and their covert intelligence gathering roles. Most of their job is now done openly by reading the press, going to political meetings where their presence is officially known or by personal unpaid contacts within social or political organizations. Their work may be very close to journalism and they must be able to distinguish reliable information from mere gossip and boasting especially when there are competing groups within a political party. *Renseignements Généraux* also regularly use public opinion polls they themselves carry out and which seem to be very accurate. For instance in relation to Presidential elections they predicted in 1965 that Général de Gaulle would have to go to a second ballot, that Giscard d'Estaing would do better than Chaban Delmas in 1974, and that Mitterrand would win in 1981. In fact, in a very French way, the Home Secretary Roger Frey did not tell Général de Gaulle about the result of the 1965 opinion poll because he did not dare to do so. Jacques Chirac when Home Secretary in 1974 made it public as a way of undermining Chaban's position. Nowadays *Renseignements Généraux* for predicting elections also use a data processing programme to analyse by-election results.

One important tool of police work has always been files, and *Renseignements Généraux* keep a lot of them. There were probably 600,000 manual files in 1990 so there is a quite general threat of being held on file. It may be a hollow threat but for young people entering into political activity in the sixties it could be rather deterring. Data processing of files began at that time. It was probably not very efficient but it had the potential to be so and it was the first point at which political policing began to be regulated by norms, as we shall see in more detail later.

Undercover work is different and must be limited to terrorist groups. It is not very different from Special Branch activity in Britain. *Renseignements Généraux* still use informers, phone tapping and some practical techniques such as the use of concentric circles for the identification of terrorists. After a bomb attack in 1978 in Guadeloupe three lists were drawn up. The first was made up of 600 persons said to be in favour of independence, while the second was made up only of 200 names and the third of 20 names and which led to arrests.[5] Most recently, *Renseignements Généraux* have dealt with social movements, urban violence, Islamism and so on.

Steps to regulate police work

Everything began with the Act of 6 January 1978 which does not deal principally with policing but which states that data processing must not interfere with human rights or privacy or civil liberties. It also establishes the *Commission nationale de l'informatique et des libertés* (CNIL) which is independent of the Government. This National commission on computers and civil liberties must give approval to public authorities before they can establish any databanks containing information on named individuals. If the Commission refuses, the authority may seek authority from the *Conseil d'État*, the highest administrative court. Section 31 of the Act forbids the keeping of personal information on racial origin, political, philosophical or religious opinion or membership of a trade union in a data processing system except where permission is given on public order grounds by the National commission.

In February 1990, after ten years of endeavour by CNIL, the Government headed by Michel Rocard decided to acknowledge and regularize the collecting of exactly this kind of sensitive information by *Renseignements Généraux*. There was general protest and Rocard withdrew his proposal.

Eventually the following year on 14 October 1991, a milder version of it was enacted by executive order. The files of *Renseignements Généraux* may refer to political 'activities' but not political 'opinions' and to 'physical peculiarities' but not 'racial origin' (which amounts to about the same thing). And individuals will be allowed to know what is written on their files except in terrorist matters.

An Act of 10 July 1991 deals mainly with the privacy of phone calls. The principle of privacy is established and may be limited in only two ways. First, by decision of a *juge d'instruction* (examining magistrate). Secondly, and exceptionally, by a written and reasoned order of the Prime Minister or one of his two delegates after a written and reasoned application by the Secretary for War, the Home Secretary or the Secretary in charge of Customs. In this case phone tapping is for intelligence linked with 'national security, the safety of essential parts of the scientific or economic infrastructure of France, prevention of terrorism, prevention of organized crime or the revival of prohibited political groups'. The law also establishes a National Commission for the Control of Security Interceptions (*Commission nationale de contrôle des interceptions de sécurité*) headed by a person appointed for six years by the *Président de la République* from a short list of four names drawn up by the highest judicial authorities. Two members of Parliament are also included in the Commission. But in any case the role of the Commission is only to give advice to the Prime Minister or Ministers who take the final decision. According to Paul Bouchet, a member of the *Conseil d'État* and former barrister famous for his work representing trade unionists and who chairs the Commission, about 3000 telephone lines out of 30 million were tapped in 1995. At the end of November, the maximum number of taps in operation simultaneously (1192) exceeded slightly the quota permitted (1180) due to terrorist threat and bomb attacks. Nearly two thirds of this phone tapping was linked with prevention of terrorism. The Commission issued an opinion opposing the Government's request for a tap 43 times and in reaction in 40 of these cases the Government dropped the request (*Le Monde*, 29 March 1996).

Last but not least, there is the Act on Security of 21 January 1995, which deals with videosurveillance and order maintenance. 'Big Brother is watching you'. Those comments, in English, were among the first offered by socialist MPs when they referred part of the law to the *Conseil Constitutionnel* (Constitutional Court), the highest court in France. In the parliamentary debate they had compared the use of video to that employed either in Eastern Germany by the STASI or in China against students. The French Home Secretary Charles Pasqua answered on the contrary that as before there had been no legal framework for videosurveillance his law gave a new protection to citizens. In fact *Conseil Constitutionnel* accepted that most of the law was constitutional, merely finding part of section 10 unacceptable. This declared that if there was no reply from the *Préfet* to a request to install a system of videosurveillance of public spaces, after four months this could be treated as an approval. This was contrary to the general principle in French law that no reply from a public authority must be taken to be refusal.

Under section 10 of the 1995 Act public authorities may install video-cameras and keep the video on record only to protect public buildings, to preserve the given safety of places significant to national defence, to regulate road traffic, to prevent driving offences and threats to the safety of persons and property in places with a high risk of assault and theft. But the inside of blocks of flats must not be recorded, and furthermore, their entrances must not be recorded 'specifically'. Which means this may be done if it is part of a more general shot.

Any public videosurveillance device must be approved by the *Préfet* after he or she has been given advice by a local commission. Within one month at most, the records must be destroyed unless a judicial investigation is being held. Illegal recording can lead to three years' imprisonment. And any 'interested person' has a right of access to any recording connected with him or her. (Though this may be refused for reasons of state security.)

Limitations

There are several kinds of limitations to this regulation. Some are connected with the texts themselves. For instance section 20 of the Act of 1978 allows the Government not to publish materials dealing with the safety of the state, defence and public security. That applies to files of the DST, DGSE (*Direction générale de la sécurité extérieure* – the equivalent of MI6) and the agency of military security, DPSD (*Direction de la protection et de la sécurité de la défense*).

The 1995 Act dealing with videosurveillance does not say who will choose the members of the local commission or its Chair. It merely states that the Chair must be a magistrate. According to an executive order of 17 October 1996 the other members must be a judge specializing in adminis-trative law, a mayor, a member of a Chamber of Commerce and a fifth 'qualified person' chosen by the *Préfet*. The commission has only a power of advice and anyway the opportunities for installing videosurveillance seem very extensive as it may be allowed for many reasons. Moreover, MPs from the left wanted CNIL to deal with videosurveillance. It will not because the records do not contain the names of individuals and are thus considered to be outside the remit of the Commission.

Later an executive order of 9 November 1995 allowed the *Gendarmerie* to 'collect, keep and process' in regional files information about named persons who had undermined the State's authority by terrorist acts or by supporting such acts. This also extended to those in a permanent relationship with such persons and to victims of terrorism. The information might include physical peculiarities, political, philosophical or religious opinions and trade-union membership. Although this text was published by *Journal Officiel* on 16 November it was not publicly debated until the quality news-paper *Le Monde* criticized it and stimulated protests on 15 December (*Le Monde*, 16 December 1995). As barristers, civil liberties groups and the biggest police union all thought it was a threat to civil liberties the Government withdrew the order the next day.

The other limitation to attempts to regulate such practices has been simply unlawful police practice. First, in relation to *Renseignements Généraux*: their remit is to obtain intelligence not to arrest people (which is the role of the judicial police). In July 1990 a homosexual parson was found dead after being followed and illegally bugged by inspectors of the Paris *Renseignements Généraux*. One officer was dismissed. On 19 June 1994 another agent of *Renseignements Généraux* was supposed to get information after a private meeting of the Socialist Party. But after introducing himself he asked to use the phone and by chance managed to overhear what was being said at the meeting and thus knew before journalists about the dismissal of Michel Rocard. After a few days *Le Canard Enchaîné* made the affair public (6 July 1994) and two heads of the Parisian *Renseignements Généraux* were sacked. In fact the agent's investigations only meant that he got the information half an hour before journalists but the point of principle was that this was an intrusion into a meeting of a legal political party.

Because of the autonomy and discretion that the police have in their work and the weakness of internal controls, public scandal and controversy are probably the best safeguards of the rule of law and civil liberties where *Renseignements Généraux* are concerned. Police unions may also play a significant role.

We must also bear in mind the role of the presidential unit against terrorism which in fact was used between 1983 and 1986 to bug writers (notably Jean-Edern Hallier), journalists and others. One of its main aims seems to have been to conceal the existence of President Mitterrand's illegitimate and secret daughter Mazarine. This unit lasted until 1988 when the Right came back to Government. A court decision in autumn 1996 suggested that those in charge of it might be prosecuted on the basis of infringement of the right of privacy. Yet Constantin Melnikhas, who was in charge of intelligence and security services between 1959 and 1962, has written that phone-tapping under Mitterrand was merely 'child's play' compared to what went on at the start of the Fifth Republic (*Le Monde*, 22 October 1996).

From time to time we hear of phone tapping done without the consent of the national commission or an examining magistrate. But the main problem seems no longer to be public authorities but rather private persons or firms. According to Paul Bouchet there are more than 100,000 illegal phone tappings per year (*Le Monde*, 29 March 1996). So one could say controls have improved but perhaps do not deal with some of that which should be controlled.

Proactive political policing has clearly been one of the main features of the French police system. Nowadays it is mainly done by *Renseignements Généraux*. Their work is to gather intelligence – whether openly or covertly. Legal reforms have started a process of regulation. But the effectiveness of this process has been limited for reasons linked to the legal framework itself and to illegal police practice.

Notes

1 The Chouans were pro-Royalist counter-revolutionaries.
2 The July Monarchy is the period of French history 1830-1848 when France was ruled by Louis Philippe.
3 The Carlists supported the Bourbons who ruled France until the 1830 Revolution.
4 This deals with the investigation of serious crime.
5 This, according to a *Commissaire* who taught on the activities of *Renseignements Généraux* at the *École Nationale Supérieure de Police,* the central Police College, and who had been working in the West Indies, *Lyon Figaro*, 10 February 1987.

References

Bollenot, Gilles (1982), Police politique police secrète à Lyon d'après les archives Gasparin (1831-1835), *Annales de l'Université de Saint-Étienne*, pp. 95-162.

Brunet, J.P. (1990), *La police de l'ombre. Indicateurs et provocateurs dans la France contemporaine*, Paris: Seuil.

Buisson, H. (1950), *La Police, son histoire*, Vichy: Wallon.

Dobry, M. (1992), *Le renseignement politique interne dans les démocraties occidentales, état de la recherche*, Paris: Institut des Hautes Études de la Sécurité Intérieure.

Emsley, C. (1983), *Policing and its Context*, 1750-1870, London: Macmillan.

Gleizal, J.J., J. Domenach and C. Journès (1993), *La police, le cas des démocraties occidentales*, Paris: Presses Universitaires de France, Thémis.

Harstrich, J. and F. Calvi (1991), *R.G., 20 ans de police politique*, Paris: Calmann-Lévy.

Journès, C. (ed.) (1988), *Police et politique*, Lyon: Presses Universitaires de Lyon.

Journès, Claude (1993), The Structure of the French Police System: Is the French Police a National Force?, *International Journal of the Sociology of Law*, 21, pp. 281-287.

Fijnaut, C. and G.T. Marx (eds.) (1995), *Undercover: Police Surveillance in Comparative Perspective*, The Hague: Kluwer Law International.

Oved, Georges (1988), La contribution des services spéciaux à la politique de la France au Maroc de 1920 à 1955, in: C. Journès (ed.), *Police et politique*, pp. 69-99.

Zamponi, F. (1994), *La police, combien de divisions?*, Paris: Éditions Dagorno.

6 Special police methods of investigation: new legislation in the Netherlands

THEO DE ROOS

Introduction

In 1993 a scandal emerged which led to the dissolution of the police Interregional Team Noordholland-Utrecht. This unit had specialized in investigation of organized crime and had relied heavily upon intelligence work and investigative methods and techniques which were controversial and sometimes new (at least in their application on such a scale). As a result of the ensuing political storm, in which two ministers (the Minister of Justice and his colleague for Home Affairs) were forced to resign, a parliamentary enquiry was set up in 1995. It was commissioned to establish the extent and the nature of organized crime in the Netherlands, to make a survey and critical evaluation of the use of special methods of investigation by the police and of the way in which they were supervised (or rather: not supervised) by the responsible authorities. The lack of control of 'unorthodox' methods of investigation generally was perceived as the real cause of the IRT conflict and the crisis in the criminal justice sphere that had been its immediate consequence. In February 1996 the Parliamentary Committee of Inquiry (PEC[1] or the Van Traa commission as it is frequently called after its Chair, the Labour MP Maarten van Traa) presented its final report.[2]

In June 1997, a Bill was sent to Parliament containing new regulations governing methods of investigations, which are to be laid down in the Code of Criminal Procedure.[3] This Bill was preceded by a draft Bill which was broadly discussed by representatives of professional organizations. In this contribution, I shall present a survey of the main characteristics of the proposed regulations.

In accordance with the PEC, the proposals stress the overwhelming importance of the legality principle. That is to say, that all investigation acts should have a (written) legal basis. Where methods of investigation affect the rights and freedoms of citizens, a general legal authorization is not sufficient: specific regulations must justify the intrusion. On the one hand the Constitution and Human Rights treaties demand it (see for instance Article 8.2 European Convention on Human Rights); on the other, it is indispensable for clarifying the limits of wide-ranging police powers, the conditions under which they can be used, and the ways in which they should be controlled and evaluated in the criminal process.

The Bill, particularly its explanatory memorandum, may be read as a critical evaluation of the conclusions and recommendations of the PEC report. On some crucial points, the proposals of the Department of Justice involve different choices and encompass departures from the recommendations of the PEC. In the following, I shall examine those differences, asking what they mean for the structure and functioning of criminal procedure as it is laid down in the 1926 Code of Criminal Procedure. As a starting point I shall take the case law in the courts, which is playing a major role in the debates about legislation. In a recent decision, the Supreme Court decided some key questions regarding the legality of special methods of investigation.

In this chapter, I shall limit myself essentially to these special police methods of investigation, which is at the core of what the PEC called the threefold crisis of justice: a normative crisis, an organizational crisis and a crisis of legitimacy. First, an important recent decision of the Supreme Court (*Hoge Raad*) will be discussed, as it furnishes the background against which the debate is taking place. To a large extent, the Bill is inspired by the boundaries set out by the Supreme Court in this decision. Subsequently, the most important features of the proposals will be discussed. Finally, I shall present in broad lines an evaluation of the general approach of the Bill.

The Zwolsman case

The Supreme Court held that the Court of Appeal of Amsterdam had understood the law correctly in reasoning as follows: where police methods and/or techniques are used – whether in 'proactive' or regular ('re-active') investigations – for which rules have not yet been formulated in legislation or case law, such rules have to be established by the court. The fact that there are no written regulations regarding a particular method does not in itself necessarily imply that using these methods and/or techniques is against the law. Police activities in the proactive phase generally find their legal basis in the Code of Criminal Procedure insofar as it assigns to the police the general task of investigating criminal acts. This must be read in conjunction with Article 2, Police Act 1993 from which it can be deduced that it is part of the police task to investigate those acts as far as is possible. This competence is only restricted by legal regulations which assign the task of investigation to other authorities. However, this general basis for action is not sufficient if rights and freedoms of citizens as laid down in the Constitution or international treaties are violated – or indeed other legal regulations. If however it is a question of breach of a specific legal prohibition, police activities may be justified by the interest in the investigation of criminal offences if this is deemed of greater importance than the interests protected by those specific regulations (e.g. police infiltrators committing crimes), and/or may be admissible under conditions which are specified in the case law (such as the Tallon criterion) which entrench the proportionality principle (discussed below).

The decision of the Supreme Court quotes approvingly a list of techniques and methods which the Court of Appeal thought admissible on the basis of the abovementioned considerations: surveillance (secretly following suspects), the taking of photographs, the use of localization equipment, for instance for the purpose of tracking or tracing vehicles, the use of video-equipment in support of observation in public places, the use of mobile phone scanners with a limited range.

The Supreme Court continues with a discourse about the legal state of affairs concerning the proactive phase. Methods of investigation used during that phase which infringe upon the rights of citizens must be justified by reference to specific legal provisions: general competence provisions are too vague a basis for action given the conditions formulated in the Constitution (Article 10) and the Human Rights treaties, especially Article 8.2 of the European Convention on Human Rights. To meet the standards developed by the Strasbourg case law, infringements on privacy must be regulated in such a way that the citizen is able to foresee under what conditions he may be subject to them. This will be the case if, in accordance with the Constitution, there are clear standards laid down in 'formal' law (i.e., acts approved by parliament and the Crown, as opposed to ministerial regulations or mere guidelines). The Police Act 1993, however, does not provide such standards, nor do the general articles in the Code of Criminal Procedure which define police functions (Articles 141, 142). The change in attitudes towards privacy in combination with technological progress in surveillance techniques requires a more precise legal legitimation of police activities in the proactive sphere.

The Supreme Court makes a distinction between 'limited' and serious violations of the right to privacy. Limited violations, such as taking photographs and making video-recordings in public, are sufficiently legitimated by Article 2, Police Act 1993. This distinction has been happily adopted now by the authors of the Bill on police surveillance methods, as I shall explain in what follows. So, scanning mobile telephones does not *per se* amount to a serious violation of privacy, for – the Supreme Court argues – a person who uses such a device must expect interception of his communication by others (including the police), and therefore, to a certain extent at least, must accept such interception. The same argument is used to justify the searching of rubbish bags (one of the disputed methods in the Zwolsman case). Only when the scanning operation is executed in a systematic way, for the purpose of obtaining a full insight into aspects of the personal life of the person involved, will this be regarded as a serious violation.

A quite different point concerns the procedural conclusions that should be drawn where a serious violation has been established. The most severe sanction which the court may apply is to dismiss the case (denying the Public Prosecution Service the right to prosecute the case before the court: *niet-ontvankelijkverklaring*). However, case law reserves this sanction to rather exceptional cases, in which due process principles are violated in a flagrant way (for instance: consciously presenting misleading information to the court and the defence). A less draconian sanction is to exclude evidence from trial proceedings if it has been obtained by methods involving (serious) violations of legal regulations and/or fundamental rights as laid down in Human Rights treaties. This sanction, however, will help the accused and the defence only if in fact evidence has been assembled by such methods, and the prosecution has to rely on it for a succesful trial result. In the Zwolsman case, as in many other cases of its kind, the operations took place in the proactive phase and were not meant specifically to obtain evidence, the investigative aim being first and foremost to get a complete picture of the Zwolsman hash-gang.

Surveillance

The explanatory memorandum distinguishes different types of surveillance:
- Static surveillance, that is surveillance from a more or less fixed point of observation;
- Dynamic or mobile surveillance (also called 'following', *volgerij*): the goods or persons to be surveyed are followed and secretly observed.

A second division can be made between:
– Surveillance with special technical equipment;
– Surveillance without such technical equipment.

These differences, however important as they may be in practice, are not decisive for the form of legal regulation. In determining that issue, the authors of the Bill think the real distinction is between intensive and superficial forms of surveillance. A static surveillance, they argue, may be as superficial or intrusive as a dynamic or mobile one. The intensity depends on the target of the operation. This is also true for surveillance with – for instance – a videocamera or surveillance without such a device. In the proposed text, only intensive forms of surveillance are regulated, superficial forms (in the eyes of the authors) being sufficiently legitimated by the general authorizations in the Code of Criminal Procedure.[4]

According to the model proposed in the Bill, intensive surveillance is identified with systematic surveillance (as opposed to non-systematic, superficial surveillance). This, in my opinion, is a rather doubtful proposition. It goes without saying that systematic surveillance by videocamera is more likely to penetrate into the private life of citizens than such surveillance carried out non-systematically. But obviously a surveillance operation of a more occasional nature might quite possibly impinge on privacy in a dramatic way (e.g. a static videocamera directed for a short period on a house).

The explanatory memorandum defines as systematic surveillance those methods which might provide a more or less complete picture of (certain aspects) of someone's personal life, for instance, his contacts within the criminal milieu or his financial means. The surveillance that needs specific regulation is not necessarily a long term operation. What is decisive is that it aims to provide a complete picture of (aspects) of the personal life of a person or a group of persons, e.g. to identify their pattern of activities within the framework of the criminal organization. Consequently, when a surveillance team is formed with six or seven participants to follow a person, an authorization of the Public Prosecutor will be obligatory. In actual practice there's no official role for the Public Prosecutor.

The proposal contains some other formalities and restrictions. The surveillance order has to be issued in a written form, but in urgent cases the Public Prosecutor may give the order orally, on condition that he or she confirms the order in writing within three days. This provision serves to enhance control, for in the written order the 'facts and circumstances' which establish suspicion of a crime (*misdrijf*), and also the name, or at least an accurate description of the suspect, have to be set out, as well as the place or places where the operation will take place and the period for which it is issued. Thus, the trial judge and the defence will be able to check and challenge the legality of the way in which the investigative method has been used.

Also important is the limitation in time. The order is given for a maximum period of three months. If the abovementioned conditions for the application of the surveillance still exist at the end of this period, the order can be extended. The proposals do not provide for a limitation of the number of extensions. Obviously, the longer the operation continues, the more likely it is that further extension will violate the 'proportionality principle'.

So much for surveillance in 'normal' criminal investigations, in which the commission of a specific crime is suspected. But the proposals also present a provision dealing with surveillance in the investigation phase which is commonly called 'proactive'. In this phase, there is not yet a clear suspicion of specific crime(s). The Bill introduces a new, broader concept of suspicion, which is linked exclusively to organized crime. If from 'facts or circumstances', a 'reasonable suspicion' arises that serious crimes (i.e., crimes for which long term pre-trial detention is possible because their nature or their connection with other crimes constitute a grave violation of the legal order) are 'planned or have been committed' (for instance trafficking of drugs, arms or people), surveillance can be ordered.[5] As is the case for 'normal' surveillance, the police are entitled systematically to follow people, verify their presence at a certain place or monitor their behaviour, provided that this is done 'in the interests of the investigation'.

In its regulation of surveillance, the Bill takes a course that differs from that presented by the PEC on this topic. The PEC took duration as a starting point for its regulation, and accordingly distinguished between operations of a maximum of 6 hours, one week, one month, and operations that take longer than a month. The longer the operation continues, the stricter the conditions to be met. The explanatory memorandum criticizes the solution of the PEC (not unfairly, I think) as being only seemingly objective, measurable and controllable, because – as has been pointed out above – it is not the duration, but the intensity of the surveillance which is decisive. Moreover, the PEC proposal is hardly practicable.

Special attention should be given to the proposed power to enter places in order to plant technical surveillance devices. A separate authorization by the Public Prosecutor is obligatory. Moreover, the police will only be entitled to enter places for this purpose in cases of suspicion of serious crimes, that is crimes which would justify longterm pretrial detention because their nature or their connection with other crimes is such as to amount to a grave threat to legal order. It is, however, not admissible to enter houses. In the opinion of the authors of the Bill, this would disproportionately impinge on privacy. On the other hand, one should not forget that surveillance that reaches into houses from the outside, for instance with a video camera, could readily have such an effect. The proposal on the use of technical devices contains two restrictions, the first being that no 'communication' may be recorded, and the second that a technical device may be placed on someone only with their consent.[6] But this intrusive method is allowed for all crimes, not only serious ones, and even when there is no suspicion of 'organized crime'. The PEC, quite understandably, did not want to go as far as that, and accordingly suggested the restriction of this method to cases of suspicion of serious crimes. But neither the PEC nor the Bill propose a restriction to cases of organized crime.

Informers and infiltrators

According to the PEC, the police are entitled to make use of civilian informers, on a casual as well as a systematic basis, provided that they are sufficiently controlled by the competent authorities and as long as they do not commit offences.

Infiltration, however, is only deemed acceptable if it is carried out by the police. The risk of using non-police infiltrators who participate in the criminal milieu (which is in fact what makes them useful in effective criminal investigations) is perceived as too great. So-called 'controlled delivery' should be permitted under strict conditions. Actually letting drugs through to final consumers should not be allowed, with the exception of an occasional 'line test' of *soft* drugs. By this method, a shipment for example is allowed through in order to make a criminal organization believe that all is safe. (One member of the PEC dissented; he considered an occasional test consignment of a limited amount of hard drugs acceptable.) The Public Prosecution Department did not completely agree with the PEC on this issue: they felt line tests of drugs (including hard drugs) were acceptable.

Letting through amounts of drugs however, with the purpose that an infiltrator may achieve a position at or near the top of the organization should not be allowed. On this topic there seems to be no dispute at the moment. The Public Prosecution Department agrees with the Van Traa commission because experience has shown that it is too difficult to control this method. But, the prosecutors follow the dissenting opinion within the

PEC in concluding that it ought to remain possible to allow shipments to pass, if only under strict conditions and only in very special cases. 'A total ban of this method would under certain conditions stand in the way of an effective fight against organized crime'.[7]

This is a very interesting issue, as in using this method the Netherlands took a leading position in Europe. In their reaction to the PEC report, the leading police officers took a more cautious position. They stressed the usefulness of the method, in that it might produce insights into the overall 'chain' of criminal activities within the organization, but they also recognized the dangers that had been pointed out in the PEC report. In their view, the legislator should decide this issue.

What position has the government taken on this issue? It sees the method of letting through goods as an application of the 'opportunity principle', which gives a margin of discretion to the Public Prosecution Department to decide on criminal prosecution based on Article 167, section 2 of the Code of Criminal Procedure. The Prosecution is entitled to balance investigation interests against (possible) disadvantages for society that might flow from refraining from prosecution (for the time being, that is).

Police infiltration

Police infiltration traditionally is a typical method of investigation in organized crime cases. The explanatory memorandum of the Bill states that infiltrating criminal organizations provides the opportunity to observe from within, to discover which persons are engaged in the planning and execution of crimes, to establish which crimes are committed and which methods used. The aim of the operation may be to obtain a picture of the organization as a whole as well as to assemble evidence for trial. But what exactly is 'infiltration'? The explanatory memorandum gives this definition: the participation in or cooperation with a group of persons engaged in the planning or committing of criminal acts, *or* participation in or cooperation with a 'criminal organization'. So, infiltration is not exclusively applicable in organized crime investigations. Groups operating in a more loose and opportunistic style may also be the target of the undercover agent. The memorandum mentions as examples a youth gang, an entreprise suspected of large scale environmental pollution, or of fraud and bribery. Where in practice the boundaries between such groups and 'criminal organizations' should be drawn is highly questionable.

The memorandum pays attention to some classical drawbacks of the method, which are described extensively in relevant literature. Police infiltration is hampered by moral dilemmas and physical risks. The infiltrator will not be able to avoid committing crimes. To maintain his credibility, he will have to play an active role, which means that often he will be involved in crimes of a type even more serious than just involvement in a criminal organization, which is punishable under Article 140, Criminal Code. The professional infiltrator also runs the risk of moral contamination by his criminal environment, especially when the operation is over a long period. Thorough preparation and training, as well as good psychological support and 'debriefing,' should limit these effects as much as possible, but obviously, success is not guaranteed. The physical risks concern not only the danger to the wellbeing or even lives of the agents themselves, but also those of their families and other relations.

Cooperation of civilians in criminal investigations (informers, infiltrators)

Catching scoundrels has to be done by using scoundrels, according to a professional police slogan (if not a popular wisdom). The use of civilians, especially members of the criminal milieu, in the everlasting fight against crime, has a very long tradition and is still practised all over the world.

The Bill proposes a legal basis for the activities of civilian informers. A person who is not a police agent ('an investigation officer') may, in the interest of the investigation, be entrusted with assisting the inquiry by systematically gathering information about a suspected person or a person who can reasonably be suspected of being engaged in the planning or committing of serious crimes within a criminal organization.[8] There are, again, some procedural prescriptions: each investigation officer (*opsporings-ambtenaar*) may allocate the task to the informer, but only after this officer has received a written order from the Public Prosecutor, which, in order to facilitate judicial control, sets out the essential data regarding the operation and the way it should be executed, the person or organization to be targeted, and a time limit.

Infiltration by civilians will also be regulated. It is to be expected that this sensitive issue will receive much academic and political attention, given the findings of the PEC. The scandal concerning the Interregional Team Noordholland-Utrecht in 1994 (the 'IRT affair'), which was subsequently investigated by the PEC, involved essentially a dramatic lack of control and accountability in relation to an infiltration project in which the undercover operator was 'run' by the intelligence service of the criminal police (CID Kennemerland[9]). This person had the job of penetrating or 'growing into' a criminal organization called Delta (at the head of which there was thought to be a triangle of three leading individuals). To gain the confidence of these top guys, the infiltrator became deeply involved in the importation of huge amounts of soft drugs, and eventually even hard drugs from Latin America. The PEC, in its final report, considered this method unjustified. It declared that it had been unable to establish that the method had been used with due regard to the Infiltration guidelines of 1991. This conclusion was reached on the basis of the following elements:

– Large shipments of drugs, of which the police (or at least some CID officers) were aware, were allowed through onto the market, without seizure and confiscation;
– The position of the criminal infiltrator was largely independent;
– The infiltrator was allowed to keep his criminal profits, which were considerable;
– The CID officers played an important facilitating role;
– The police used money, acquired from criminal activities, to finance the operation.

In short, the most important reason for the PEC's repudiation of this, the so-called 'Delta method', was that steering and control was impossible, raising the question: who was running who? The fate of the judicial authorities was to become hostage to those whom they should have been controlling.

However, the explanatory memorandum to the Bill argues that the technique of using civilians rather than police officers as infiltrators cannot be renounced completely. It argues for instance, that, in order to maintain credibility in a certain environment, an infiltrator may need a very specific expertise which the police do not possess. This environment might include a group preparing a kidnapping (where infiltration is admissible if there is suspicion of a specific crime, i.e. suspicion in the narrow, old fashioned sense). It might also include penetration of a criminal organization of the mafia type (then infiltration at the 'proactive' stage is also admissible). As for the required expertise, one could think of financial experts (accountants for instance), who could operate in so called front stores.

The regulations expressly exclude the use of non-police infiltrators when the use of police infiltrators is a viable method (an application of the subsidiarity principle). It does not exclude, however, the use of *criminal* infiltrators. Here there is a major departure from the recommendations of the PEC, which suggested that non-police informers should not have the right to commit punishable acts, and that all infiltration by civilians (not just criminals) must be excluded totally. This point of view was obviously the result of the trauma of the IRT scandal.

The explanatory memorandum correctly underlines the fact that it is unthinkable that an infiltrator could avoid committing (serious) criminal acts without undermining his credibility. It is not convenient – so the argument continues – to forbid or restrict the use of informants in the Code of Criminal Procedure. It is however necessary, by means of specific guidelines, to restrict the use of infiltrators from the criminal milieu to very exceptional cases. In principle, the method should be banned. However if, by using it over a short period, a decisive step forward in the investigation can be achieved, the most senior body of the Prosecution Service (*College van Procureurs-Generaal*), on the advice of the Central Review Committee,[10] may permit its use. If it does so, it has to inform the Minister of Justice, who – as politically responsible authority – has the right to cancel the decision.[11]

Thus, the method is only permitted in extreme cases such as kidnapping, murder, the taking of hostages etcetera, and then only once, for a short period, for well defined activities and under permanent and strict control.

This means that longterm projects in which, as in the Delta case, criminal infiltrators are used, are forbidden. These operations are the exclusive preserve of police infiltrators. The argument that police infiltration is not sufficient because the criminal milieu is very hard to penetrate, is in the opinion of the authors of the Bill not a justification for maintaining such a risky and problematic investigation technique. It should be kept in mind, however, that the text of the Bill allows a much wider field of application. It is to be doubtful whether the view expressed in the explanatory memorandum will turn out to be the final word on this controversial issue.

The way in which rewards for non-police infiltrators will be treated in the future is also worth noting. As I have pointed out, one of the objections the PEC had to the Delta method was the fact that the infiltrator (who, by the way, was systematically but incorrectly described by the authorities as an informer!) was able to keep his considerable profits from criminal activity. The Bill says nothing on the subject. The explanatory memorandum dedicates only a few sober lines to it: the Public Prosecutor who takes the decision to employ the civilian infiltrator must draw up a contract, which is in accordance with the terms of the (written) order authorizing infiltration, and which lays down the mutual rights and obligations of the parties, such as the task of the infiltrator, the duration of the project and the reward.

The general legal conditions which should be fulfilled in employing infiltration techniques have been developed in case law since the late 1970s, although this method was already being used (without any public debate or political decision) from 1973. This case law resulted in some general criteria, which were then incorporated into guidelines from the Public Prosecutor's Office. In 1979, the Supreme Court confirmed a ruling of the lower courts which had held that the suspect should not, by the employment of under-cover agents, be led into the commission of criminal acts which he or she had not previously intended to commit.[12] This criterion has become known as the Tallon criterion, after the name of the suspect in the case, Bruce Tallon. The meaning of this formula is not evident. Thus the PEC see it as a prohibition on inciting the suspect to illegal acts, but that interpretation is based on too narrow a concept of 'intention'. In a more recent decision, the Supreme Court has ruled that the undercover agent may provoke illegal acts provided that the suspect would have ended up committing these acts, or acts of the same nature, without the intervention of the undercover agent. His or her readiness to act may appear from different factors, such as previous convictions for similar offences, the time delay within which the suspect is able to supply drugs or the amount of the drugs that can be supplied.[13]

As with all investigative acts, especially those which affect the fundamen-tal rights of citizens (in particular their right to privacy), the courts and guidelines require the observance of the principles of proportionality and subsidiarity. The proportionality principle entails the balancing of the seriousness of the (presumed) crime against the drawbacks of this drastic method in its effect on the freedom of citizens. In practice, this does not involve a very significant restriction, as the method is generally accepted by the court not only in drugs cases and other organized crime cases, but also for instance in illegal gambling cases. The subsidiarity principle entails the obligation to establish that no other, less intrusive means is available that might be effectively used in the investigation of the particular case. As drugs trafficking takes place secretly and in a covert, organized way, it is not easy for the police to get hold of the really important people if it can only operate 'from the outside'. Therefore, examples of court decisions establishing violations of the subsidiarity principle are rare.

One thing is certain: control over criminal non-police infiltrators, even if they are used under strict conditions, very exceptionally and for a short period, will remain extremely problematic.

To a somewhat lesser extent, the same is true for informants who are 'run' by the police (the 'spontaneous' informant is not to be the object of legislation). There is not only the problem that these informers are rewarded for their services (in this, there is no difference with spontaneous informers, whether within or outside the criminal milieu). The real problem is that the police and the Public Prosecution Service do not have a firm grip on the civilian informer; neither legally nor from a psychological or social point of view.

The recording of communication

In 1993, a Bill[14] was put before parliament to authorize the police to record conversations in organized crime cases. In practice, the police were already using this method, but without an adequate legal basis. In essence the PEC adopted this 1993 legislative proposal, which had been withdrawn for reconsideration after a change of government. The Bill also wants to introduce this method of investigation but with some important alterations. In the first place, it replaces the term 'conversation' in the original Bill with the term 'communication'. This is to prevent the regulations from getting obsolete as a consequence of technological innovations, for instance encrypted electronic mail. The use of this term also takes into account the possible simultaneous use of different means of communication, such as sound, text or images.

A more important difference from the PEC proposal concerns the scope of the regulations presented by the Bill. The PEC did not want to extend the use of bugging to the proactive phase, without a specific suspicion that a crime has been committed. The authors of the Bill, in accordance with original 1993 proposals, argue that this method is aimed very much at the struggle against organized crime. So, in the future, as soon as there is a 'reasonable suspicion', based on 'facts and circumstances', that a person is involved in serious organized crime, the Public Prosecutor will be entitled to issue an order that communication in which this person is participating shall be recorded by special technical devices. This is the broad concept of 'suspicion', for it is not necessary that this person be suspected of having already committed crimes. The 'involvement' criterion is rather vague, and seems to be free from moral connotations. In principle, this involvement might appear rather innocent (and, by the way, might actually turn out to be completely innocent). A person can be involved in covert criminal operations but be unaware of the fact that he is rendering services to those operations (for instance by money-laundering or the transporting of drugs).

The explanatory memorandum recognizes that this power does entail considerable consequences for the privacy rights of citizens. So, the Bill provides for judicial control, analogous to the regulation of wire and fax tapping as laid down in the Code of Criminal Procedure. The Public Prosecutor may only give his permission after having obtained authorization from the Investigating Judge (*rechter-commissaris*),[15] except where a police officer himself is participating in the communication.

It is only a matter of consistency that the tapping and recording of communication via the telecommunication infrastructure should also be possible in criminal investigations. It goes without saying, that the person who is the object of these secret operations does not have to be notified beforehand. To meet the standards of the European Court of Human Rights, however, notification post factum, when the investigation is finished, is obligatory,[16] as is judicial control. Notification and judicial control are now laid down in the Code of Criminal Procedure (Article 125g) insofar as 'classical' investigation into crimes already committed, is concerned.

Evaluation

The parliamentary inquiry on investigation methods, its conclusions and recommendations, the subsequent debates among government, politicians, criminal law professionals (police, public prosecutors, magistrates, the bar) and experts, when considered alongside the recent developments in case law, do appear to confirm a tendency towards a new balance between effective crime fighting and due process, and between effective policing and control. The PEC showed a firm, probably rather naive belief in fixed legal rules, far stretching restrictions to police operations and elaborate control mechanisms in which the magistracy takes a dominant position. The main criticisms concerned, as might have been expected, the strait jacket the Van Traa commission allegedly want to force upon the police, the impracticability of some of the proposals, the tendency to regulate via legislation what might be better laid down in guidelines, and a unfortunate allocation of control competences (a too prominent position given to the investigating judge; a taking of too much responsability away from what should be seen as the central authority, i.e. the Public Prosecution Service).

Not all of this criticism is beside the point. To assign, for example, the control competence for infiltration operations to the investigating judge by demanding his prior authority involves drawing the authority of the *rechter-commissaris* much more into investigation practices, which could in the end mean a threat to its independent position. On the other hand, one could ask what will be changed if (most of the) proposals presently in the Bill became law, as compared with the present situation which has provoked so much criticism? Of course, the working out of the different police methods of investigation and the regulation of the proactive phase must be seen as a necessary and useful improvement. But as far as control and organizational safeguards are concerned, it is obvious that much more room is left to the criminal law agents and institutions than the PEC thought desirable.

The discussion about the judicial control of methods of investigation will be a test case for the adequacy of the organization of criminal procedure, as it is currently laid down in the Code of Criminal Procedure. The choice of a central role for the investigating judge not only entails the necessity of improving the quality and status of this function by training and recruitment measures (which the PEC suggested), but also means a step towards a different model of criminal procedure, in which the *rechter-commissaris* becomes a *juge d'instruction* comparable with the French and Belgian systems. That, in its turn, might result in a debate about the need for a fundamental reform of criminal procedure in the Netherlands. The government prefers the opposite course. This option implies, whether that is the intention of the legislator or not, an orientation towards a more adversarial practice, which has already been evident in the court room, especially in the 'mega-cases' such as the *Zwolsman* case. It is hard to believe that, if this tendency becomes dominant, that the practice of counter-investigation by the defence will remain at its present modest level.[17]

Notes

1 PEC stands for *Parlementaire Enquête Commissie* (Parliamentary Committee of Inquiry).
2 *Inzake opsporing* (1996), Enquêtecommissie opsporingsmethoden, The Hague: Sdu.
3 Bill on Special competences of investigations methods, TK 1996-1997, 25 403, nrs. 1-3.
4 See Article 148 in combination with Article 141 and Article 142 CCP.
5 Bill, Article 126o.
6 Bill, Article 126g, 4.
7 Speech Mr Gonsalvez E.I.P.A. Congress, Maastricht, March 1996.
8 Bill, Article 126v.
9 CID stands for *Criminele Inlichtingendienst* (Criminal Intelligence Unit).
10 The *'Centrale Toetsingscommissie'* (CTC) on which both police and prosecutors are represented.
11 This is in agreement with the contents of the provisional Guidelines on infiltration, issued by the College van Procureurs-Generaal in 1996.

12 Supreme Court 4 December 1979, NJ 1980, 356.
13 Supreme Court 24 October 1989, NJ 1990, 239.
14 Number 23 047, concerning overhearing and registration of communication with a technical device.
15 Bill, Article 126s, 4.
16 Bill, Article 126bb.
17 In relation to defence investigation see the contribution of Ed Cape and Taru Spronken in this volume.

7 Proactive investigation: a Belgian perspective

CYRILLE FIJNAUT AND FRANK VERBRUGGEN

Introduction

A tradition of proactive policing

Like all European countries, Belgium has a long history of proactive policing, in the political as well as in the criminal field.[1] Traditional literature put the use of secret informers, the covert surveillance of people or goods, the metering of telephone calls and the infiltration of criminal organizations under the heading of 'police inquiries', the preliminary phase of criminal investigations that neither the Code of Criminal Procedure nor the Police Laws regulate.[2]

In the distant past it was political undercover policing that sparked most controversy. Serious scandals in connection with the large scale gathering of ongoing information on the private life of citizens and with the infiltration of radical leftist parties nourished the general distaste for this category of proactive policing (Van Outrive and Cappelle 1995). Undercover policing within the framework of criminal investigations, on the contrary, was widely accepted, as long as the police did not provoke the commission of crimes by the persons they were deceiving. Before World War II, police officers writing their *memoirs* referred to these methods and police manuals addressed the advantages and disadvantages of their use (Goddefroy n.d.; Louwage n.d.). What's more the authors candidly stressed that the successful use of ruses to catch criminals reflected the professional qualities of the policemen concerned. Belgian criminal law scholars of the time, like their counterparts elsewhere in Europe, did not pay any attention at all to these police practices. They were usually academics, lawyers or magistrates and considered these police actions to fall outside of the framework of criminal procedure. Apparently they silently accepted some forms of proactive policing as a necessary preliminary means to reach the point of official investigation in the stricter, legal, sense of the word.

Fall from grace: the methods and their application lose their self-evidence

The situation radically changed in the 1970s and 1980s, when it transpired that special undercover units within the Ministry of Justice and the gendarmerie had ended up in a quagmire of police crime and corruption. Furthermore, a parliamentary committee of inquiry established that the national police services (*gendarmerie* and *judicial police*[3]) practised undercover policing methods in a very unprofessional and even counterproductive manner. In the meanwhile, privacy concerns had made an inroad into Belgian doctrine and case law, particularly under the influence of the European Court of Human Rights. Modernization and professionalization of police investigation lead to an increased use of technology and economies of scale, adding new privacy-concerns.

In 1990, the Justice Minister responded to this evolution by issuing secret guidelines on the use of the so-called 'special investigative methods', entrusting the most risky ones to specially trained and equipped police units. Parliament adopted laws on the metering of calls and the interception of private communications. The political debate has not yet come to a standstill though. In a number of high profile cases the Belgian criminal justice system had already shown some distressing malfunctioning. A most upsetting case of child kidnap and murder, directly linked to paedophilia and child pornography and indirectly to car theft rings, was the straw that broke the camel's back. Especially after the Court of Cassation removed the investigating judge – who had become a kind of white knight to public opinion – because he had fraternized with some of the victims, the entire criminal justice system plunged into an unprecedented legitimacy crisis. One of the particularly nasty episodes was a public clash between different police services and between police and public prosecutors over proactive investigations. Several parliamentary commissions are now trying to sort things out. The federal government promised fundamental reforms. The creation of a coherent legal framework for the application of proactive police investigations should be one of them.[4]

In this chapter, we will describe the recent development of proactive investigation in Belgium itself, its current regulation and organization, and the ongoing reform debate as it has been fuelled by new scandals. We will also briefly address cross-border proactive investigations from a Belgian perspective. Consciousness of the problems is growing, but there is not much information available, so many questions remain unanswered.

The development of the 'new' proactive policing in Belgium

The setting-up of new undercover units

In 1971, Justice Minister Vranckx established[5] the Department of Criminal Information (BIC), a special undercover unit within his Ministry. He justified his decision by arguing that the drugs trade – and organized crime more generally – posed a real threat to Belgian society and that the classical methods of criminal investigation were no longer adequate to contain them. Time had come, he emphasized, to modernize criminal investigation by introducing so-called 'new' forms of undercover policing. He borrowed his ideas for renewal from the American federal police services (especially the DEA). In the framework of the Nixon Administration's international war on drugs, they made a great effort to push for the introduction of the 'new' American methods of undercover policing in Western Europe and other parts of the world. The BIC's task would be to penetrate organized crime circles in order to collect information which could be used as a starting-point for so-called operational criminal investigations, i.e. aiming at the arrest of the relevant perpetrators and the seizure of the stolen or illegal goods.

Its members did not have the special legal status of 'officers of the judicial police'. That implied that they would not really perform the tasks of the 'judicial police', the standard criminal investigation under the super-vision and authority of the prosecution service or an investigating magistrate, and would lack the corresponding powers (arrest, search, seizure, use of force, etcetera). Control and authority would thus stay exclusively with their superiors in the Ministry. The Minister justified the withholding of this status by pointing out that the unit's members would only collect information and would not be involved in the operational aspects of criminal investigations as such.[6] They had to hand over the relevant information they gathered, to the established units of the *judicial police* and to the criminal investigation departments of the *gendarmerie*.[7] Later on, however, it was made public that the gendarmerie at the same time had established its very own special undercover unit – National Bureau of Drugs (NBD) – within its general headquarters. And again, American officials were the back seat drivers, or at least heavily supported this initiative (Fijnaut 1983; Nadelmann 1993).

The NBD was headed by Captain François, who would give his name to a scandal that burst out in the beginning of 1980s.

From the very beginning, political party spokesmen, legal scholars and even prominent members of the Prosecution Service, protested against the renewal of undercover policing. First of all, they claimed that there was no adequate legal basis for the systematic use of undercover methods, which could easily infringe upon the private life of citizens. This legal objection was supplemented by an organizational one: the establishment of the BIC would needlessly stir up the 'police war' between the national police services. In a third and more functional objection, they stated it was wrong to separate 'information' from 'action' in criminal investigations, because they are two sides of the same coin. The final argument was a social one: should the use of the 'new' but very risky methods go wrong, not only the police services involved, but the entire criminal justice system would be disgraced. Successive Ministers of Justice did not feel strongly about these objections. On the contrary, time after time they defended the units, in spite of strong indications that their operations had got out of hand.

In 1980-1981 it became undeniable that in the foregoing years several members of the BIC and the NBD had not only committed a wide variety of crimes but had become completely corrupt. The Tribunal of First Instance in Brussels found them guilty, not only of falsifying and suppressing official documents but also of earning a lot of money by cooperating with important drug-traffickers. On 14 April 1982, it sentenced them to (completely or partially suspended) prison sentences from one to four years. This scandal of course put undercover policing in a very unfavourable light: it really became a taboo subject in political circles, in the *gendarmerie* and in the Ministry of Justice. The ambiguous reaction of some of those in charge in the police and elsewhere in the criminal justice system, only fomented the distrust of public opinion towards the entire system. In that context, nobody dared to take the initiative to establish a legal framework for the use of proactive methods in criminal investigation.[8]

Case law

Under Belgian law, the courts cannot set binding precedent, but case law nevertheless is an important source for the interpretation of the law. It filled the vacuum to some extent. In a 1984 case of a *pseudo-buy* of drugs, the Court of Appeal of Brussels stated the conditions under which this form of infiltration is admissible:

1. the suspect may not be entrapped, meaning that the agent may not 'implant' the intention of committing a crime into the suspect's mind;
2. the method may only be used for serious crimes (proportionality-requirement);
3. the undercover-agent may not commit crimes, except in the case of an emergency,
4. and his (police) superiors should supervise and conscientiously control the agent's action.[9]

In the subsequent years courts all over Belgium followed this rule, making it also the main point of reference for police services considering whether to use the pseudo-buy technique.

Case law was less coherent in its evaluation of another often used investigative method: the metering of telephone numbers. For a long time, guidelines issued by the Minister of Justice in 1923 which allowed an examining judge to order such metering, were widely accepted as sufficient (Traest 1992, p. 322). Under the influence of the European Court of Human Rights case law, particularly the *Malone* case (2 August 1984), opinions started to differ. While some courts stuck to the traditional viewpoint that the guidelines were a sufficient basis for this practice, others came to the conclusion that the creation of a more adequate legal framework was necessary (Lemmens 1984-85; De Nauw 1982-83).[10] In May 1990 the Court of Cassation sided with the latter view, thus forcing the legislator into action.[11] In the meantime, the – completely prohibited – tapping of the telephone calls themselves had also become more and more of a public issue. In particular, the inability of the police and Prosecution Service to prevent or solve cases like that of the so-called 'Tueurs du Brabant/Bende van Nijvel', who perpetrated a series of very violent raids on shops, restaurants and supermarkets in the first half of the 1980s, inflamed the public debate on issues like phone-tapping, infiltration or the use of informers. Many observers pointed out that Belgium was the only country in Western Europe where telephone-tapping was completely prohibited.

Parliamentary inquiry and the Whitsun-plan

In 1988 the infamous *warehouse murderers* had not been brought to justice[12] and all kinds of rumours about infighting and obstruction surrounded the continuing investigations. Parliament (the Chamber of Representatives) therefore established a committee of inquiry into the way in which the fight against organized crime and terrorism was organized. On 30 April 1990, this committee published its report, based upon the consultation of a number of *dossiers*,[13] several fact-finding missions in Belgium itself and in neighbouring countries, and a long series of public hearings. It found that in previous years at least some components of the 'new' undercover policing had been organized in a more professional way. The 23rd (national) squad, created within the *judicial police* in 1987, could call upon its own small special surveillance unit. Much more important however, was the surveillance capacity that had been built up within the *gendarmerie*. Apart from its national squad for special interventions, founded in 1972 after the terrorist drama at the Munich Olympic Games, which was well-equipped and trained for surveillance operations, this police force had also set up (in 1984) five regional units, with the surveillance of (groups of) serious criminals as one of their main tasks.

The committee pointed out that in the field of proactive investigations still a lot of legal and operational problems subsisted, so it recommended that Parliament should develop as soon as possible a legal framework for the use of the well-known forms of short-term infiltration (pseudo-buy, flash-roll) as well as for the tapping of telephone conversations. The committee believed that the running of informers remained indispensable to solve difficult criminal cases, but that the internal law enforcement control mechanisms should be strengthened in order to prevent all sorts of problems: the entrapment of potential suspects by informers, informers who manipulate their runners or play off policemen against each other, etcetera.[14]

The government anticipated the main conclusions and recommendations of the parliamentary committee of inquiry. It developed a comprehensive programme, the so-called Whitsun-plan,[15] in order to restructure the police system and to modernize the criminal justice system, particularly in relation to pre-trial proceedings. A first major step in the reform of pre-trial proceedings had already been taken: a new law (1990) on pre-trial detention. It had become an absolute necessity for different reasons. On the one hand, there were just too many people on remand, even when it was not strictly necessary, with desperately overcrowded prisons as a result. On the other hand, parliamentary inquiries had only reinforced existing suspicions about police abuses during detention, particularly during interrogations. Whether the legislator realized it at the time is not clear, but by adopting the law on pre-trial detention, it gave proactive policing a new push. First of all, investigators were forced to produce stronger evidence before they could justify detention. Secondly, the law introduced an exception to the principle that criminal investigations are secret and gave the defence the right to consult the file every time the detention had to be prolonged. It is an effective way for the defence to keep investigators under pressure to make progress. For investigators, it has therefore become important to investigate as long as possible without having to rely on pre-trial detention. According to some critics, law enforcement is circumventing the law by creating secret files parallel to the criminal case-file itself.

The current legal framework of proactive investigation[16]

Framework

Unfortunately, the drafters of the Whitsun-plan did not grasp the opportunity to bring about a coherent legal regulation of proactive investigations, and consequently it is anything but easy to describe its current legal framework. The secret guidelines, issued by the Minister of Justice on 24 April 1990, still constitute the basic regulatory instrument. They mainly relate to the use of informers, surveillance and infiltration. Often the use of these techniques will result in a privacy-infringement under Article 8.1 of the European Convention of Human Rights. Secret guidelines cannot possibly be regarded a formal source of law and as such they fail to meet one of the basic quality standards the European Court of Human Rights has developed for the notion of 'law' in Article 8.2 of the European Convention. Even though they are sometimes referred to in court proceedings (especially to rebut a defendant's argument that the police acted illegally), secret guidelines can of course not be considered by the trial judges.

Other aspects of proactive investigation have in recent years indeed been regulated, or at least been touched upon, in specific formal laws. Some changes (in 1991 and 1995) to the Code of Criminal Procedure allowed the monitoring or interception of communications in exceptional circumstances. The 1992 Law on the Police Function (WEPA)[17] and the Law for the Protection of Private Life vis-à-vis the Processing of Personal Data (WEBER),[18] contain provisions regarding the collection, storage and use of information by the police.

Within the local prosecution services, so-called 'prosecutors of confidence' were given responsibility for sensitive proactive operations. They are to be the privileged partner of the police service, but their relation with other prosecutors within their district is not clear.

The general collection, storage and use of information[19]

Although notably the (original version of the) Law on the Gendarmerie (*Wet op de Rijkswacht*, from 1957) contained some provisions on the gathering of information, it was in the WEPA that this basic task of all police services got a specific legal basis for the first time. Under its Article 39 the police services, when performing their duties (in the administrative as well as the judicial field), may collect information, process personal data and store documentation with respect to events, groupings and persons which are of a concrete interest for the performance of the named duties. The police services can not exert this power on their own authority: they always operate within the respective areas of responsibility of the competent administrative and judicial authorities. Although Article 39 WEPA does not exclude covert policing methods, they were not mentioned explicitly in the preparatory works. Nowadays, however, it is widely accepted that via this article in combination with Article 5 WEPA (the power of the Minister of Justice to issue general guidelines in the field of judicial policing) the secret guidelines got an explicit legal basis post factum (Bourdoux et al. 1992).

Nobody doubts that respect for the private life of citizens implies limits on the police services' powers, but – apart from the legal regulation of the interception of communications – this basic point of departure has only been transformed in positive law with respect to the processing of personal data (Bourdoux and De Valkeneer 1993) and the royal decrees implementing it. Interestingly enough, this law was adopted because the Schengen-Convention requires that participating states meet the conditions set in the Council of Europe Treaty on the Protection of Persons against the Automated Processing of Personal Data and the 1987 Recommendation R(87)15 of the Committee of Ministers of the Council of Europe regulating the Use of Personal Data in the Police Sector.[20] Although the WEBER goes beyond the demands of the 1981 Convention, the legislator seems to have overlooked Recommendation R(87)15. The law does contain several articles which also relate to the processing of personal data by the police services, but is still quite unsatisfactory as a legal framework.[21] Where the rights of citizens are at stake, the data bases of the police (and intelligence) services are systematically exempted.[22] If somebody wants access to a police data system or wants to correct data that has been recorded in such a system, he or she has to turn to the official Commission for the Protection of Private Life (Dumortier 1993). A royal decree implementing Article 17 WEBER on the way the Commission has to be notified when a data base is set up, lists four 'purposes of computing' for 'Police and Justice':

1. *public security*: the gathering and follow-up of information on persons who are deemed to pose a risk to public security;
2. *tracing*: circulating the description of, and tracing suspected persons;
3. *administration of justice*: the administration of justice and the taking of minutes;
4. *penal records*: registration of criminal convictions.

The obligations and powers of the police under the privacy law were made explicit in royal decree nr. 8 of 7 February 1995.[23]

Basic principles concerning the use of informers, surveillance and infiltration

As we already said, in 1990 three of the core methods of proactive investigation (the use of informers, surveillance and infiltration) were set out in a set of secret guidelines, issued by the Minister of Justice. To a large extent, they embodied the norms which case law had developed in the preceding years.[24] The specific guidelines for each of the three core methods of proactive investigation are guided by common principles:

1. the methods in question may only be used in such a way that fundamental human rights and the dignity of the judicial process are respected;
2. they may *never* be used to *provoke* the commission of a crime;
3. they may only be applied if the case meets requirements of *proportionality* (serious crime and/or organized by a gang) and *subsidiarity* (the necessary pieces of evidence can not be collected by other investigative methods);
4. the deployment of these methods takes place under the control and authority of *the Prosecution Service*;[25] in a number of cases that will not *only* be the local public prosecutor but (one of) the (two) so-called 'federal magistrates', high-ranking members of the Service, who coordinate criminal investigations of (inter-)national importance (De Hert and Vanderborght 1996a);
5. when the application of these methods may result in a minor crime being committed, the Prosecution Service has to approve the proposed operation in advance; in exceptional circumstances a (minor) crime – in proportion to the seriousness of the crime that has to be solved – may be committed by the person involved, but he must report this to the local public prosecutor as soon as possible.

The running of informers

The guidelines only concern informers themselves implicated in the *milieu* of organized crime or who obtain information about this milieu other than by chance. Every informer gets two runners in the police who in turn are controlled by a senior officer. The runners and their supervisor of course have to know the identity of the informer, but in their reports they may only identify him/her by his/her identification number. A copy of all the reports that have been made, should always be sent to a regional information centre (within the gendarmerie and/or the judicial police). In a number of cases, however, a copy also has to be transmitted to the national information centres (within the named federal police services). To prevent different police services paying or running the same informer, all of them are recorded in a central register under the responsibility of the federal magistrates.

In accordance with prevailing theory and practice, the guidelines state that police officers are under no obligation to disclose the identity of the informer to the trial court, when they believe that secrecy is necessary for the informer's safety and the efficiency of the fight against crime. The local public prosecutor, on the contrary, has the power to ask that policemen reveal the identity of their informers to him.

If the Prosecution Service wants to use information provided by an informer as evidence and – in other words – wants to turn the informer into a witness, the secrecy obviously becomes a very critical issue. Under Belgian law, in exceptional cases and under a number of specific conditions (see the *Kostovski* case, ECHR 20 November 1989) the statements of an anonymous witness may be used in evidence. The Code of Criminal Procedure does not address the problem. It will be up to the investigating judge to interrogate the informer/anonymous witness (De Nauw 1985-86a; De Wilde 1988, 1990). Belgium does not have any official witness protection program yet.[26]

Although it is far too soon for definitive conclusions, the 'missing children' case demonstrated that a great number of important informers are still not registered (they even refuse to provide information if they are). Most informers it seems, are not paid cash for the information. They hope law enforcement agencies will take their help into account when stumbling on offences committed by the informer.

Surveillance

Even though in recent years police surveillance has been modernized considerably through the establishment of special surveillance units and the evolution of tracking and visual observation technology, it has not yet become an issue in case law and legal writing discovered it only recently (De Hert 1994; De Hert and Gurwith 1994; De Schutter 1996). The guidelines admit that long-term surveillance and/or surveillance with the help of special devices may infringe upon the privacy of the persons under surveillance or third parties. They do not address the use of short-term and unsophisticated forms of surveillance. The Minister – vaguely – defines in-depth surveillance (*observation*) as the gathering, in a discrete way, of information or evidence concerning specific persons or matters. The guidelines only apply to the extent that the surveillance aims at arresting the perpetrators of crimes or the gathering of criminal evidence.[27] Surveillance operations may be deployed in order to support the use of other proactive methods of investigation or they may be set up independently from the employment of such methods. In any case, they can only be ordered when the criteria of proportionality and subsidiarity are met. The local public prosecutor or the relevant investigating judge must be informed about the start of surveillance operations as soon as possible. They have the power to terminate such operations if, in their opinion, the privacy of certain persons is violated in an irresponsible way. The local police authorities merely need to be notified that surveillance actions are being conducted (by the national units).[28] Finally, the guidelines provide that if the results of surveillance operations are used as evidence in a criminal trial, the police officers involved have to remain anonymous and the means which have been used, have to be protected.

Infiltration

There is infiltration within the meaning of the guidelines[29] when a police officer using a cover identity contacts a group of persons who participate in serious criminal activities or who – on the basis of objective data – are supposed (to be about) to commit serious crimes, and tries to enter into extended interaction with its members.[30] This method may only be used to collect evidence on criminal activities or to identify the persons involved in them with a view to their subsequent prosecution. Apart from the general conditions listed at the beginning of this paragraph, the guidelines stipulate that:

1. Only short-term infiltration may be practised and it must never lead to the undercover agent participating in the perpetration of serious crimes;

2. A local public prosecutor or, if the operation takes place within the framework of a judicial investigation, the investigating judge always has to give written permission beforehand;
3. The police service entrusted with the infiltration must keep the public prosecutor or the investigating judge informed about the course of the operation;
4. Infiltration may only be executed by a group of police officers especially trained and given support for this purpose;
5. If possible, the results of an infiltration must be used as a means of evidence before the relevant court.

The guidelines clearly distinguish a pseudo-buy and a controlled delivery. Only for a pseudo-buy may civilians act as undercover agents, and even then, only in exceptional cases and with the permission of the public prosecutor. Controlled delivery, typically aimed at identifying those who are behind a particular transport of illegal goods, may also be used in order to protect an informer or undercover agent. The federal magistrates play an important role in the coordination of (international) controlled deliveries.

Like those on surveillance, the guidelines on infiltration state that in the end its results should be suitable as evidence for the Prosecution Service, provided that the police officers involved remain anonymous. Defence lawyers heavily criticized this provision and particularly the corresponding practice that undercover agents are interrogated by the investigating judge (if there is one). They regularly put forward that this procedure was a clear infringement of Article 6.3.d of the European Convention, granting every person charged with a crime the right to question the witnesses *à charge* and *à décharge*. In its well-known *Lüdi* decision of June 1992, the European Court of Human Rights of course proved them right (Scheers 1994).

Proactive metering and tapping of private communications?

The Belgian regulation on the metering and registration of private communications, does not permit the strictly proactive use of this method, so one is tempted to think it falls beyond the scope of this contribution. Particularly in this area it is hard to draw the borderline between proactive and reactive criminal investigation. We will show that some communications can already be tapped, even though the suspected persons have not been exactly identified yet. They also deserve our attention because in the public debate on the necessary modernization of criminal investigation, the police services put proactive metering and tapping of communications high on the agenda.

The metering of communications

When in the late 1980s the lawfulness of the existing rules on the metering of telephone calls had become extremely questionable, the Minister of Justice introduced a Bill proposing the insertion of an Article 88a in the Code of Criminal Procedure, to give this traditional practice an appropriate legal basis. After a lot of discussion resulting in numerous amendments, the Bill was eventually passed in January 1991 (Deruyck 1991-92).

Under Article 88a the investigating judge (and, except in a very limited number of urgent cases, not the public prosecutor), when he believes that the metering of telephone calls is necessary, can order the telephone company to register for a certain telephone apparatus the numbers of all phones from which incoming or to which outgoing calls are made.[31] In the warrant the judge not only has to give reasons for his decision, he must also explicitly state the duration of the warrant's validity. The maximum is two months, but it can be prolonged indefinitely by new warrants. In the course of the parliamentary discussions it was made clear that the related provisions were also applicable to the metering of telephone numbers which are used for sending faxes.

The tapping of communications

In September 1993, the Minister of Justice, in furtherance of the parliamentary inquiry's conclusions, introduced a Bill inserting a clause making tapping by judicial order an exception to the law on the protection of privacy against the interception of communications (Lambert 1990; Blontrock and De Hert 1991-92). Both inside and outside Parliament this Bill faced a lot of criticism. In particular, the gendarmerie raised a number of objections.[32] Some of these critical comments led – after a sharp discussion in Parliament – to major amendments to the Bill before it was finally passed. The act, inserting the new Articles 90b-90decies in the Code of Criminal Procedure, was published in the official bulletin (*Belgisch Staatsblad*) in January 1995 and came into force on 3 February 1995.

As the provisions with respect to interception are rather complicated and detailed, we will only give an outline of the basic rules (Verstraeten 1995; Verspeelt 1995). In principle only the investigating judge has the power – within the framework of a judicial investigation – to order the tapping of private communications. Who can be subjected to the measure? Both persons who, on the basis of precise indications, are suspects of the crimes for which the investigation was started and persons who, on the same basis, are likely to come into regular contact with the suspect(s). According to the accompanying parliamentary discussion paper, it is not necessary that the identity of all the persons in question be clear at the moment that the decision to tap their communications is taken. Two important conditions have to be fulfilled before the investigating judge can order police officers to apply this method. The alleged crime should be included in the list of serious crimes enumerated in Article 90(b)2 (extortion, arson, violent theft, drugs trade, etcetera) and other means of investigation should be incapable of revealing the truth about the crime. In cases of flagrante delicto linked to kidnapping and extortion the local public prosecutor also has the power to order the tapping of private communications. The investigating judge, however, must confirm this decision within 24 hours. The investigating judge's warrant, which has to meet a lot of substantive and formal requirements, is valid for at the maximum one month but can be repeatedly prolonged for one month, up to a maximum of six months.

Electronic 'bugging'

Whereas in other countries the issue sparked vivid debate, Belgian parliament did not really dedicate special attention to the fact that the 1995 law allows the direct recording of private conversations under the same conditions as the interception of telecommunications, even if special technical devices are used, and even if the persons or goods bearing the technical device enter private homes. Whether a judicial warrant allowing bugging implies the possibility of break-ins (in cars or homes), or entering under false pretences to place or remove the bugs, is not clear.

The sanctions on illegal behaviour

In theory, police officers and members of the Prosecution Service may always be prosecuted for offences they commit while investigating. In the course of proactive criminal investigations they may commit ordinary crimes like the falsification of official documents or specially constructed crimes, like the one that has been inserted in the Criminal Code (Article 259a) as a result of the Interception of Communications Act (1995). It says that public officers who, in the course of their duties, tap private communications in circumstances outside those laid down in the law and without following the prescribed procedures, can be punished with a prison sentence of six months to two years and/or a rather severe fine. Of course, in case of justifiable error or higher orders which are not manifestly illegal, the lower officers will go free. It is not at all excluded that (in addition to a criminal charge or not) disciplinary proceedings will be started against them for breach of the legal rules and/or the internal guidelines.

Apart from these personal consequences there are of course also the procedural consequences of such behaviour in a given criminal case. The general rule, developed and strictly applied over the years by the courts, is that evidence (and the 'fruits' of it) that has been obtained illegally has to be excluded. In cases where the judges decide to remove such evidence from consideration, they then have to ask themselves whether the remaining untainted evidence nevertheless constitutes a sufficient basis for a conviction. An even more radical sanction exists. Particularly in infiltration case law the standard rule is that provocation requires the quashing of the Prosecution Service's case (Traest 1992; Verstraeten 1993).

That is of course the theory. In practice, it will be hard to detect offences and to find out who is responsible. Furthermore, the inevitably vague phrasing of the law allowing tapping, results in a quite heavy burden of proof for anyone alleging wrongdoings. For investigative measures other than wiretapping not even such vague touchstones are available. Without a more complete legislation, the basic rule, that police can do everything which is not explicitly forbidden, entails a deplorable lack of control on activities which do not lead to evidence on trial. Thus, it is particularly the innocent who have little remedy if their privacy is invaded.

Coordination

One of the most painful and difficult issues is the coordination of different investigations and the flow of information. Whereas the police have their central units who can take care of very rapid processing and dispatching of information, similar institutions do not exist for the prosecutors or investigating judges. As they are the actual leaders of the investigation and as such responsible for the case, the current situation with de facto the police guaranteeing the coordination, was bound to result in trouble. In the 'missing children'-case, some information – which later turned out to be vital – obtained in one district did not reach the investigating judge of another district in written form. The prosecutor believed the gendarmerie would pass it on, whereas the gendarmerie believed that was the task of the prosecutor. As the prosecutor did not require written affidavits about a (fruitless) investigation against a suspect, the gendarmerie did not make them. They explained that they did not spontaneously write everything down, because that would endanger their informer.

As the problem had already been an important ingredient of the troubled investigation of the 'warehouse murders', the post of federal magistrate was created. These high-ranking prosecutors (at the moment there are two, but there will be a third one soon) have a coordinating role, but they lack central analysis capabilities to spot concurring or overlapping investigations. To complicate things, it has not yet been clarified what authority they (as members of the Prosecution Service) have over (unwilling) investigating judges (members of the Bench).

Cross-border proactive investigation[33]

What makes transnational investigations different from national ones?

However difficult and sensitive entirely national proactive policing and undercover investigations might be, the difficulties and dangers multiply when the Belgian borders are crossed. Organized crime (like almost all lucrative trade) is often international. In Belgium, a small, open country in the heart of Western Europe, that is even more so. We believe it therefore fair to say that a serious organized crime or terrorism investigation which remains wholly limited to Belgian territory is virtually impossible.[34]

Legal problems

In many areas of private law, countries started tackling the consequences of internationalization a long time ago, by working out rules for the settlement of conflicts of law on an international level. When merely private interests are at stake, states can react in a rather flexible way and give the concerned individuals or corporations a large degree of autonomy in deciding what the applicable law will be. As soon as the international situation concerns matters which a society deems crucial, international consensus on solving conflicts of law is often lacking. A state's decision to use criminal law to sanction certain behaviour and use the instruments of force at his disposal to obtain obedience, often indicates that it considers the matter to be of utmost importance to his society.[35] The willingness to give leeway to other states and their vision or policy will be very low. The notion in which this autonomy is embedded in an international context, is – of course – that of sovereignty. And under international public law, the exercise of 'sovereign powers' is in principle limited to the national territory.

International public law is by nature rather vague and mouldable. National policy-makers will be able to use the available manoeuvring space (and even try to push against the outer limits) or refrain from doing so. Small countries like Belgium (the notion 'small powers' is an oxymoron) face more difficulties in blowing against the wind: they lack the political weight and operational capacity to export their own rules, let alone to elevate them to the level of standards. They will also be disproportionately punished by international disapproval, isolation or other sanctions. To the extent that they lack the tools of power that are the trumps in international politics,[36] they are forced to follow suit. That does not exclude the existence of a certain amount of autonomy in criminal matters, as the domestic political importance of criminal policy makes countries willing to pay a price on the international level to stick to their (tolerant or repressive) criminal policies. To the despair of international human rights activists and of some law enforcers, that price will rarely be high. On the other hand, the lack of political clout, also means that small countries do not carry the same ballast and can be creative contributors to negotiated arrangements.

When considering the application of Belgian law ratione loci, one should distinguish between substantive criminal law, police law and the law of criminal procedure. Furthermore, one still has to assess to what extent Belgium, when it has granted its institutions jurisdiction, but facts (also) imply the territorial jurisdiction of another state, considers itself bound by the law of that state. For instance, an informer of the Belgian police intercepts a conversation between two suspects in a Dutch bar, while respecting Belgian, yet not necessarily Dutch rules. The current framework of international instruments regulating international treaties on extradition and mutual assistance in criminal matters looks seriously outdated in respect to the evolution of crime and policing.

Practical problems

Legal scholars have a tendency to focus on legal impediments, but in daily police practice the practical difficulties may create the biggest strain on cross-border investigations. The cross-border investigator will have to overcome differences in language, culture, and legal system. He or she will have to consider the sensibilities and priorities of local politics. And probably the most important problem is that cross-border investigations are expensive. Often the police agency will not have the necessary means at its disposal, and if it does, bureaucratic logic will require justifications for the money spent. When police officers are sent abroad, they lose the opportunity of using the tools of power available in a domestic setting: they lack authority. Particularly in undercover operations, the limited supervision that domestic superiors can exert and the operational independence of their agents, entail tremendous risks (Passas and Groskin 1995). Whereas national proactive police operations can be blown by uninformed law enforcement personnel, interference of territorial authorities in extraterritorial police operations will be even more damaging and embarrassing for the participants in the 'unveiled' operation.

Belgium, international law and covert operations

Belgium traditionally adopted a quite moderate position with respect to its territorial criminal jurisdiction. Only for the classical exceptions under international law, was Belgian criminal law applied extraterritorially. Of course, that is a lot easier if you give a broad interpretation to the notion of 'Belgian territory'. Case law indeed chose to adopt the so-called ubiquity-theory, which meant that as soon as any of the elements constituting the offence was located in Belgium, the whole offence was deemed to have been committed within the territory. In recent years, in a very broad interpretation of the universality principle, Belgium granted itself jurisdiction over war crimes and genocide wherever they were committed.

Claiming jurisdiction is one thing, enforcing one's laws yet another. In the sphere of criminal law enforcement Belgium has always taken a rather conservative stance. The official line is one of non-interference and enforcement within strict territorial boundaries. This even applies to 'passive' covert operations, where the foreign policemen do not use coercive powers (meetings with informers for example, or surveillance). Trust and good neighbourliness are seen as the key to success. Belgian police officers have often been active promoters of international cooperation and the federal government has joined them. The necessity of consent from the state on whose territory the operation is taking place (the 'territorial state') is the cornerstone of that policy. Often that is feasible, because there are few fundamental differences in criminal policy between Belgium and its immediate neighbours,[37] although on some concrete issues there have been some confrontations.[38] The 1990 Schengen Convention provided one of the first formalizations of proactive policing on an international level, and as such a moderate attempt to remedy the deficiency of classical legal assistance treaties. Schengen is a framework, which is being implemented in bilateral agreements, exchanges of letters and so on. In other instruments, like the Europol Convention, the 'formalization' of transnational policing is continuing. It is too soon to assess what their practical impact will be.

Foreign elements in Belgian investigations

As we said, it is anything but rare that an ongoing Belgian investigation turns out to contain foreign elements. If that happens, there are plenty of formal and informal channels to obtain more information.[39] If more formal action has to be taken (arrests, searches, interrogations, etcetera) the classical 'rogatory commissions' (the delegation by investigating magistrates of investigative acts) will have to be used. With the exception of border regions (unfortunately, the size of the country means that almost the whole territory is composed of border regions) all international information exchanges should use the national clearing house within the General Police Support Service within the Ministry of the Interior. That is where the Belgian element of most international networks (Interpol, Europol, Schengen, etcetera) is situated.

To facilitate cooperation with foreign authorities, an increasing number of Belgian liaison officers are being sent to other countries. Although they should also be available for local law enforcement, their primary function is clearly that of laying reliable links and knocking on the right doors for the benefit of Belgian investigations. Belgian police services are particularly pleased with the assistance provided by the liaison-officers.[40] The Ministers of Justice, of the Interior and of Foreign Affairs jointly issued guidelines for both Belgian liaison officers abroad[41] and foreign liaison officers in Belgium. Some initiatives have been taken to formalize their status, if possible, at a European level. One problem is of course the difficulty of controlling them.[42] Another problem is the cost: the build-up of a liaison-network is quite expensive. Initiatives to cut costs by pooling Benelux-liaisons have, up to this moment at least, failed to come to anything.[43] Apparently, 'centralized liaisons' through Europol Liaison-officers (ELOs) as an alternative for liaison-officers in individual European countries also meets with scepticism. They cannot be as effective as a man on the spot. Still, it is particularly outside of Europe that the intervention of Belgian liaison-officers seems decisive for the success of the investigation.

We cannot assess what value foreign criminal information receives in Belgium law or whether there is any control on how it was gathered. Trust and non-interference in a foreign state's affairs might be the guiding principles, but especially with regard to 'soft information' a dose of scepticism, distrust of sources and a margin of error are an essential ingredient of law enforcement activity. What if foreign law enforcement agents acted illegally and passed on some of the resulting information to their Belgian colleagues? The Belgian Court of Cassation distinguishes information that merely triggers a Belgian investigation from information used as evidence or for the gathering of evidence (on the use of extraterritorially obtained evidence, see Traest 1996; Gane and Mackerel 1996). The former is not considered to be problematic. With respect to the value of extraterritorial evidence and criteria for its admissibility, the Court is rather more scrupulous. It not only reviews the compatibility of foreign evidence gathering with local laws, but additionally it reviews whether the foreign rules (on investigation and/or evidence gathering) respect international standards, particularly those ECHR.[44] Such an attitude means that as a national court it passes judgement on foreign legislators and authorities. As such, it risks causing embarrassment to the Belgian government. Defence lawyers feel quite uncomfortable about the current situation, for they are rarely in a condition to control the foreign elements in the investigation.

Little is known about extraterritorial operations by Belgian officers. Some cases have been revealed in which Belgian officers acted as pseudo-buyers at the request of foreign colleagues. They should strictly comply with local legislation and instructions of local authorities while doing so. A lot more complicated is the extraterritorial use of Belgian police informers and infiltrators. In spite of all the formal rules, it seems impossible to keep foreign authorities informed about all extraterritorial contacts and meetings.

Although it is not clear whether it often happens, it seems that in the past threatened witnesses have been taken (ad hoc) abroad for protection.

Foreign services' operations on Belgian soil

Under standing doctrine, any activity of foreign services on Belgian soil is conditional upon approval by the Belgian authorities. That is of course pure fiction, especially in areas where the thin line between political and criminal intelligence blurs (terrorism, arms trade, nuclear proliferation, economical espionage etcetera). In practice, most of those activities will take place without Belgian authorities having a clue. Furthermore, it seems that sometimes Belgian authorities will be willing to turn a blind eye to operations of 'friendly' police and intelligence services.[45] Belgium's willingness to cooperate can however often serve as a cheap and safe alternative to clandestine foreign operations. Not hampered by excess of pride, Belgian police services have shown willingness to accept the assistance of foreign services to Belgian operations. That should nevertheless happen in an accountable way.

The shadow of foreign services who might have manipulated Belgian officers still hangs over some scandals of the recent past. Hardly anything is known about the use and hiring of a foreign service's agents or informers, value of foreign grants of immunity and plea bargains in Belgium.[46]

Belgian police can supply foreign counterparts with information necessary for the detection, prevention of crime or proactive policing. Three conditions must be met: the existence of a bi- or multilateral treaty, a minimum standard of data-protection observed by the requesting country and a respect of the 'finality'-principle (the information should not be used for any other purpose than the one for which it was granted) (Joubert and Bevers 1996, p. 503). Controlling this in daily practice is of course difficult: the whole system is built on mutual trust.

International coordination and compatibility of national proactive investigations

On a national level operations should be coordinated by central police units, under supervision of the federal magistrates. As we pointed out, the latter do not have any formal powers to overrule unwilling local prosecutors or investigating judges. These federal magistrates are also the main recipients of foreign requests for help or information. In several international instruments, Belgium has pledged to assist foreign partners in proactive investigations. It nevertheless retains the right of any competent prosecutor or investigating judge to intervene if he believes that to be necessary. That can happen for instance, if he believes that foreign partners would allow shipments of illegal goods to be released into the market, to protect informers or inflate their status within the criminal organization.

Transnational proactive investigations?

International cooperation gets plenty of soundbytes, particularly Europol, which to some should become the nerve-centre of transnational investigations. It seems that in real life, the picture is less clear. In many important cases, cooperation happens ad hoc. Many people in Belgium argue that all police information exchange is part of – or destined to become part of – the criminal investigation. Consequently, they believe that authority and leadership should stay with either prosecutors or judges. That is why the creation of liaison-prosecutors or liaison-judges is being considered. It is not clear whether this should happen ad hoc or on a permanent base, nor what their actual competencies would be. Others believe that police can exchange both 'administrative' and 'judicial' information. Only the latter would have to involve judges and prosecutors.

Another institution, the Commission's *UCLAF,* which is supposed to coordinate transnational EC-fraud investigations, gets plenty of vocal support but seems to remain a marginal player in daily practice.

The ongoing demand for reform

Franchimont commission

In another initiative in furtherance of the Whitsun plan, in 1991 the Minister of Justice asked an official commission, consisting of well-known law professors and senior officials, to draft proposals for a fundamental restructuring of pre-trial proceedings. It is somewhat perplexing that in its final report this so-called Franchimont commission did not pay any attention to proactive investigation. Perhaps its members feared that the insertion of this sensitive matter would hamper the quick approval of their other, politically less explosive, suggestions for change. Or maybe they shared the opinion of the previous Minister of Justice that there was no ground for creating a formal legal basis for the use of proactive methods, in any case not within the framework of the Code of Criminal Procedure. Strangely enough, the experts themselves suggest from time to time that their use may amount to a violation of Article 8.1 of the European Convention.[47]

The drafting of a legal framework

For several reasons the current government (Dehaene II) promised in its coalition agreement that it would investigate whether it is necessary or not to develop a coherent legal framework for proactive criminal investigation.

In the first place, legal scholars and members of the law enforcement community kept offering reminders that such a framework was necessary, not only because fundamental human rights are endangered by the systematic use of intrusive methods of proactive investigation, but also with a view to the legal security of everyone who is involved in the application of such methods (Verstraeten 1995).

The second factor is, we guess, that prominent police officers not only have demanded a more structural extension of proactive criminal investigation, but also have argued that it should also be used outside of the realm of traditional organized crime. They think of serious fiscal, financial, and economic crime, against which they would like to deploy even more sophisticated forms of infiltration, like the setting-up of front stores for instance (Deridder 1994; Doraene 1995).

Thirdly, in recent years at least one new scandal has erupted. On 25 January 1995, the Head of the Brussels brigade of the judicial police was convicted (of falsification of official documents and violation of professional secrecy) by the Brussels court of first instance. The officer gave his blessing to the setting-up of a front store by one of his informers, in an attempt to obtain information on VAT fraudsters. The informer clearly got out of hand and made use of the front store to earn a lot of money without providing any significant criminal information. On appeal the policeman was acquitted on the most important charges, but the case illustrated once again the risky nature of infiltration and the need for a well-regulated and strictly-controlled framework for proactive policing in the judicial field.[48]

The federal government has established a working group to comply with the promise of its coalition agreement. At this moment it is not at all clear what will come out of it. The scandals that rocked the country in the summer of 1996 have put a lot of extra pressure on the government. Parliament, responding to the widespread media coverage, has decided to grasp the initiative.

An interesting point in any event, is that in the debate a lot of attention is being paid to the actual legal developments in the neighbouring countries. In particular the activities of the Dutch parliamentary committee of inquiry into proactive policing (under the chairmanship of MP Maarten van Traa) has attracted a lot of attention. Its final report and notably the conclusion that all forms of proactive criminal investigation should be regulated in the Code of Criminal Procedure, met with a lot of response south of the border, although at the same time most observers stressed this conclusion was not automatically and completely valid in Belgium (Janssens and Naesen 1996; Berkmoes 1996; Bruggeman 1996).

The case of the 'missing children' highlights one of the most painful dimensions of proactive investigation. Many of the special investigative methods were designed for so-called 'consensual' or 'societal injury' crimes, which would justify their secret use and a postponement of police intervention. Unfortunately, such strategically well-founded choices risk leaving victims of ongoing criminal activities in the cold, by either exposing them to physical danger or by failing to provide them with information as to the progress of the investigation. Prostitution may be a 'victimless' crime, forced prostitution is not. Insider trading may be 'consensual', embezzlement is not.

The classical dilemma still stands: how many 'minor offences' can you afford to disregard in order to discover networks or organizations and instigators, which would easily regenerate after rash police intervention? The climate in society is very much in favour of victim's rights.

Changes to the law on the interception and registration of private communications

The fairly recent regulation of the interception and registration of private communications has not eliminated all criticism either. Critics consider the list of serious crimes incomplete. The trading of illegal hormones – which has developed into a most lucrative, and sometimes violent business – was an obvious example. Furthermore, the obligation to make written records of everything that is being said, regardless of its relevance, whatever language is being used, is also proving to be a nightmare for the police. Although in the future speech technology might come to their rescue – the computer putting words into writing – they do not want to wait that long. Finally, the wish of the police forces that truly proactive tapping in the field of criminal investigation should also be made possible, has not been fulfilled. The government now envisages amendments to the law to make its application more practical. It would give the police the chance to select which data from the wiretap are relevant, add hormone-trade to the offences for which wiretaps can be allowed and, as for tracing of calls with the compulsory help of the telecom-operator, extend the possibilities for the public prosecutor, and in extremely urgent cases even the police, to act autonomously.[49]

Conclusion

Belgium has a long history of policing which nowadays would be labelled 'proactive'. In the last two decades the awareness has grown that a legal framework has become indispensable. On the one hand a series of scandals painfully illustrated the dangers and difficulties of proactive policing and, on the other hand, European case law and legal certainty require formal legislation. The legislator has only partially complied with these obligations. A lot of important proactive investigative techniques are regulated only in secret guidelines, a choice which reflects the outdated opinion that they are an internal matter of the law enforcement community. In the fields where formal legislation exists (wiretapping and eavesdropping with the use of recording devices), it reflects profound distrust of the police, but gives rather broad powers to prosecutors and investigating judges. There is, for example, no prohibition against direct recording of private communications inside homes. To be able to bear the extra responsibilities such extra powers necessarily engender, their training and organizational structures (specialization, better coordination) will have to be modernized urgently.

The urgent necessity of a complete legal framework is the only thing everybody agrees on. Parliament will have to decide on painful questions like the monopolization of proactive policing in the criminal procedure (or leaving space for proactive policing outside criminal process), the role of the different players and the relations between them, the sanctions and the amount of openness the system can afford (vis-à-vis trial judges and juries, defence and third parties (particularly victims)).

Any account of proactive policing in Belgium is therefore doomed to end in a 'To be continued ...'

Notes

1 Criminal law enforcement employs 'classical' undercover methods to obtain evidence that persons, who at the outset of the covert investigations are only vaguely suspected of having committed a crime or of being about to commit one, can be considered with good reason as suspects against whom the classical means of coercion (arrest, search, interrogation, custody, etcetera) may be applied. Under the influence of American rhetoric, however, such methods are in Belgium more and more defined as the main elements of proactive (judicial) policing. Indeed, most of the time police uses these methods on their own initiative to convert a mere suspicion against individuals into the evidence of their guilt.

2 In Belgium, the label 'proactive', in our view indicating that law enforcement is taking initiatives which should enable it to prevent crimes from occuring or to be present when there are committed, is therefore often used as a synonym for either 'undercover police activities' or for 'special investigative methods'. The blurry terminology is somewhat complicating the debate.

3 Particularly in a notorious case of extremely violent raids upon supermarkets.

4 It was envisaged in the coalition agreement (June 1995) anyway.

5 This happened in June 1971, by the way of a royal decree, i.e. as an administrative decision, without explicit Parliamentary approval.

6 In an attempt to reinforce law enforcement's information position, Parliament in 1975 amended drugs law so as to reward suspects incriminating other suspects with the reduction of their sentence and even with immunity (see De Nauw 1985-86b).

7 Their position resembled that of members of the *Staatsveiligheid/Sécurité d'état* (counterespionage and domestic political intelligence service).

8　The constitional reform of the state, the federalization process, and economic emergencies also absorbed a lot of the political world's time and energy. Criminal justice simply was not a high priority.

9　Court of Appeal Brussels 19 November 1984, *Rechtskundig Weekblad*, 49, pp. 2563-2568. See also De Nauw 1987.

10　See further Court of Appeal Liège 21 January 1985, *Jurisprudence de Liège,* 92 (10) 1985, pp. 165-168, and Court of Appeal Brussels 30 April 1986, *Jurisprudence de Liège,* 93 (39) 1986, pp. 664-666.

11　Court of Cassation 2 May 1990, *Arresten van het Hof van Cassatie,* 1989-1990, nr. 516.

12　Suspects of some of the early raids were set free after a jury trial.

13　Indirect: by former magistrates.

14　*Parlementair onderzoek naar de wijze waarop de bestrijding van het banditisme en het terrorisme georganiseerd wordt; verslag namens de onderzoekscommissie,* Kamer, 1989-1990, nr. 59/8-1988.

15　This document has been published in Fijnaut and Lauwaert 1995.

16　See De Hert and Vanderborght 1996b, p. 635; Joubert and Bevers 1996, pp. 127-140, 170-171, 174-185, 187-197, 202-203, 207-209, 224-225, 232-242, 443-464, 501-504.

17　*Wet op het Politieambt* (WEPA) 1992.

18　*Wet tot Bescherming van de Persoonlijke Levenssfeer* ten opzichte van de Verwerking van Persoonsgegevens (WEBER), 1992.

19　See De Schutter and De Hert 1995 and De Hert 1995.

20　The 1995 Europol Convention does the same.

21　The law does not explain how the police has to notify its files to the privacy-commission, how judicial data may be used, whether data bases may be linked, whether it may pass on its data to foreign police etcetera.

22　For example: a person must always be informed that he is registered in a data system, but not in the case of a system that is maintained by the police (Article 9 *io* Article 11). De Schutter and De Hert (1995, p. 2) state that these provisions are at odds with Recommendation R(87)15. Everybody, says Article 10, has a right to get access to the data which have been stored about him in a data collection, but not if this is a collection of a police service (Article 11).

23　Koninklijk besluit nr. 8 van 7 februari 1995 tot vaststelling van de doeleinden, de criteria en de voorwaarden van toegestane verwerkingen van gegevens bedoeld in artikel 8 van de wet van 8 december 1992, *Belgisch Staatsblad*, 28 februari 1995.

24　Court of Cassation 26 February 1986, in *Journal des Tribunaux*, 106, 1986, p. 328 and further Court of Appeal Liège 8 January 1986, in *Jurisprudence de Liège,* 93 (15), 1986, 231-235 and Court of Appeal Brussels 30 April 1986, in *Journal des Tribunaux*, 106, 1987, pp. 335-336.

25 Under the Belgian Code of Criminal Procedure the prosecutor – or the investigating judge, if a so-called judicial investigation is initiated – leads the investigation. The (narrow) space the police has for autonomous proactive investigation depends therefore on the exact moment in which the police can be deemed to have acquired knowledge of the offence. Case law has made it clear that the police can collect some supplementary information before notifying the Prosecution Service (see De Nauw 1990-91).

26 Under Article 11 WEPA, the Minister of Home Affairs has to look after the special protection of persons and goods, a duty which also covers the protection of an endangered (non-anonymous) witness. In some cases it can be deduced from the police measures which have been taken, that a witness has got special protection. Toussaint (1996) suggests a crucial endangered witness might have received plastic surgery.

27 Surely it would be a serious mistake to deduce from this that surveillance would not be allowed for other purposes. We do not know whether other secret guidelines deal with these types of surveillance.

28 Understandable as this rule may be (prevention of interference), it is questionable whether this is workable in practice, especially when observing vehicles, highly mobile persons or movable goods. For surveillance through the covert use of technical tracking devices, it will normally not be necessary nor convenient to notify, so we doubt whether the rule is actually applied in those cases.

29 Some municipal police forces use officers dressed up as innocent tourists or joggers in order to arrest potential pick-pockets. Others use undercover patrolling in drug areas (Wils 1995). Apparently this is not considered to be infiltration, because it is not the police taking the initiative to contact the criminals and no lengthy relations are envisaged.

30 The definition limits infiltration to the *gerechtelijk onderzoek*, but other provisions indicate that this notion cannot be limited to its meaning under the Code of Criminal Procedure (investigation by an investigating judge) and also embraces the Public Prosecutor's autonomous investigations.

31 Although the burdensome procedure of the 'judicial investigation' is disproportionate for this kind of delinquency, there is no way the police can trace 'harassing phonecalls': without a judicial order, the telephone-company will not hand over the caller's number. A Bill proposes the insertion of an Article 46a into the Code of Criminal Procedure, which would allow the Prosecutor to order the phone company to hand over the number from where a certain call was made, and in urgent cases even upon autonomous decision of a police chief, which then needs a posteriori confirmation by the judicial authorities.

32 It complained that the cases in which tapping could be ordered were much too limited, that the validity of a tapping warrant (in the initial Bill only two days, possibly renewable for two days) was much too short. It also deplored the lack of provisions regarding the interception of communications in what it calls the 'proactive phase of investigations', that is at the moment that certain persons are

merely suspected of planning serious crimes (see Berkmoes 1994, pp. 23-38).

33 Compare the Dutch Parliamentary Inquiry into Investigative Methods, which dedicated some special attention to the complications of international investigations: Enquêtecommissie Opsporingsmethoden (1996), *Inzake Opsporing, Bijlage V: opsporingsmethoden,* pp. 422-454.

34 Often the international character of criminal activities is used in definitions, as a criterium hinting that a certain group might be an 'organized crime organization'.

35 By criminalizing a certain behaviour, one also depicts it as immoral, uncivilized, despicable. Calling the adversary a criminal is therefore a strong rhetorical tool, both in a national and in an international context. If 'criminalization' is used too often, however, it does lose impact.

36 Military power, geostrategic position, population, economic resources, Security Council membership, etcetera.

37 But what if the counterpart cannot be deemed trustworthy? The investigators who obtained the arrests of the members of one of Belgium's most notorious gangs, after they had sought refuge in South America (apparently in collusion with some local authorities) really worked on the edges of due process. The Belgian Court of Cassation applies the male captus, bene detentus rule, thus circumventing some thorny questions. As cooperation with countries like Turkey, Morocco, Central and Eastern Europe will be of crucial importance for the fight against criminal organizations in Belgium, sooner or later a policy on this explosive subject will have to be developed.

38 France refuses full implementation of the Schengen convention alleging Belgian laxism towards the transit of soft drugs from the Netherlands into France. Belgium is not really pleased with the French reluctance to help Belgian investigations into white collar crime perpetrated by French 'captains of industry'. Another conflict, with Spain, regarded the political offence exception to extradition of presumed ETA-collaborators.

39 Research has demonstrated that law enforcement rank and file are somewhat baffled by the panoply of channels for information exchange. For urgent or sensitive information they still rely very much on their personal informal networks.

40 At the moment there are nine: six of them in EU-countries (Germany, Austria, Spain, France, Italy and the Netherlands), one in Colombia, one in the US and one in Russia. The UK, Turkey, Canada and Pakistan are under consideration.

41 *Ministerial guidelines concerning the legal position and the operational rules for the liaison officers of the Belgian police services stationed abroad,* Brussels, 4 October 1993, not published. See also De Hert and Vanderborght 1996b, pp. 95-105.

42 Newspapers suggested that the liaison-officer in The Hague went out of line and was privy to suspicious 'uncontrolled' deliveries of drugs. The man sued the (Dutch) newspaper that produced the story for libel and wanted 'rectification' in

the Belgian press. The Court granted part of the rectification he had demanded. Soon afterwards however, investigating judges caused further embarrassment when they conducted searches in the man's private home as well as in his office at the Belgian embassy. The investigation is still going on.

43 'De verbindingsofficieren van de Europese Unie: enkele cijfergegevens',*Politeia,* September 1996, p. 5.

44 Evidence from foreign wiretaps could therefore be used in Belgian procedures, even though wiretaps were completely forbidden under Belgian law.

45 There even is a strong argument to be made that customary international law allows certain extraterritorial 'sovereign' actions (secret 'intelligence gathering' and – more controversial – covert action).

46 The only exception is the Schengen Convention, which contains a rather broad 'double jeopardy' clause.

47 *Verslag van de Commissie Strafprocesrecht* (1994), Liège-Antwerpen: Ed. Collection scientifique de la Faculté de Droit de Liège – Ed. Maklu.

48 Rechtbank van Eerste Aanleg te Brussel, 25 januari 1995.

49 Bill concerning the access to and the tracing of numbers of communication and telccommunication and amending the Articles 90ter, 90quater, 90sexies and 90septies of the Code of Criminal procedure (not yet published).

References

Berkmoes, H. (1994), De georganiseerde misdaad, in: *Mensenrechten; jaarboek van het Interuniversitair Centrum Mensenrechten,* Antwerpen-Apeldoorn: Maklu, pp. 23-38.

Berkmoes, S. (1996), Het eindverslag van de (Enquete)commissie Van Traa: 'Cut and paste' of 'Read Only'?, *Vigiles-Tijdschrift voor Politierecht,* 2 (1), pp. 36-43.

Blontrock, P. and P. de Hert (1991-92), Telefoonaftap: Trounet, Peureux, Derrien, Huvig, Kruslin et les autres, *Rechtskundig Weekblad,* 55, pp. 865-871.

Bourdoux, G.L., E. de Raedt and J. Seurynck (1992), *De wet op het politieambt; handleiding voor de leidinggevende politieambtenaren,* Brussel: Politeia.

Bourdoux, G.L. and Ch. De Valkeneer (1993), *La loi sur le fonction de police,* Bruxelles: Larcier.

Bruggeman, W. (1996), Van Traa: crisis in de opsporing of een nieuwe start, *Politeia,* 6 (3), pp. 14-16.

Deridder, W. (1994), De relatie openbaar ministerie-rijkswacht, in: *Een eigentijds openbaar ministerie,* Brussel: Imbel, pp. 247-257.

Deruyck, F. (1991-92), De wet van 11 februari 1991 tot invoeging van een artikel 88 bis in het wetboek van strafvordering betreffende het opsporen van telefonische mededelingen, *Rechtskundig Weekblad,* 55, pp. 10-15.

Doraene, J-P. (1995), *C.D.G.E.F.I.D.- Activiteitenverslag* 1994, Brussel.

Dumortier, J. (1993), *Wet tot bescherming van de persoonlijk levenssfeer*, Gent: Mys & Breesch.

Fijnaut, C. (1983), *De zaak François; beschouwingen naar aanleiding van het vonnis*, Antwerpen: Kluwer Rechtswetenschappen.

Fijnaut, C. and K. Lauwaert (1995), *Het Belgische politiewezen; wetgeving, beleid en literatuur*, Antwerpen: Kluwer Rechtswetenschappen, pp. 195-211.

Gane, C. and Mackerel, M. (1996), The Admissibility of Evidence Obtained from Abroad into Criminal Proceedings – The Interpretation of Mutual Legal Assistance Treaties and the Use of Evidence Irregularly Obtained, *European Journal of Crime, Criminal Law and Criminal Justice*, pp. 99-119.

Goddefroy, E. (n.d.), *Mémoires de police*, Bruxelles: Larcier.

Hert, P. de (1994), Het verzamelen en gebruiken van visuele informatie: foto's, videosurveillance en verkeersradars, *Politeia*, 4 (8), pp. 8-18.

Hert, P. de (1995), De geïnformatiseerde verwerkingen van persoonsgegevens: richtlijnen voor politiekorpsen, *Politeia*, 5 (5), pp. 19-22.

Hert, P. de, and S. Gurwirth (1994), Camera's tussen controle en privacy-bescherming, *Journal des Procès*, nr. 257, pp. 24-25.

Hert, P. de, and J. Vanderborght (1996a), Magistraten met aanleg voor politiewerk: de nationale magistraten, *Vigiles-Tijdschrift voor Politierecht*, 2 (1), pp. 1-19.

Hert, P. de, and J. Vanderborght (1996b), *Informatieve samenwerking over de grenzen heen*, Brussel: Politeia

Janssens, S., and Y. Naesen (1996), Ik zou wel eens willen weten, de gespecialiseerde politiezorg, *Politeia*, 6 (4), pp. 29-31.

Joubert C., and H. Bevers (1996), *Schengen Investigated, A Comparative Interpretation of the Schengen Provisions on International Police Cooperation in the Light of the European Convention on Human Rights,* The Hague-London-Boston: Kluwer Law International.

Lambert, P. (1990), Les écoutes telephoniques, *Journal des Tribunaux*, 109 (5571), pp. 10-11.

Lemmens, P. (1984-85), Het afluisteren van telefoongesprekken en het registreren van uitgaande en binnenkomende oproepen, *Rechtskundig Weekblad*, 49, pp. 1735-1739.

Louwage, F.E. (n.d.), *Police criminelle; technique et tactique*, Ninove: Anneessens.

Nadelmann, E.A. (1993), *Cops cross borders; the internationalization of U.S. criminal law enforcement*, Pennsylvania: The Pennsylvania State University Press.

Nauw, A. de (1982-83), Het afluisteren van telefoongesprekken op bevel van de onderzoeksrechter, *Rechtskundig Weekblad*, 46, pp. 2369-2380.

Nauw, A. de (1985-86a), De anonieme getuige, *Rechtskundig Weekblad*, 49, pp. 1873-1891.

Nauw, A. de (1985-86b), Overzicht van rechtspraak; tien jaar vernieuwde drugwet, *Rechtskundig Weekblad*, 50, pp. 833-852.

Nauw, A. de (1987), De toelaatbaarheid van de politie infiltratie in België, in: *Naar eer en geweten, Liber Amicorum J. Remmelink,* Arnhem: Gouda Quint, pp. 443-454.

Nauw, A. de (1990-91), De beoordelingsruimte van de politie in de opsporing en het strafprocesrecht, *Rechtskundig Weekblad,* 54, pp. 65-74.

Outrive, L. van and J. Cappelle (1995), Twenty years of undercover policing in Belgium: the regulation of a risky police practice, in: C. Fijnaut and G.T. Marx (eds.), *Undercover: Police Surveillance in Comparative Perspective,* The Hague: Kluwer Law International, pp. 141-153.

Passas, N., and R. Groskin (1995), International Undercover Investigations, in: C. Fijnaut and G.T. Marx (eds.), *Undercover: Police Surveillance in Comparative Perspective,* The Hague: Kluwer Law International, pp. 291-312.

Scheers, J. (1994), Infiltratie, provocatie en undercover-agenten, in: *Mensenrechten; jaarboek van het Interuniversitair Centrum Mensenrechten,* Antwerpen-Apeldoorn: Maklu, pp. 67-76.

Schutter, B. de, and P. de Hert (1995), Is België klaar met zijn politieprivacywetgeving?, *Vigiles-Tijdschrift voor Politierecht,* 1 (3), pp. 1-12.

Schutter, O. de (1996), La videosurveillance et le droit au respect de la vie privée, *Journal des Procès,* nr. 296, pp. 10-14, nr. 300, pp. 20-21.

Toussaint, Ph. (1996), L'affaire Bongiorno et consorts: une vérité insupportable?, *Journal des Procès,* nr. 301, pp. 6-7.

Traest, Ph. (1992), *Het bewijs in strafzaken,* Gent: Mys & Breesch.

Traest, Ph. (1996), De internationalisering van het bewijsrecht: over telefoontap en de eisen die aan in het buitenland verworven bewijs moeten gesteld worden, *Recente arresten van het Hof van Cassatie,* pp. 142-152.

Verspeelt, F. (1995), De wet op het afluisteren van communicatie: een kennismaking, *Politeia,* 5 (1), pp. 17-20.

Verstraeten, R. (1993), *Handboek strafvordering,* Antwerpen-Apeldoorn: Maklu.

Verstraeten, R. (1995), Opsporingsmethoden: regulering en controle in België en Frankrijk, *Delikt en Delinkwent,* 25 (6), pp. 605-642.

Wilde, L. de (1988), Anonimiteit in het strafproces, in: A. de Nauw, J. D'Haenens and M. Storme (eds.), *Actuele problemen van strafrecht,* Antwerpen: Kluwer, pp. 59-86.

Wilde, L. de (1990), *De anonieme getuige: een preadvies,* Vereniging voor de Vergelijkende Studie van het Recht van België en Nederland.

Wils, J. (1995), Infiltratieteam bij Schaarbeekse politie, *De Standaard,* 14 June, p. 3.

8 Intelligence services and undercover operations: the case of Euromac

NIKOS PASSAS AND JACK A. BLUM

Introduction

Although intelligence services have less work to do after the end of the Cold War, they are not about to issue redundancy notices. As the expensive and energy-consuming fight against communism is over, a new cause has emerged. That is the fight against international organized crime, which is perceived as a serious global security threat (Naylor 1995; Williams 1994). The gravity of the international crime problem is certainly not to be under-estimated. The process of globalization has increased the number of 'criminogenic asymmetries', that is structural disjunctions, power inequalities and mismatches in the spheres of politics, culture, the economy and the law (Passas, in press). These asymmetries create opportunities for economic misconduct, motives to avail of such opportunities and control weaknesses. In addition, geopolitical changes in the 1990s have brought about new conflicts conducive to illegal markets, inter alia, in technology, arms and drugs (OGD 1996).

Since secret services and their agents possess information on many participants in such markets, it may be reasonable to suggest that they pass that information on to law enforcement agencies. The question, however, is how far such collaboration can or should go. Should secret services be enlisted in the business of law enforcement? Should we envisage joint intelligence and police operations? Many regard undercover investigations as the most effective instrument in the fight against sophisticated criminality (Greany 1992; Stavsky 1985). Should spies initiate or participate in inter-national undercover operations?

The argument in this chapter is that the functions of intelligence agencies and law enforcement are not compatible. The numerous risks arising from this incompatibility outweigh any potential benefits. Combining the two functions is likely to cause unjustifiable violations of citizens' privacy and civil rights. Many of the problems can be highlighted by the case of Operation Quarry, which was led by the US Customs Service in collaboration with the British Customs and Excise, and under the watchful eye of British military intelligence and the CIA.

The target was Euromac, a company allegedly involved in the illegal transfer of sensitive technology to Iraq before the Persian Gulf war. The authorities argued that its two executives, Ali Daghir and Jeanine Speckman, tried to illegally export electric capacitors, which could only be used as triggers for a nuclear bomb. They are the only persons to be gaoled for any illegal-arms-to-Iraq activity in the United Kingdom. Both their targetting by an undercover operation and trial have been questioned in the light of the very evidence produced by the investigation and the findings of the United Nations-International Atomic Energy Agency Team in Iraq. It emerged that Euromac and its managers had nothing to do with the arming of Iraq, which involved other companies massively exporting dual-use technology and military material with the knowledge and secret support of Western governments (Mantius 1995; Phythian 1996). The involvement of secret services and the fact that the publicity surrounding this case served to prepare public opinion for the Persian Gulf war, has prompted arguments that Operation Quarry's aims extended beyond any ethically or legally acceptable law enforcement objectives.

The case study is based on primary data such as Euromac correspondence, prosecution evidence and the complete set of cassettes containing the secretly recorded conversations between the undercover operatives and the targets of the investigation. In addition, extensive interviews have been conducted with Daghir, a British Customs official involved in the prosecution and two expert witnesses in the trial. The first was Dr. Hassard, a nuclear physicist at the Imperial College who has studied the Iraq nuclear programme for six years, who has taught a course on Arms Control Verification and Nuclear Proliferation for students from the UN, Ministry of Defence, the Foreign and Commonwealth Office and serving military officers from several countries. The second expert was Mr. Tillford, director of a company making high-speed flash equipment for the MOD and the German government. Finally, account has been taken of the press reports on the case.

Problems with joint intelligence-law enforcement operations

Strict and effective controls of cross-border undercover investigations are indispensable (Blum and Passas, this volume). International law must be observed, differences in cultural and legal traditions must be respected, sovereign functions must be honoured, and civil rights must be protected. The good management of undercover investigations is vital for the achievement of these goals. Even if these investigations are technically well managed, however, serious problems can arise when high-level officials pursue goals outside the conventional and legitimate law enforcement agenda. The combination of ordinary policing goals with intelligence gathering and the pursuit of political objectives, domestic or international, is dangerous for at least two reasons (in this chapter, we are not concerned with other dangerous deviations from licit practices, such as the use of a government agency for personal purposes).

Firstly, these objectives are bound to clash in such a way that the attainment of one undercuts the other. There are plenty of examples of this problem from the recent past. Given the huge amounts of money and power involved in the illegal markets of arms, technology and drugs, secret services wish to know who are the main players and how they operate (OGD 1996). Intelligence agents have occasionally directly participated in illegal markets, in order to raise funds for off-the record covert operations (Kwitny 1987; Labrousse 1991). Prosecutors and agencies involved in the 'war on drugs' and acting against arms proliferation in the US have seen their efforts frustrated by the protection extended to their targets in the name of national security (Bullington and Block 1990; Kerry Report 1990). Many undercover investigations appear to be fruitless not because serious offenders were not identified, but because these were granted immunity, had their charges dropped or enjoyed diplomatic status. The practices and networks involved in the Iran-Contra affair (Coburn 1987; Scott and Marshall 1991) and the arms-to-Iraq scandal (Mantius 1995; Phythian 1996) clearly illustrate the crime facilitative effects of 'realist' foreign policies.

Secondly, efforts to blend intelligence and policing roles have disturbing consequences for innocent parties and civilians, who may be practically recruited to perform government tasks without their knowledge or consent. Their privacy is violated and their entire lives or careers may be completely ruined by overzealous police agents and intelligence 'patriots' who pursue covert foreign policies. Ken Walker, for example, the Canadian broker who is still trying to recover from the unethical tactics of law enforcers, has alleged that Customs agents asked him to spy on other Canadian businessmen and join 'Team USA' in exchange for having his manufactured charges dropped (Fialka 1994; Passas and Groskin 1995). In a personal interview, Walker has also suggested that one of the main reasons for the sting operation that framed him was to discredit some witnesses who were about to testify before the US Congress; specifically people who participated in business transactions underlying the so-called 'October surprise' affair – the alleged delay of the release of US hostages held in Teheran until the elections that brought Reagan to the White House (Parry 1993).

The use of civilians for both intelligence and policing roles is risky, and more often than not inappropriate and unethical. The cooperation of unwilling civilians is obtained by deceit, when individuals are completely unaware of their own functions, or by force – for example under the threat to press criminal charges against them. Those agreeing to collaborate in order to avoid criminal convictions have strong incentives to make up crimes against others, incriminate them or actively incite them into offending. Thus motivated civilians and *agent provocateurs* constitute a serious risk to the integrity of law enforcement operations and can undermine the cause of justice.

Other individuals may volunteer their services for money or ideological reasons – as in the private funding of the Contras in Nicaragua (Walsh 1993). This sort of privatisation of foreign policy, intelligence collection, or of law enforcement operations leads to diminished accountability. Whenever a secret operation goes wrong or is disclosed to the public prematurely, there is easier deniability on the part of government agents and agencies. Scapegoating is another unfair outcome of such alliances, as we have seen in the attempt to convict a Matrix Churchill executive who worked for British intelligence (Phythian 1996) and in the conviction of one bank manager at the Atlanta Branch of the Banco Nazionale del Lavoro (BNL) for the billions of dollars illegally lent to Iraq for military purposes (Friedman 1993; Mantius 1995). When political objectives are promoted by particular undercover operations, the media may also be exploited to broadcast prejudicial half-truths or distorted facts about the cases and people implicated. Selective leaks to the press, always eager to report exclusive stories, can have a major impact on public opinion and devastating consequences for defendants. Undoing the damage caused by inaccurate media reports is virtually impossible, even when the innocence of suspects is eventually acknowledged.

In addition, victims of force or fraud by undercover operations often find that civilian participants enjoy protective shields against remedial actions. Walker, for instance, has been trying for many years to sue the Bank of New York, whose high-level executives acted in concert with US Customs and repeatedly deceived him about the legitimacy of the client he was considering doing business with. The Bank of New York has so far successfully argued that it enjoys state immunity for this action (Francis 1994; Walker 1994). Interestingly, motivated by the Walker case, the Canadian government has taken action to clarify the law stating unequivocally that no private party could claim such immunity in similar cases.

Any undercover investigation must be subjected to ex ante scrutiny for its legality and probable cause. Predisposition must be carefully demonstrated, especially in sensitive and international cases. The critical questions of 'how targets should be picked', 'how much temptation should be offered', and 'how much pressure should be exerted on someone to do something against the law' must be answered in advance. Investigations need to be constantly monitored to ensure that no operation strays from its target and established parameters. We have too much serious crime in real life to keep adding further criminogenic influences and create criminals out of law-abiding citizens. The police are not in the business of examining corruptibility but corruption (Marx 1982; 1988). All these issues become far more critical when undercover operations incorporate intelligence and political components.

Police and intelligence agencies have different mandates, methods and roles. Whereas police operations must be based on knowledge of, or reasonable suspicions about, specific offending practices of particular individuals or organizations, intelligence operations seek new information about *what may be happening*. Secret services can and most often do engage in 'fishing expeditions'. Mixing the two has obvious civil rights implications.

Further, the role of law enforcement is to ensure that laws are not broken and law violators are apprehended. By contrast, intelligence agents are in a sense trained to violate laws, domestic as well as those of other countries. This is understood and routinely accepted by spy agencies which explain to their operatives that their work abroad is usually illegal. An important difference between spies and police operating abroad is that spies do not have to testify in court about what they have done. They are not subject to cross examination. When they present information, they do not have to prove that it was obtained in a legal and untainted manner. Relying on spies to do police work, therefore, will effectively undermine some of the most fundamental legal principles and constitutional guarantees against power abuses by state authorities against civilians.

In this context, it should be noted that international operations, even with solely law enforcement agents and aims, increase the risk of violating individuals' civil and legal rights. The US Supreme Court, for example, has ruled that foreigners do not enjoy the same constitutional protections Americans do with respect to arrests or even kidnapping of suspects, as well as illegal searches and seizures (Abramovsky 1990; Oppenheim 1991; Semmelman 1992; Yered 1994). In such cases, individuals can be deprived of rights they have both under their domestic legal system and under that of the USA, where they face trial and punishment.

In any event, law enforcement and secret service roles should not mix. Representatives from these agencies ought not to initiate or conduct undercover police operations. When they do, there is a higher risk of abuses of state power, injustices, civil rights violations, and unacceptable invasions of innocent parties' privacy. When the involvement of state agencies in such practices is revealed, future law enforcement collaboration with the states concerned is likely to suffer, as will the allegiance of third parties to international law and procedural rules. All this, therefore, can ultimately undermine the legitimacy of the international legal order. That the above problems and risks are not merely theoretical is amply demonstrated by the case study below.

Operation Quarry

The roots of Operation Quarry (known as operation Argus in Britain) can be traced back to the criminal importation of electric capacitors with hazardous PCBs from Colombia into the USA by a Californian company, CSI Technologies (CSI). The company agreed to collaborate with the US Customs Service in future cases in exchange for settling the charges. In September 1988, Kowalsky, the President and Chief Operating Officer of CSI, received from CSI's agent in the UK a request for information about the existence of any US 'embargo on supplying goods to Iraq' and how current laws might affect the sale of capacitors to Iraq. This request for information had been originally received from Michael Hand, a Euromac employee, on behalf of Al-Qaqaa. Al-Qaqaa was a state organization controlled by the Iraqi Ministry of Industry and listed in a booklet published by the British Department of Trade and Industry with the title 'Doing Business with Iraq'. Euromac was a company established in the outskirts of London in 1987 in order to take advantage of the trade initiatives promoted by the DTI following the end of the Iran-Iraq war. It was managed by Ali Daghir, an Iraqi with British citizenship.

The specifications for the 100-200 capacitors Al-Qaqaa was interested in made it clear that the capacitors had many civilian applications. Their export was not prohibited by UK laws. No mention of capacitors with the same or similar parameters was made in the 1989 Export Control Guidelines. Nevertheless, Kowalsky immediately contacted the CIA and Supnick, a Customs Service special agent, suggested to them that the capacitors Al-Qaqaa was inquiring about were intended for the making of a nuclear bomb. The decision was made to start an undercover investigation, Operation Quarry. An internal memorandum highlighted the fusion of law enforcement and intelligence goals. The operation's objectives included,

> 3) To enter into an agreement to provide the controlled technology to the subject UK-based firm through either a US-based contact (individual or firm) and then either damage or substitute the goods and trace their route from the US via England to Iraq ...
>
> 5) To develop additional intelligence and information concerning the Iraqi nuclear missile program for purposes of initiating other spin-off and collateral investigation (US Customs internal memorandum, 4 August 1989).

Supnick instructed Kowalsky to respond positively and offer a low price (Goodwin and Watts 1994). The fax, dated 29 September 1988, stated: 'We are researching Iraq embargo question but do not anticipate problem as US is relaxing its position with the winding down of the Iraq-Iran war.' Supnick began to act as CSI manager under the false name of Daniel Saunders.

In the following six months, several communications took place between Supnick and Euromac, but no order was placed. Euromac had intervened merely for good will purposes and stood to make no profit for the proposed transaction. So, when Hand left the company, Euromac had no interest in pursuing the deal. CSI's agent in England faxed a note to Kowalsky letting him know that 'Mike Hand has left the company and the project with Baghdad has been terminated' (fax dated 17 April 1989).

One might have thought this would bring about the end of the undercover investigation. Yet, Supnick and Kowalsky continued the operation and persistently sought to revive the project. In the period between September 1989 and March 1990, there were fifty faxes and calls from CSI to Euromac, all of which were tape-recorded by Supnick and most of which were unsolicited. The lack of interest on the part of Euromac is obvious also from the unresponsiveness of Daghir and his sales manager Jeanine Speckman, a French citizen who replaced Michael Hand. They returned only two of these communications. Their indifference about the whole project becomes even clearer by the tone of the voices when they answered some of these telephone calls. They repeatedly suggested that CSI contact directly the Iraqis. They also sent to Al-Qaqaa CSI's address, telex, fax and telephone numbers, and referred to Kowalsky as the contact person: 'CSI have been in touch with us several times and are keen on helping you. Do you still have a requirement for these capacitors. If you wish, you could get directly in touch [sic] with the manufacturer: CSI Technologies Inc., Capacitor Division...' (Speckman telex dated 21 April 1989). It is plain that the Euromac executives had had enough of these capacitors and attempted to put the parties in direct contact, so that they could get on with their business independently, if they so wished.

Paradoxically, the UK and US authorities' interest in the case was growing. The UK Customs and Excise joined forces with the US Customs Service and briefed the then Prime Minister Margaret Thatcher on the ongoing operation. The Americans were told that she was 'very much interested in its progress and successful outcome' (US Customs internal memorandum, 4 August 1989). British military intelligence was also involved. It is quite remarkable, however, for Thatcher to show this interest in a case where no illegality had been committed or planned, the targets of the investigation had proceeded with care and due diligence to ensure that no country's laws would be violated, and the items under discussion were on CSI's and their UK agent's published catalogue. Dr. Hassard has pointed out that Al-Qaqaa had interests in aerospace technologies and nuclear weapons, and it had a worldwide network of procurement companies. It had been known that Al-Qaqaa was trying to obtain technologies for, inter alia, a flashlamp camera system, which can be used for ballistics research. Flashlamps and discharge laser systems can also be used in range-finding, pollution monitoring, atmospheric studies etc. (Dr. Hassard personal communication). No one in the intelligence community should have expected anything new or significant to come out of the comparatively trivial order at the centre of the Operation Quarry.

It was later alleged that Euromac was a front for the Iraqi procurement effort. Yet, neither Daghir nor Euromac had any previous deals with the Al-Qaqaa establishment (Euromac had been asked in the late 1980s to export photographic cameras with fast discharge capacitors, but refused to do so after the DTI had denied an export license). The initial contact had been made by the Department of Trade and Industry, whose representative called Daghir to ask if he would like to meet an Iraqi delegation (Goodwin and Watts 1994).

The undercover operation continued with CSI constantly contacting Euromac's managers, refusing to deal directly with Al-Qaqaa and turning down the invitation to visit their headquarters in Baghdad. At this point, one wonders why they did not make that visit, if the chief objective was to gather as much intelligence as possible on Iraqi procurement networks and nuclear plans. The official version is that Supnick did not have the necessary travel authorization. In view of the stated objectives of the undercover operation, however, only gross incompetence and lack of elementary planning could account for the absence of such authorization. Alternatively, the priorities and aims of this operation lay elsewhere.

CSI's persistence led to a meeting at the Cavendish hotel in London between Kowalsky, Supnick (always as Saunders), Daghir, Speckman and two Iraqi engineers from Al-Qaqaa. The secretly recorded discussions at this hotel confirm that Daghir and Speckman understood virtually nothing about the technical terms, specifications and details of the capacitors in question. The Americans unsuccessfully tried to interest the Iraqis in items that might indeed be used for nuclear devices at this meeting. One of the engineers suggested that all they needed was capacitors listed in the Walmore (CSI agent's) catalogue. Supnick's response was 'let's forget about the catalogue'.

In the end, Supnick got the Iraqis to agree to the inclusion of military specifications to the order. Daghir, in any event, was merely facilitating the meeting, ordering drinks and contributing virtually nothing to the conversation. The official transcripts of the Arabic conversations contained a number of mistakes. For example, the Iraqis are claimed to have said 'We take our orders from the very top', when they actually said 'we want to go to the original specifications' (i.e. those without military applications!). Later they mention a contact in Baghdad 'But I cannot mention his name, by God', implying a reference to Saddam Hussein, but which should have been translated as 'I cannot remember his name, by God'. Some of these erroneous translations were picked up and quoted by the media after the close-down of the operation.

Finally, the Iraqis placed an order for forty capacitors, the total value of which was US$ 10,500. Euromac still tried to have them shipped directly to Baghdad, but ended up serving as transit agent at the insistence of the Americans. The Iraqi engineers had stated that the end use of the capacitors was for laser photography. The prosecution argued that these were nuclear triggers. Setting carefully the stage, Supnick suggested that the capacitors should be described as for use in air-conditioning system in order to avoid any difficulty with the US authorities. Yet, it was later alleged that this suggestion had been made by Daghir. Although Daghir and Speckman apparently believed the Al-Qaqaa version of the end use, they eventually agreed to do this, thereby complicating the matter for their defence.

On the 19th March 1990, the capacitors were sent to Heathrow in a box that stayed in TWA's cargo hanger for a few days before delivery to Euromac's premises. In the meantime, they were replaced with inoperable capacitors by Customs and Excise. The shipment was received by Omar Latif, the Iraqi Airways station manager and a reputed member of the Iraqi intelligence. As the box was about to be loaded on an airplane bound for Iraq on the 28th of March 1990, Daghir and Speckman were arrested and charged with the attempt to illegally export prohibited items to Iraq. Latif was immediately deported.

There was originally no intention to put Daghir to trial (Gillie 1991). The Immigration and Nationality Department notified Daghir of his deportation order in a letter stating that his 'departure from the United Kingdom would be conducive to the public good for reasons of national security of relations [sic] between the United Kingdom and other countries and for other reasons of political nature ...' (IND letter dated March 1990, p. 1). In fact, 'documents prepared by the immigration authorities were dated 10 days previously, showing that this plan had been well considered' (Gillie 1991, p. 3). In their rush to get rid of Daghir, the authorities neglected the fact that he was a British citizen who had no intention of leaving the country in which he was entitled to stay.

The arrests triggered a media frenzy that was extremely prejudicial to the defendants because it effectively disseminated false and misleading information about the whole affair and its significance. Mistranslations of the conversations at the Cavendish Hotel and uncritical presentations of the prosecution's case appeared everywhere (e.g., *Time Magazine*, 9 April 1990, p. 44). US Customs had invited a NBC News crew to film the loading of dummy capacitors in California before their export to the UK, the surveillance team's work in England and the arrests. As the case became one of the most visible world wide, the international coverage was absolutely sensational with references to the 'nuclear thieves of Baghdad' and celebrations about a 'nuke bomb gang held'. NBC quoted authorities as stating that 'the man at the top of the Iraqi operations is Ali Daghir, who was sent to London from Baghdad almost two years ago' (Associated Press, 29 March 1990).

Margaret Thatcher sent the following letter to the Customs and Excise Commissioner: 'Dear Mr. Unwin, May I ask you to pass on my warm congratulations to all those engaged in the operation to prevent the illegal export to Iraq of components for a nuclear weapon. It must have required the highest professional standards, as well as great patience and skill, and the whole nation has reason to be grateful to those concerned' (letter dated 2 April 1990). Against the shocking revelations following the Matrix Churchill fiasco and the BNL scandal, she was still prepared to state before the Scott Inquiry that it was these 'nuclear capacitors that had alerted me to ask for more information' about Iraq's procurement efforts (Inquiry into Exports of Defence Equipment and Dual Use Goods to Iraq, Day 48 – Evidence of Lady Thatcher, 8th December 1993, pp. 203-204; see also pp. 60-61).

In the meantime, public comments by British and American officials fuelled the media discussion about krytrons by insisting that the capacitors could only be used in a nuclear bomb. Some may have been genuinely surprised when expert witnesses testified at the trial that the capacitors had several more likely uses, including the laser photography use claimed by the Iraqis. According to Dr. Hassard,

> '[T]he capacitors were of a type consistent with the triggering of the chemical explosives – like most capacitors, but the Crown contended that these capacitors could only be used for triggering a fission bomb. ... I happen to think that the capacitors were either part of an elaborate and entirely contrived sting, to get a result during a time of great proliferation by German and UK sources, or that they were for the separation stage of a two stage Scud. On balance, I think it was the former, but I can be absolutely certain that there is no way that Ali Daghir exported these capacitors as nuclear components knowingly' (personal communication).

After reviewing the IAEA/UN Inspection Team's findings on the Iraqi nuclear bomb and the capacitors which were to be used to detonate it, Dr. Hassard concluded:

> 'In every parameter, the Daghir capacitors are different. ... it is my opinion that the Daghir capacitors were not intended for the Iraqi nuclear bomb detonator. They could have been used in many other applications outside this programme. I am aware this document may be used in legal proceedings' (letter to Daghir's lawyer dated 19 February 1992).

Anthony Tillford, the director of a British company dealing with high speed flash systems, has provided additional evidence as to the use of the Daghir capacitors. He purchased two identical capacitors from CSI through a business colleague in the US, declared them at Heathrow as samples for research by his company, and showed the cashier a document he was given that there was no duty payable for them. 'There were no further questions' he noted and added,

> 'I can recount that my colleague in the U.S., Dr. John Cooke spoke with Tylene Williford, Sales Administrator for CSI Capacitors when we placed our order. Tylene Williford was also involved with the original Euromac order. I requested the capacitors to be identical to those supplied to Euromac and specified them by the same CSI part number, Dr. Cooke

was told that the original capacitors manufactured for the Euromac order had been, after the trial, been put back into stock at CSI and were sold to any customers who required similar items" (Tillford letter dated 6th February 1995, p. 1).

Strong exculpatory evidence was presented at the Daghir/Speckman trial, in spite of Public Interest Immunity Certificates (PIIs) issued by the British government depriving the defence from access to documents of vital importance. The climate at the completion of the Persian Gulf war, the media and other public reports on the defendants and the transparent dislike the trial Judge Dennison took to Daghir did not help the defendants' cause. When a prosecution witness gave evidence with a screen covering his face – for reasons of national security, according to a letter from Tom King – the judge pointedly looked at Daghir and said that it was to prevent terrorists from killing the witness. Mr. X, a prosecution expert witness testified that the capacitors could only have been used for the nuclear bomb programme. His identity being secret, the defence was unable to cross-examine him. In any event, his expertise (if not good faith) is now seriously undermined by the IAEA/UN findings. Finally, in summing up the judge asked the jury to decide the case on the basis that the capacitors were intended for any military use, not necessarily for a nuclear bomb. Given that there is hardly any capacitor without some kind of military use, there was not much room left for declaring the defendants not guilty. Daghir was sentenced to five years imprisonment and Speckman to 18 months.

The press kept on promoting the government's story and exaggerating its importance. An article in the *Financial Times* stated that the 'verdict appears to have vindicated US and UK Customs officers in their conviction that their joint operation prevented Iraq from pursuing a programme which, had it been allowed to be completed, may have altered the balance of power in the Middle East' (Burns and Donkin 1991, p. 9). The protagonists of the sting operation continued to receive kudos for their deeds. US Representative Henry Gonzalez introduced Kowalsky at a Congressional hearing on the laundering of funds from trade with Iraq as 'indeed ... an American hero. He received several awards for thwarting Iraqi efforts to obtain nuclear warhead detonators, alerting and worked with the US and UK Customs Services and the FBI on an undercover sting operation to stop this traffic' (Federal News Service, 9 April 1991).

Strong exonerating evidence emerged from the investigative work of the UN/IAEA in the aftermath of the war against Iraq. The names of Daghir and Euromac did not appear on any list of procurement agents or companies found in the course of post-war investigations. This was confirmed also by the DTI to Daghir's solicitors (DTI letter dated 5 March 1992). In addition, the capacitors due to be exported via Euromac were not needed for Iraq's nuclear programme. In fact, Iraq could have made them in any case within six months (Dr. Hassard interview). Yet, Daghir and Speckman are the only persons to be gaoled for any illegal-arms-to-Iraq activity in the United Kingdom. In contrast, those who did export billions of dollars worth of sensitive technology and material to Iraq have enjoyed immunity, had their charges dropped or made profits by writing books about the affair.

After many months behind bars, Daghir and Speckman prepared their appeal. The prosecution suggested that procedural matters be dealt with before substantive grounds. The jury misdirection problem was more than sufficient to quash the convictions and the fresh evidence was not considered. Successful as the appeal was, it failed to restore justice. Prosecutors, politicians and media could still argue that the case was overturned 'on a technicality', implying that the two were in fact guilty. Supnick did not cease to extol his courage and self-importance after the appeal and was quoted in a *Common Cause Magazine* feature article as saying about Daghir and the Euromac case:

> (There are) all these things you have to think of when you are an agent, when you go into these things', Supnick says. 'Is one of these guys going to pull a gun? Are they going to invite us to the Iraqi embassy and the recording device on my back will be exposed with the magnetometer? Are these guys going to lead us away from here and am I going to wind up in the Thames the next day?' (Lutterbeck 1994).

It is appalling that anyone at this stage could persist in referring to Operation Quarry as 'an all-too-rare story of an undercover arms export investigation that worked' (ibid.). Moreover, the US indictment remains in place. Telephone calls to the prosecutor's office in California with questions about the status of the case in 1997 for this paper were not returned. Daghir still fears that upon his departure from the UK, he may be arrested and sent to California for another trial. The inability to travel practically kills any chances of rebuilding his business. It is interesting to note, however, that a Customs and Excise official did not believe in 1996 that Daghir had anything to be afraid of. In that official's words, 'what does he worry about? *Entrapment is not allowed in the States!*' (personal interview; emphasis added).

Daghir's life and career have been irreparably harmed by the sting operation. He has lost millions in the last five years, his health is damaged, his marriage is all but destroyed, his son dropped out of school in embarrassment and tried repeatedly to commit suicide. In 1996, he decided to sue Customs and Excise for malicious prosecution, but the case is still pending.

Conclusion

There are many questions that remain unanswered, particularly with respect to the real purpose of this operation, the entrapment and aggressive prosecution of people who appeared to play no role in the arming of Iraq. Even if the charges were true as to the military applications of the CSI capacitors, the whole case pales by comparison to the gigantic volume of military and dual-use items exported by Western companies. The revelation that the British, American and other governments were aware of this trade and actively encouraged it raises further doubts as to the good faith of Operation Quarry.

Why bother with Euromac? Why involve the Prime Minister? Why generate a media circus with distorted facts, half-truths and mistranslations? Why ruin the lives of people who showed no predisposition to break the law and clearly told the undercover agent that they did 'not want any trouble' (tape-recorded telephone conversation)? One can only speculate. At the very best, this was a case of scapegoating rendered easier by the targetting of foreigners. Hypocrisy, duplicity and abuse of state power is the worst case scenario. Predictably, a Baghdad newspaper seized the opportunity to argue that 'the West's democracy, respect for human rights and credibility have come into question' and that the 'fabrication of the capacitors story' was meant to 'mislead public opinion in the West, especially in the United States, and fabricate justifications to convince legislative and other bodies of the need to launch a war against Iraq' (BBC Summary of World Broadcasts; 27 May 1994; The Middle East; Iraq; Me/2007/Med).

Another hypothesis is that Western governments wanted to warn Iraq about their knowledge of efforts to manufacture a nuclear bomb. They could not reveal how they knew about it because that would prevent the collection of intelligence from the same source. As Alan Clark has stated to the Scott Inquiry: 'There is an absurd paradox, that the intelligence was telling you what the machines were going to be used for, but the machines had to be provided in order to protect the source that was telling you the purpose for which they were going to be used' (quoted in Phythian 1996). By pressing ahead with and publicising a trivial or fabricated case, the message could be conveyed to Iraq without jeopardizing intelligence operators. At the same time, the public opinion climate was effectively prepared for the war against

Iraq. Whether intended that way or not, these were real consequences of Operation Quarry.

At any rate, cases like this highlight in sad detail the devastating human consequences of police-intelligence operations or undercover law enforcement investigations that combine political and intelligence objectives. We are clearly better off if intelligence services and law enforcement agencies keep their activities and mandates separate and independent of each other. Collaboration should take place only under strict conditions and should be formally monitored. In addition, we must concentrate our efforts on the prevention of unwarranted invasion of people's privacy and other official deviance.

There is an obvious need for controls in advance, during and after the closing down of undercover operations. Scandal, the disclosure of public misconduct, acquittals, embarrassment and diplomatic tensions operate as ex post facto controls for future cases. Hopefully officials learn their lessons and do not repeat the same mistakes. In order to strengthen the deterrent effect of such forces, it is imperative to allow and facilitate private law suits against all participants in unethical or illicit operations. Private parties must not get involved in official operations for profit, under duress or through deceit. If they do, they should not be able to shield themselves behind any type of state immunity for their involvement. State immunity ought not to impede the quest for some redress by victims, such as Ken Walker, Ali Daghir and Jeanine Speckman.

Agencies should introduce guidelines for both internal and external accountability purposes. The FBI, for instance, has certain controls in place, such as high level review of cases deemed to be sensitive. If agencies are unwilling to establish guidelines, these should be legislated. Matters to be covered include the better protection of foreign nationals, who are particularly vulnerable to scapegoating and unfairness. Another issue is the degree of temptation that may be offered to a target of investigation. Offers must not exceed real world situations. Another question is how many times can targets be approached before calling off an investigation. The use of informants and previous offenders must also be regulated and closely monitored.

When guidelines are not followed, those responsible must be sanctioned and seen to be sanctioned. External controls, such as judicial supervision, are nevertheless essential. Both domestic and international bodies, such as the tribunal proposed by Blum and Passas (this volume), need to play a leading role in establishing probable cause, appropriate methods, respect of international laws, and jurisdiction. In addition, the media must play a more critical and responsible role in reporting and assessing government operations. It is one thing to cite press releases of a given agency and quite another to report everything in such a release as a fact. Police integrity and noble motives should not be taken for granted. The internal logic and consistency of their stories must be scrutinised carefully.

Finally, we need to conduct evaluation studies on the need for, effectiveness and success of undercover operations. Have they disrupted or eliminated criminal organizations? Have such groups recovered or been replaced by others? Has there been any displacement of criminal activities? How can we evaluate the net consequences of the use of undercover operations? How can we work toward the establishment of criteria for evaluation of the effectiveness of undercover investigations? Do they provide deterrence or incentives for better organization of crime? How can we tell? How can we establish criteria for operations that are not mere fishing expeditions? Answering these questions will assist policy makers who rely on cost-benefit analyses to determine whether, and if so under what conditions, we should accept international undercover operations.

References

Abramovsky, A. (1990), Extraterritorial Jurisdiction: The United States Unwarranted Attempt to Alter International Law in *United States v. Yunis, Yale Journal of International Law*, 15, pp. 121-161.

Bullington, B. and A. Block (1990), A Trojan Horse: Anti-Communism and the War on Drugs, *Contemporary Crises*, 14 (1), pp. 39-55.

Burns, J. and R. Donkin (1991), Customs Draw the Sting from Iraq's Nuclear Tale, *Financial Times*, 13 June, p. 9.

Coburn, L. (1987), *Out of Control,* New York: The Atlanta Monthly Press.

Fialka, J.J. (1994), Customs Service's 'Stings' to Curtail Arms Sales Draw Blood (Its Own) as Cases Collapse in Court, *Wall Street Journal*, 18 March, A12.

Francis, D. (1994), Liberals Should Come to Ken Walker's Aid, *The Financial Post,* 10 March.

Friedman, A. (1993), *Spider's Web: The Secret History of How the White House Illegally Armed Iraq,* New York: Bantam Books.

Gillie, O. (1991), Two Convicted of 'Iraqi Bomb Triggers' Plot; The Thwarting of a 'Nuclear Parts For Baghdad' Scheme was not the Sting it Seemed, *The Independent*, 13 June, p. 3.

Goodwin, B. and M. Watts (1994), Atom-powered Sting Paralysed Justice, *Sunday Telegraph*, 29 May, p. 14.

Greaney, G.M. (1992), Crossing the Constitutional Line: Due Process and the Law Enforcement Justification, *Notre Dame Law Review*, 67, pp. 745-797.

Kerry Report (1990), *Drug Money Laundering, Banks and Foreign Policy,* Washington, DC: GPO.

Kwitny, J. (1987), *The Crimes of Patriots: The True Tale of Dope, Dirty Money, and the CIA,* New York: W.W. Norton & Co.

Labrousse, A. (1991), *La Drogue, L'Argent et les Armes,* Paris: Fayard.

Mantius, P. (1995), *Shell Game,* New York: St. Martin's Press.

Marx, G.T. (1982), Who Really Gets Stung? Some Issues Raised by the New Police Undercover Work, *Crime and Delinquency,* (April), pp. 165-193.

Marx, G.T. (1988), *Undercover: Police Surveillance in America,* Berkeley: University of California Press.

Naylor, R.T. (1995), From Cold War to Crime War: The Search for a New 'National Security' Threat, *Transnational Organized Crime,* 1 (4), pp. 37-56.

Observatoire Géopolitique des Drogues (1996), *The Geopolitics of Drugs: 1996 Edition,* Boston: Northeastern University Press.

Oppenheim, M.A. (1991), *United States v. Verdugo-Urquidez*: Hands Across the Border – The Long Reach of United States Agents Abroad, and the Short Reach of the Fourth Amendment, *Brooklyn Journal of International Law,* 17 (3), pp. 617-638.

Parry, R. (1993), *Trick or Treason: The October Surprise Mystery,* New York: Sheridan Square Press.

Passas, N. (in press), Globalisation and Economic Crime, in: Ulrich Beck (ed.), *Globalization: Controversies, Political Answers, Everyday Experience.* To be published in English (Sage) and German (Suhrkamp).

Passas, N. and R.B. Groskin (1995), International Undercover Operations, in: C. Fijnaut and G.T. Marx (eds.), *Undercover: Police Surveillance in Comparative Perspective,* The Hague: Kluwer Law International, pp. 291-312.

Phytian, M. (1996), *Arming Iraq: How the U.S. and Britain Secretly Built Saddam's War Machine,* Boston: Northeastern University Press.

Scott, P.D. and J. Marshall (1991), *Cocaine Politics: Drugs, Armies, and the CIA in Central America,* Berkeley and Los Angeles: University of California Press.

Semmelman, J. (1992), Due Process, International Law, and Jurisdiction over Criminal Defendants Abducted Extraterritorially: The *Ker-Frisbie* Doctrine Reexamined, *Columbia Journal of Transnational Law,* 30, pp. 513-576.

Stavsky, M.M. (1985), The 'Sting' Reconsidered: Organized Crime, Corruption and Entrapment, *Rutgers Law Journal,* 16, pp. 937-989.

Walker, J. (1994), Immunity for Extraterritorial Enforcement Measures in Canada – The *Walker* Case, *Canadian International Lawyer,* 1 (1), pp. 17-23, 67, 73.

Walsh, L.E. (1993), *Final Report of the Independent Counsel for Iran/Contra Matters,* Washington, DC: US Court of Appeals for the District of Columbia Circuit.

Williams, P. (1994), Transnational Criminal Organisations and International Security, *Survival,* 36 (1), pp. 96-113.

Yered, J.J. (1994), Defendant Forcibly Abducted at Request of United States Government Agents Subject to Jurisdiction of United States Courts Despite Extradition Treaty: *United States v. Alvarez-Machain*, 112 S. Ct. 2188 (1992), *Suffolk Transnational Law Review*, 17, pp. 218-229.

Part II
The new information gathering: some new sources

9 Sun Tzu goes electronic. The changing nature of proactive methods in (criminal) intelligence

BOB HOOGENBOOM

Introduction

'Subtler and more far-reaching means of invading privacy have become available to the government. Discovery and invention have made it possible for the government, by means far more effective than stretching upon the rack, to obtain disclosure in court of what is whispered in the closet' (US Supreme Court Justice Louis Brandeis, 1928).[1]

The concept of proactive investigation refers to a variety of (criminal) intelligence gathering techniques which, stripped to their bare essence, are euphemisms for spying. Sun Tzu, 2500 years ago, laid down the principles of the profession: 'Thus, what enables the wise commander to strike and conquer, and achieve things beyond the reach of ordinary men, is fore-knowledge. Now this foreknowledge cannot be elicited from spirits; it cannot be obtained inductively from experience, nor by any deductive calculation. Knowledge of the enemy's dispositions can only be obtained from other men' (Sun Tzu 1988, p. 168). Hence the need for spies.

In ancient China watchtowers were erected from which surveillance took place and spies were recruited to obtain intelligence. Watchtowers, surveillance, intelligence and spying have taken on an entirely different meaning in the information society with an:

- Increasing capacity of systems and technologies, both in quantitative and in qualitative terms;
- Increasing connectivity of systems and technologies, making organizational boundaries more diffuse and making limitations of time and space obsolete;
- Integration of systems, media, and technologies, and increasing matching of data in computer systems;
- Increasing successes in the development of virtual reality and

- Increasing significance of tracking devices which enable the combination of all sorts of 'electronic traces' (Frissen 1996).

With the advent of the information society the nature of intelligence gathering is changing. This chapter traces some of these changes. The human spy, although his importance should never be underestimated, is making way for the electronic variant. Human intelligence (humint) has always been a very important factor in proactive investigations, especially in the field of domestic subversive activities and crime control. The informer is generally considered the most powerful (and intrusive) means of penetration. Sun Tzu is all about humint, as is the subject of this chapter. The dominant perspective is on informants, undercover operations, surveillance and observation. All these proactive methods essentially have some form of face-to-face interaction in common.

In the information society intelligence is less a matter of penetrating secrets through humint: increasingly, sophisticated technologies (technical intelligence) and more recently the use of data bases and electronic networks (open source intelligence) have gained in importance.

Technical intelligence (techint) and open source intelligence (oscint) go far beyond anything Sun Tzu could have imagined. New technologies, mostly developed by the defence industry, are spreading into law enforcement, civilian agencies and private companies. Forms of technological intelligence tend to be subtle, invisible, scattered and involuntary. They are often not defined as surveillance, and many people are unconscious of them. 'People are often unaware of the extent to which surveillance has become embedded in everyday relationships' (Marx 1988, p. 3).

The aim of this chapter is to broaden the discussion on intelligence-gathering by introducing electronic and open source intelligence both in the public and the private domain. The chapter has predominantly an introductory character.

In the second section examples of electronic intelligence will be given with special reference to their use in law enforcement. In the third section we enter cyberspace and discuss the increasing use of data bases and on-line information systems (Internet) in law enforcement and the business community. An introduction will be given to concepts like cyberspace, business intelligence, artificial intelligence and cybercops.

Although the legal possibilities of intelligence-gathering have increased dramatically there still is a need for clandestine operations. In the fourth section attention will be given to cyberspies involved in economic and industrial espionage, hackers and electronic infiltration and more generally the discussion on infowars or cyberwars.

In the fifth section some conclusions will be drawn with regard to the social impact of these new intelligence-gathering techniques (intrusion of privacy); the political consequences (democratic control) and the academic challenges these new developments pose for a scientific community (criminal law, criminology) predominantly occupied with the most visible form of intelligence-gathering: humint.

Most of the material for this chapter has been collected through a series of Internet surfing expeditions. In this way it has become an example of desktop research which is basically the subject of the chapter.

Technological intelligence

Surveillance is the systematic investigation or monitoring of the actions or communications of one or more persons. It has traditionally been undertaken by physical means such as prison-guards on towers. It has been enhanced through image-amplification devices such as binoculars and high-resolution satellite cameras. Electronic devices have been developed to augment physical surveillance and offer new possibilities such as telephone 'bugging'. In this section examples wil be given of new developments.[2]

Identification numbers

In 1961, the Internal Revenue Service (IRS) began using Social Security Numbers (SSN) as a tax identification number and slowly other agencies followed. Since banks and other non-governmental entities can legally turn away customers who refuse to supply a SSN, its use in the private sector is virtually taken for granted in everything from medical insurance to telephone to credit applications (Banisar 1996).

Identification cards

In addition to name, address, and identification numbers, the identification cards can include photographs, fingerprints and magnetic strips or microchips which automatically enter the data into leading devices. Cards originally designed for a single-use are being expanded to link multiple data bases. In Thailand, a company (Control Data Systems) set up a universal ID card to track all citizens.[3]

Smart cards have an embedded microchip that can hold several pages of information. Columbia/HCA Healthcare Corporation recently announced that it was providing 50,000 Florida residents with cards that could hold medical records, including X-rays. Multifunction cards are the next step. Utah is one of several states considering a single smart card for such diverse services as motor vehicle registration and libraries. Other federal government proposals for reforming government call for a single card for welfare benefits, food stamps, and other federal government functions. Florida and Maryland have already experimented with the concept. Active badges, already in use in numerous high-tech companies, transmit their location and, of course, that of the wearer.

Biometrics

Biometric identification refers to a system of identification through unique physical characteristics (Clarke 1994). The evolution of information technology is likely to result in intimate interdependence between humans and technology.[4] Some applications of biometric identification technology are now cost-effective, reliable, and highly accurate. As a result, biometric systems are being developed in many countries for such purposes as social security entitlement, payments, immigration control and election management.

The use of biometric verification through unique physical characteristics began in the late 19th century with fingerprinting. Recently, automated systems which electronically scan and digitalize fingerprints have taken the technology beyond its traditional role in criminal investigations.[5] The FBI has spent several hundred million dollars over the last few years creating an Automated Fingerprint Identification System (AFIS). Because of the improvements in access, fingerprints are now used for more applications at the state level as well. California and New York require all welfare beneficiaries to be fingerprinted. Even after a New York survey revealed that little fraud was actually detected by the massive fingerprinting effort, the state expanded its programme to include all members of the recipient's family. And, as in so many other cases, the technology is moving from the margins of society into the mainstream. California is now requiring thumbprints on drivers' licenses; several banks in the Southwest are fingerprinting non-customers who wish to cash checks; and a proposed California referendum would require all newborns to be fingerprinted and issued an official ID card.

DNA

The complex molecular structure that holds a genetic code unique to each individual is present in even the smallest sample of hair, tissue, or bodily fluids. The FBI has developed technology and infrastructure to create a computer network to link the state data bases to create a de facto central registry.

Hand geometry

A system based on hand geometry measures the length and distances between fingers. In a pilot program travelers when passing through Customs present the card and place their hand in a reader that verifies their identity and links into numerous data bases. The member countries have signed an international agreement facilitating information sharing and agreeing to require eventually all international travelers to use the cards. Hand geometry was used at the last Olympics in Atlanta.

Facial recognition

Facial recognition is based on measuring facial curves from several angles, digitizing the information, and doing a computer comparison with existing images in a data base or on an ID card. NeuroMetric, a Florida manufacturer, claims that its system can scan 20 faces a second, and by 1997 will be able to scan and compare images against a data base of 50 million faces in seconds. The Immigration and Naturalization Service has a pilot program using video cameras and computer data bases to identify known illegal and criminal aliens, terrorists, drug traffickers and other persons of special interest to the US government at airports, checkpoints and other ports-of-entry.

A.C. Neilson, a large market research company, recently patented a system using facial recognition for covertly identifying shoppers to track their buying habits around a particular region.

Facial thermography measures the characteristic heat patterns emitted by each face. Mikos Corporation claims that its Facial Access Control by Elemental Shapes (FACES) system can identify individuals regardless of temperature, facial hair, and even surgery, by measuring 65,000 temperature points with an accuracy level surpassing fingerprints. It estimates that by 1999, with a price tag of only $1000, the devices could be used in automated teller machines, point-of-sale terminals, welfare agencies, and computer networks. One serious drawback, they admit, is that alcohol consumption radically changes the thermograms (Banisar 1996).

Advanced microphones

The FBI's Rapid Prototyping Facility at the Virginia Quantico Research Laboratory is producing microminiature electronics systems involving unique surveillance equipment customized for each separate investigation. The FBI has developed a solid-state briefcase-size electronically steerable microphone prototype, that can discreetly monitor conversations across open areas. On the state and local level, jurisdictions such as Washington, DC, and Redwood City, California, are considering microphone systems first developed to detect submarines. Placed around the city, they would hear gunshots and call in the location to police headquarters.

Closed Circuit Television Cameras (CCTC)

Technical developments have increased the capabilities and lowered the cost of video cameras, making them a regular feature in stores and public areas. In the UK, dozens of cities have centrally controlled, comprehensive citywide CCTC systems that can track individuals wherever they go, even if they enter buildings. Effective even in extreme low light, the cameras can read a cigarette pack 100 yards away. Baltimore recently announced plans to put 200 cameras in the city centre. The FBI has miniaturized CCTC units it can put in a lamp, clock radio, briefcase, duffel bag, purse, picture frame, utility pole, coin telephone, book and other objects and then control remotely to pan/tilt, zoom and focus.

Forward Looking Infra Red (FLIR)

Originally developed for use in fighter planes and helicopters to locate enemy aircraft, FLIR can detect a temperature differential as small as 0.18 degrees centigrade. Texas Instruments and others are marketing hand-held and automobile- and helicopter-mounted models that can essentially look through walls to determine activities inside buildings. Law enforcement agents are pointing them at neighbourhoods to detect higher temperatures in houses where artificial lights are used to grow marijuana. They are also using FLIR to track people and cars on the Mexican border and search for missing people and fugitives.

Massive millimetre wave detectors

Developed by Militech Corporation, these detectors use a form of radar to scan beneath clothing. By monitoring the millimetre wave portion of the electromagnetic spectrum emitted by the human body, the system can detect items such as guns and drugs from a range of 12 feet or more. It can also look through building walls and detect activity. Militech received a $2 million grant from ARPA's Technology Reinvestment Project to fund development of working systems for local police.

Van Eck Monitoring

Every computer emits low levels of electromagnetic radiation from the monitor, processor, and attached devices. Although experts disagree whether the actual range is only a few yards or up to a mile, these signals can be remotely recreated on another computer. Aided by a transmitting device to enhance the signals, the FBI reportedly used Van Eck Monitoring to extract information from spy Aldrich Ames' computer and relay it for analysis.

Intelligent Transportation Systems (ITS)

ITS refers to a number of traffic management technologies, including crash-avoidance systems, automated toll collection, satellite-based position location, and traffic-based toll pricing. To facilitate these services, the system tracks the movements of all people using public or private transportation. As currently proposed by TRW, a leading developer of the technologies involved, the data collected on travel will be available for both law enforcement and private uses such as direct marketing. Automated toll collection is already in operation in several states, including New York, Florida, and California. Tracking systems for counterintelligence purposes are already in place in New York City, where the FBI has set up a permanent real time physical tracking system. On a commercial level, insurers are pushing car owners to install the 'Lojack', which is supposed to help retrieve stolen cars by sending out location signals once the system is remotely activated. Since cellular phones transmit location information to the home system to determine call routing, they can also be used for automated tracking of the caller's movements. In 1993, fugitive Colombian drug kingpin Pablo Escobar was pinpointed through his cellular phone. Currently there is an effort to develop a 999 system for cellular systems that would give location information for every cellular phone.[6]

Intelligent Vehicle-Highway Systems (IVHS)

The application of computing and communications to road management systems is set to become far more sophisticated. A great many of the projects involve identification of vehicles, and directly or indirectly of their occupants.

Cyberspace and data bases: open source intelligence

New technologies have enhanced the ability to see through walls, overhear conversations, and track movement. At the same time, dataveillance following people through the trail of their computerized records has become part of daily life. Detailed information on nearly every conceivable subject – usually in electronic form – is inexpensively accessible to anyone with a desktop computer. Information is routinely transmitted around the world on high speed networks for synthesis and analysis.[7]

It is the world called cyberspace. The word cyberspace was coined by the science fiction author William Gibson, when he sought a name to describe his vision of a global computer network, linking all people, machines and sources of information in the world, and through which one could move or 'navigate' as through a virtual space (Gibson 1984).

Every digital transaction leaves fingerprints somewhere in cyberspace. Huge data bases of personal information have begun to accumulate. Efficient software has been written to collect fragments of information from multiple locations in cyberspace and put them together to form remarkably complete pictures of how we are conducting our lives. Life in cyberspace generates electronic trails as inevitably as soft ground retains footprints.

Open source intelligence (Oscint)

Open source intelligence refers to information that is publicly available and potentially useful in the political arena, the business world, the intelligence community and more recently law enforcement. Increasingly, open source intelligence is recognized as a substitute for, and a complement to, more expensive, or unavailable, classified intelligence, or – in the private sector – industrial espionage. The political costs of (industrial) espionage, or penetrations of other governments to divine 'plans and intentions', are unacceptable when contrasted with the benefits of open source intelligence (Hoogenboom and Cools 1996).

Data bases and law enforcement

The US government maintains hundreds of data bases with information on individuals. One of the largest, the FBI's National Crime Information Center (NCIC), contains over 24 million records and connects over 500,000 users in 19,000 federal, state and local agencies. Over the past several years, NCIC has grown to include juvenile records, and in 1994 it incorporated records of suspected gang members and terrorists. Every year, over a million NCIC records are accessed for criminal investigations and civil background checks. Motorola Corporation is offering wireless access to the NCIC data base, bar code scanning of drivers' licenses, and cameras for instant transmission of pictures.

At the same time, the private sector has been increasing its capabilities. Using purchase records, surveys, credit reports, department of motor vehicle and medical records and numerous other files, direct marketing companies are gobbling up information about individuals to create comprehensive records for targeted selling. Donnelly Marketing claims to maintain records on 86 million households and 125 million individuals. Many of these data bases are also being used by the federal government. A number of online services now specialize in providing a menu of sensitive information – credit reports, motor vehicle records, criminal background checks, insurance files and telephone usage, among other things – to subscribers that pay about 200 dollars to sign up.

In addition, most state and city offices and departments, including motor vehicle bureaux, are computerizing their public records – mortgage and tax files, driver histories, and civil and criminal proceedings – and offering them through their own systems to third parties. With the hunger for confidential data increasing, especially among investigators, attorneys, journalists, researchers and marketers, more general-interest online services are gingerly stepping into this market. Nexis, for instance, carries a nationwide listing of real estate records that includes a list of property owners, how much they paid for the property, the account number and amount of the mortgage, and which bank issued it.

CompuServe has gone even further. Its data base, offered by Arlington, Va.- based CACI, provides information, sorted by postal code, on how many people have credit cards, what kinds of cards, how much they spend each month and what they buy. Another CompuServe data base has a file of the dead that lists each Social Security number, dates of birth and death, and where the life insurance payout was made. Online information service Employers Information Service (EIS) offers upward of a million files on workers throughout the United States who have applied for worker's compensation. Hundreds of subscribers to the EIS data base – especially companies in the accident-prone oil, gas and construction industries – use this information as a litmus test for hiring, say critics of the Gretna, La., information provider. If EIS has a record on a job applicant, he is out of the running, even though filing for worker's compensation is a right and not a crime, these opponents say.

Cybercops

'The day is coming very fast', says the director of the Federal Law Enforcement Center (FLETC), Charles Rinkevich, 'when every cop will be issued a badge, a gun and a laptop'. Adding a high-speed modem, cellular phone, cryptography textbooks and a bulletproof vest to that arsenal might also be prudent because 'crime involving high technology is going to go off the boards', predicts FBI Special Agent William Tafoya, the man who created the bureau's home page on the Internet, the worldwide computer network.

Of the various anti-hacker activities of 1990, Operation Sundevil had by far the highest public profile. The sweeping, nationwide computer seizures of 8 May 1990 were unprecedented in scope and highly, if rather selectively, publicized. Bruce Sterling in 'The Hacker Crackdown. Law and Disorder on the Electronic Frontier' described the activities of Cybercops working for the Secret Service and a number of private companies.

Business intelligence

Real-World Intelligence, Inc. delivers customized Business Intelligence Systems through its private online information service, 'Lookout Point'. This enables any company to identify and monitor those key trends in business, economics, geo-politics, science, and technology relevant to its unique strategic objectives. The company give their clients custom-built BI Systems operating from profiles and data sources specific to business or activities. Training and assistance in analysis transforms raw information into Intelligence in the form of strategic Alerts and Reports. To obtain 'Real-World Intelligence' an analyst must be able to access and capture the widest possible number of information sources and facilities, and then to discern the wheat from the chaff. The Internet is only a means to an end. A vast network of raw data has opened itself up which we can all get on and make the most of. But information is only as valuable as the context in which it can be evaluated.[8]

This is just one of the companies advertizing on the Net. Business or corporate or competitor intelligence has become a central feature of the business world.

Artificial Intelligence (AI)

The more comprehensive and interconnected systems use Artificial Intelligence (AI) to detect patterns and relationships. Once information is gathered and linked using the unique identifiers and networks, it can then be analysed using artificial intelligence and eventually disseminated. Data bases supplemented by artificial intelligence systems can scan through the vast quantities of information and detect patterns and relationships. Artificial intelligence is defined as a 'multi-disciplinary field encompassing computer science, neuroscience, philosophy, psychology, robotics, and linguistics; and devoted to the reproduction of the methods or results of human reasoning and brain activity'.[9] By 1984, Security Pacific, Citibank, Chase, Chemical, American Express and other major financial corporations had formed AI groups, or had at least started a project using some sort of AI technique or tool. Most of the initial financial applications involved decision making systems, including commercial and individual loans, credit card applicant screening and fraud pattern detection. There are different varieties of artificial intelligence systems. The Case Based Reasoning (CBR) system relies on the similarity of new situations or cases to other, previously solved occurrences. The system recognizes these similarities and suggests a similar course of action be taken. Once these similar cases are retrieved they are further filtered down to fewer cases by asking appropriate questions of the operator. The CBR system can then present the operator with a list of possible actions and solutions that worked in the past for similar cases. CBR systems allow problem resolution without expensive and labour intensive problem solving. Genetic Algorithms (GA) and Genetic Programming (GP) are relatively new technologies which are inspired by the Darwinian Theory of Evolution. A population of individuals, each representing a possible solution to a problem, are initially created at random. Then pairs of individuals combine to produce offspring for the next generation. The system is run for dozens or hundreds of generations. Because the probability of an individual reproducing is set to be proportional to the goodness of the solution it represents, the quality of the solutions in successive generations improves 'automatically'. The process is terminated when an acceptable or optimum solution is found, or after some fixed time limit.

Neural Networks (NN) are particularly applicable when a business expert is not available in order to supply business IF...THEN...ELSE rules, or when these rules cannot be expressed clearly or are simply not known. In such cases NNs can be used to 'learn' from historical data bases. The process is not unlike conventional statistical analysis. In effect it is the process of data base mining for patterns from existing historical data. These patterns can then be used to categorize or score new data at very high speed.

AI in law enforcement

There are several types of AI used in law enforcement, including link-analysis, which can explore relationships between different pieces of information; neural networks, which attempt to emulate the human brain to make inferences about information; and expert systems, which process data based on rules entered into the computer by experts. One of the largest users of intelligent systems is the Treasury Department, to help it detect money-laundering and drug trafficking. The Financial Crimes Enforcement Network (FinCEN), a data base of data bases, links hundreds of government data bases, including ones containing suspicious transaction reports, DEA files, and commercial information. After applying an expert-based system to analyse information and assign scores rating each transaction, FinCEN then uses link-analysis. The FBI is also using AI to track organized crime, drug enforcement, and counterterrorism through its Multi-Domain Expert System (MDES) which also links associates, phone calls, and relationships of suspects.

Clandestine actions: cyberspies

In Sun Tzu's world spies infiltrated enemy territory to obtain intelligence. In cyberspace electronic spies do the same.

Electronic blackmail

The 2 June 1996 *Sunday Times* from London front page headline reads: 'City Surrenders £400 million to Gangs, HERF Guns, electromagnetic pulses and sophisticated logic bombs may be responsible'. A trading house in London was blackmailed into paying to unknown extortionists who demonstrated they could crash the company's computers at will. According to officials in Washington, Whitehall, London, City of London Police, the National Security Agency, Kroll Associates, Bank of England and others the threats are credible. The attackers have the clear ability to bring trading and financial operations to a halt – exactly when they say they will. 'Banks, brokerage firms and investment houses in America have also secretly paid ransom to prevent costly computer meltdowns and a collapse in the confidence among their customers', sources said in the article. 'According to the American National Security Agency (NSA), they have penetrated computer systems using "logic bombs" (coded devices that can be remotely detonated), electromagnetic pulses and "high emission radio frequency guns" which blow a devastating electronic "wind" through the computer systems.'[10]

Cyberwar

The National Security Agency, along with intelligence units in the Army, Navy and Air Force, has been researching ways to infect enemy computer systems with particularly virulent strains of software viruses that already plague home and office computers. Another type of virus, the logic bomb, would remain dormant in an enemy system until a predetermined time, when it would come to life and begin eating data. Such bombs could attack, for example, computers that run a nation's air-defence system or central bank. The CIA supposedly has a clandestine program that would insert booby-trapped computer chips into weapons systems that a foreign arms manfacturer might ship to a potentially hostile country – a technique called *chipping*. In another program, the agency is looking at how independent contractors hired by armsmakers to write software for weapons systems could be bribed to slip in viruses. 'You get into the arms manufacturer's supply network, take the stuff off-line briefly, insert the bug, then let it go to the country', explained a CIA source who specializes in information technology. 'When the weapons system goes into a hostile situation, everything about it seems to work, but the warhead doesn't explode'.

Infowar weapons may be even more exotic than computer viruses. Los Alamos National Laboratory in New Mexico has developed a suitcase-size device that generates a high-powered electromagnetic pulse (emp). Commandos could sneak into a foreign capital, place the emp suitcase next to a bank and set it off. The resulting pulse would burn out all electronic components in the building. Other proposals combine biology with electronics. For instance, Pentagon officials believe microbes can be bred to eat the electronics and insulating material inside computers just as micro-organisms consume trash and oil slicks.

Infowar will aggressively foster new intelligence-gathering techniques. The Pentagon has satellites, spy planes and unmanned aircraft with cameras aboard to watch the enemy on the ground. In the future, thousands of tiny sensors may be sent airborne or covertly planted on land. M.I.T.'s Lincoln Laboratory is trying to build an unmanned aerial vehicle about the size of a cigarette pack that can take pictures. Miniature aerial sensors might even smell out the enemy. For example, aerosols would be sprayed over enemy troops, or chemicals would be clandestinely introduced into their food supply. Then biosensors flying overhead, says Thomas Baines at Argonne National Laboratory in Illinois, would 'track their movement from their breath or sweat', so they could be targeted for attack. Recently, the US government has made it possible for private citizens and the business community to hire capacity or launch spy satellites. The company Space Imaging claims its satellite will be able to photograph details up to one square meter.[11]

Internet: 'browsing patterns'

Information sent over the Net may pass through dozens of different computer systems on the way to its destination. Each of these systems may be managed by a different system operator ('sysop'), and each system may be capable of capturing and storing online communications. Furthermore, the online activities of Internet users can potentially be monitored, both by their own service provider and by the sysops of any sites on the Internet which they visit.

Many types of online activities do not involve sending e-mail messages between parties. Internet users may retrieve information or documents from sites on the World Wide Web (WWW), or from 'gopher' or 'ftp' sites. Or users may simply 'browse' these services without any other interaction. Many users expect that such activities are anonymous. They are not. It is possible to record many online activities, including which newsgroups or files a subscriber has accessed and which Web sites a subscriber has visited. This information can be collected both by a subscriber's own service provider and by the sysops of remote sites which a subscriber visits. Records of subscriber 'browsing patterns', also known as 'transaction-generated information', are a potentially valuable source of revenue for online services. This information is useful to direct marketers as a basis for developing highly targeted lists of online users with similar likes and behaviours.

Conclusions

Developments in the field of technical and open source intelligence are relevant from a sociological, political and academic point of view.

From a sociological perspective commentators like Roger Clark and Gary Marx pose questions like:
- What is the quality of the data and consequently the decisions being made on the basis of this information?;
- Do we have enough knowledge of the changes taking place?;
- To what extent will integration take place between techniques and systems?;
- What are the consequences for privacy protection?;
- Is there a danger of blacklisting; arbitrariness; a-contextual data merger; witch hunts; ex-ante discrimination and guilt prediction; selective advertising or the inversion of the onus of proof;
- Is there a chance of unknown accusations and accusers and a denial of due process?

What are the risks to society? Is there a possibility of a prevailing climate of suspicion and adversarial relationships between people who no longer trust each other? A weakening of society's moral fibre and cohesion?

From a political perspective commentators point to a destabilization of the balance of power and a repressive potential for a totalitarian government. On the other hand the privatization that is taking place raises question about the extent to which the state can control activities of the private security industry. The ancient idea – reflected in the Oxford definition of a community as a 'body of people living in one place, district, or country' is eroding; a community may now find its place in cyberspace.

Within cyberspace, social contacts will be made, economic transactions will be carried out, cultural life will unfold, surveillance will be enacted, and power, both by the state and the business community, will be exerted. Who will have access to it and under what circumstances? Will information of different kinds be kept separately, or will there be ways to assemble it electronically to create close and detailed pictures of our lives? Several public interest groups touch upon the sociological and political issues raised here. They have extensive information about privacy issues available via their online archives.

Finally, these developments and newly formulated questions raise questions for academics. The subject matter of criminology and criminal law is to a large extent limited to street crimes, organized crime and to a lesser extent organizational crime. With regard to the discussion on the (criminal) investigation process there is a limitation with regard to the study on intelligence-gathering: the informer in all sorts of varieties is the main focus. The gap between 'normal science', in the words of Thomas Kuhn *Structure of Scientific Revolutions* (1962), and the anomalies (empirical evidence of the rapidly changing nature of electronic data-gathering) discussed in this chapter is increasing more and more.

It forces us to redefine the concept of proactive investigations. There is an evident need to broaden the discussion on concepts like proactive methods, surveillance, intelligence, privacy and democratic control. New theoretical frameworks must be developed to understand what intelligence in the information society is all about. New technologies, mostly developed by the defence industry, are spreading into law enforcement, civilian agencies, and private companies. They tend to be subtle, invisible, scattered and involuntary. They are often not defined as surveillance, and many people, including academics, are unconscious of them.

Notes

1   Banisar 1996.
2   Some of the examples have been found on Roger Clarke's Web-site (roger.clarke@anu.edu.au). In 'Dataveillance and Information Technology', originally published in Communications of the ACM, May 1988 we find examples of the use of different techniques in surveillance.
3   The Thailand Central Population Database and ID card system, developed by US-based Control Data Systems, involves sophisticated intelligence that has been used by the Thai military for political control. (Similar ID card and smart card systems have been marketed to more than two dozen developing countries.) The government-issued ID card features electronic fingerprint and facial imaging, and is linked to an electronic data base covering the entire population. The data base spans most government agencies and is controlled by the powerful military/police-dominated Interior Ministry. After extensive discussions with Thai authorities, Control Data designed a system which accesses a staggering variety of data bases, including: Central Population Database, National Election System, Political Party Database, Political Member Database, Voter Listing, Electronic Minority Group Registration System, Electronic Fingerprint Identification System, Electronic Face Identification System, Population and House Report System, National Tax Collection System, Village Information System, Secret Information System, Public Opinion System, Criminal Investigation System, National Security System, Social Security System, Passport Control System,

Driver Control System, Gun Registration System, Family Registration System, Alien Control System, and Immigration Control.

4 S. Davies, *Touching Big Brother: How Biometric Technology Will Fuse Flesh and Machine*. Davies' paper directly confronts the likelihood that emergent biometric technologies, such as fingerprints, retinal scanning, hand geometry and DNA-profiling, will have very significant impacts on fundamental freedoms and civil liberties. This will be so, even if their applications remain partitioned off, with, say, each employer, consumer services provider and government agency developing their own, largely independent systems. The problems will be particularly acute should biometrics be used as a basis for a ubiquitous, multi-purpose scheme. See: simon@privint.demon.co.uk.

5 http://weber.ucsd.edu/~pagre/identification.html.

6 In *Information Technology & People*, Special Issue on Identification Technologies and Their Implications for People, Volume 7 Number 4, 1994 these examples are discussed more broadly.

7 http://www.anu.edu.au/people/roger.clarke.

8 http://www.lookoutpoint.com/look.

9 http://www.webcom.com/~bsmart/aidcf.html.

10 For a complete description of HERF Guns (coined by Schwartau in 1990), see *Information Warfare: Chaos on the Electronic Superhighway*, Thunder Mouth Press, 1994.

11 'Vanuit de ruimte in buurmans achtertuin koekeloeren' ('To watch someone's backyard from space'), in *de Volkskrant*, 11 February 1997.

References

Banisar, D. (1996), Big Brother Goes High-Tech, *CAQ Magazine*.

Clarke, R. (1994), Human Identification in Information Systems: Management Challenges and Public Policy Issues, *Information Technology & People*, 7, 4 December, pp. 6-37.

Frissen, Paul H.A. (1996), *De Virtuele Staat. Politiek, bestuur en technologie, een post-modern verhaal*, Schoonhoven: Academic Service.

Gibson, William (1984), *Neuromancer*, New York: Harper Collins.

Hoogenboom, A.B. and M. Cools (1996), *Kwetsbare kennis. Over bedrijfseconomische spionage en informatiebeveiliging*, Alphen aan den Rijn: Samsom Bedrijfsinformatie (Vulnerable knowledge. Economic espionage and information security).

Kuhn, T.S. (1962), *The Structure of Scientific Revolutions*, Chicago: University of Chicago Press.

Marx, G.T. (1988), *Undercover: Police Surveillance in America*, Berkeley: University of California Press.

Sun Tzu (1988), *The Art of War*, Boston: Shambhala.

10 Data bases – positive policing or civil liberties nightmare?

FIONA DONSON

Introduction

The gathering and storing of information, which is fundamental to the ability of police forces to undertake effective proactive strategies against individuals and groups of potential offenders, has historically been limited by the practical physical difficulties involved in establishing and maintaining information systems. These limitations have been compounded by the difficulty in ensuring adequate resources in order to set up and run information handling systems effectively. Whilst information gathered from different policing techniques[1] has for a long time had an important role to play in policing methods, the development of computer technology has helped to revolutionise and dramatically expand proactive policing over the last three decades in the UK.

The creation of police data bases can be found at both the local and national level within the UK, with the national context developing links with European policing networks. However, the development of computerized data bases which store and process police and other intelligence to be used by police organizations has developed in the UK largely unnoticed. Whilst this may not be surprising in the context of local police forces, the creation of a national policing organization dedicated to the development and control of information is a significant shift in the traditional approach to policing in the UK and the limited debate surrounding this change is perhaps, therefore, cause for concern.[2] Whilst technological developments appear to further the use and efficiency of proactive policing, questions of privacy and control arise in the context of civil liberties which ultimately require consideration.

This chapter considers the potential dangers involved in the use and development of data bases, and considers what protections might help to achieve a more appropriate balance between 'law and order' interests, in particular the interests of the police in preventing crime by invasive policing techniques, and the need to safeguard the public from invasive policing which gives rise to issues of privacy. More generally, the wider public interest must be considered in relation to the amassing of information, which, if not adequately guarded from commercial interests, might impact upon an individuals attempt to gain insurance and employment.

Computing and police work

As in many other professions, the development of computer technology has had a significant impact upon police work. Indeed, policing is based to such a significant extent upon the collection and utilization of information that it is hardly surprising that the police have seen computer technology as a method of enhancing their capability to operate and achieve 'results' in an increasingly proactive based system.

The information-based work of the police relies upon both the public to provide information, and a system within police forces to obtain, record and use the resulting intelligence to its maximum efficiency. Computer technology can offer a system by which this method of policing can be enhanced but the effectiveness of such a project is reliant upon the ability of the organization itself to adapt to new systems of working.

The efforts to develop a computing strategy within the British police has not been without its difficulties. In particular, a tension has developed between local and national systems, with development being hampered by rivalries and limited cooperation. However, a further requirement in the success of the development of computer technology, is the need for an overall strategy designed to have a significant impact upon the traditional working methods and to provide adequate training to allow the operators of the system to understand fully and maximize the system they are using. With the development of different systems and approaches, both in relation to proactive policing strategies and computerization, created on a local level and separate from the national developments, this has not necessarily taken place (Westwood 1994; Maguire and John 1995).

The development of data bases as a source of utilizing information within regional police forces has tended to develop on a system by system basis as different technologies and opportunities have shown themselves. Thus data bases on such diverse aspects of police work as domestic violence, football intelligence and firearms exist but remain largely separate with little real attempt to interlink the systems adequately. Although unsurprising, given the general ad hoc development of such systems, it is inefficient and can result in duplication.

On the national level, although the UK continues to regard a national police force with suspicion, the development of nationally based intelligence systems has created a de facto national organization. Although the first national computer was developed in 1968[3] at the Police National Computer (PNC) in Hendon, it was not until 1992, with the creation of the National Criminal Intelligence Service (NCIS) that a more high profile, strategic intelligence system began operating. NCIS was not initially placed on a statutory footing[4] but instead came under the auspices of the Home Office. Its overall aim is to 'combat the top echelons of crime and [to seek] the ultimate arrest or disruption of major criminals in the UK'. It is trumpeted by the UK government as being 'one of the first services to be set up in Europe to deal with the development of criminal intelligence on a national scale'.[5] To this end its current mission statement sets out its organizational aim as being 'to assist law enforcement and other relevant agencies: by processing intelligence; giving direction; and providing services and strategic analysis – to combat serious criminal activity'.[6]

With the enactment of the Police Act in Spring 1997 a clearer idea of the role of NCIS has emerged with the statutory basis for the organization finally being established. Section 2 of the Act provides that one of the main functions of NCIS is to 'gather, store and analyse information in order to provide criminal intelligence'. The organization, with an annual budget of £25 million and 500 staff, has already set up a number of data base systems. Its specialist Intelligence Branch consists of units dealing with organized crime, economic crime, drugs and assorted 'specialist crimes' which include paedophile crime and football violence. As a result, the paedophile index held by NCIS has around 4000 convicted or suspected names on it[7] and the hooligan data base created by the football unit has approximately 6000 people on it.[8]

NCIS regards itself as being at the 'forefront of criminal intelligence' and clearly sees itself developing its computerized intelligence 'services' into many other areas. In particular the adoption of the Europol Convention[9] means that NCIS will have a stronger European role to play in acting as the national unit liaising with Europol. Greater mobility of people, goods and capital has meant that police forces have come to consider the need to develop cross-border cooperation. Data bases and other computerized systems appear to provide an efficient system of sharing information and resources in a mutually beneficial way. The development of cooperation between customs and police forces within Europe has, under the Schengen

Agreement, seen the development of the Schengen Information System – a data bank which should facilitate the tracing of suspects, aliens and others sought by the police (Den Boer 1992).

The development of national data bases designed to work as a provider of intelligence services to local police forces clearly requires a partnership between local and national police organizations with the necessity of mutual assistance and efficient access to such information. However, this requires strong safeguards to prevent abuse of such systems and the information they contain. Clearly the courts are not unaware of the need to act in this area:

> '... One of the less welcome consequences of the information technology revolution has been the ease with which it has become possible to invade the privacy of the individual. No longer is it necessary to peep through key holes or listen under the eaves. Instead, more reliable information can be obtained in greater comfort and safety by using the concealed surveillance camera, the telephoto lens, the hidden microphone and the telephone bug. No longer is it necessary to open letters, pry into files or conduct elaborate inquiries to discover the intimate details of a person's business or financial affairs, his health, family, leisure interests or dealings with central or local government. Vast amounts of information about everyone are stored on computers, capable of instant transmission anywhere in the world and accessible at the touch of a keyboard. The right to keep oneself to oneself, to tell other people that certain things are none of their business, is under technological threat.'[10]

The difficulties they face will be discussed below.

Developing the UK DNA data base

One of the most high profile and publicly debated moves to create a national data base in the UK can be found in the development of Home Office policy on the creation of a national DNA data base. In February 1994 the Home Secretary announced that the Forensic Science Service and the Metropolitan Forensic Science Laboratory were to carry out a pilot study into the feasibility of establishing such a data base.

The pilot study announcement was combined with the publication of what was to become the Criminal Justice and Public Order Act 1994 which went beyond the recommendations of the Royal Commission on Criminal Justice.[11] That report, set up to consider the criminal justice system in the light of a series of high profile miscarriages of justice, dealt briefly with gathering of samples and the use of DNA profiles. However, a reading of the particular recommendations gives a clear indication of the influence which the police have been able to exert over the development of criminal justice policy. The RCCJ recommended that the police should be given the power to take non-intimate samples, without the consent of the suspect, where they had been arrested for a serious offence, even where DNA was not relevant to the offence being investigated. Such samples could be held on an offender data base where the person is subsequently convicted of the offence for which he or she was arrested. The argument for extending this power was that '[t]he police service argued that this power is necessary as many people who are arrested for sexual offences have previous convictions for other serious offences, such as burglary'.[12] It is unclear whether the police service provided the Royal Commission with any evidence to support this view. However, the conclusion is evident: 'coercive powers are justified where a crime may be committed at some unspecified time in the future' (Creaton 1994, p. 213).

The powers introduced by the 1994 Criminal Justice and Public Order Act allowed that under the new section 63A of the Police and Criminal Evidence Act a non-intimate sample[13] could be taken without consent where a person has been charged with or informed that s/he will be reported for a recordable offence. Where a suspect is subsequently convicted no provision is made within the legislation for their sample to be destroyed, and it may therefore be available for use in future investigations.

Non-intimate samples can be taken even where DNA evidence is not relevant to the investigation at hand and can therefore be used to build up a DNA data base which will allow speculative searches to take place during future investigations. Thus the Act provides for the creation of a large data base to be used for investigative purposes and made up of samples from those convicted of a 'recordable offence',[14] a term which covers a very wide sweep of offences, including those of a minor nature.

A statistical data base is also being developed which will be used to determine the likelihood of a given DNA profile occurring in an individual chosen at random from the population. The information is not to be used in an investigatory role, and will include samples from those acquitted of offences. The actual samples taken from suspects subsequently acquitted of an offence do not have to be destroyed where they were taken for the investigation of an offence for which another person has subsequently been convicted.

The provisions of the 1994 Act are, according to the claims of Michael Howard, the world's first 'national' DNA data base. The potential scale of the system set out in the legislation is massive – according to the Association of Chief Police Officers, there are potentially 675,000 recordable offences testable for DNA each year – although cost requirements have meant that the numbers have tended to be limited so far to the more serious categories of offence. However, claims for the new crime fighting wonder are based upon the assumption the DNA profiles[15] provide solid forensic evidence which will be acceptable to courts.

DNA profiling clearly has strong evidentiary value in cases involving offences against the person, and has been seen as a crucial development in relation to sexual offences and murder. There is, however, an expectation that DNA profiling will expand to be useful in other contexts. However, it is suggested that the criminal justice system should not necessarily accept such technological development without some critical evaluation of the potential limitations and problems inherent in the use of such profiling.

Since its discovery, strong claims have been made for the use of DNA fingerprints in the criminal justice system. Its evidentiary value in helping investigations and establishing sufficient evidence to use against someone accused of a crime combined with the underlying assumption that scientific evidence is an impartial and trustworthy 'witness' to crime have long since won the argument on the benefits of its development. It is also argued that those who are innocent of crimes will find it easier to clear themselves by providing a sample for DNA analysis. Further, it is argued that DNA can aid in the clearing up of old crimes where body and forensic samples have been preserved. The apparent benefits of compiling a data base of such information leads to the argument that such a system will allow police officers to have easy access to a centralized, accessible and reliable method of identification.

Against these arguments are the conclusions of the research study carried out by Beverley Steventon (1993) for the Royal Commission on Criminal Justice. She discovered two particular problems – disclosure of the existence of DNA evidence to defence and the need for that disclosure to be made early enough to allow the defence to obtain their own expert evaluation and the difficulty for defence lawyers in obtaining independent experts and the need for legal aid to cover the costs of such an expert.

Given the overall concerns of the report, it is perhaps surprising that the final report of the Royal Commission appeared to embrace the usefulness of DNA profiling and the need for the development of a DNA data base so uncritically.

Further cause for concern has been apparent problems in the reliability of the technology and the laboratory processes. Accidental mismatches are not unknown and concerns have been raised about the use of probabilistic methods of interpretation of DNA evidence by expert witnesses which tend to minimize the level of doubt that might benefit the defendant (Alldridge 1992).

Civil liberties concerns

Whilst the concept of privacy can be defined in relatively wide, and perhaps rather vague terms to encompass 'the desire of individuals for solitude, intimacy, anonymity, and reserve',[16] in the context of a discussion of the development of data bases the idea of privacy can be narrowed down to focus upon the idea of 'information privacy'. This can be seen as the claim that others should not obtain knowledge about an individual without their consent – 'the claim of individuals, groups or institutions to determine for themselves when, how, and to what extent information about them is communicated to others' (Westin 1967, p. 7).

James Michael poses a crucial question in his discussion of information privacy in *Privacy* when he raises the issue that if individual choice

'... Is central to personal privacy, both in the sense of allowing physical intrusions and of sharing information, how can privacy be said to be invaded by the obtaining of information about an individual and its processing by automatic means if the individual has no knowledge that this is occurring?' (Michael 1994, p. 268)

Clearly the obvious response to this question lies in the idea of the 'chilling-effect' on peoples behaviour[17] with the assumption being that individuals actions may be restricted by the notion that one's activities and thoughts are subject to surveillance:

'In such cases ... the result would be an increase in the incidence of tension-induced mental illness or at least a decrease in imaginativeness and creativity of the society as a whole.'[18]

However, this view is not convincing in itself where the individual is unaware of the surveillance, a position which proactive policing will seek to maintain in order that intelligence gathering is successful.

The creation of data-protection legislation generally developed in the name of privacy, seeks to reinforce the democratic relationship between the people and the government. The development of supervisory systems seeks to protect individuals from objectionable surveillance even where they may be unaware of its presence. It also sets out a system which attempts to achieve some balancing process between privacy on the one hand and the interests which claim that surveillance and data collation is necessary on the other.

The Data Protection Act 1984, although not the direct result of the Younger Committee on Privacy which reported in 1972,[19] was strongly influenced by the core principles it set out as requiring observation in the context of automatic processing of personal data and mirror those at the heart of the 1981 Council of Europe Data Protection Convention. These were that:[20]

1 The information to be contained in personal data shall be obtained, and personal data shall be processed, fairly and lawfully.

2 Personal data shall be held only for one or more specified and lawful purposes.

3 Personal data held for any purpose or purposes shall not be used or disclosed in any manner incompatible with that purpose or those purposes.

4 Personal data held for any purpose or purposes shall be adequate, relevant and not excessive in relation to that purpose or those purposes.

5 Personal data shall be accurate and, where necessary, kept up to date.

6 Personal data held for any purpose or purposes shall not be kept for longer than is necessary for that purpose or those purposes.

7 An individual shall be entitled:
   (a) at reasonable intervals and without undue delay or expense
      (i) to be informed by any data user whether he holds personal data of which that individual is the subject; and
      (ii) to access any such data held by a data user; and
   (b) where appropriate to have such data corrected or erased.

and where personal data is held by data users, or where services are provided by those carrying on computer bureaux:

8 Appropriate security measures shall be taken against unauthorised access to, or alteration, disclosure or destruction of, personal data and against accidental loss or destruction of personal data.

The first seven principles apply to personal data held by data users, whilst the eighth applies to both data users and to data held by computer bureaux. The statute sets about to establish that as a general rule the holder of data must observe the data protection principles. The Act required the creation of a register of data users, to be maintained by the Data Protection Registrar and also allows for the use of the criminal law in relation to acts of registered data users.[21] The Data Protection Registrar has made it clear in a recent report that the basis for the legislation is rooted in the concept of privacy:

> 'Data protection legislation is about the protection of individuals rather than the regulation of industry. It is civil rights legislation rather than technical business legislation.'[22]

The 1984 Act provides an exemption, however, for data systems where it is certified by a Cabinet Minister that such an exemption is necessary in the interests of national security. For non-certified systems, including those operated by the police, the provisions providing for subject access do not apply where it is likely to prejudice the specified purpose of preventing or detecting crime, apprehending or prosecuting offenders or the assessment or collection of a tax.[23]

Both the Data Protection Registrar and the Courts have a key role in enforcing the provisions of the statute. The police work under their own Codes of Practice which incorporate the provisions of the 1984 Act. However, the sheer weight of numbers of systems, and costs involved in searches has prompted some to question the ability of the access provisions to operate effectively (Baxter 1990, p. 217).

The role of the courts is also crucial in assessing the ability to effectively achieve privacy protection. For this to occur, the development of the law relating to data protection must be rooted in an understanding of the potential for its misuse. A recent case in the House of Lords illustrates the difficulties that can arise. In *R v Brown*[24] a police officer, checking the vehicle registration numbers of people who owed money to a friend's debt collecting agency, was able to retrieve information on the computer screen which fell within the provisions of the statute. He was prosecuted under section 5 of the 1984 Act but the House of Lords, by a majority, held that he had not 'used' the information, as required in the act, as the ordinary and natural meaning of 'use' requires more than retrieving the information from the data base and displaying it in a readable form on the screen.

However, Lord Griffith, dissenting, argued that a more purposive interpretation should be used in looking at the provisions of the statute. By having regard to the Council of Europe Convention on Automatic Processing of Personal Data, which the Data Protection Act was meant to bring into domestic law, and in particular having regard to the aims of the conventions:

'The purpose of this Convention is to secure in the territory of each party for every individual, whatever his nationality or residence, respect for his right and fundamental freedoms, *and in particular his right of privacy*, with regard to automatic processing of personal data relating to him.'[25]

Given that Lord Griffith considered that the act should be interpreted in accordance with the Convention, he concluded that the retrieving of information and subsequent reading of it amounted to an invasion of privacy, given that no legitimate purpose could be found in defence of the reading.

In the light of this approach, Lord Griffith therefore concluded that the word 'use' could include mere retrieval and reading of the vehicle registration. The important point is that the integrity and security of the information is not protected if the word 'use' does not include the reading of information. He points out that the nature of information means that

'Once information has entered the public domain it is impractical to attempt to place any restraints on its use or further dissemination. The Act therefore concentrates its protective provisions in s5 upon those who hold or have access to personal data, in an attempt to ensure that they do not abuse the data, and confine it to its proper purpose for which it is required.'[26]

The decision of the majority of the House of Lords effectively means that improper retrieval of data protected under the statute cannot be prosecuted where there is no subsequent misuse of that information. Indeed, Lord Hoffman recognizes that the result of the decision is that

'... Unfair or unlawful forms of processing do not fall within the criminal sanctions of s 5.'[27]

The response of the Office of Data Protection Registrar to the decision of the House of Lords was on the whole positive. It welcomed the 'natural and ordinary meaning' approach and stated that it found the emphasis on the protection of personal privacy 'especially pleasing'.[28] However, whilst it pointed out that an employee who 'browsed' personal data could potentially be prosecuted under the Computer Misuse Act 1990, the inability to prosecute such behaviour under the Data Protection Act 1984 was a worrying development:

'Employees accessing a data base for their own use or amusement causes concern about security, integrity and confidentiality of personal information.'[29]

Unfortunately, such abuses have already occurred within NCIS. Following a corruption case involving ex-DC John Donald who was found to have sold information relating to the interception of communications to defence lawyers and sentenced to eleven years imprisonment, an inquiry was undertaken into the administrative processes surrounding the NCIS telephone intercept facility. The inquiry found that procedural lapses in dealing with notebooks took place on a massive scale resulting in police officers failing to return notebooks to NCIS. It was further found that the Service itself failed to keep a proper register of data given to individual officers. Whilst NCIS stated that '[t]he investigation revealed that faults were mainly administrative ...'[30] the trial of Donald and the findings of the resulting inquiry go to undermine the claim that NCIS provides an intelligence gathering and storage system which can be trusted by the public not to infringe privacy.

Whilst corruption of those employed to handle information in systems which lack basic safeguards to prevent misuse gives rise to a major concern in relation to data bases, a second issue concerns the accuracy of information stored. Inaccurate information, once part of a data base system, takes on a strong legitimacy simply by being part of that system. With the development of interlinked data bases throughout the European Union, the need to ensure that intelligence is accurate, and that information which is less than fact is identified as such, takes on an increased importance.

The battle undertaken by Welsh football fans following their visit to Belgium in 1992 to watch Wales under-21s play illustrates some of the present difficulties. Alun, Gwilym and Rhys Boore discovered that a routine inquiry in Belgium two years earlier had resulted in their names being placed on hooligan registers in a number of European Countries. After a long campaign during which the Home Office, although originally denying their names were on a blacklist, finally admitted that NCIS held their names on its hooligan data base, the brothers obtained a decision by the European Commission that their freedom of movement had been restricted for no reason. As a result, in 1996 Britain, Belgium and Luxembourg agreed that their names should be removed from their hooligan blacklists. However, they are left unsure as to whether any other countries might have received intelligence from those three countries and registered them on similar lists thus resulting in a perpetuation of false information. The difficulty in challenging data base mistakes was graphically illustrated by the *Observer* newspaper:

'The brothers had been obliged to go to the Home Office, Foreign Office, NCIS, South Wales Police, Data Protection Registrar, British Embassy in Brussels, Belgium and Luxembourg Embassies in London, Belgium police, Belgium Ministry of Justice, Belgium Ministry of the Interior,

European Commission and European Ombudsman to clear their names'
(*Observer*, 21 July 1996, p. 7).

Concerns around the establishment of DNA data bases include those already
considered but are complicated by the fact that there may be two different
types of information to be stored – the DNA fingerprint itself, and the
sample from which it was taken. These raise different issues and different
levels of concern.

In relation to an individual's DNA profile, the question arises as to what
interest he or she has in it? There are also concerns over who has access to
the information and what protections are made available to prevent the
unauthorized use or publication of the information? Finally, concerns will
be raised as to what happens to the DNA fingerprint if a suspect has been
acquitted of the offence for which it was created?

A second set of questions arise in relation to the sample of blood, saliva
or hair follicle from which the DNA fingerprint has been obtained. Is the
sample destroyed after the DNA profile has been obtained and defence
lawyers have had the opportunity to employ their own experts? Is any other
genetic testing allowed on the sample? Who has access to the sample? What
protections are in place to prevent unauthorized access to the sample and
testing?

The fundamental question in relation to the creation of a data base of this
sort is whether the criminal justice benefits can be seen to outweigh the
privacy interests of the public? A clear danger in the storage of samples
from which DNA is taken is that genetic information, which is personal and
inherently sensitive, may be stored in a system which is not truly secure and
through this the police, security services, government and commercial
organizations may be able to obtain access to information which, if known,
may damage the individual. Failure adequately to secure such genetic
information may clearly lead to discriminatory treatment and the stigmati-
zation of individuals within society.

Conclusion

Proactive policing, with its emphasis on the collection and collation of
intelligence, clearly gives rise to fundamental problems in achieving a
balance between the interests of 'information privacy' on the one hand, and
'law and order' concerns on the other. Problems arise in relation to distinguishing between facts and opinions, if no clear method of distinction is

employed, rumours and gossip will very quickly become validated as usable intelligence. A system of auditing the accuracy of information is crucial if mistakes such as occurred in the case of the Boore brothers are not to become commonplace. Equally, if an information system becomes 'unreliable' due to damaging errors, and therefore loses its credibility, the basis of proactive policing is dramatically undermined.

Improper access to information, and leakage, such as occurred in the Brown case, and that of *R v Loat*,[31] where a civilian employee made use of the Police National Computer to pass on information to a burglar alarm company and was prosecuted under section 2 of the Official Secrets Act 1911, suggests that information could ultimately be used to very damaging effect. An individual could be excluded from many basic aspects of normal life if genetic information, or general policing information were passed on to employers, insurance companies and banks. The Data Protection Act 1984 can only provide a remedy for someone who has become suspicious that such a problem may exist.

Although the Data Protection Act 1984 seeks to protect the interests of the individual in relation to privacy, as we have seen, in the policing context its ability to achieve this may be limited. Article 8 of the European Convention provides the nearest the UK has to a right to privacy when it states that 'Everyone has the right to respect for his private and family life, his home and correspondence' (Article 8.1). This right is limited where a public authority, 'in accordance with the law' finds that it is necessary to do so 'in the interests of national security, public safety or the economic well-being of the country, for the prevention of disorder or crimes ...' (Article 8.2). The European Court of Human Rights has taken a broad view of the concept of the 'right to a private life' concluding it amounts to a right to lead a life without outside interference.[32] The limitation that any interference with the right should take place 'in accordance with the law' is viewed as requiring that it complies with domestic law and that it is compatible with the rule of law.[33] In effect this would seem to require that safeguards should exist within the legal framework to prevent arbitrary use of methods and actions which would infringe the Article 8 right.

When considering whether the development of data base systems in the UK fulfil the requirements under Article 8 the lack of strong external controls on such developing computer systems gives rise to concern. With the establishment of the statutory framework for the development of NCIS it becomes clear that no system of external information auditing exists. Equally, the development of the Europol system which NCIS will be central to in the UK requires that each member state designate a national supervisory body to independently monitor the functions of the national liaison unit in relation to the gathering and distribution of personal data. As the system develops, it appears that in the UK that body will be the Data Protection Registrar. However, insufficient powers currently exist under the Data Protection Act 1984 in order to meet the requirements of the role. It appears that auditing powers would be necessary so that compliance can be pursued.[34] The development of European wide information systems indicates that the balancing process between privacy and proactive policing is crucially important if confidence in the quality and fairness of police information gathering process is to be maintained. It is not enough for Government to say that NCIS can be trusted to ensure that fairness will be ensured by voluntary compliance with the wishes of the Data Protection Registrar. As long as the Registrar does not have the power to enforce compliance where it is claimed that to do so would be likely to prejudice prevention or detection of crime, then it will be hard to maintain that the police meet the first data protection principle that information must be obtained and processed fairly and lawfully. In such a context, proactive policing remains a serious threat to civil liberties generally[35] and privacy in particular.

Notes

1   These include general contact with the public, the use of informants and the use of surveillance techniques such as bugging.
2   See discussion below of the creation of the National Criminal Intelligence Service.
3   Although it did not receive its first computer until 1972, see Baxter 1990.
4   The Police Act 1997 finally provides a statutory framework within which NCIS will work.
5   Foreign and Commonwealth Office Background Brief, FCO Information Department, April 1995.
6   NCIS Annual Report 1995/6.
7   *The Observer,* 25 August 1996.
8   *The Guardian,* 8 August 1995.
9   European Office of Police, adopted 26 July 1996.
10 Per Lord Hoffman *R v Brown* [1996] 1 All ER 545, at p. 556.
11 RCCJ Report, (1993), London: HMSO.
12 RCCJ para 2.34.
13 For example, a sample taken from a nail, saliva, non-pubic hair; all fall within the definition of non-intimate samples.

14 The term covers all offences punishable by imprisonment, plus a number of other specified offences.
15 Profiling is a scientific technique which allows a scientist to compare two biological samples in order to determine the likelihood that the samples originate from the same source.
16 See Michael 1994, p. 266 using Professor A. Westin's definition in (1967) *Privacy and Freedom*, New York: Atheneum.
17 *Federal Constitutional Court, Karlsruhe,* Census Act 1983 partially unconstitutional, 15 December 1983, (1984) 5 HRLJ 94.
18 The Younger Committee, para. 111.
19 The Committee recommended the development of voluntary codes of practice and the creation of a standing committee to monitor the growth of computer technology and systems affecting privacy in the public sector – Cmnd 5012, ch. 20. These recommendations were not adopted.
20 Section 2 and part I of Schedule I.
21 See section 5(2) for a list of prohibitions.
22 Tenth Report of the Data Protection Registrar HMSO 1994.
23 Section 28.
24 [1996] 1 All ER 545.
25 Per Lord Griffith, ibid., at p. 554, his italics.
26 Ibid. at p. 555.
27 Ibid. at p. 561.
28 Press release, Office of the Data Protection Registrar, 12 February 1996.
29 Ibid.
30 NCIS Press release 21 January 1997.
31 [1985] *Crim LR* 154.
32 ECHR 16 December 1992, Series A, vol. 251-B (*Niemietz v Germany*).
33 ECHR 24 April 1990, Series A, vol. 176-A (*Kruslin v France*).
34 Hansard, House of Lords Debate, 26 November 1996, col. 187.
35 The potential oppressive misuse of the DNA data base can be found in a report of the eviction of two squatters from a beach chalet. Arrested for possessing a juggling stick, which was defined as an offensive weapon, the law allowed for samples to be taken from them for DNA testing.

References

Alldridge, Peter (1992), Recognising Novel Scientific Techniques: DNA as a test case, *Criminal Law Review* 687.
Baxter, J. (1990), *State Security, Privacy and Information,* London: Harvester Wheatsheaf.

Boer, M. den (1992), *Working Paper V: 'Schengen: Intergovernmental scenario for European Police Co-operation'*, Edinburgh: University of Edinburgh.

Creaton, J. (1994), DNA Profiling and the Law: A Critique of the Royal Commission's Recommendations, in: M. McConville and L. Bridges (eds.), *Criminal Justice in Crisis*, Aldershot: Eward Elgar.

Maguire, M. and T. John (1995), *Intelligence, Surveillance and Informants: Integrated Approaches,* London: Home Office.

Michael, J. (1994), Privacy, in: C. McCrudden and G. Chambers, *Individual Rights and the Law in Britain*, Oxford: Clarendon Press.

Steventon, Beverley (1993), *The Ability to Challenge DNA Evidence*, Research Study No 9, London: HMSO.

Westin, A. (1967), *Privacy and Freedom,* New York: Athenaeum.

Westwood, S. (1994), The computer peace treaty, 10 *Policing* 23.

11 Financial investigation and privacy in Britain and the Netherlands

ROAN LAMP, MICHAEL LEVI AND WANDA KERVER-POLDERVAART

Introduction

Financial information has become an important source for law enforcement agencies investigating serious forms of crime for gain, especially 'organized crime' which – whether reasonably or not – has become a major political issue for European governments during the 1990s. These concerns (or, to the more cynical, 'moral panics') arose as the end of the Cold War freed up the Foreign Offices and Security Services of many countries to think about the more diffuse threat posed by the post-modern plethora of Central and Eastern European States, replacing the (at least perceived) monolith of the Soviet Union.[1] Concerns about moral hazards for bank depositors (and their insurers, the taxpayer) and for 'society', which was being harmed by the laundering of the proceeds of crime, led both to legislation and to Codes of Conduct, though the balance varied between societies over time and place. Both as cause and effect (and stimulated not only by politicians and the Financial Action Task Force[2] but also by the technical and organizational skills of competent legal bureaucrats such as Hans Nilsson, formerly of the Council of Europe and then of the Council of the EU), the impetus for dealing *internationally* with the criminal aspects of money has been sustained by the UN Convention against illicit traffic in narcotic drugs and psychotropic substances 1988, the Basle Declaration of (banking) Principles of 1988, the Council of Europe Convention on Laundering, Search, Seizure, and Confiscation of the Proceeds of Crime 1990, and the EC Directive on Money-Laundering 1991.[3] Indeed, with continuing developments in international legislation on corruption, asset confiscation, and money-laundering, this globalizing legislative process is by no means at an end in 1997.

The challenge that deep-structured 'organized crime' poses for traditional police methods, including even the use of informants and undercover infiltrators, is clear, since it is seldom possible to connect high level organizers with street-level criminals. Therefore, in constructing the evidential web of culpability, there has been an increasing resort to covert surveillance (such as electronic eavesdropping) and to financial data. Bank statements, tax returns, telephone and credit card usage data are all potential sources of importance to the modern police-unit (though by no means all such units may be modern, and the extent to which the police use financial investigations as part of their strategy is variable). This information is of interest not only for the investigation of individual crimes but also for the gathering of general intelligence on crime networks that are involved in serious criminality and money-laundering, which in turn may feed into their disruption rather than into the sort of criminal justice intervention that might end up before the European Court of Human Rights.

These methods can be used because traditional methods of responding to reported crimes give insufficient forensic clues to convict high-volume offenders who are believed – rightly or wrongly – to be committing a large proportion of the traditional crimes such as burglary and car theft in particular areas. But they also can be (and more often are) used in more strategic, longer term investigations carried out by organized crime squads, howsoever labelled. Information about criminals' financial affairs can help in asset freezing and confiscation – one of the new areas for European police forces. Furthermore, unless the audit trail is broken by legal protection and/or offender deviousness, this information can enable the investigation of relationships with professional advisers (such as accountants, bankers and lawyers) and other domestic and overseas intermediaries. These relationships might not be readily discovered, given budgetary constraints, via covert surveillance or other means.[4] Such financial intelligence can be obtained following requests by police or customs officers, or unprompted by the authorities, via reports of suspected money-laundering.

The latter emanate from financial institutions covered by money-laundering regulations, which – at least formally – have been harmonized in Europe (Gold and Levi 1994; Gilmore 1995). In both cases, there are implications for the freedom of individuals from surveillance, but the availability of financial data to the authorities following a court order of some kind at least resembles the extension of the domestic search warrant to external financial 'homes'. The extent to which such information is *used*, especially where it relates to people who are not already suspects, is open to question, largely as a result of the time taken to follow them through and modest resourcing in financial investigation units.

In 1986, before any international conventions and agreements relating to money-laundering, the English government had taken the initiative to make it a crime for bankers within the jurisdiction of the English courts[5] *not* to pass on their suspicions of *drugs* money-laundering, and had given bankers immunity from lawsuits for voluntarily disclosing suspicions of *non-drugs* money-laundering (see Drug Trafficking Offences Act 1986). In the UK, since the coming into force of the Criminal Justice Act 1993 and the Money-Laundering Regulations 1993, there is criminal liability for bankers who assist in disposing of what they suspect to be the proceeds of drugs trafficking or terrorism; bankers can report with civil as well as criminal impunity, transactions that they suspect to be the proceeds of fraud or robbery; and there are imprisonment sanctions for the Money-Laundering Reporting Officers that have to be designated by regulated institutions, however small, should they fail to keep the sort of account-holder records required by the Regulations. Although the Netherlands started slightly later, there are similar obligations in relation to money-laundering as in the UK.

These changing obligations may be usefully distinguished in terms of 'proactive' obligations (such as, in the context of money-laundering, the duty to inform the authorities about customer transactions of which criminal investigators and regulators may be ignorant) and 'reactive' obligations (the duty to respond to investigative enquiries about persons who are already criminal suspects). In a *reactive* context, UK financial institutions and professionals are regularly in receipt of (a) instructions from the Director of the Serious Fraud Office (*without* the need for any court order) to disclose information under section 2 of the Criminal Justice Act 1987 – a power that since the Criminal Justice Act 1993 has been exercisable on behalf of overseas serious fraud enquiries (such as those by the Italians against Silvio Berlusconi's company Fininvest) and (b) Production Orders made by circuit judges in England and Wales under Schedule 1 of the Police and Criminal Evidence Act 1984 to disclose details of bank accounts and background papers of suspected offenders and even material witnesses. The Proceeds of Crime Act 1995 has extended powers to examine records in the course of a financial investigation whose exact nature does not have to be specified. This is a dramatic change from the situation applicable prior to 1984, when records were lawfully viewable only *after* 'the institution of criminal proceedings'. Thus, there has been a two-pronged development (i) in easing violations of privacy in pursuit of already opened criminal investigations, and (ii) in using the private sector as an extension of the public, to generate information about 'suspicious persons'. However, one would not like to *over*estimate these changes from the traditional, reactive model of law enforcement: apart from the generalized obligation under the Council of

Europe Convention and EC Directive to establish 'adequate' money-laundering reporting systems, to obtain adequate identification from customers, and to keep records of transactions, etcetera, no-one is punished for failing to suspect things that 'objectively' (at least in retrospect) actually *were* money-laundering.[6]

The most important and radical of the proactive measures is the introduction in several countries of an obligation upon financial institutions to report to centralized law enforcement agencies financial transactions variously described as 'unusual' or 'suspicious'. These systems of disclosure have several problematic aspects. First, and most importantly, they raise serious privacy concerns when the state, through its investigatory agencies, gets access to large amounts of financial information on its citizens, without necessarily having an *individualized* justification for the intrusion. (In this sense, they represent 'actuarial justice'.) The US and Australian systems with their routine reporting requirements for large cash deposits and wire transfers are more intrusive than the suspicion-based reporting systems that exist in Europe, for in practice, suspicious *transaction* reporting often amounts to direct suspicion of *individuals* (behaviour based on their style of self-presentation), or assumptions of suspiciousness based on the inconsistency between what is known or believed about particular individuals, corporate accounts and their money movements.

The legal question salient to this chapter is whether any or all of these suspicions of their customers *by financial institutions* constitutes a breach of Article 8 of the European Convention on Human Rights which reads:

> 1. Everyone has the right to respect for his private and family life, his home and his correspondence.
>
> 2. There shall be no interference by a public authority with the exercise of this right except such as is in accordance with the law and is necessary in a democratic society in the interests of national security, public safety or the economic well-being of the country, for the prevention of disorder or crime, for the protection of health or morals, or for the protection of the rights and freedoms of others.

Article 8 was not even mentioned in the discussion of human rights issues in money-laundering regulation by Gilmore (1995). Yet arguably, financial details are a part of the private life of account-holders, especially if they are personal rather than business accounts, but even if they are the latter: see, for example, the extensive view of 'home life' adopted in *Niemietz v Germany*.[7] No-one has seriously argued that European money-laundering legislation per se is a fundamental breach of human rights, but the 'necessity' criterion may depend on acceptance of arguments about the damage done by money-laundering *and/or* by its contribution to the prevention of crime. In our view, it is an open question whether or not money-laundering controls actually contribute significantly to the prevention of crime, though they are intended to do so. This is because many offenders would have no particular need to save or re-invest (Van Duyne 1994; Levi 1997), as well as because too little policing input currently exists to make serious inroads into crime networks via financial investigation. However, those who make very large profits from crime *do* have a need to launder, not least because they would be unable to spend all that they make. So although there are grounds for scepticism regarding the 'necessity' of money-laundering to encouraging criminal behaviour *in an individual case*, the leap required to undermine the crime control merits of the legislation itself would be too great.

Nonetheless, there is some form of (probably unconscious) actuarial prejudice in the operation of money-laundering suspicions: a person from a drug source country making transfers may be viewed as being 'more suspicious' than the same behaviour from a non-drug source country; and ethnic minorities may be more often suspected than are Caucasians, especially if they do not have a British passport (Gold and Levi 1994). Someone from a wealthy background may be less suspected than a *nouveau riche*, because unless there are person-specific suspicions, the former may be viewed as less of a 'criminal type'. But someone without a known commercial base may (reasonably) be regarded as more suspicious than either if large domestic or international transfers are made. Conversely, though such a system exists in no European country, the total capture of financial data in Australia or the US may be more intrusive but less discriminatory: discrimination enters in those regimes when one examines corporate exemptions from reporting requirements or, perhaps, the decision to follow up particular cases.

Another problematic aspect of this type of legislation is that the question of control is unclear. When the police make use of powers that are given to them, this usage is subject to the control of the judiciary when the case comes to court. In such a case, the presiding judge will re-evaluate whether the police made proper use of a certain power. When it is not the police investigating but rather a financial institution which discloses the information to the police 'voluntarily' under the money-laundering provisions, it becomes unclear where the system of checks and balances occurs, for neither the citizen nor any independent party normally has any knowledge of the violation of privacy. Because it is connected with the prevention of crime, the conduct also lies beyond the powers of Data Protection Registrars to regulate, though if the banks were to link their data bases to search for people and activities that were not already subject to suspicion, they might be held to infringe Data Protection legislation. In other words, once one becomes a 'suspected person', one's right to privacy is diminished in English law.[8]

In this chapter we will look at the disclosure systems in England and Wales and in the Netherlands as instruments of proactive financial investigation. In the discussion of the two systems, we shall review the problematic aspects briefly summarized in this introduction, as well as other issues relevant to effectiveness.

Financial investigation

General

The use of financial information in the investigation of crime is not new. Information about the financial situation of suspects has always enjoyed the attention of some law enforcement agents, at least in principle, but until recently, it played only an incidental and happenstance role. It was mostly a matter of coincidence if the police, for example through the search of premises, encountered information relating to the financial dealings of suspects which might then be used in further investigation and/or assist the subsequent prosecution (though it is impossible to know how often such information was available and then either ignored totally or its significance not appreciated).

The financial investigation of crime entails what we view as being a potentially fundamental change to the above situation. By financial investigation of crime we refer to more than the sole use of financial data as evidence in a criminal case, but also to the generation of further non-financial inquiries and the construction of evidence of a relationship between individuals – perhaps via computer software such as I-2 – a relationship which would otherwise be very difficult to uncover.[9]

Financial investigation is not a legal concept but a strategy of police investigation. It entails a change in the subject of analysis, from the human suspect and physical forensics at the crime scene to general financial information about criminal lifestyles and networks. It also entails a change of expertise. In a traditional crime investigation, even against so-called 'organized crime', the most valuable asset of a law enforcement agent is his knowledge of the criminal milieu – a certain accumulated street wisdom –

but when investigating crime financially, the law enforcement officers must depend on their knowledge of and contacts in the financial world to build up a profile of the people in whom they are interested. To do their job well and avoid wasting time, officers must be able to distinguish between plausibly legitimate and plausibly criminal economic behaviour. This has consequences for the necessary skills in police work, and for the training of existing officers, though in most countries, such changes are slow in coming and currently affect only a minority of the police.

The concept of financial investigation of crime is of American origin, reflecting the American view that in cases of organized forms of criminality, whatever that is (Van Duyne 1996), the top of the organization has links to the operational part on only two fronts, namely communication and finance (Schaap 1995). Consequently, American law enforcement agencies – in particular the FBI and the DEA – found it necessary to investigate systematically the finances of individuals suspected as a result of wiretaps, surveillance, etcetera. This focus on the financial side of criminality has also led to exceptionally broad forfeiture possibilities in the USA, though often via forfeiture of property by professional people who act as intermediaries (see Levi and Osofsky 1995). In the UK, it has been spurred on by the work of the Audit Commission (1993) and by Her Majesty's Inspectorate of Constabulary working from the Home Office: the result is that many forces in the UK have re-allocated detectives from reactive (following up recorded crimes) to proactive investigations which focus on collecting information about known or suspected offenders and their associates (Maguire and John 1995), a process that started during the 1970s in the Netherlands and was also halted there earlier, due partly to Dutch policing scandals. Little of the *British* work on proactive policing has paid attention to financial transactions, however.

Legislative changes

In the late 1980s, the British and Dutch police and, following not far behind, British and Dutch politicians started showing an interest in the financial side of serious forms of criminality. This interest had two different aspects. Firstly, there was concern about the problem of money-laundering. Even though neither the British nor the Dutch police or governments had a clear picture of the extent or nature of the problem in their countries, they assumed – partly at the instigation of the US agencies and partly prompted by some larger investigations of their own – that by analogy with the principle that without fences there would be no thieves, attacking money-laundering was one way of choking off the financial life-blood of 'criminal organizations', and the governments felt it essential to counteract the threat. As a consequence, since 1986, England and Wales[10] have passed the Drug Trafficking Offences Act 1986, the Criminal Justice Act 1988, the Criminal Justice (International Co-operation) Act 1990, the Prevention of Terrorism (Temporary Provisions) Act 1991, the Criminal Justice Act 1993, and the Drug Trafficking Act 1994 (leaving out some minor legislation). Over the same period, the Netherlands has criminalized money-laundering, has passed three preventive anti-money-laundering laws – namely the Financial Services Identification Act, the Disclosure of Unusual Transactions Act and the Bureaux de Change Supervision Act – and has established the Disclosures Office. Of these, the Disclosure of Unusual Transactions Act 1994 and the establishment (based on this Act) of the Disclosures Office are the most significant for our purposes. They and their differently organized British equivalents play an important role in the gathering of financial information in the proactive phase of criminal investigations.

Secondly, the confiscation of proceeds and instrumentalities of crime has increased in importance. Here, the British were first, reflecting frustration at the inability of the courts to confiscate £750,000 of assets – some of them in France and Switzerland – in the possession of people convicted of running a major domestic LSD factory, since these were not used in committing the crime.[11] Thus, the Drug Trafficking Offences Act 1986 was intended to confiscate all assets of convicted drugs traffickers that came into their possession or control over the previous six years and that the convicted persons could not prove to have been acquired lawfully. Hitherto, provided they are not retrospective in their impact before the legislation came into existence, these 'reverse onus of proof' rules have not been prohibited by the European Court, possibly because they apply post-conviction and have not been used in cases that were plainly disproportionate. Much more limited rules, however, were applied to both the reporting of suspicions and the confiscation of the proceeds of other offences (the proceeds had to be linked to a specific offence of conviction under the Criminal Justice Act 1988), reflecting the *realpolitik* 'principle' that legislation depends upon what the political market will bear, and there is more unambiguous support for a law and order perspective in drugs and terrorism in England than in other spheres such as fraud. By the mid-1990s, the political climate in Europe had changed and the Proceeds of Crime Act 1995 was passed in the UK, making similar but not quite as severe confiscation provisions for non-drugs as for drugs trafficking cases. The legislation also gave the police power to examine financial records *without a warrant from a judge* in cases of fraud, since they did not have to specify a particular offence as they did under the already tolerant Production Orders under the Police and Criminal Evidence Act 1984 (Hewson 1993), only that they were investigating the proceeds of crime. Since 1983, it has been possible under Dutch law to confiscate proceeds received from prosecuted and proven criminal offences. But according to the Dutch government, this possibility was too limited: only proceeds from proven criminal offences could be confiscated and the Dutch regulation did not create the possibility of a criminal investigation focused on criminal earnings. The 1993 Forfeiture Act eliminated these limitations.

Let us now deal systematically with the Dutch legislation.

The Disclosure of Unusual Transactions Act

Stimulated by a change in the Dutch law on handling (including the handling of money – i.e. money-laundering) which increased the risk of criminal liability for financial institutions, a number of major Dutch banks started reporting transactions which they considered to be of a suspicious nature to the financial desk of the Central Investigation and Information Division (CIID) of the national police unit in 1992. The disclosure of this information occurred on a voluntary basis and was not regulated by legislation. Both the banks and the Dutch government were of the opinion that legislation was needed. The banks wanted to see their position legally regulated where they had disclosed information to the police about clients in spite of their contractual duty of secrecy. The prospect of civil claims by clients against financial institutions which had passed on information based on unspecified suspicions of money-laundering was not appealing. On the part of the Dutch authorities there was a desire to implement a legal obligation of disclosure to replace the existing voluntary practice. In that way the Dutch authorities could themselves decide what information should be passed on and so end their dependence on a variable supply from financial institutions. This desire was also spurred on by the international consensus that legislative measures were of paramount importance to an effective fight against money-laundering. The 1991 EC Directive and the recommendations of the Financial Action Task Force are good illustrations of this. The final proposal for the introduction of the Disclosure of Unusual Transactions Act came from a task force on money-laundering which consisted of representatives of the relevant governmental agencies.

The most important feature of the Disclosure of Unusual Transactions Act, which came into force in February 1994, is the intermediary position of the Disclosures Office, which receives and processes the information passed on by Dutch financial institutions. The Dutch government was of the opinion that financial institutions should not be given complete responsibility for separating out that information which might be relevant to the investigation of crime from that which was not. According to the government this process is an investigative process and is essentially a governmental task. In addition, unlike the UK government, the Dutch government found excessively intrusive any system whereby the Dutch police could get access to all – or a great deal of – the data of financial institutions and themselves sift for relevant information. At issue, according to the government, was the right to privacy of individual citizens whose financial transactions would, in such a system, become known to the police without there being any suspicion or probable cause. Quite apart from this, the Dutch government thought that a system whereby the police received large amounts of information from financial institutions was likely to be inefficient, because the police would have to go through a large proportion of irrelevant information.

The structure of the Act is such that the filtering of information is partially done by the financial institutions themselves and partially done by the (administrative) Disclosures Office, which in turn – under certain conditions – passes on the information to the police. The first disclosure of information is done by the financial institutions to the Disclosures Office, the second one by the Disclosures Office to the Financial Police desk (Finpol) at the Central Intelligence and Information Division.

Financial institutions

The disclosure of information by the financial institutions is regulated by indicators set by the Dutch government. Financial transactions which meet at least one of the indicators are called 'unusual transactions' and must consequently be passed on to the Disclosures Office. The indicators set by the government cannot be too stringent if one wants to avoid relevant information passing through financial institutions without being reported. On the other hand, the indicators cannot be so broad that the Disclosures Office is flooded with information that is for the most part irrelevant and 'innocent'.

Article 9 of the Act states that anyone who commercially or professionally offers a financial service must disclose immediately any unusual transaction – whether intended or already performed – to the Disclosures Office. Further financial services can be included by executive order. To come within the terms of the Act the financial service must take place in the

Netherlands. Accordingly, a Dutch subsidiary of a foreign financial institution falls under the act but a foreign subsidiary of a Dutch bank does not. A disclosure by a financial institution must include the identity of the client, the nature, time, place, origin and destination of the transaction and, lastly, the circumstances which made the transaction unusual.

As we have mentioned before, indicators guide the decision to regard a particular transaction as unusual or not. These indicators for disclosure were set out by the Ministers of Finance and Justice after preparatory work by the Disclosures Office and the Assistance Committee created by the Act. The indicators must be approved by executive order within six months to remain valid. The types of indicators are two-fold. On the one hand, there are those indicators which can be established objectively. An objective indicator is, for example, any transaction exceeding NLG 25,000 – or the equivalent thereof in another currency – in which small denomination notes are exchanged for larger ones. In such cases, disclosure of the transaction by the financial institution to the Disclosures Office is mandatory. There is little need for judgement on the part of the financial institution. Clearly, this is not the case with subjective indicators, where financial institutions must decide whether the circumstances surrounding a particular transaction suggest a preference for structuring transactions below the objective threshold (referred to by the Americans as 'smurfing'), thereby evading routine disclosure under objective indicators. In these 'subjective' cases a disclosure is obligatory if in the view of the financial institution one of the indicators is applicable. Only the institution providing the financial service is in a position to determine this.

The Act imposes on financial institutions an obligation of secrecy with regard to the reports they pass on to the Disclosures Office. Thus it is an offence for a financial institution to inform a client that certain transactions of his have been disclosed. Without this provision clients would argue that it is a civil obligation of financial institutions to report all relevant information to the client if there is no legal obstacle to do so. For a client disclosure of a transaction to a third party would certainly be relevant information.

Financial institutions are guilty of a criminal offence under Dutch law if they handle money which they know or might reasonably suspect represents proceeds of crime. Therefore, if financial institutions know or suspect that transactions handled by their institution are part of an effort to launder proceeds of crime, they are reporting their own criminal behaviour to the authorities when they disclose information about them. Given that the Disclosure of Unusual Transactions Act was not intended to tackle financial institutions involved, in all good faith, in money-laundering schemes, but rather to direct law enforcement agencies more effectively at those involved in (serious) crime, the Act had to find a solution to this situation. Accordingly, Article 12 provides a limited criminal exoneration by stating that information disclosed by financial institutions cannot be used in the investigation or prosecution of the disclosing financial institution for a money-laundering offence.

Article 13 of the Act gives an exemption from responsibility in civil law to financial institutions. This exemption depends on the reasonableness of the acts of the financial institution. If a client can show that in his particular case, the decision to report was unreasonable, the institution remains liable for damages. (Under English legislation consolidated in the Criminal Justice Act 1993, there is immunity for disclosures made in good faith).[12]

The Disclosures Office

The primary function of the Disclosures Office is to filter the received information. The Disclosures Office must collect, register and analyse the incoming data and separate the information which might be of importance for the prevention and investigation of criminal behaviour from information that cannot be related to crime. For this purpose, the Disclosures Office can collect additional data from other police registers, although the more sensitive and secret police registers are off limits to the Office. The Disclosures Office can also – like anyone else – make use of public sources.

It is important to note that even though the Disclosures Office falls under the responsibility of the Minister of Justice, and the register of the Disclosures Office is designated as a police register (and therefore falls under the Act on police registers), the Disclosures Office is separate and independent from the police. This means that information received by the Disclosures Office is not available to the police unless certain conditions are met. When these conditions are met, in the terms of the act, an 'unusual transaction' is upgraded to a 'suspect transaction', which allows communication to the police via the Finpol desk at the Central Intelligence and Information Division.

The Dutch Act and Order on Police Registers are measures of information regulation. They are intended to prevent unjustified use of sensitive police information and form a legal structure within which Dutch law enforcement agencies must gather, store and exchange information. The Disclosures Office must operate within this framework. Article 4 of the Act states that information can only be stored in a register within the meaning of the Act if two conditions are met, namely that the information is legally obtained and that the information is necessary for the purpose for which the register operates. The purpose of the Disclosures Office is the prevention and investigation of crime.

Article 12.1.d of the Order of Police registers determines when the Disclosures Office must relay information to the police, in other words, the cases in which 'unusual transactions' become 'suspect transactions'. Here we will discuss the two most important criteria of the Article. The first instance in which information can be released from the Disclosures Office is when the disclosed transaction and further investigation by the Disclosures Office leads to a reasonable suspicion of a criminal act. This is a judgement that the Disclosures Office must make on its own. It is difficult to know when and how the Disclosures Office decides that a unusual transaction raises a reasonable suspicion. What can be said is that a reasonable suspicion can not be easily created by a single unusual transaction without any further incriminating information. It has to be a combination of facts which together can support a suspicion that may be regarded as both objective and reasonable.

A second category of information which can be released is an important one in the context of proactive policing. It is also the biggest category, being the basis on which over half of the transactions are passed on by the Disclosures Office to Finpol (Terlouw and Aron 1996). The Disclosures Office runs the names of those reported to them through two registers of the Criminal Intelligence Service (CIS), namely the index of subjects and the 'grey-field' register. The subject index contains natural or legal persons that in the opinion of the CIS are – or may be in the future – suspected of criminal behaviour that represents an assault on the legal order of Dutch society because of its serious nature, its frequency or the organized manner in which it is planned or committed. The 'grey-field' register contains those natural and legal persons who are being considered – in a broader context and with the use of other information – for upgrading to CIS subjects and addition to the subject index.[13] If there is a match between an unusual transaction and presence in one of the two registers it means that information about this person has thus been gathered through sources other than the Disclosure of Unusual Transactions Act. In these cases, the 'unusual transactions' of this person – natural or legal – are upgraded to 'suspicious' ones and can be passed on to the police.

Finpol

The intermediary role between financial institutions and law enforcement agencies that is performed in the Netherlands by the Disclosures Office is a role found in several other continental European countries, for example, Belgium and France. In the Netherlands it is not the function of the Disclosures Office to lead the criminal investigation into the disclosed transactions. The Disclosures Office does some investigating prior to the disclosure to Finpol, but its main purpose is to function as a filter of financial information. This limited investigatory function is in line with the impartial and administrative character of the Disclosures Office. If the Office had broad investigatory powers, the distinction between the Office and law enforcement agencies would be a slight and inessential one.

Once the Disclosures Office has established that certain transactions are suspect and has done – limited – further investigation into these transactions, the Office passes on the information to the financial police desk (Finpol) of the Central Investigation and Information Service. Finpol manages the incoming flow of suspect transactions and functions as a coordinating point for the distribution of the information to the various regional police units. Within police circuits it was thought to be important that there be one central unit from which the financial information can be distributed. This unit can, because of its position, keep an oversight over the distribution process as well as develop an expertise in money-laundering methodology.

It occurs on occasions that a financial institution contacts the police directly with a suspicion of money-laundering. These cases are also dealt with by Finpol. Finpol will decide in these instances whether the financial institution should allow the transaction to take place or not. If Finpol advises the financial institution to allow the transaction, the public prosecutors office must guarantee that the financial institution will not in the future risk a criminal prosecution for knowingly being involved in a money-laundering scheme.

Problematic aspects

Privacy

During the implementation of the Disclosure of Unusual Transactions Act the Dutch government acknowledged that the Act interfered with the privacy of individuals whose financial transactions are disclosed. On the other hand, the Dutch government was of the opinion that the Act met the criteria set by Article 8 of the European Convention of Human Rights as interpreted by the European Commission and Court of Human Rights. To limit the intrusion into the privacy of individuals, the Dutch government chose the administrative status and the filtering function of the Disclosures Office. Before financial information falls into the hands of the Dutch police, it must meet certain criteria proscribed by law and operationalized by the Disclosures Office. This system is meant to prevent financial information in relation to individuals about whom no adverse information is known falling into the hands of law enforcement agencies.

The Dutch government was also of the opinion that the separation of data on suspicions from general financial information constitutes part of criminal investigation – a public function – and should not be solely placed into the hands of financial institutions. This is the reason that banks in the Netherlands do not disclose 'suspect transactions' but rather 'unusual transactions', and that the Disclosures Office is meant to be the organization that makes the final selection.

This system depends on the genuineness of the selection done by the Disclosures Office. The incoming data must genuinely be analysed for evidence of criminal origin. If this function is not taken seriously the intermediary position of the Disclosures Office has no real content and the improvement compared to systems of direct disclosure is only symbolic. But if an intermediary organ like the Disclosures Office analyses all incoming data independently from the police and on the basis of that analysis separates out suspect transactions, the intermediary position of such an organ does signify an improvement.

But in the Netherlands, reality does not always live up to theory. Under the first criteria – reasonable suspicion – disclosure arises out of the information that the Disclosures Office has analysed. In such a case, the Disclosures Office must have come to the conclusion – through independent investigation – that the financial transaction is probably linked to a criminal act. Here the final judgement is solely done by the Disclosures Office and the office does indeed function as an intermediary between financial institutions and the law enforcement community.

In our opinion, this genuine intermediary role does not apply in practice to the second ground for release of information by the Disclosures Office, under which a majority of transactions are being transferred to Finpol. When an individual is included in one of the two mentioned registers of the Criminal Intelligence Service and is also involved in an unusual transaction, it automatically follows – in terms of the legislation – that this individual becomes a suspect and that the transaction is a suspect transaction. On this basis, the transaction can be disclosed to the police. In these situations the intermediary function of the Disclosures Office is in our opinion only symbolic. From the moment it has been decided by the Criminal Intelligence

Service to add an individual to one of their registers, the actual consequence is that all unusual transactions by that individual are by definition 'suspect' and are, thus, automatically passed on to the police. In these cases there is no independent assessment done by the Disclosures Office and the selection function of the office is nullified. One might as well have given the police the power to demand from financial institutions the release of all unusual financial transactions in which individuals registered by the Criminal Intelligence Service are involved.

Judicial control

'Rule of law' principles dictate that the use of police powers must always be under the control of the judiciary. Ordinarily it is when the case comes to court that the presiding judge will evaluate whether the criteria for the actions taken by the police were met. If the court considers that they have not been met, the evidence has been obtained unlawfully and cannot be used in a criminal prosecution in the Netherlands. Within the context of the Disclosure of Unusual Transactions Act, financial institutions, the Disclosures Office and the police – especially the Criminal Intelligence Service – all make judgements which can have serious consequences for the individual involved. These judgements are all regulated by law in one way or another. But these general legal rules will have to be interpreted in specific cases. This interpretation is naturally going to be influenced by the interests of the interpreter, for example to minimize the risks that the banker confronts or rather, perceives that s/he confronts. These risks include financial loss and also criminal prosecution and in both the Netherlands and the UK, actual experience of these risks – especially the criminal ones – is very rare and thus 'market knowledge' is highly imperfect. In the abstract, we may hypothesize that a financial institution will be likely to report a transaction when the *expected* risks involved in reporting are smaller than the risks involved in not reporting. However, this is merely a defensive hypothesis, not reflecting any extra 'good citizenship' motivations, including the desire to protect a customer from the risk of expected fraud by getting the police involved in an investigation.

With regard to the Disclosure of Unusual Transactions Act, it is unclear how scrutiny of reasonableness and lack of bias in interpretation is achievable, and what the role of the judiciary might be in this process. What are the consequences of a mistake by the banks? The Act states that the banks will not be liable for damages in civil law. But what are the consequences in a criminal case? What are the consequences if the Disclosures Office discloses information which it is not supposed to? Will this be considered in the Netherlands as illegally obtained evidence and thrown out of the dossier? What if the Criminal Intelligence Service adds an individual to one of their registers which does not meet the relevant criteria? Has the information subsequently disclosed by the Disclosures Office been obtained illegally? These are all questions as to the role of the criminal courts in cases where the line between public and private criminal investigations becomes blurred.

One thing is clear: the Dutch judge confronted with a case which is based, partially or wholly, on evidence received through disclosures by financial institutions must, if necessary, be able to retrace all the steps taken by the financial institutions involved, the Disclosures Office and the police. The judge must be able to scrutinize the decisions of all the parties concerned. This means that the whole process must be accounted for in the dossier. The question remains, what if something went wrong? What if someone made a mistake?

In principle the rule should be that if information which the police received from the Disclosures Office is found to be unjustifiably disclosed, the disclosure loses its legal foundation and the information is illegally obtained. This is most easily said in situations where the police deliberately abuse the system. If, for example, an individual is added to the registers of the Criminal Intelligence Service by the police with the specific intent of receiving financial information from the Disclosures Office, knowing that the criteria for inclusion in such a register are not met, the received information is 'illegally obtained' and may not be used as evidence in a criminal prosecution. The question becomes more problematic in cases where the mistake was made by somebody other than the police, but there seems to be no rational basis for not applying the same principle to them. However, in practice, how is anyone to know that the police deliberately put the person on the register with intent to by-pass the controls? This raises the question of whether adequate scrutiny of police decision-making is likely or even possible in this area. This in turn may relate to how seriously money-laundering is perceived and the sympathy extended to those officers with the task of combating the menace of organized crime: a cultural challenge to the principle of the Rule of Law itself.

The UK system: a contrasting jurisprudence

The approach adopted within the UK was to be relatively unconcerned about fundamental principles but to look pragmatically at how to improve the flow of information to the law enforcement authorities without imposing 'unreasonable' and expensive burdens upon financial institutions (or, for that matter, upon public institutions in the UK's decentralized, cost-conscious policing sector). There was some internal opposition within individual financial institutions to breaches of the principle of customer confidentiality, but by 1991, this had been resolved and industry representatives had chosen a path of cooperation and active involvement in framing legislation and industry guidelines (separate for retail banking, wholesale banking and insurance, and later, stimulated by their obligations under the Money-Laundering Regulations 1993, for lawyers and accountants). Furthermore, staff training was actively promoted in a process that tended to merge with a general trend towards staff training in compliance with financial services regulation. But privacy issues were essentially left to individual institutions and their Money-Laundering Reporting Officers, who had discretion to decide whether or not a transaction was 'suspicious', but who risked being held liable (with a potential imprisonment sentence) should they, having suspected a transaction, not pass on that suspicion if the transaction was proven to be money-laundering. Issues of 'transferred suspicion' became significant, i.e. what happened if a police or customs officer told the banker that s/he was suspicious of a particular account holder and the banker failed to give them information? Or what happened if the bank's Money-Laundering Reporting Officer decided wrongly that a transaction, about which a junior clerk had expressed a suspicion, was *not* money-laundering? Some institutions, partly to save money by not investigating and partly from fear of taking responsibility by *not* reporting onwards the suspicions of their counter staff, screened out few internal reports before passing on the data to the National Criminal Intelligence Service (NCIS); other institutions were more concerned about customer confidentiality (or, to the more cynical, protecting their customer base), and screened out a greater proportion of their internal suspicions.

Unlike the Dutch system, which is premised upon regulating *activities* and covers casinos and safe deposit services, the UK system regulates institutions in different sectors – retail banking, wholesale banking, and investments. The expectations of feedback among Dutch bankers are lower than in the UK, with only formal acknowledgement of the reports in the Netherlands, but much greater agreements to feed back information about results of reports in the UK (viewed negatively by British bankers – see Gold and Levi 1994). As in the UK, disclosure gives Dutch bankers both civil and criminal immunity, except that civil liability exists in the Netherlands where it can be shown that, given all the facts and circumstances, a disclosure should not have been made. Again, how real this risk is is questionable, dependent as it is upon the clarity of guidelines. The Dutch branch is given discretion to decide whether or not to execute a transaction they suspect to be money-laundering, though if they are certain it is the latter, it should not be executed.

The volume of notifications to the Dutch Disclosures Office is greater than in the UK, reflecting the system of reporting *unusual* rather than *suspicious* (or, as we would prefer, *suspected*) transactions. In 1994, there were 23,000 and in 1995, 25,000 notifications (compared with 14,000 and 16,000 respectively in the UK). Between 13 and 15 per cent of Dutch notifications are passed on to the financial investigation units of the police. As in the UK, where Gold and Levi (1994) discovered that less than half a per cent of reported suspicions led to prosecution or to a major impact on an investigation (see also Levi 1995), the measurable yield for the Dutch police is modest, with some 30 cases in 1994 giving rise to new investigations; 900 adding to existing investigations; and the rest simply being put on the data base. However, though this may be a much lower figure than was believed at the outset, it also reflects the problems of re-shaping policing in a finance-oriented way and the inherent limitations of reports as a guide to scarce investigative time.

So in the UK, from an initial expected rate of 250-300 reports per year in 1986, the number of reports rose to 16,000 in 1995. Arguably, what happened next demonstrated the lack of *practical* (as opposed to legal) invasion of privacy rights. NCIS acted as a clearing house, to redistribute reports to the financial investigation units (FIUs) of the individual police forces in the areas where the account-holders lived. However, those underfunded FIUs often did little more than run the name against their central and force intelligence data bases and, if the person was not 'known' already, normally would do nothing further unless the context of the report suggested that something 'clearly criminal' had happened. This is partly a subjective decision. So although the personal financial data were passed on via NCIS to the police and customs without the central screening safeguards in the Dutch system – however illusory some of the screening is – the net effect was not dissimilar. Thus, as the capacity of the UK system to process the reports diminished, the initial proselytizing approach of the police and customs – 'bring us all your suspicions' – became transformed into a plea not to drown the system in defensive reporting – 'bring us the things you *really* think are suspicious' – and for the banks to invest more in filtering. In neither the British nor the Dutch systems, however, was any real guidance given to institutions beyond looking for conduct inconsistent with what the institution knew about their personal and corporate account-holders and for 'smurfing'. Hence, the variation in reports between, at the high scale end, transfers of millions where the banker did not understand what the transfer could be for, and, at the lower end, the reporting of one social security claimant account-holder who deposited £20 in two-penny pieces (which was presumed to be the proceeds of crime)! As with Rule of Law principles generally, the under-resourcing and inefficiency of the State is a poor basis upon which to rest confidence in privacy rights. In the UK, there is no strict limit to the length of time that data on persons who are suspected – rightly or wrongly – of money-laundering can rest in the computer systems of the individual police forces, Customs & Excise, and NCIS: indeed, the police hope that this is one of the ways in which the long-term yield of money-laundering reports can be increased, for example as multiple reports on the same person over time can trigger the use of scarce investigative time to examine the background fully, or as the name makes more sense to police investigators who have received information or have been conducting surveillance. Unlike the Dutch system, there are no criteria strictly applied to regulate the data-keeping activities of the police, nor the information given by financial institutions, provided that the data relate to the exceptions to the Data Protection Act 1984, inter alia information held for the purpose of crime prevention. A similar logic applies to information held by industry associations and State regulators for the purpose of fraud prevention, provided that the Data Protection Registrar can be satisfied that the records apply to persons who are genuinely and reasonably suspected of fraud.[14]

Some enthusiasm has been expressed by hi-tech enforcement personnel for the development of 'neural networks' or other large-scale data-analysing mechanisms for generating suspicion other than by human methods, as a way of filtering the 50 billion non-cash domestic payments in the 15 EU countries plus Norway and Switzerland in 1994. However, such systems – which would not be allowed, for example in Germany, if conducted by the State – may be unlawful under Data Protection laws as well as currently impracticable. The European Banking Federation claims that because electronic payment systems are transaction-oriented, not customer-oriented, it is not possible to build up a customer profile on them, nor is it possible to develop automated indicators of suspicion on SWIFT messages for funds transfer.[15]

Privacy is legally protected in that neither law enforcement authorities nor other persons are permitted to communicate the financial disclosures to persons other than for crime investigation or prevention purposes. Thus, in addition to protection against civil and criminal lawsuits for breach of confidentiality – which are protected in the UK as they are in the Netherlands – it is a criminal offence for anyone to disclose that there has been a financial disclosure to NCIS or that there is a money-laundering investigation. So arguably, though privacy 'rights' – if they exist under these circumstances – have been invaded, no other harm is done unless the suspected account-holder is indeed a money-launderer.

On the assumption that both the Dutch and the UK approaches would be upheld as lawful by the European Court of Human Rights, this chapter illustrates the interaction of different jurisprudential and cultural traditions in countries with high-powered financial institution infrastructures and broadly similar concerns about 'organized crime'. There are similarities, then, with the Anglo-Dutch differences observed in other contexts in this volume, with UK structures demonstrating a relative lack of interest in philosophical fundamentals, and the preponderance of 'order' over 'law' in its preoccupation with a crime control rather than due process orientation. We have demonstrated, however, that even though the Dutch formally may be at the 'due process' end of the regulatory spectrum, the system of money-laundering reporting is structured so as to permit itself to be overridden in practice. Whether this means that in both countries (and, a fortiori, in their dependent territories), bank secrecy is dead is more questionable: one might rather put it as that under normal circumstances, customer confidentiality is preserved, but where institutions, applying their equivalent of the beat police officer's instincts, choose to convey their suspicions to the authorities, not only is there no legal obstacle to their doing so but there are powerful personal and institutional reasons why they *should* do so, especially since they are not prevented from doing the business and thereby satisfying the organization's economic needs. Indeed, inasmuch as the risk-averse prefer not to take responsibility for holding back from the State, contemporary legislation encourages the commercial equivalent of Neighbourhood Watch. In neither case is there a massive observable benefit in crime prevention – though money-laundering prevention is harder to judge, since the data are less valid – but in both cases, people *feel* that something is being done about social problems which concern them. In sum, whatever the longer term prospects for action in response to the considerable amount of private sector money spent on money-laundering detection and reporting, the extensive privacy infringements arguably have occurred for a very modest law enforcement gain. On the other hand, perhaps because of the representations of the *beneficiaries* of 'banking secrecy' as corrupt dictators and drugs traffickers, civil libertarian outcry has been very muted, as it also has been over greater powers of access to the private information of white-collar crime suspects.

Notes

1 In an alternative, cynical version, the end of the Cold War required those parts of the West to create a new threat to justify their bureaucratic role and resources: see, for some varied perspectives, Sterling 1993; Van Duyne 1996; Levi 1997.

2 FATF, established by the Group of 7, Economic Declaration of 16 July 1989.

3 For a good legal history sponsored by the Council of Europe, see Gilmore 1995.

4 See, for an international perspective, Fisse et al. 1992.

5 This *excludes* the subsidiaries of British banks overseas, and excludes the colonies, Crown Dependencies, and UK dependent territories, which are constitutionally separate jurisdictions.

6 In law and theory, the UK Prevention of Terrorism (Temporary Provisions) Act 1989, did allow for prosecution for failure to report suspicions of laundering the proceeds of terrorism: but there were no prosecutions at all under these provisions, not least because it had to be proven that the funds *were* the proceeds of terrorism.

7 ECHR 16 December 1992, Series A, vol. 251-B (*Niemietz v Germany*).

8 After the implementation of the 1995 EU Data Protection Directive, such protection as there is will also apply to manual records.

9 Though computerized charting simply makes a method that was theoretically possible before far less laborious and time consuming, and therefore less expensive and more likely to be used.

10 In Scotland and Northern Ireland legislation exists but differs in its detail.

11 See *R v Cuthbertson* [1981] A.C. 470.

12 It is, however, not clear whether in-house documents relating to internal suspicions of money-laundering are disclosable to civil plaintiffs in the course of civil actions for breach of constructive trust, where banks are civilly liable for frauds of which they are negligent intermediaries: legally, disclosures can be revealed only 'to a constable'.

13 It is important to note that the intention and actual use of these two registers is mainly proactive. The most important individuals and companies in them are those considered by the police to be linked to organized crime. The information in the registers is therefore used mainly to analyse the operation of these organizations.

14 See, for example, the role of the Credit Industry Fraud Avoidance System, discussed by Levi et al. 1991 and subsequently expanded.

15 Personal communication.

References

Audit Commission (1993), *Helping with Enquiries*, London: HMSO.

Duyne, P. van (1994), Estimates in Fog, *Journal of Asset Protection*, 2 (1), pp. 58-76.

Duyne, P. van (1996), The Phantom and Threat of Organised Crime, *Crime, Law and Social Change*, 24 (4), pp. 341-377.

Fisse, B., D. Fraser and G. Coss (eds.) (1992), *The Money Trail*, Sydney: the Law Book Co.

Gilmore, W. (1995), *Dirty Money*, Strasbourg: Council of Europe Press.

Gold, M. and M. Levi (1994), *Money Laundering in the UK: an Appraisal of Suspicious Transaction Reporting*, London: Police Foundation.

Hewson, B. (1993), *The Seizure of Confidential Material*, London: Butterworths.

Levi, M. (1991), *Pecunia non olet*: Cleansing the money-launderers from the Temple, *Crime, Law and Social Change*, 16, pp. 217-302.

Levi, M. (1997), Evaluating the New Policing: Attacking the Money Trail of Organised Crime, *Australian and New Zealand Journal of Criminology*, 30: 1, pp. 1-25.

Levi, M., P. Bissell and T. Richardson (1991), *The Prevention of Cheque and Credit Card Fraud*, Crime Prevention Unit Paper 26, London: Home Office.

Levi, M. and L. Osofsky (1995), *Investigating, seizing and confiscating the proceeds of crime*, Police Research Group Paper 61, London: Home Office.

Maguire, M. and T. John (1995), *Intelligence, Surveillance and Informants: Integrated Approaches*, Crime Detection and Prevention Paper 64, London: Home Office.

Reuter, P. (1983), *Disorganized Crime*, Cambridge, Mass: MIT Press.

Schaap, C. (1995), Dat andere aspect van criminaliteit en criminaliteitsbestrijding, in: A. Hoogenboom, V. Mul, W. van Peski (eds.), *Financieel Rechercheren*, The Hague: VUGA Uitgeverij B.V.

Sterling, C. (1993), *Crime without Frontiers*, London: Little, Brown.

Terlouw, G. and U. Aron (1996), *Twee Jaar MOT*, The Hague: WODC, Gouda Quint.

12 Police intelligence gathering and access to journalists' materials[1]

CHRISJE BRANTS

The core of the first part of this book has been an examination of the significance of the development of proactive policing, defined as secret investigative methods targeted at particular individuals or groups and put into operation before the offence is committed or (at the very least) before there is reasonable suspicion against the target. But this can be seen as part of a broader development in policing: the development of new possibilities for intelligence gathering. One element of this has been the growth of the power of policing agencies to secure information held by third parties unsuspected of criminal activity themselves. One such development has been the rise of police access to journalistic materials. This raises particular and acute problems.

The problem of the protection of journalists and their sources is one that affects any democratic country in which free media are expected to fulfill the role of public watchdog, while at the same time not overstepping the boundaries of criminal law. In all countries, the fundamental dilemmas are the same: the profession of journalism is governed by certain ethics and ideology – of which the public-watchdog-duty to bring the truth into the sphere of public debate forms an integral part – but also by commercial considerations and the professional interest of individual journalists in uncovering facts that will bring the kudos of a scoop. In their professional work they are dependent on sources and on those sources' belief in their integrity, for the source is likewise dependent on the journalist for his or her protection. The criminal justice authorities are also interested in facts, but not necessarily in bringing them into the public domain. Given this common interest in the same information, it is hardly surprising that a certain interdependence may exist between journalist and authorities in matters of crime and criminal justice, or that conflict may arise when interests in what should happen to that information do not run parallel.

However, if the fundamentals of the problem are the same for both the United Kingdom and the Netherlands, there are nevertheless substantial differences in the way in which it manifests itself and is resolved. In both countries the public interest in the free flow of information is weighed against the interests of justice, but the outcome of this balancing act seems to differ considerably. Indeed, while originally in the Netherlands journalists were, at least at law, worse off than their British counterparts, the situation seems now to have reversed. Dutch courts are increasingly recognizing a public interest exception or defence for journalists if they seek to protect their sources when called to testify in court, or their material against confiscation for the purpose of criminal investigations, or even if they themselves have committed a criminal offence in obtaining information (although this latter point is as yet not entirely clear). In Britain the interests of justice – defined very much as the interests of investigation and successful prosecution – are inclined to outweigh the interests involved in the exercise of freedom of expression.

These differences reflect fundamental differences in the situation in both countries: in criminal policy and the ideology that surrounds it, in the organization, role and self-image of the media and in the legal system itself. To start with the latter, it should be noted that Dutch courts have integrated the European Court's decision in *Goodwin* into their standard reasoning when faced with decisions on the protection of journalists' sources.[2] One of the more surprising aspects of *Goodwin* is that very little importance is attached to the fact that the source had obtained his information illegally. So too in the Netherlands the way in which information is obtained is apparently of minor significance in the face of an undertaking by a journalist to protect the source's identity. In the United Kingdom, where at present unlawful behaviour with regard to obtaining or disseminating information seems to outweigh other factors and where Strasbourg case law cannot be invoked directly, it remains to be seen whether *Goodwin* will have the same impact.

Again in the United Kingdom, the reliability and probative value of evidence is a major factor in decisions on whether or not to allow it in court. In the Netherlands, unlawful conduct on the part of the criminal justice authorities – i.e. actions not based on any legal provision or flagrantly at odds with due criminal procedure – may suffice to exclude evidence, however reliable. In common law countries such as England and Wales moreover, the rule of law in the continental sense that places the police on a different footing from the citizen with regard to investigative powers – in the sense that these do not exist unless explicitly provided for in law – does not apply. Neither are there entrenched constitutional notions of citizens' rights to privacy. The effect of this is the gathering of information by the police stands at the same level as fact-finding by journalists and both can be weighed on the same scale.

With regard to criminal policy and ideology, in Great Britain greater reliance is placed on criminal law in dealing with social problems than in the Netherlands. On the other hand, organized crime has yet to figure on the public agenda in the way it does in the Netherlands and the notion of proactive policing as being a means of pure intelligence gathering rather than a step on the road to prosecution – as the visible and politically necessary maintenance of law and order – has not yet taken hold. Except, that is, in the field of terrorism and the activities of specialized police forces and military intelligence. Thus, it is noteworthy that some of the most important cases in Britain concerning the media also concern terrorism and the Prevention of Terrorism Act, while in the Netherlands they are often part of large and complex criminal cases against organized criminals.

The Netherlands have in a way been fortunate in having the excesses of proactive policing exposed during the Van Traa hearings, where the role of the media was also discussed at some length. However much journalists might have got themselves involved in dealings with organized criminals, it is also evident that a great deal of police misconduct would not have been exposed without the help of investigative journalism. Historically, the criminal justice authorities have enjoyed the cooperation of journalists, which reflects in general the more consensual nature of Dutch society and the somewhat misplaced trust – as it now turns out – in the lasting commitment of those authorities to legitimate justice. In the wake of Van Traa, courts may well be inclined to regard the activities of investigative journalism more benignly, especially since journalists themselves can be seen to be taking the professional problems it poses seriously.

In the United Kingdom, there is, traditionally, much less faith in the good intentions of the state. The press is continually at odds with the government on any number of issues – ranging from tabloid coverage of the royal family to attempts by serious broadsheets and broadcasting companies to expose government misconduct (including activities of the police and military intelligence services). Unlike the Dutch media, British journalists have always considered themselves a thorn in the side of authority and have paid more than lip service to this role. But in this they are often regarded by both judges and juries more as serving their own professional and commercial interests than the interests of democracy. And notwithstanding a substantial number of spectacular miscarriages of justice, no general press disavowal of the police and the methods they use has occurred. Investigative journalists have not played the complex mediating role between organized crime, proactive policing and the public sphere that they have in the Netherlands. Journalists have been generally accepting of police claims for the crime control value of proactive methods especially as they have been directed at the traditional villainy of street-crime. They have not generally been at the forefront in exposing dubious police proactive practice by their own investigations, tending to derive stories from court cases where informers and undercover operations have gone wrong[3] and new legislative developments, especially the Security Services Act 1996 and the Police Bill 1997. But then the proactive wheels do not seem to have come off so spectacularly as they have in the Netherlands. Generally, the fight against crime and against terrorism is still seen much in terms of the end justifying the means, and figures in this way on the agenda of both major political parties.

Finally, it should be noted that in some ways the media situation in the Netherlands is coming to resemble that of the United Kingdom: professionalism and commercialism, and in their wake an increased interest in crime-reporting and the rise of specialized investigative journalists, are very much features of the Dutch media now. Journalists too seem both more aware of their duty as public watchdogs and have more opportunities for acting as such. The clash of interests however that comes with that role, occurs in a very different social and legal situation. It will be interesting to see whether these differences will continue to be as stark as they now sometimes appear.

The two chapters that follow reflect the varying breadth of interaction between journalism and proactive policing: the chapter on the UK by Ruth Costigan focuses on journalistic materials as a potential resource for police intelligence while Chrisje Brants discusses more widely the complex interactions between journalism and secret police operations in the Netherlands.

Notes

1 Editors' note: this short chapter forms a comparative introduction to the more detailed chapters (on the Netherlands and the United Kingdom) that follow.
2 *Goodwin v United Kingdom*, ECHR 27 March 1996, Judgement nr. 16/1994/463/544.
3 See national newspapers 15-20 September 1994 for coverage of the Colin Stagg case and D. Graves and N. Darbyshire, Storm over killer lured into Britain, *Daily Telegraph* 14 September 1995. For a more representative (uncritical) look see D. Rose (1995), Eagle eyes home in on city streets, *Observer*, 29 November.

13 Journalists and the protection of sources of information in the Netherlands

CHRISJE BRANTS

Introduction

As is to be expected, the increasing concern in the Netherlands in recent years about the rise of organized crime and the development of proactive methods of policing as a means of dealing with it, has been reflected in the media in a number of ways. The events that gave rise to the parliamentary inquiry conducted by the so-called Van Traa commission also prompted a marked increase in investigative journalism specifically directed towards both organized crime and the criminal justice authorities. Indications of the existence of organized criminal groups with sometimes colourful personalities in leading positions, police activities such as controlled deliveries that have brought large quantities of drugs into the country to be sold on the 'open market', deals with criminal informers that have allowed them to keep the proceeds of controlled deliveries, the secret financing of further undercover and proactive police work from money obtained through controlled drug transactions, corruption, crooked lawyers, incompetence and power-struggles within the police and prosecution service, these are the things that good stories and scoops are made of.

In that sense, media profit and journalistic prestige have been important factors in changing the nature of crime reporting in the Netherlands. But at the same time, proactive policing and all of the problems of democratic control of the police and criminal justice authorities it involves, have enhanced the role of the media as a democratic watchdog. It is a role that, until recently, sat ill with traditional journalistic structures and perceptions in the Netherlands. Perhaps nowhere, at least in Western Europe, has there existed such a symbiotic relationship between the press and the criminal justice authorities – the traditional sources of information on crime and related matters – as in the Netherlands (see for a detailed account: Brants

1993). It has been characterized by a lack of critical attitude towards the information that these authoritative sources provide, by an inclination to self-censorship and to identification with what the state considers appropriate reactions to crime and information fit to be published. If non-Dutch readers find this hard to swallow, it should not be forgotten that faith in (the good and democratic intentions of) state institutions in general has traditionally been a peculiar feature of Dutch society in general and the criminal justice system in particular.

The more cynical form of investigative journalism that has now developed has, of course, much to do with a breakdown in traditional media structures (among other things the coming of cable broadcasting and increasing commercialism), but there are other factors at work too. On the one hand, the criminal justice authorities have not been averse to using journalists to further their own interests. In the course of increasingly bitter struggles between police departments and between the police and the prosecution service, the leaking of information to the press has proved a useful, if not always completely reliable, instrument. Again, as the fight against organized crime as viewed from the police point of view became a war of information and disinformation, media-leaks about certain criminal organizations have been part and parcel of police tactics. On the other hand there has been the growing realization among journalists that there is more information to be had about policing than that which the police themselves are willing to provide.

The advent of proactive policing and the development of investigative journalism have made the problem of the protection of journalistic sources particularly pertinent. It is in the nature of proactive and/or undercover investigations that certain activities be kept secret and it is in the nature of investigative journalism to uncover secrets. The sources upon which journalists must rely if they wish to reveal the type of secret information involved in proactive police work, are most likely to have a very special interest in a guarantee of anonymity. For they will usually be either involved in the criminal activities that are the target of police investigations, or belong to the criminal justice authorities themselves (the police, the public prosecution service) and therefore be committing at the very least a breach of discipline by passing on information to the media. Information provided by the source will therefore often be illegal information, either because of the means by which the journalist or the source obtained it, or because the source or the journalist may be committing an offence in passing it on or publishing it. It is evident that in such cases the interests of the source and the journalist in guaranteeing the anonymity of sources of information, and of the authorities in knowing them, will clash violently. In the final event, the journalist may be called as a witness in a (criminal) case and the decision will be made in court, where a particularly difficult balancing act is required to determine which interest shall prevail.[1]

An extra complication

It is equally evident that the same balancing act, sometimes even more precarious, is needed if journalists themselves are prosecuted for receiving or passing on illegally obtained secret information. The matter of protecting sources is secondary here (often, the journalist will not know the source or be at pains not to find out), and within the scope of this chapter I can do no more than point to the obvious parallels. The whole issue of the protection of sources arises because journalists may need to guarantee protection in order to do their job. In matters of proactive policing, an extra complication arises as the journalist will need to become increasingly involved in cultivating vulnerable sources in the circles of the criminal justice authorities and the criminal organizations they are targeting, who may only be able to pass on information by illegal means. If, as has been the case, illegal methods of criminal investigation have been widely used, the public has a right to know. The police and prosecution service have their own, sometimes legitimate interests in keeping such information secret: it may reveal that evidence in a specific case has been illegally obtained and should be excluded, or it may endanger methods of investigation or individuals such as informers or undercover agents. However, disclosure to the defence in such cases has been increasingly limited in the Netherlands. Indeed, it has proved singularly difficult for both defence lawyers and courts to discover how evidence in specific cases was obtained and therefore to examine whether it is reliable and/or accurate. The chances therefore of such information coming out at trial and playing some role in the public debate, are small. It is here that the journalist may have a special role to play in exposing such matters in the interests of fair trial and justice in general, but this then might well involve deciding whether publication warrants overstepping the boundaries of the criminal law. There may be a pressing public interest in publication, but when is it sufficient to justify a criminal offence?

Recent cases in the Netherlands in which journalists have been prosecuted, have involved serious offences, with information (documents or floppy discs) being stolen from the police by criminal organizations and passed on to journalists (and from them sometimes on to defence lawyers) and published. Not only is the original theft a crime,[2] under Dutch law, the

Criminal Code (Article 139e) also forbids having in one's possession objects (e.g. floppy discs or tapes) containing information that has been illegally copied, making such information public or passing it on. By simply possessing a floppy or tape with illegally copied information or passing it on to someone else (e.g. a lawyer), or by having stolen documents in one's possession or using them in some other way (even if publishing the information they contain does not constitute the offence of receiving) journalists may lay themselves open to a criminal charge in the exercise of their professional duties. As yet, existing criteria provide no certain answers for the journalist faced with this dilemma.[3] We must wait for a body of case law to emerge, that will deal with what looks like becoming an increasingly frequent problem – just as, very gradually, the questions surrounding the protection of sources were answered.

The balancing act

There are several situations in which the problem of protecting journalistic sources may arise. First, journalists may be required by law to testify in court (or during a criminal investigation by an investigating magistrate – the so-called judge of instruction) as to the identity of their sources or as to the nature of unpublished material that would reveal the identity. Second, journalists may also be required to produce documents which would reveal the identity of a source, or these may be confiscated in criminal proceedings. Besides documents, other material that contains information relevant to a criminal investigation may be demanded or confiscated (e.g. unbroadcast film or video, or unpublished photos). Third, the criminal justice authorities may request information on telecommunication from telephone companies, or require access to computerized data that would reveal the identity of a source. Before turning to the way in which the courts now deal with these problems, we must examine the competing interests involved in the protection of sources, and the means evolved in Dutch law of dealing with the dilemmas they pose.

An undertaking by a journalist to protect the source is often necessary to obtain information: without a guarantee of protection, information in a specific case may be impossible to obtain, and eventually sources of information may dry up altogether. This is a distinct professional interest, but it corresponds to and is inseparable from fundamental interests of a democratic society: the free-flow of information, guaranteed by the right to free expression on the one hand, and the right of the public to be properly informed on the other. However, that same democratic society must also be able to rely on the accuracy of the outcome of (criminal) cases in court, so that the interests of justice require that a court of law must be in a position to establish the truth. Such interests may be private: a person seeking to pursue a private claim may need information that a journalist wishes to protect. But they may also be public.

The information the journalist seeks to conceal may be necessary in order to arrive at the truth in a criminal case: the source may be a suspect or have information on a suspect or journalistic material may reveal other information relevant to a criminal offence or future criminal offences. And finally, the journalist may possess information that exposes misconduct on the part of the criminal justice authorities (especially the police) that would, were it to become known, lead to exclusion of evidence that has been illegally obtained or at the very least cast doubt on the reliability and/or accuracy of the prosecution case. Interests of due process therefore also require that a journalist be in the position to obtain the necessary information from sources that may need protection. The more confidential, controversial or damaging to third parties (including the state) the information, the greater the pressure on the journalist by the source to guarantee anonymity. And the greater the public interest in receiving information, the greater the social interest in protecting the source.

The European Convention on Human Rights and Fundamental Freedoms

The freedom of expression is guaranteed by Article 10 of the European Convention on Human Rights and Fundamental Freedoms. It forms an integral part of Dutch law and can be invoked directly in court as a source of enforceable rights and, when applicable, can set Dutch law aside. Dutch citizens, like those of the other signatories to the Convention, also have the right to put their case before the European Court of Human Rights if they consider that their rights under the Convention have been infringed. Article 10.2 of the European Convention allows restrictions on the freedom of expression, but only if they are necessary in a democratic society and have a basis in law (which means that they must be foreseeable and sufficiently specific). The European Court has repeatedly stressed that the freedom of expression is fundamental to democratic societies and that it includes the right to express facts and opinions that are shocking, displeasing or inopportune. There is therefore a fundamental right to receive and impart information on the one hand, and to be properly informed on the other.

An obligation on journalists to name sources restricts these rights. The European Court's interpretation of when restrictions of the freedom of expression are necessary in a democratic society, is in itself restrictive. States have a margin of appreciation, but in considering the freedom to express political criticism or to provide information within the framework of a public debate on important or controversial matters, the European Court is inclined towards a 'European standard' in which 'exceptions must be narrowly interpreted and the necessity for any restrictions must be convincingly established'.[4] The most recent case under the European Convention is that of *Goodwin v United Kingdom*.[5] It concerns a complaint by a British journalist that a disclosure order to reveal the identity of his source in a private law suit (brought by a corporation in connection with imminent publication of a stolen document) interfered unjustifiably with the freedom of expression as guaranteed by Article 10 of the European Convention. It has a direct bearing on our problem because of the reasoning applied both by the English House of Lords and the European Court.

An appeal by the journalist was dismissed by the House of Lords. It reasoned that, under English law, disclosure may be ordered if the interests involved are one of four matters of public concern: interests of justice, national security, prevention of disorder or prevention of crime – in this case the interests of justice. Decisive factors in determining which interest shall prevail (justice or journalistic freedom) are: the nature of the information – the greater the public interest, the more important the protection of sources (e.g. revealing corruption); the manner in which the information was obtained – if legitimately, then the greater the importance of protecting the source, whereas if obtained illegally this would reduce the importance of protecting the source, to be outweighed only by a clear public interest in publication (e.g. exposure of iniquity). In this case the source's complicity in illegally obtaining information diminished the importance of protection and was held to be outweighed by the interests of the company in identification.

The European Court however, reasoned as follows: 'protection of journalistic sources is one of the basic conditions for press freedom, as is reflected in the laws and professional codes of conduct in a number of contracting states and is affirmed in several international instruments on journalistic freedoms ... Without such protection, sources may be deterred from assisting the press in informing the public on matters of public interest. As a result the vital public watch-dog role of the press may be undermined and the ability of the press to provide accurate and reliable information may be adversely affected. Having regard to the importance of the protection of journalistic sources for press freedom in a democratic society and the potentially chilling effect an order of source disclosure has on the exercise of that freedom, such a measure cannot be compatible with Article 10 of the Convention unless it is justified by an overriding requirement in the public interest.' The important issue is therefore whether any restrictions to the freedom of expression, and an order to disclose sources is such a restriction, can be said to be necessary in the interests of democratic society. Conceding that national authorities still possess a margin of appreciation when it comes to determining what the public interest is in a specific case, the Court goes on to say that the interest of a democratic society in ensuring and maintaining a free press weighs heavily indeed in determining whether restrictions are proportionate to the legitimate aim pursued. It found that, in this case, they were not.

Dutch law on testimony and confiscation of material

Despite the incorporation of the European Convention and despite the fact that the Netherlands is obliged to bring its laws into accordance with the Convention's provisions, as far as the protection of journalistic sources is concerned, Dutch law proceeds from the opposite starting point. The Convention assumes the protection of sources, unless this is outweighed by other interests. Dutch (case) law offers no protection, unless exceptional circumstances so require. Journalists in the Netherlands are in exactly the same position as any other citizen: the Criminal Code makes refusing to appear as a witness or, if the witness does appear, refusal to testify a criminal offence (with stiffer penalties if the case concerned is a criminal one), while the Code of Criminal Procedure allows a court, if urgent interests of investigation so require, to imprison a reluctant witness in order to force him to speak.[6]

Articles 217 and 218 of the Code of Criminal Procedure provide immunity from testifying for certain categories of witnesses: members of family and those who are bound to secrecy by reason of their profession (traditionally, the doctor and the priest, but of late also the tax inspector). These original categories now also include those who have a functional duty to secrecy deriving from the nature of their profession: e.g. the lawyer, notary public, legal aid worker and sometimes the social worker or probation officer. Here the duty to speak as a witness in order to further the cause of justice (defined here as truth-finding by the court) is outweighed by the public interest that everyone must be able to seek confidential help and to rely on confidentiality. An important argument here is that such professions usually have a code of ethics and a disciplinary body and that therefore the necessary weighing of interests can be left to the profession itself. Journalists do not come into this category.

The law seems to preclude immunity for journalists. Until 1977 this was also the position in case law.[7] However, in 1977, the Supreme Court ruled that '... although *in general* it cannot be said that journalists enjoy immunity from testifying, the interests of truth-finding by a court to protect private interests of those damaged by publication who need to know the identity of the source of information to claim compensation, must be weighed against the protection of journalistic sources in order to safeguard the ensured and continued publication of matters of public interest, which depends, among other things, on confidential sources being assured of protection.'[8] The principle of non-immunity remained, but here there was an opening where previously there was none.

In later cases, the circumstances in which journalists would be allowed to protect their sources were gradually established. The granting of immunity from testifying depends on: the nature of the public interest in publication, which in its turn depends on the nature of publicised facts (e.g.: information leading to the exposure of government corruption will carry greater weight than a tip providing sensational photo of bank robbery); whether protection of sources makes publication in itself possible, that is whether the public would not be informed if the source could not be protected, or whether publication simply serves to allow commercial interests of media to prevail; and whether hearing the journalist is a reasonable means of obtaining information for the criminal justice authorities.[9] That there is no automatic immunity for journalists was again established in 1989, when a journalist published an article naming a certain Bengali woman N in connection with intimidation and threats to Bengali workers in the Netherlands. N filed a suit for damages against the newspaper and the anonymous source. The former was granted, but the damages suit against the workers depended on the journalist revealing the names of his sources. He refused, because this would endanger them. The court ruled that the plaintiff's interest in the identity of the source was overridden by necessity: the safety of the source being more important than the need to know their identity.[10]

With regard to confiscating documents and material, Dutch courts take the same position as with regards to testimony: no immunity, unless there are exceptional circumstances. In a case in which a demonstration had become violent, a TV company fought a confiscation order placed by the prosecution service on its uncut video material, arguing that the public function of the journalist in passing on important information of public interest would be severely curtailed (demonstrators would refuse to allow journalists to be present if the confiscation of their material was a possibility). The court considered confiscation justified: there were no other means of identifying the perpetrators of these public order offences, while confiscation was a reasonable measure in the light of the seriousness of the disturbance.[11]

Telecommunications data and access to computerized data

One is inclined to think of journalistic material as being written text, film or photos. Journalists, however, not only make frequent use of the telephone as a means of obtaining information, they also use computers to write articles and store data. Obviously, telephone conversations in which confidential information is passed, or computer files on which that information is stored, may be of great interest to the criminal justice authorities. As to what is said on the telephone, the rules on telephone tapping apply. But it may be equally interesting to know with whom a journalist has spoken, when and for how long, and the new technology that telephone services use for reasons of efficient administration and billing provides just such information. And again, while some professionals are protected against search and seizure of electronic data, this does not apply to the journalist.

The Dutch telephone service keeps specified data (date, number, length of conversation etcetera) for 120 days and then destroys them; information on ex-directory numbers is never provided. There are two ways in which it may be procured. An investigating magistrate may demand such data in the course of a criminal investigation, if a suspect is thought to have been a party to a telephone conversation.[12] Under the Registration of Personal Data Act, the telephone company may hand over such data after it has weighed the interests involved. According to the telephone company, this weighing of interests will often be impossible in cases of criminal investigations, because the necessary information will be too confidential and therefore not forthcoming from the police or prosecution service. However, such a case did arise in the Netherlands. Although a journalist had refused to name his source when asked to do so by the investigating magistrate, the public prosecutor had subsequently discovered it by requiring and receiving information from the telephone company on telephone conversations between the journalist (at home and at work) and his source. The prosecutor's action was thought to be justified, because the journalist himself had taken insufficient steps to guarantee anonymity (for example by arranging for phone calls on public telephones).[13] As far as access to computerized data is concerned, Articles 125-125n of the Code of Criminal Procedure provide for access during a criminal investigation, subject to a warrant from the investigating magistrate. There is an exception for data held by those with an immunity from testifying under Article 218 of the Code of Criminal Procedure for reasons of a professional obligation to secrecy. The journalist, as we have seen, is not among them.

Recent developments

A Bill of law is currently being debated in the Netherlands which proposes to bring Dutch law into line with the European Convention on Human Rights. It is based on the principle that journalists have a right to protect their sources and to refuse to testify as to their identity, and it seeks to prevent the confiscation of documents, uncut film or video and computerized data that would reveal the identity of a source; requests for telecommunications data on journalists would be governed by the same rules as now apply to those with a professional obligation to secrecy. The Bill distinguishes between civil and criminal law: in civil cases immunity is to be absolute, in criminal cases it may be overridden by 'important social interests'. 'No, unless ...' will become 'Yes, unless ...' It is doubtful whether this Bill, currently in the final stages of parliamentary procedure, will actually be passed. The Dutch Council of State has serious objections. One being that, although the principle complies with the requirements of the European Convention, there are no indications as to how these 'important social interests' are to be established, nor as to what the position is if information has been illegally obtained. As we have seen, in the light of the current developments in proactive policing, it is the latter that has become particularly urgent in the Netherlands.

Moreover, the Bill now seems no longer necessary since it has recently been overtaken by the case law of the Supreme Court of the Netherlands, which – following the European Court in *Goodwin* – has finally recognized the principle of the protection of sources.[14] The same case provides some indication of what will happen if the source has committed an offence in passing on information. In 1994, journalists were present when the police searched the home of a former mayor suspected of corruption. Contrary to disciplinary rules, they had been tipped off that the search was imminent by someone within the prosecution service. The mayor subpoenaed the journalists in civil proceedings, in an attempt to discover the source against whom he wished to initiate a damages suit. The journalists refused to testify and their refusal has now been recognized as legitimate by the Supreme Court: the public interest in the media being able to bring the misconduct of public officials to the attention of the general public – which may require that journalists protect the identity of their sources – outweighed the interests of the plaintiff in having the source named. In this case there were indications of serious structural misconduct by the mayor, about which the state had been unable to provide clarity within a reasonable time; the fact that the source had acted contrary to disciplinary rules was not regarded as decisive.

Conclusion

Certainly since the latest decision by the Supreme Court, there is great similarity in the criteria applied in both the case law of the Dutch courts and of the European Court as far as the protection of journalistic sources is concerned, even if the basic starting point in Dutch law is very different. The problems that have arisen as a result of proactive policing in the Netherlands suggest even more strongly that there is a case to be made for the protection of journalistic sources and possibly for the protection of journalists themselves against prosecution if their aim is to further the interests of democratic justice, regardless of the offence with which they are charged. Publication by a journalist of illegally obtained material could be justified if we assume, as surely we must, that it is unacceptable under the rule of law that the police should use illegal methods and so at the very least lay themselves open to the charge of subverting the course of justice. The exposure of police misconduct by the media, the necessity of using secret information from vulnerable sources who require a guarantee of anonymity if they are to continue to provide it, the fact that such information will often, by its very nature be illegally obtained, are all factors that could be decisive in regarding publication of such material as of greater public interest than forcing journalists to reveal a source or even prosecuting reporters themselves – shooting the messenger (De Roos 1995).

Restricting journalists to the point of making it impossible for them to obtain and pass on information in such a situation cannot be in the public interest or, more narrowly, the interests of justice. They need to be able to protect both their sources and their means of communication, and to raise a public interest defence against prosecution if their legitimate aim is to impart information that would otherwise not be available on matters of serious public concern, although the latter is infinitely more complicated when it comes to striking the correct balance. However, there is another side to the coin. Scoops and stories about problems in the police force and about organized crime are likely to be sensational, so that the journalist's professional interest in his scoop will be inextricably linked to the public interest and even more difficult to disentangle than usual. There is a lot of money involved in a good story and even more financial potential in contacts with criminal organizations, while disinformation tactics are part and parcel of proactive investigations on the part of both investigators and investigated. There is also growing evidence that journalists themselves in the Netherlands have not always managed to keep their hands clean and have allowed themselves to be used both by the police and by criminal organizations in the sense that the source has not only provided information but also determined how it is to be used.[15]

There is also a well-nigh insolvable dilemma if journalists are to assume a task of 'policing society': who is to police the journalist? One of the main arguments in the Netherlands for allowing certain categories of professionals immunity from testimony (and, in the case of doctors, a defence of justification in medical matters such as euthanasia) has always been that the members of these professions must belong to a professional society, that has a code of ethics and can conduct its own disciplinary proceedings. The Dutch Association of Journalists has always regarded obligatory membership in itself as contrary to the freedom of expression – an argument of principle that is very difficult to refute, although it hardly absolves the journalist absolutely from the responsibility of continually assessing the ethical limits of professional conduct.[16] Dutch journalists adhere to a voluntary code of ethics that has come under growing pressure as commercial concerns increase and investigative journalism leads journalists on an ever more urgent search for new sources of information. The profession's own disciplinary body, the Council for Journalism, also operates on a voluntary basis. Its decisions do carry moral weight, but are not enforceable. It recently attempted to formulate criteria for journalists who find themselves in possession of illegally obtained information, but it will not be easy to find a means of internal discipline that is effective.[17] This leaves the decision on recognizing the protection of sources and material and, if necessary, on a public interest defence, in the hands of a court of law. Which is perhaps where it should be, considering the gravity of the interests that are at stake.

Notes

1 Although I will be concentrating on criminal cases and investigations, it will be impossible to leave civil law (in the Continental European sense of the law that governs private law suits) out of the picture. Even if the underlying problems have arisen in a criminal case, the actual decision on the protection of sources may have to be made by a civil court. Much Dutch case law is, therefore, not part of criminal law but of civil law.

2 Although prevailing opinion holds that such actions do not constitute receiving or using or passing on stolen goods because the articles governing receiving and or fencing apply to material goods only, and not to information (see De Roos 1996).

3 Until now, courts in Holland have been quite clear about public interest exceptions if journalists commit offences: there are none. See e.g. HR 27 June 1995, NJ 1995, 711 (journalist attempts to obtain driving license under false pretences in order to expose negligence of the authorities). Recently, the District Court of Amsterdam acquitted a journalist accused of violating Article 139e Criminal Code, but failed to fully address the fundamental problems or to establish the scope of a public interest exception (District Court Amsterdam 2 January 1996, *Mediaforum* 8 (1996) 2, p. B30-B35).

4 ECHR 23 October 1994, Series A, vol. 298 (*Jerslid v Denmark*); see also ECHR 23 May 1991, Series A, vol. 204 (*Oberschlick v Austria*).

5 ECHR 27 March 1996, Judgement nr. 16/1994/463/544.

6 Articles 192 and 444 CC and Article 289 CCP: the imprisonment order may last for 30 days. An investigating magistrate may order imprisonment for 12 days (Article 223 CCP). The word used here is 'gijzeling', which literally means 'holding hostage'. In 1979, in a civil case concerning journalists, the Supreme Court decided that 'coercive payment – so much for every day that a witness persists – may also be imposed in order to force the witness to speak, in this case to reveal their sources of information' (HR 18 May 1979, NJ 1980, 213).

7 The principle that journalists have no right to immunity from testifying was established by the Supreme Court of the Netherlands in 1949, when a journalist refused to name the source of secret information concerning Dutch decolonisation politics in Indonesia (Lingadjatti decision: HR 14 December 1949, NJ 1949, 95). As late as 1975, a district court dismissed as irrelevant a journalist's claim that he could only exercise his profession if verification of information is possible and that this often includes confidential information from other sources to be used as unpublished background information; if he were to be forced to reveal this, these sources would dry up (District Court Alkmaar 27 May 1975, NJ 1977, 200).

8 HR 11 November 1977, NJ 1979, 399.

9   District Court Zwolle 4 March 1985, NJ 1985, 490: a journalist had published photographs of, and was therefore apparently an eye-witness to, the 'liberation' of chincillas by animal rights activists. The investigating magistrate allowed him the privilege of refusing to name members of the movement, a decision against which the prosecution appealed. The court ruled that, although there may be exceptions to the duty of a journalist to testify, this was not one of them.

10 Appeals Court Amsterdam 16 February 1989, NJ 1990, 533.

11 HR 19 February 1991, NJ 1992, 50.

12 Article 125f Code of Criminal Procedure.

13 This approximates the type of reasoning by US courts in similar cases. See Korthals Altes 1995.

14 HR 10 May 1996, RvdW 1996, 112.

15 See the final report by the four criminologists who researched the extent and nature of organized crime for the Van Traa commission. They identify a number of situations which point to a serious potential for investigative journalism to go off the rails in this sense.

16 For this reason it is divided on the issue of allowing journalists a right to protect their sources: some feel that such a right would necessarily involve obligatory membership.

17 Decision of 24 November 1995, see De Roos 1996.

References

Brants, C. (1993), Justice Done and Seen to be Done? The institutionalized relationship between the press and the criminal justice system in the Netherlands, *International Criminal Justice Review*, 3, pp. 60-76.

Korthals Altes, Willem F. (1995), De Telegraaf en de telefoongegevens, *Mediaforum*, 7, 5, pp. 60-62.

Roos, Theo de (1995), Journalist, strafrecht en algemeen belang, *Mediaforum*, 7, 5, pp. 56-59.

Roos, Theo de (1996), De zaken Salverda en De Vries: principiële uitspraken over informatie-heling, *Mediaforum* 8, 2, p. 24.

14 Journalistic material in the UK criminal process

RUTH COSTIGAN

Introduction

The use of journalistic information, particularly photographic and film material, in the investigation and prosecution of offences is a relatively new but increasingly important issue. This usage both reflects and engenders changes in the criminal justice system on a number of levels from the gathering of potential evidence through to its actual presentation at a criminal trial, and may even affect post-trial considerations (such as parole in the case of those incarcerated for (filmed) violent offences). At the core of these developments is police exploitation of new technology: once film is regarded by the police as a useful resource in the detection and prosecution of offences then it is inevitable that camera surveillance will increase, that journalists will be routinely approached for their material and that film will become a common item of evidence in court.

The seizure of journalistic information is a logical consequence of a proactive policing agenda: a broadcast or published item might bring (potential) crimes to the notice of the police for the first time; in many instances, journalists will have conducted their own investigation; and journalists will often have access to sources more elusive to the police who might otherwise have to deploy undercover detectives or involve MI5 to obtain intelligence. Journalistic information enables police to bolster intelligence files and, if in the form of film, provides a particularly powerful source of evidence. The courts, in recognition of the value of journalistic material in the criminal process, have facilitated police access to it and have smoothed the path of admissibility and use of film so that the law is exploiting the powerful medium of film to be the detective's partner, the advocate's junior, the jury's mentor.

Although the police in the UK are increasingly looking to journalists to provide them with information to be used both as intelligence and as evidence, there are few reported cases. Police requests for material are arguably more likely to enter the legal process when presented to large news organizations and national newspapers, whilst local media (more dependant upon the police) might be under greater pressure to deal with the matter at an informal level. Furthermore, the scope for challenging an order to seize journalistic material is limited: the recipient of the order must challenge by way of judicial review, so only the legality and not the merits of the decision to grant the order is reviewable. Before reviewing cases in which the acquisition of journalistic material was challenged, it is necessary to examine the provisions in the Police and Criminal Evidence Act 1984[1] (hereinafter PACE) governing seizure of such information.

The law relating to seizure[2]

At common law, there existed no general power to seek warrants authorizing searches for evidence and the specific powers would not have been applicable to journalists who were not themselves suspected of criminal conduct. Journalists did not, however, enjoy immunity from search and seizure powers and the decision in *Ghani v Jones*[3] rendered their material more vulnerable to confiscation. Lord Denning stated in *Ghani* that if the police held a reasonable belief that a serious offence had been committed, then they had the power to seize from premises anything reasonably believed to be material evidence. There was no general power to enter premises but if police were on journalists' premises by consent, then material was potentially open to confiscation under *Ghani*. The power of seizure was exercisable even though the journalist was not herself suspected of criminal activity: Lord Denning significantly extended common law powers of seizure by declaring that an unreasonable refusal to provide the police with items that they considered to have evidential value could justify confiscation. It is clear from Lord Denning's judgement that 'unreasonable refusal' would be easily satisfied for the purposes of a search under *Ghani*.

When entry, search and seizure powers were rationalized and extended under PACE, a special regime was created to afford sensitive material enhanced protection from police seizure. Protected information was organized hierarchically: that which has a claim to legal professional privilege,[4] 'excluded material',[5] and 'special procedure material'. Although journalists generally opposed distinct treatment on principled and pragmatic grounds,[6] journalistic information was designated special procedure material.[7] 'Journalistic material' was unhelpfully defined in section 13(1) as 'material acquired or created for the purposes of journalism'. This definition extends to information received from a person who intends it to be used for the purposes of journalism. Material will only remain 'journalistic' for so long as it is possessed by a person who acquired or created it for the purposes of journalism; thus, once information has been passed to a non-journalist it ceases to be protected under the special procedure provisions.

The police may seek access to special procedure material either by means of a production order[8] or a search warrant, but the present discussion is confined to production orders since there are to date no reported cases involving acquisition of journalistic material by the more difficult route of a PACE search warrant.

The PACE provisions governing police seizure of protected material are contained in section 9 and Schedule 1. Before a production order can be granted, a circuit judge must be satisfied that one of the two sets of access conditions detailed in the Schedule is fulfilled. The first set of access conditions will be met if there are reasonable grounds for believing: that a serious arrestable offence has been committed, that there is special procedure material on the premises specified in the application, that the material is likely to be of substantial value to the police investigation and that it is likely to be relevant evidence. The police must show further that other methods of obtaining the material have been tried without success or have not been attempted because they would, in the view of the police, inevitably fail. The judge must also be satisfied that a production order is in the public interest, having regard to the benefit likely to accrue to the investigation if the material is obtained and to the circumstances in which the material is held.

Although a production order in respect of special procedure material may be obtained under either of the two sets of access conditions, it is easier for the police to satisfy the first set and indeed nearly all the applications have been made in this way.[9] The police are much less likely to petition for an order on the second set of access conditions since these require that they identify an Act which, pre-PACE, provided for the granting of a search warrant in respect of the type of material now sought.[10] Furthermore, they require that the police satisfy the judge that the issue of a warrant under that Act would have been appropriate. PACE has afforded the police access to certain types of information for the first time so on occasions it might be impossible for the police to find prior legislative authorization for a search warrant. However, journalistic material could be seized under warrant authorized by the Official Secrets Act 1911 as, indeed, it was in the infamous 'Zircon affair'. In 1987, the BBC decided not to broadcast a programme exposing the Ministry of Defence's failure to notify Parliament of the £500 million 'Zircon' spy satellite project, but details of the documentary were published in the *New Statesman* magazine. Warrants issued under the secrecy legislation enabled the police to search for and seize a vast amount of material from journalists' premises and the BBC's Glasgow office. Since the enactment of the 1989 Official Secrets Act,[11] the special regime in PACE can no longer be circumvented in this way: journalistic material must be sought under PACE in England and Wales. Nevertheless, the previous availability of the power of seizure under the secrecy legislation opens an avenue for the police under the second set of access conditions in PACE.

Seizure of journalists' material

The jurisprudence concerning the PACE special procedure reveals that the courts are facilitating police intelligence gathering by undermining obstacles designed to protect sensitive material from police scrutiny. One of the most important safeguards of the special procedure is that disclosure must be in the public interest, having regard to 'the benefit likely to accrue to the investigation if the material is obtained and to the circumstances under which the person in possession of the material holds it.'[12] Judicial construction of this nebulous requirement has, however, rendered it a safeguard devoid of significance. This is powerfully illustrated by *R v Central Criminal Court, ex p. Carr*,[13] in which Glidewell LJ opined: 'If documents of the kinds referred to in the information are on any of the applicant's premises, it is obvious that they are likely to be of substantial value to the investigation, that some or all of them will be relevant evidence, and therefore that it is in the public interest that such documents should be produced.' This dismissal of the public interest requirement was reinforced by *R v Northampton Crown Court, ex p. DPP*, in which Taylor LJ held that once a judge had concluded that a serious arrestable offence had been committed he should not refuse an application for a production order as it was 'hardly consistent to find anything other than that it was an offence for which there was a public interest in bringing the matter to justice.'[14] The decision in the *Northampton* case exhibits blatant disregard for the letter and the spirit of the legislation; the Court created a looking glass world in which the special procedure designed to protect sensitive material from police seizure became a convenient vehicle for information and evidence gathering.

The courts' selective view of what is required by the public interest where the police seek to obtain protected material is manifested also in those cases involving journalistic information. Journalists have argued that allowing police access to their material will compromise the impartiality of the media and threaten the personal safety of reporters who collectively might come to be viewed as agents of the police. These public interest arguments have, however, left the judiciary largely unmoved. In the *Bristol Press and Picture Agency* case[15] (an application to quash a production order in respect of photographs of the 1986 disturbances in the St. Pauls district of Bristol), the Divisional Court declined to interfere with Stuart-Smith J's conclusion that the order should be made in view of the 'very great public interest that those guilty of crime, and particularly of serious crime involving widespread public disorder, should be brought to justice.'[16] In the case arising from the 1987 disturbances at the Wapping plant of News International (in May 1988, *The Independent*, *The Observer*, *Mail on Sunday*, Independent Television News, Thames Television and four freelance photographers were ordered to surrender to Northamptonshire police unpublished film and photographs of the demonstration[17]) the Court decided that the public interest required that the police be given access to the material because it had been taken at crucial times and places during the disturbance. In 1988, the Royal Ulster Constabulary obtained, by threat of prosecution under section 11 of the 1984 Prevention of Terrorism Act,[18] RTE footage of the assaults on the two corporals murdered in West Belfast in March of that year. The police formally obtained film from several other news organizations including the BBC, ITN and a French network. Journalists were summoned to give, anonymously (Marcus 1990), evidence in the trials arising from the investigations based on the film material. In another prominent affair, several news organizations were ordered to provide the police with film of the 1990 demonstration in London against the poll tax; in all, the police studied seventy hours of video and nearly four thousand photographs and then released 'wanted' pictures to the media. In November 1993, Butler J ruled that the public interest required production orders against the BBC, ITN, Sky News and London News Network in respect of a violent disturbance outside the Royal London Hospital where a man was seriously ill after a racist attack. The judge observed that the pursuit of offenders 'far outweighed perceived loss of integrity' of the broadcast companies.[19] The following month, the same judge granted the Metropolitan Police access to film of an anti-Nazi demonstration. The order was directed at the BBC, ITN, Sky, London News Network, *The Guardian*, *The Observer*, *The Sunday Times*, *The People*, *News of the World*, *Daily Mail*, *Mail on Sunday*, *London Evening Standard* and the *Financial Times*. This decision allowed the police to supplement their own photographs and video recordings of the disturbance. In none of these cases does one gain the impression that the judge found himself grappling with competing public interest arguments of equal importance. Judges often concluded that journalists would not be exposed to increased risk of physical harm or to attacks on their professional integrity because they could advert to the fact that they had been compelled by a court to surrender material to the police. But it is naive to claim that this reasoning will be appreciated by those caught up in an urban disturbance, for instance. The real motive for these decisions is the facilitation of police intelligence gathering and, where film is concerned, the securing of power-fully probative (but inherently flawed) evidence.

Protection of sources

It is not, of course, only the police who have an interest in obtaining jour-nalistic information. Commercial organizations,[20] tribunals of inquiry,[21] government departments[22] and plaintiffs in civil actions,[23] have sought access to such material to further private or public interests. In 1981, Parlia-ment enacted the Contempt of Court Act to afford journalists a qualified immunity (in the Hohfeldian sense[24]) from compulsory disclosure of sources, but prior to the Act the common law gave little recognition to the importance of protecting journalistic confidences. In the absence of a general entitlement to maintain assurances of confidentiality,[25] the only protection for journalists resided in the court's discretion to refuse to order disclosure where the interests of justice were not sufficient to defeat confidences owed by journalists.[26] The Contempt of Court Act has changed the common law approach by asserting a presumption against disclosure: 'No court may require a person to disclose, nor is any person guilty of contempt for refusing to disclose, the source of information contained in a publication for which he is responsible, unless it be established to the satisfaction of the court that disclosure is necessary in the interests of justice or national security or for the prevention of disorder or crime' (section 10). The exis-tence of section 10 recognizes that freedom of the press (with related public interests attendant upon the free flow of information) depends in part upon the maintenance of journalists' confidences. Yet in the construction and application of section 10, the courts have continued to accord little weight to these public interests when they are asserted against state or private agencies seeking access to journalistic information.[27]

An important challenge to the courts' interpretation of section 10 was presented to the European Court of Human Rights in the case *Goodwin v*

UK.[28] The journalist Bill Goodwin had been ordered by the High Court in 1989 to disclose material which would reveal the identity of the source of commercially sensitive information about Tetra Ltd. When Bill Goodwin, who had given the source an assurance of anonymity, declined to comply with the disclosure order, he was convicted of contempt of court and fined £5000. On appeal in the House of Lords,[29] Lord Bridge opined that section 10 required a balancing exercise, considering a range of factors in each case to determine whether the preponderance of interests was in favour of disclosure. For Lord Bridge, possibly the most significant factor in assessing the importance of protecting the source was the manner in which the information was obtained by the source. This reasoning, however, devalues the essential concern of section 10 in the free flow of information: it is the nature of the material which is of prime importance to the question of source anonymity – the way in which the material was acquired is of marginal relevance here. But by focusing on any wrong-doing by a source, such as obtaining information in breach of confidence, the claim for disclosure can appear more pressing and, sometimes, doubt can be cast on the reliability of the source. In the instant case, the judges were anxious not to protect a source who had come by information as a result of a breach of confidence: Lord Bridge decided that 'interests of justice' for the purposes of section 10 was not limited to legal proceedings and could extend to ordering disclosure to enable an employer to identify and dismiss a disloyal employee. This significant undermining of section 10 does not sit easily with the purpose of the provision.

Although the European Court of Human Rights agreed with Bill Goodwin that the order requiring disclosure of his source infringed the qualified right to free expression contained in Article 10 of the Convention, the decision does not represent a fundamental condemnation of section 10 of the Contempt of Court Act. The Court's decision must be seen in the light of the High Court injunction secured by Tetra prohibiting revelation of the sensitive information acquired by Bill Goodwin. The European Court observed that the injunction (of which notice had been given to all national newspapers and relevant journals[30]) had prevented the dissemination of the confidential information and examined what further purposes the disclosure order might serve. In contrast to the view taken by the House of Lords, the Court did not find Tetra's interest in identifying a disloyal employee sufficient to defeat the public interest in protecting Bill Goodwin's source. It is to be hoped that UK courts will, in the light of the judgement in *Goodwin*, accord greater weight to public interest arguments raised by journalists contesting orders to disclose their sources.

Returning to police acquisition of journalists' material, it should be noted that section 10 of the Contempt of Court Act will not assist the journalist who has been served with a production order, for such an order is evidence that it is in the interests of justice or of crime prevention for that journalist's sources to be disclosed. Discussion of the *Dispatches* case will elucidate the consequences of this for freedom of information.

In 1991, the Prevention of Terrorism Act 1989 (hereinafter PTA) was used for the first time to seize journalists' material: Channel Four Television and Box Productions Ltd were ordered to provide the police with information which would have revealed the identity of their source for a *Dispatches* documentary alleging collusion between the Royal Ulster Constabulary and Loyalist paramilitaries in sectarian killings in Northern Ireland. Researchers for the programme had given an assurance of anonymity to 'Source A', whose life would be in danger if his identity was disclosed. The failure of the companies to comply fully with the production order led to a conviction for contempt of court and a joint fine of £75,000.[31]

In contrast to the PACE special procedure, an application for a production order under the PTA is heard ex parte, so journalists do not have the opportunity to counter police arguments. Furthermore, not only is section 10 of the Contempt of Court Act of no avail to the journalist who decides not to comply with a production order, the PTA stipulates that an order 'shall have effect notwithstanding any obligation as to secrecy or other restriction on the disclosure of information imposed by statute or otherwise.'[32] There can be no doubting, then, that the obligation to comply with a PTA production order is absolute, notwithstanding professional mores of confidentiality. All that Channel Four and Box Productions could do, when the Attorney-General moved against them for contempt, was to argue that it was in the public interest for the identity of 'Source A' to be protected.

The *Dispatches* programme provided first-hand evidence of collusion between state security forces and terrorists, about which rumours had been circulating for years, culminating in the establishment of the Stevens inquiry in 1989. Without the guarantee of anonymity to 'Source A', the documentary could not have been made and the circumstances of the murders examined by the programme would not have entered the public domain. Liz Forgan, then director of programmes at Channel Four, explained to the court that 'It is a serious journalistic problem to have an anonymous source and it arises only in wholly exceptional circumstances if the story is of exceptional importance ... We decided to carry out the interview because the public interest seemed to us to be overwhelming.' When faced with the contempt action, Channel Four found itself in a dilemma: it could either honour the guarantee of anonymity to 'Source A' and so risk contempt of court, or it could comply fully with the production order and expose its source to virtually certain death.

The Divisional Court accepted that the journalists found themselves in 'a genuine dilemma', but declared their justification for guaranteeing anonymity to the source to be 'in law an impermissible approach'. The companies had 'themselves created that dilemma'. Despite the unprecedented use of the PTA in this case the Court stated that 'both Box Productions and Channel Four should have appreciated that because of the provisions of the 1989 Act they should not have given an unqualified undertaking to A'.

The solutions offered by Woolf LJ to the dilemmas presented by a source requiring anonymity were unrealistic. His Lordship said that journalists should offer a qualified undertaking that identity would be protected unless disclosure was ordered by a court. This is clearly unworkable, especially where a potential source is in fear of her life. Alternatively, Woolf LJ suggested, Channel Four and Box Productions could have sought advice at the 'highest level of government ... as to the propriety of the action they were proposing' – presumably to obtain an assurance that the companies would not face legal action. This, however, is naive: a promise of anonymity usually has to be given before a source reveals her information. Further, such consultation would be inappropriate when the subject of the exposé is itself a state agency.

One of the most disturbing aspects of the *Dispatches* case is the all too familiar conflation of criticism of law enforcement agencies with vilification of the rule of law itself, a misapprehension which permeates the judgement of the Divisional Court. According to Lord Justice Woolf, Channel Four and Box Productions 'should have borne in mind that what they were proposing to do would inevitably undermine not only the reputation of the RUC but also ... the rule of law and must help to achieve the very result that the terrorists on both sides in Northern Ireland are seeking to bring about.' Rather than acknowledging that evidence had been uncovered which might assist the apprehension of murderers, the court took the view that by concealing A's identity the companies 'could be collaborating in the continuation of the killings' in Northern Ireland. This inversion is reflected in Pill J's judgement, where he states that the conduct of Channel Four had deprived the authorities, the courts and the public of the opportunity to have the allegations properly investigated. (The Court did not elucidate the difficulty of investigating the allegations without the identity of 'Source A'.) The concern felt by the Court over the effect on the rule of law of Channel Four's stance is in marked contrast to its disregard of the far-reaching consequences of requiring journalists to supply police with intelligence data and potential evidence.

A further determinant of the finding of contempt was the court's irritation at Channel Four's definition of the public interest. Lord Justice Woolf endorsed the view of Lord Bridge in *X v Morgan-Grampian*[33] that,

> The journalist cannot be left to judge in his own cause and decide whether or not to make disclosure. This would be an abdication of the role of Parliament and the Courts and ... would be tantamount to conferring an absolute privilege ... [T]o contend that ... a journalist or anyone else has a right of 'conscientious objection' which entitles him to set himself above the law if he does not agree with the court's decision is a doctrine which directly undermines the rule of law and is wholly unacceptable in a democratic society.

Journalists generally do not, however, seek to be above the law. The problem here is the disparity of perception between the judiciary and the media. As the preceding analysis has illustrated, UK courts have not embraced the prospect of a public interest paramount to the maximally efficacious investigation of a specific crime. Thus, when journalists raise the public interest of maintaining source anonymity, they are accused of attempting to claim an esoteric and sectional privilege. But the role of the media is vital in investigating illegality and immorality in institutions whose very function is to protect the public from such conduct. Responsible investigative journalism is not subversive, but educative. Public confidence in state authority is enhanced by access to information and by the certainty that matters of corruption will be rooted out. The *Dispatches* case struck at the heart of a mainstay of free society: the ability of the media to keep the public informed of issues of moment.

Conclusion

There is a real need for the problems attendant upon the use of journalists' material in the criminal process to be addressed. Journalists are not a resource of the criminal justice system yet are expected to take an increasingly active role in assisting the detection and prosecution of offenders. It is vital that the media has the freedom to fulfil its role: to record history, to highlight popular protest, to educate, to communicate, to inform. If the media is seen as a resource of the police, (photo)journalists and camerapersons will not be regarded as neutral recorders of events but as plainclothes detectives and their presence at a disturbance, for instance, will be received in the same way. There has traditionally been a symbiotic relationship between the police and the media in the UK, but the association is becoming characterized by exploitation. The police, aided by the judiciary, have succumbed to the dangerous temptation of relying on journalistic information as a source of intelligence and evidence, eroding recognition of the special importance of the media to a free and democratic society. It will be to the detriment of us all if freedom of information is sacrificed before the altar of crime control.

Notes

1 The Prevention of Terrorism Act 1989 also provides for the seizure of journalistic material: see Costigan 1996.
2 A substantial part of this section was originally published in [1996] *Criminal Law Review* 231-39 and is reproduced by permission.
3 [1970] 1 QB 693.
4 For discussion of legally privileged material, see Stone 1988.
5 Categories of confidentially-held data such as medical and counselling records, specified in section 11. In *R v Cardiff Crown Court, ex p. Kellam* [1993] 16 BMLR 76, an order of certiorari was granted to quash production orders made by Rutter J who had wrongly concluded that records detailing the movements into and out of a hospital for mentally ill people were not excluded material. The Divisional Court held that such records 'related to' the mental health of the patients and were therefore within the definition of excluded material.
6 See, inter alia, Hansard, 42 H. C. Deb., col.s 155-57; 60 H. C. Deb., col.s 266-68 (cf. col.s 269-71); 452 H. L. Deb., col.s 428-46; 454 H. L. Deb., col.s 113-26.
7 This category of material also covers information acquired or created in the course of any business or profession which is held subject to an obligation of confidence: section 14. For journalistic material to be classified as excluded material it would have to be held in confidence (section 11(3)), a requirement which will rarely be satisfied since journalistic material is usually intended for publication. (Assurances of anonymity given to journalists' sources might create obligations of secrecy but will not usually affect the status of the material itself.)
8 A production order requires the possessor of the material sought to relinquish it to the police, usually within seven days (PACE, Sch. 1, para. 4). Para. 6 brings material obtained by production order within the compass of sections 21 and 22 of the Act, providing for copying and retention of the material.

9   See Lidstone 1989, p. 344, n. 35: the police in England and Wales have obtained more than 2000 production orders and search warrants under the first set of access conditions compared with 9 under the second set. An unsuccessful application for a production order was made under the second set of access conditions in the hearing that was the subject of the application for judicial review in *R v The Independent Newspaper, ex p. DPP,* unreported, 30 March 1988, Queen's Bench Divisional Court. This case is also noteworthy because it was the first application made against a newspaper under the second set of access conditions.

10 Section 9(2) of PACE repeals all previous legislative provisions insofar as they relate to the granting of search warrants for legally privileged information, excluded material or special procedure material in the form of documents or other records.

11 Section 11(3).

12 PACE, sch. 1(2)(c).

13 Unreported, 27 February 1987, D.C.

14 (1991) 93 Cr. App. R. 376, 381. The Divisional Court granted the DPP's application for judicial review of the decision by Hall J that it was not in the public interest for a firm of solicitors holding the material on behalf of their client to have to produce the material. Taylor LJ found the judge's decision *Wednesbury* unreasonable.

15 (1987) 85 Cr.App.R. 190.

16 (1987) 85 Cr.App.R. 190 at 196, cited by Glidewell LJ.

17 Re- an Application under Section 9 of the Police & Criminal Evidence Act, *The Independent,* 27 May 1988.

18 Re-enacted as section 18 of the 1989 Act. That the RUC threatened prosecution was revealed to the author in an interview with RTE journalists in Belfast, May 1992; see also, Walker 1992, pp. 141-143.

19 *The Guardian,* 26 October 1993.

20 *British Steel Corporation v Granada Television* [1981] AC 1096; *X v Morgan-Grampian* [1991] 1 AC 1; *Handmade Films v Express Newspapers plc.* [1986] FSR 463.

21 *AG v Mulholland, AG v Foster* [1963] 2 QB 477.

22 *Secretary of State for Defence v Guardian Newspapers Ltd.* [1984] 3 All ER 601; *Re An Inquiry under the Company Securities (Insider Dealing) Act 1985* [1988] 1 All ER 203.

23 *Senior v Holdsworth, ex p. Independent Television News Ltd.* [1976] 1 QB 23.

24 Hohfeld, 1913.

25 *AG v Mulholland, AG v Foster* [1963] 2 QB 477; *British Steel Corporation v Granada Television* [1981] AC 1096.

26 *AG v Lundin* (1982) Cr App R 90.

27 See, for example, *Secretary of State for Defence v Guardian Newspapers Ltd.* [1984] 3 All ER 601, *Re An Inquiry under the Company Securities (Insider Dealing) Act 1985* [1988] 1 All ER 203.
28 (1996) 22 EHRR 123.
29 *X v Morgan-Grampian Ltd.* 1 [1991] AC 1 (CA & HL).
30 It was confirmed by the House of Lords in *A-G v Times Newspapers* [1991] 2 All ER 398 that a publisher with notice of an injunction is liable in contempt notwithstanding that the publisher is not party to the injunction.
31 *DPP v Channel Four Television Co. Ltd. and another* [1993] 2 All E.R. 517.
32 Sched. 7(4)(5).
33 [1991] 1 AC 1, at 48-49; cited by Woolf LJ at [1993] 2 All ER 530-31.

References

Costigan, Ruth (1996), Fleet Street Blues: Police Seizure of Journalists' Material, *Criminal Law Review*, pp. 231-239.

Hohfeld, W. (1913), Some Fundamental Legal Conceptions as Applied in Judicial Reasoning, *Yale Law Journal* 16.

Lidstone, K. (1989), The Police and Criminal Evidence (Northern Ireland) Order 1989: Powers of Entry, Search and Seizure, 40 *NILQ* 333.

Marcus, Gilbert (1990), Secret Witnesses, *Public Law* 207.

Stone, R.T.H. (1988), PACE: Special Procedures and Legal Privilege, *Criminal Law Review* 498.

Walker, Clive (second edition, 1992), *The Prevention of Terrorism in British Law*, Manchester: Manchester University Press.

15 The privilege against self-incrimination in proactive policing

PETER ALLDRIDGE AND BERT SWART

Introduction

The privilege against self-incrimination is an enigmatic right. The central use of the privilege is that it exempts witnesses from answering questions if by answering they would incriminate themselves. The archetypal situation is that in which the witness has to appear before a court and has taken an oath. The court need not be a criminal court but may also be a 'civil' court or, for that matter, any judicial body. The privilege usually extends to other situations in which a person has to take an oath before testifying as a witness or is otherwise liable to punishment for telling untruths, for example in congressional or parliamentary hearings. The Canadian Charter of Rights and Freedoms makes it a constitutional principle (Canadian Constitution Act 1982 Article 13), as does the United States Constitution (USCA 4 and 14). Yet in spite of the high value which can be attributed to anything regarded as worthy of constitutional enshrinement, a perfunctory glance at four different legal systems (USA, UK, the Netherlands, Germany) immediately reveals considerable differences in recognizing the privilege, those differences reflecting differences in principle as to why it exists at all. Significant differences include:

- In the USA federal jurisdiction the privilege is recognized only in so far as it relates to testimonial evidence and applies to the production of documentary evidence only if the act of producing the evidence would itself provide the authorities with new information (*Fisher v United States* 1976; *US v Doe* 1984);[1]
- In the UK, in the absence of contrary statutory provision, the privilege also rules out the compulsory production of documentary evidence (*Video Information Exchange v Rank Film Distributors* 1982);[2]
- In Germany (Kleinknecht 1989, p. 17) and the Netherlands (Reijntjes

1996) the privilege rules out any duty of the suspect or accused actively to contribute to an investigation. The person is only under a duty to 'tolerate' the investigation and may not offer resistance. In the Netherlands the distinction between 'active' and 'passive' forms of cooperation does not seem to have a strong appeal in case law and doctrine any more; it is frequently dismissed as irrelevant and difficult to apply in practice. In Germany, on the other hand, it is still a basic distinction, carefully observed by legislation and case law.

Having for many years regarded the presumption of innocence as rather more of a *mantra* to be recited than anything with a real pull on the criminal justice system (Ashworth 1994; 1996), we now need to consider it more fully to determine its rationale and what limitations follow from the rationale. A system of criminal justice cannot operate with a rule that the state is not allowed to collect *any* evidence generated by the accused. Evidence of criminal activity will almost always be generated by the accused. What is in issue are the limits, and the degree of participation which cannot be demanded of a defendant.

Rationales and limits

Few rights in criminal justice are absolute. In respect of any of the competing justifications, there is the possibility of abridging the privilege for the sake of protecting competing values. The questions which must be addressed are, why should the privilege against self-incrimination exist at all and what competing values can legitimately be taken to displace it? The main justifications for restrictions upon the extent to which a defendant can be compelled to give evidence against him/herself (or to have adverse inferences drawn from failure to respond) seem to be as follows.

Protecting the innocent?

Here the argument is that having a testimonial privilege protects someone who may otherwise be tricked into a confession or some kind of statement contrary to interest. The problems with this as an account of the privilege against self-incrimination is that it ignores the whole corpus of law on the interrogation of suspects. If the criminal justice system were to set out to avoid circumstances in which the accused may behave contrary to interest and have privileges in respect of many of them, the entire investigatory process will have radically to alter.

A necessary consequence of the presumption of innocence?

This is a strange argument which surfaces from time to time. It states that *because* the burden of proof is upon the prosecution to establish guilt beyond reasonable doubt (or whatever the test is) *it follows that* the accused need not give evidence and must be afforded at least a testimonial privilege. Now at a simple level this argument is obviously wrong. There is nothing inconsistent as a matter of formal logic with leaving the burden on the state but allowing inferences to be drawn, for example from the silence of the accused.

A concomitant of the right to privacy?

The claim that the privilege against self-incrimination was a subset of the right to privacy was relatively popular in the 1970s. The claim of privacy has been made yet more metaphysical (by Galligan 1988):

> Privacy is important because it protects personal identity and autonomy. Without a zone of privacy, identity, autonomy and personality cannot exist. This is easily shown: suppose that your every action could be monitored, that every thought urge and desire could be known and recorded, to be used for any purposes by a stranger. Identity and autonomy, let us use the general term personality, under such conditions would be seriously distorted if not destroyed. It follows that a zone of privacy is essential to personality.

The privacy argument was used in the US Supreme Court when it was trying to explain why there was no Fifth Amendment privilege in respect, for example, of blood samples.[3] There are two obvious problems with this account. First, the right to privacy is a relatively weak right, frequently able to be defeated. So far as concerns the jurisprudence of the European Convention on Human Rights, one of the reasons for making as many as possible of these arguments within the framework of the right to a fair trial (Article 6.1) and as few as possible in terms of the right to private life (Article 8) is that the Article 6.1 rights are not defeasible by the interest of the state. Article 6.1 contains none of the usual savings relating to those derogations from rights which can be justified as necessary in a democratic society. Second, even if the right were strong enough, the right to privacy (or to private life) is not co-extensive with the privilege against self-incrimination.

A protection from cruel choices?

Then it is argued that the privilege against self-incrimination exists to protect from the choice between being punished on account of having confessed and being punished on account of not having testified. Dennis (1995) claims that unlike the other theories this rather assumes that the suspect is guilty: if the suspect is innocent, so the argument runs, s/he has nothing to lose by answering truthfully. Dennis follows this point to its conclusion.

> Once the true nature of the premise is recognized, the argument loses much of its claim to moral force. It becomes difficult to accept that the interest of a guilty person in escaping conviction by not disclosing evidence of the crime is worthy of official legal protection.

Notwithstanding Bentham's critique, to which Dennis refers (and see Lewis 1990), the issue is not as simple as this. There may be suspects who do not want to answer the question for reasons other than that they are guilty. Nonetheless, Dennis' general point is correct, if rather lengthily made. That is, that the 'traditional' justifications advanced for the privilege do not give a satisfactory account either of how the law presently stands or of how it might rationally be developed.

Protection of freedom of expression

The European Commission for Human Rights has made the argument that the right to freedom of expression, protected by Article 10 of the European Convention on Human Rights, implies freedom to choose whether or not to express oneself (*K v Austria* 1993),[4] but this seems to be far-fetched.

To rule out unreliable evidence?

The argument has from time to time been run that the purpose of the privilege against self-incrimination is to exclude unreliable evidence. Assuredly, one of the functions of any system for controlling proof is to rule out unreliable evidence. There are many rules in each of the systems under consideration which do rule out such evidence. Either those rules (in respect of the admissibility of hearsay, opinion and confession evidence) perform their function, in which case no further rules (in particular the privilege against self-incrimination) are necessary to achieve the purpose, or, if they do not, it is unreasonable to expect the privilege against self-incrimination to do it.

As an instrumental means by which to protect other 'substantive' rights (human dignity, privacy, fair trial)?

Finally, there is the instrumental argument that the privilege against self-incrimination is deployed as a means to protect other rights (Dennis 1995). Again this argument implies that if those rights could be afforded adequate protection otherwise than by the adoption of the privilege against self-incrimination, there would be no independent case for the privilege. It will not be pursued further.

Constitutional status and history

The constitutional status of the doctrine in England and Wales was fairly clear before the intervention of European Human Rights Law. What happened was that the courts of Star Chamber and High Commission under the Stuarts sat in secret, used torture as a means of gathering evidence and compelled people to take the oath and give evidence. In the 1630s and 1640s John Lilburn, a dissenter, the leader of the Levellers, famously and successfully argued for the right to have his case heard in public and not to be compelled to testify. By the late Eighteenth Century that history was used in English legal discourse for denouncing continental Europeans, Stuarts and Catholics and for complacent self-congratulation by common law writers and judges.

There was a privilege against self-incrimination, but the privilege was a 'common law doctrine' and as with any other common law doctrine it could be overridden by statute. Thus, for example, it was in the early nineteenth century that it was first held that the privilege against self-incrimination was of no avail in proceedings in bankruptcy (*Ex p Cossens* 1820; *R v Scott* 1856).[5] Now, in English criminal law the defendant was not a competent witness at his/her own trial until the Criminal Evidence Act 1898, so the ramifications of the privilege in criminal proceedings against the person claiming the privilege did not arise. The legislation which made the accused a competent witness also provided that s/he could not be compelled to give evidence (Criminal Evidence Act 1898 section 1(a)), and that no adverse inference could be drawn from failure to testify. It is that which was altered in 1994 (Criminal Justice and Public Order Act 1994 sections 34-39).

A typical common law application was in *Video Information Exchange v Rank Film Distributors* (1982). There was civil action for breach of copyright arising from video piracy, at the outset of which an order was made that the defendants should allow the plaintiffs to enter upon the defendant's premises and search for evidence. The defence was run that this could not be allowed to occur because it would expose the defendants to criminal charges under the Copyright Act 1956 (the penalties for which were negligible, in comparison to the substantial civil damages which would have been payable). The House of Lords held that the privilege against self-incrimination was indeed available and would stand in the way of the proceedings. Again typically, it was overruled almost immediately afterwards by statute (Supreme Court Act 1981 section 72).

In many jurisdictions there are duties to inform the authorities of some criminal activity. Thus, in the UK, there is an active duty to inform the authorities of terrorist offences (Prevention of Terrorism (Temporary Provisions) Act 1989 section 18). One of the most important developments in recent years is the increasing tendency in many states to impose duties of disclosure upon third parties to assist in investigations by providing information, and there too, there have been statutory attenuations of the privilege. Banks, other financial institutions, accountants, journalists, the legal profession, all have to cope with the desire of modern governments to make them useful tools in investigating crime. Legislation compelling the reporting to the authorities of suspicious financial transactions (Criminal Justice Act 1993 (UK)) is but one example (see Lamp et al. in this volume). One aspect of the duty of third parties to provide information is that they may, on occasion, be forced to incriminate themselves. Article 12 of the 1993 Dutch Act (*Staatsblad* 1993, 705) on the reporting of unusual transactions states that information which incriminates its provider may not be used as evidence in a criminal trial against that person nor may it be used within the framework of a criminal investigation against him. Nonetheless the information must be provided. Otherwise the Act would have the odd consequence that information would have to be supplied by bankers except where the banker was party to a criminal conspiracy with the customer. At no moment during the Parliamentary Debate on the Bill[6] did anyone raise the possibility that the privilege against self-incrimination might be the justification for the provision. The government only advanced the argument that the provision would promote compliance with reporting duties by banks and other financial institutions. In other words, they might also decide to abolish the provision if its usefulness is doubtful.

Mechanisms

There is a wide range of legal mechanisms which implement the privilege against self-incrimination. The following is an inexhaustive enumeration:
- Full privilege against self-incrimination: questions directly or indirectly from agents of the state need not be answered and no inference may be drawn from there being no answer.
- As above but separate crime of failing to supply the information/evidence.
- Privilege against self-incrimination but adverse inferences can be drawn from reliance upon the privilege.
- Privilege against self-incrimination but legally enforceable guarantee of immunity from subsequent prosecution may/must be accepted.
- No privilege against self-incrimination but evidence given only admissible in these proceedings.
- No privilege against self-incrimination but evidence given only admissible in these proceedings unless witness subsequently makes inconsistent statement.
- No privilege against self-incrimination. Self-incriminatory answers or evidence obtained in consequence of them, admissible. Failure to answer punishable.

Fuller treatment of each of these rules would include consideration of the 'fruit of the forbidden tree' issue. Suppose that evidence is obtained in breach of the privilege (however expressed) and that the evidence is consequently excluded. Is evidence which is obtained lawfully but gained in consequence also to be inadmissible? Since this is not an issue relating specifically to the privilege against self-incrimination, it will not be dealt with here.

The European Convention on Human Rights

After a period during which it was unclear whether or not the privilege against self-incrimination was recognized for protection under the European Convention on Human Rights, *Funke v France* held that Article 6.1 of the Convention, which protects the right to a fair trial, extends to include a version of the privilege against self-incrimination.[7] It prevented Funke being convicted of an offence of failure to supply documents to customs authorities. On the face of it *Funke* holds that Article 6.1 includes the right of anyone charged with a criminal offence to remain silent and not to contribute to incriminating himself. The applicant had been convicted for failing to deliver documents to French customs' officials, and the Court held the legislation purporting to create the obligation to deliver was a violation of the part of Article 6.1 which protected the privilege against self-incrimination.

> 'In one sentence the court gave the privilege the status of an entrenched constitutional right which could not be removed by a legislative enactment in comprehensive terms' (Dennis 1995, p. 372).

Murray v UK[8] has now restricted *Funke* with a suggestion that so far as concerns Article 6.1 the rationales for the privilege against self-incrimination which rely upon a paradigm of interrogation do not apply.

What has the privilege against self-incrimination to do with proactive policing?

Informers and undercover agents are useful tools of investigation. Part of their usefulness lies in the fact that the target of investigation will tell them things that s/he would never have told to an uniformed policeman or other authority. In a sense, the target is incriminating himself and is purposely induced to do so by the informer or undercover agent. This may be a very effective means not only of gathering information but also of gathering evidence, especially if conversations have been tape-recorded. No court has ever accepted the argument that the privilege has been violated in situations where evidence is gathered without the knowledge of the suspect. However, a variety of reasons could be given for this rejection. They include:
- The privilege only applies to those who have already committed offences and thus not those who are proactively targetted;
- The privilege does not rule out some forms of pressure;
- There is no compulsion at all in such situations;
- S/he who engages in criminal activities must be aware that s/he runs the risk of encountering an undercover police officer.

What, then, does the privilege against self-incrimination have to do with proactive policing? Surely the privilege against self-incrimination comes in where proactive policing ends? The privilege is something to be asserted in response to questions from someone who is (known to be) acting on behalf of the state. But the developments are cognate ones.

In recent years proactive policing has developed, and with it the attempt to generate legal mechanisms to generate purchase against it. Reactive policing takes place in response to reports of crime. It involves the traditional policing techniques of interrogation, searches, seizures and so on, by police officers, whose status and identity is known to the suspect. In a system of reactive policing the traditional guarantees of rights to the suspect may or may not in fact be available, but it is fairly clear what they would involve. Due process provides an argument for access to legal advice, some knowledge of the prosecution case, the right to have interviews recorded and the right to know when an interview is taking place and when it is being recorded. To some extent at least, in the United Kingdom, the Police and Criminal Evidence Act 1984 effected such due process precepts.

These due process guarantees simply cannot be available in a system of policing which is directed towards the securing secretly of evidence against an accused, before and during the time when s/he commits an offence. Secret surveillance is incompatible with reading the suspect a statement of his/her rights to a lawyer and that interviews will be tape recorded. If every interaction between police and suspect must be prefaced by appropriate warnings, there could be no undercover police work (Brants and Field 1995, pp. 46-47). Consequently, within a system of proactive policing, arguments for rights for suspected persons are not arguments for due process, but are frequently arguments for regulating access to the suspect's private time, space and information. In this sense, the claim of privacy is to proactive policing what the claim of due process is to reactive policing.

But there is another (parallel) set of cases in which the traditional methods have proved, or been perceived as, unsatisfactory in the UK, and those have led to the introduction of inquisitorial methods, conferring upon state officials greater powers than elsewhere to require answers, frequently upon threats of imprisonment. It is now more or less usual in legislation which confers power upon any official to require documents or information to make provision for whether or not the privilege against self-incrimination is to be abrogated (Child Support Act 1991 section 15(7); Courts and Legal Services Act 1990 section 107(14); Consumer Protection Act 1987 section 47(2)). Although the governing principle (statutory precedence over common law) has been around for a long time these derogations have arisen largely since the mid-1980s, contemporaneously with the advent of a far more significant jurisprudence of human rights, and in particular, the decision in *Funke, Murray* and *Saunders*.[9]

Do these developments have anything to do with proactive policing? They certainly proceed from cognate concerns. The kinds of justifications which are advanced for derogations from the privilege against self-incrimination during the 1980s were very much the same kinds which are advanced for proactive policing, and also for derogations from standard due process rights. They are two. First, it is said that a particular type of crime is particularly evil/particularly dangerous to our society, and calls for special measures to combat it. In the past drugs, terrorism and fraud have been the targeted offences. To those we might now add paedophile offences. Take, for example, *Hamilton and others v Naviede*[10] where Lord Nolan said (at 834h):

> The type of fraud which led to the passing of the Criminal Justice Act 1987 is an exceptionally pernicious form of crime, and those who commit it tend to be as devious as they are wicked. It is not the least surprising or regrettable that Parliament should have entrusted the Serious Fraud Office with the power to call upon a suspected person to come into the open, and to disclose information which may incriminate him.

The second, frequently overlapping claim, is that the difficulties in obtaining evidence are so great that the powers in place are necessary in order to obtain any convictions. It is this claim which gave rise to the establishment in the United Kingdom of the Serious Fraud Office (SFO), and its extended powers (Criminal Justice Act 1987).

There are two sets of rules which are important here. First, those relating to the SFO itself. It is compulsory to answer an officer of the SFO (and a criminal offence equivalent to perjury to lie to him/her) and the SFO can require the production of documents, even if they were generated in the course of a DTI enquiry. The answers given to a SFO officer are not admissible in a subsequent trial unless the person questioned gives inconsistent evidence (Criminal Justice Act 1987 section 2(8)). Information discovered in consequence of such disclosures is admissible. Second, there are rules arising out of the scheme for corporate governance. Proceedings into the running (Companies Act 1985 section 431 *et seq.*) or the insolvency of a company (Insolvency Act 1986 section 236) involve the most serious derogations from the privilege against self-incrimination. The Companies Act and the Insolvency Act both contain provisions which allow the Inspector to require answers to questions under threat of imprisonment.

Saunders and the significance of 'charge'

In many states numerous statutes oblige citizens to furnish information to the authorities and make refusal to do so a criminal offence. Do these statutes violate the privilege? The Saunders litigation arose from an enquiry undertaken by inspectors from the Department of Trade and Industry (DTI) into the Guinness take-over of Distillers (Pugh 1987), acting under sections 432 to 442 of the Companies Act 1985. Section 434 of the Act provides that the officers of the Company are under a duty to assist the inspector, and that the inspector may examine them under oath. Section 434(5) provides that:

> An answer given by a person to a question put to him in exercise of powers conferred by this section (whether it has effect in relation to an investigation under any of sections 431 to 433, or as applied by any other section in this Part) may be used in evidence against him.

Section 436(2) and (3) provide that a person refusing to produce documents or to answer questions is to be treated (and punished) as if s/he were guilty of contempt of court. (Maximum penalty two years. Contempt of Court Act 1981 section 14(1).) Saunders was involved in two proceedings: first, the enquiry by the Department of Trade Inspector into the events surrounding the take-over. This was not itself a criminal proceeding. DTI inspectors, when questioned as to the role which they have under sections 434 *et seq.* of the Companies Act 1985, claim that they (in contradistinction to the police) are committed to finding out the truth of the matter, and that there is consequently no need for the kinds of procedural safeguards which might be appropriate in the case where the interrogating official has an interest in securing a conviction. The traditional use of the privilege would have been in just such a proceeding as that. But by the time of the enquiry in point it had already been decided that the privilege was not available to a person examined before an inspector, either under the Companies Act *Re v London United Investments* (1992)[11] or the Insolvency Act *Bishopsgate Investment Management Ltd v Maxwell* (1993),[12] and that failure to respond could therefore be punished as a contempt of court. Saunders therefore answered the questions. He was subsequently tried for various criminal offences arising from the take-over. Evidence was used which had been obtained by the inspector's interrogation. He was convicted. (For the last appeal, see *R v Saunders et al.* (1996).[13]) He argued that his right to a fair trial guaranteed by Article 6.1 had been violated. The British government sought to argue that the position was different because of the special status of persons conducting the affairs of public companies who enjoy a privileged position towards the public and who have a responsibility to account for it. This argument was rejected by the Commission, which held for Saunders. When the European Court of Human Rights finally decided the case, it held for Saunders that whether or not there had been a 'charge' was not a pre-requisite for the coming into existence of the privilege. Nothing in the (laconic) judgement requires there to be a charge for Article 6.1 to come into play. Before the case was heard by the European Court of Human Rights, Dennis suggested that:

> If ... [the decision of the Commission in *Saunders*] is upheld by the European Court of Human Rights, the implication will be that no use can ever be made in a criminal prosecution of any evidence obtained by means of inquisitorial powers. Certainly this will be true of statements made by and documents disclosed by the accused. If the European institutions follow their own logic it will also extend to facts discovered in consequence of such evidence, such as the existence of a foreign bank account. In the context, say, of international fraud or of money-laundering such evidential restrictions would be a major problem (Dennis 1995).

The court having decided the case in this manner, reappraisal is now required.

The Netherlands

What are the consequences of *Saunders* for criminal investigations in the Netherlands? The 1926 Code of Criminal Procedure protects the privilege against self-incrimination in two different ways. Persons who are reasonably suspected of having committed a criminal offence have a right to remain silent. Moreover, while suspects may not resist the authorities in their investigations, they are not obliged to assist them (e.g. by producing documents) in other ways. On the other hand, numerous special statutes oblige all citizens to answer questions and to produce information in certain specific situations. Tax legislation and legislation creating economic crimes provide some of the most important examples. This, inevitably, raises the question of their relationship with the privilege against self-incrimination. Case law assumes that suspects always have a right not to answer questions, notwithstanding specific legislative provisions.[14] However, the privilege does not apply to persons who are not (yet) considered to be suspects by the authorities but who would incriminate themselves by answering questions.[15] Special statutory provision may, however, grant them the right to invoke the privilege, as is, for instance, the case in most situations in which a person has to testify as a witness under oath. As far as other duties to cooperate are concerned, notably the duty to produce documents, case law has always refused to accept the point of view that a suspect may refuse to cooperate by invoking the privilege; it is up to the legislature to decide whether special statutes should make exceptions to the general rule that a suspect is not obliged to assist the authorities in their investigations.[16] Obviously, in the view of the Dutch courts the core of the privilege against self-incrimination is the right to silence. Until *Saunders*, the European Convention has been largely irrelevant where their approach to the privilege is concerned. Case law has always assumed that Article 6 of the European Convention may be invoked by a person only if he has been 'charged' within the meaning of that provision. The mere fact that a person is the target of a criminal investigation does not automatically imply that he has been 'charged': this would only be the case if there is a definite possibility that he will be prosecuted.

Comparing *Saunders* with the case law of Dutch courts one may state that there is a basic accord where the right to silence of persons suspected of having committed criminal offences is concerned, although the approach is somewhat different. While the European Court seem to accept the possibility that the imposition of a duty upon a suspect to answer questions does not in itself infringe the privilege but that the subsequent use of the person's statements in a criminal trial would, Dutch courts take the unconditional point of view that a suspect may never be compelled to give answers. But the real problems with *Saunders* lie elsewhere. The crucial question is whether the *Saunders* doctrine also applies to persons who are not yet considered to be suspects by the authorities but who may become so by making statements. Although the facts of the case show that Saunders was clearly suspected of having committed fraud, it is not entirely clear whether any form of legal compulsion to answer questions of an incriminating nature would rule out the subsequent use of statements thus obtained in a criminal trial, regardless of whether the person was already suspected of having committed criminal offences. If that were indeed to be the case, the consequences for Dutch law would be considerable.

An illustration of the importance of the question discussed here is provided by the current practices in the Netherlands with respect to euthanasia. Medical doctors who perform euthanasia have to report that fact to the authorities. The consequence of reporting such a case may be that a doctor is requested to answer a set of detailed questions as to the reasons for and circumstances of the performance of euthanasia. These answers enable the public prosecutor to decide whether a doctor has observed the accepted criteria for performing euthanasia or whether he has committed murder. It has been argued many times that an obligation to answer questions violates a doctor's privilege not to incriminate himself. The Government's response hitherto has been that at the moment a doctor has to draw up a report of his acts, he cannot yet be considered as 'charged'; therefore, Article 6 of the European Convention does not apply to the situation. Moreover, in a society that allows euthanasia in certain cases there is a clear need for supervision of medical practices. If the *Saunders* case is to be given a broad interpretation, the result would be that doctors would continue to be obliged to make a detailed report of what they did but, on the other hand, their statements could not be used as evidence against them in a criminal trial. Whether this would be a satisfying solution is another matter.

A fresh starting point – The European Convention on Human Rights and contractual models of the state

Would it not be more honest and intellectually satisfying to say that in many of the cases considered above the privilege is at stake but that there are circumstances in which it may be abridged? What we want to do is to try to argue towards a 'reflective equilibrium' in which the relationship of the citizen and the state, and how it is constructed in a given state, is the critical factor. In this way we can liken the privilege against self-incrimination to a range of other issues, for example the treatment of omissions in substantive law. The immediate structural problem with the right to a fair trial under Article 6 of the Convention is that so long as the privilege against self-incrimination is constructed as part of the right to a fair trial it is not so easily defeasible as is consistent with many national laws. This is inevitable: had those responsible for the drafting of the Convention envisaged that the privilege against self-incrimination was going to be held to be protected by it at all, then a better and more explicit provision would have been made.

The limitations of regarding the privilege as inextricably bound up with the right to a fair trial becomes apparent if one considers witnesses (other than the accused). Can one really say that the right of witnesses not to answer questions is an aspect of their right to a fair trial? At first sight this seems rather far fetched since, usually, proceedings will not be in train against the witness. This may explain why the European Commission in *K v Austria* looked to Article 10 of the European Convention as a tenet, and not to Article 6. But one may construe a link by arguing that the state may not obtain from a person indirectly what it cannot obtain directly from him (Stuart 1991, p. 328). The outcome of a later trial is inevitably affected by earlier declarations before a different forum; and a defendant's ability to defend him/herself against a criminal charge is substantially impaired. Apart from that, there is, of course, also a utilitarian argument for granting the privilege to witnesses: the social interest in encouraging people to come forward to give evidence argues for removing anything which might become an obstacle to witnesses coming forward.

The existence of the European Convention on Human Rights and the jurisprudence of the European Court of Human Rights have given rise, naturally, to it being regarded as the last place or resort in any case where an applicant appears legitimately to be aggrieved. Sometimes the attempts of the court appear as attempts to fit Procrustes to the bed. The mere fact that some systems of criminal justice guarantee greater procedural rights to defendants does not necessarily imply that there is anything wrong with those who guarantee fewer, or that, if there is something wrong, it is a human rights issue. A better approach might be to ask to what extent is the privilege against self-incrimination a human right and to what extent is it a mechanism according to which each individual state defines its relationship to the citizen. What we suggest is that, in general, the privilege against self-incrimination should be regarded as the latter, and only when there would be another breach of human rights (for example, by torture) should the discourse of human rights be invoked.

Consequently, a more appropriate place to search might be in an account of the general duties of a citizen. A fresh starting point comes from considering the roles of the privilege against self-incrimination in the cases where it is widely agreed that the privilege against self-incrimination should not be of assistance to the defendant: blood tests, taxation and in social security dealings with the state. The analogy here might be with the criminal law of omissions. There is, without more, no obligation in Anglo-American law (for example), to pull a drowning child out of the water. Legal obligations are generally not to do things, rather than to do things. The history, and the justification is the contract model – why should a person do something for nothing? There are few instances in Anglo-American culture where citizenship implies anything more than simply to refrain from actively committing crimes. There are other jurisdictions in which there is a far more active duty to assist. This says something interesting which might help to place the respective legal cultures on a continuum from individualist to communitarian, but little or nothing about human rights.

Applying a contractual model

Blood tests

It is almost universally accepted to have blood alcohol tests for drivers. A justifying account for blood-alcohol tests within a system of licensing is a contractual one. If you want to drive it requires a minimal level of competence and an undertaking to remain sober at the wheel. The inexorable concomitant of this is that in certain circumstances you will have to suffer blood tests. Whatever the privilege against self-incrimination problems elsewhere in respect of blood tests, there are none here. The argument made by the Court in *Saunders*, that there is no inconsistency with the convention in requiring blood tests, is that it is the effect upon the will of the suspect which is the central question.

> The right not to incriminate oneself is primarily concerned, however, with respecting the will of an accused person to remain silent ... it does not extend to use in criminal proceedings of material which may be obtained from the accused through the use of compulsory powers but which has existence independent of the will of the suspect such as, *inter alia*, documents acquired pursuant to a warrant, breath, blood and urine samples and bodily tissue for the purpose of DNA testing (*Saunders v UK* (1996) paragraph 69).

In the same way as the argument is sometimes made that blood-alcohol tests for drivers are justifiable as an exception to the privilege against self-incrimination as part of a licensing scheme on contractual grounds (i.e. that one of the derogations which the citizen makes from his/her general privilege against self-incrimination when applying for a license is that s/he gives up the general right not to have blood taken) an argument could be made that the persons to whom the inquisitorial procedure applies forfeit the more strongly protected privilege against self-incrimination in exchange for the right to conduct the operations of a limited liability company.

Taxation

Before the Commission in *Saunders*, the one dissenting member, Mr Henry Schermers, gave the following account:

> In my opinion, the main reason why a fair process should include a right not to incriminate oneself is that one should not put a person in a situation where he must choose between telling the truth which incriminates

him and lying in order to protect himself. The human right of protecting oneself would be brought into conflict with the human duty of telling the truth. In the criminal proceedings of the present case that situation did not arise. All statements to the DTI Inspectors had been made before the criminal proceedings started. If the applicant was put in a situation of conflict between truth and self-protection, that conflict was in the proceedings before the DTI Inspector.

Even Justice Holmes opined that

[I]t would be an extreme if not extravagant application of the Fifth Amendment to say that it authorized a man to refuse to state the amount of his income because it had been made in crime (*United States v Sullivan* (1927)[17]).

That is, they both regard it as bordering upon absurd that you could have a system of taxation which afforded the maker of unlawful profits the privilege against self-incrimination. The unspoken premise behind these utterances is that income is taxable whether it is lawful or not. In a country where unlawful income is not taxed (but may, of course be subject to legislation on confiscation), the problem doesn't arise.

In the wake of *Saunders* the major problem surrounding the privilege against self-incrimination might well turn out to be in dealing with taxation of illegally obtained income. There is a range of approaches which a country could adopt to the taxation of illegally obtained/generated income. The pure approach (that adopted, e.g., in Sweden) is not to tax it at all, but to confiscate or nothing. On this account there will never be any problem in having to justify derogations from the privilege against self-incrimination. If, on the other hand, it does, then it can not have as full a privilege against self-incrimination. Taxation is a badge of sovereignty, and it would be strange if the power to tax were altered by such a sidewind. Now there are obvious due process problems with employing the criminal law of taxation as a back up when other approaches fail, and this might well be something which argues for the purist approach.

One thing is clear, that it is inappropriate to treat differently tax returns and applications for social security benefits. Suppose that upon an application for state benefits a citizen, when called upon to disclose whether s/he had any savings which would provide germane considerations, declined, praying in aid the privilege. The application should not succeed. Yet taxation was not mentioned in the European Court of Human Rights. Again, further consideration is required.

Third party obligations

Again, on this view, the imposition upon third parties of positive obligations to inform the authorities is relatively unproblematic for the privilege against self-incrimination. The issue whether one party could maintain a privilege against informing is dealt with elsewhere, so far as concerns legal, religious and journalistic privileges. Those privileges are directed more towards the protection of a socially desirable relationship than the prevention of any particular pressure being brought (pressure to testify is the same whether or not the person against whom it is brought is a lawyer, but the lawyer-client relationship justifies the making of the exception). Within a contractual model of the state, whether or not citizens have a duty to inform, and the extent of the obligation, will be something to be fixed on a scale from individualist 'night-watchman' to communitarian, interventionist state.

Conclusions

The main conclusion of the foregoing is that the privilege is largely irrelevant to most proactive investigation methods discussed here, with the exception of the compulsory providing of information by third parties. In a way, proactive methods may make interrogations even superfluous, and with them the privilege, or they may enable the authorities to collect such amounts of information that it makes no sense to deny the charges any more.

We suggest that *Funke* and *Saunders* have misled us as to the area in which we should be looking for the privilege. There are two false dichotomies which have arisen in the consideration of these issues by the European Court of Human Rights – those between being a human right and counting for nothing and between being an absolute right or nothing. We assert that the privilege against self-incrimination can be a significant right (its significance varying from legal system to legal system) without being either an absolute or an omnipresent right. So far as concerns proactive policing, in view of the general irrelevance of the privilege against self-incrimination one had better concentrate directly on the values which it aims to protect, human dignity and autonomy, and discuss ways of protecting them adequately. The opaque language of the judgement of the majority of the European Court of Human Rights in *Saunders v UK* does little to aid clarity in this whole area.

Notes

1 *Fisher v United States* (1976) 425 US 391; *US v Doe* (1984) 465 US 605.
2 *Video Information Exchange v Rank Film Distributors* [1982] AC 380.
3 *Perez v Campbell* (1971) 402 US 637.
4 Report of the European Commission in *K v Austria* (ECHR 2 June 1993, Series A, vol. 255-B).
5 *Ex p Cossens* (1820) Buck 531; 540 *R v Scott* (1856) Dears and B 47.
6 Parliamentary debates 1992/1993, 23 009, nr. 6.
7 *Funke v France*, ECHR 25 February 1993, Series A, vol. 256-A.
8 *Murray v UK*, ECHR 8 February 1996, 22 EHRR 29.
9 *Funke v France*, ECHR 25 February 1993, Series A, vol. 256-A; *Murray v United Kingdom*, 8 February 1996, 22 EHRR 29; *Saunders v United Kingdom*, ECHR 17 December 1996, *The Times* 18 December 1996.
10 *Hamilton and others v Naviede* [1995] 2 AC 75.
11 *Re v London United Investments* (1992) Ch 578.
12 *Bishopsgate Investment Management Ltd v Maxwell* (1993) Ch 1.
13 *R v Saunders et al.* [1996] 1 Cr App Rep 463.
14 HR 26 October 1993, NJ 1994, 629.
15 Cf. HR 22 November 1994, NJ 1995, 240.
16 Cf. HR 23 October 1994, NJ 1995, 239; HR 29 October 1996, NJ 1997, 232.
17 *United States v Sullivan*, 274 US 259 (1927).

References

Ashworth, A. (1994), *Criminal Justice: An Evaluative Study,* Oxford: Clarendon Press.

Ashworth, A. (1996), The Presumption of Innocence in English Criminal Law, *Criminal Law Review* 306.

Brants, C. and S. Field (1995), *Participation Rights and Proactive Policing: Convergence and Drift in European Criminal Process,* Deventer: Kluwer.

Dennis, I. (1995), Instrumental protection, human right or functional necessity? Reassessing the privilege against self-incrimination, 54 *C.L.J.* 342-376.

Galligan, D.J. (1988), The Right to Silence Reconsidered, *CLP* 69.

Kleinknecht, T. (1989), *Strafprozeszordnung*, München: Beck.

Lewis, A.D.E. (1990) Bentham's view of the right to silence, 43 *CLP* 135-157.

Pugh, P. (1987), *Is Guinness Good for You? The Bid for Distillers,* London Financial Training.

Reijntjes, J. (1996), *Nemo tenetur,* Deventer: Gouda Quint.

Stuart, D. (1991), *Charter Justice in Canadian Criminal Law* 328, Carswell.

Part III
Accountability and control: some potential strategies

16 Controlling cross border undercover operations

JACK A. BLUM AND NIKOS PASSAS

Introduction

As criminal activities and illicit enterprises increasingly cross national borders, so does the need for law enforcement efforts to become more international. The United States of America has been doing so for some time, influencing lawmaking and law enforcement practices overseas (Nadelmann 1993). One of the methods US agencies have been using and promoting overseas is undercover investigations. Beside the problem of extraterritorial jurisdiction, this practice raises numerous issues including the invasion of privacy, the use of deception, and the involvement of police officers in criminal activities.

With police agencies often engaging in cross border undercover operations, the question then is how to control these operations and the officials who run them (Passas and Groskin 1995). Controls are essential to protect human rights, to ensure that police operations are directed at appropriate targets, and to prevent the criminal law enforcement process from provoking destructive political reactions. So, who should run the control system? How should it work? How should the needs for control be balanced against the need for operation security? Authorities responding to international organized crime, on the other hand, must be able to operate quickly and with flexibility.

In this chapter, we attempt to pave the ground for policy improvements by pointing to problems regarding control methods and international undercover operations. We will suggest the creation of an international tribunal for the express purpose of controlling such operations.

The US example: exclusionary rules

Although undercover operations are frequently used in the United States (Marx 1988), they are neither allowed nor undertaken in all criminal justice systems (Fijnaut and Marx 1995; Parry and Hunt 1994). US domestic police operations are controlled through management within law enforcement agencies and by the judiciary, which supervises and participates in the investigative process and decides ex post facto on the legality and appropriateness of police operations. The requirement that police receive judicial permission for searches, wiretaps and arrests is a central element of the control system.

In the common law and under the US constitutional framework the courts have, to a great extent, controlled the police through exclusionary rules – that is, by not allowing prosecutors to put material gained through improper investigative techniques into evidence. In the United States the courts have established the 'fruit of the poisoned tree' doctrine. Under that approach, evidence obtained improperly taints and leads to the exclusion of all evidence which is derived from it.

Even in a purely domestic American context, however, exclusionary rules have caused considerable debate. For years, police and the general public complained that guilty criminals were being released on technicalities as a way of punishing the police. Despite the lack of any evidence that such rules 'handcuff' the police (Davies 1983; Skolnick and Fyfe 1993), over a period of years the courts have whittled away at the exclusionary rule, carving out one exception after another.

In the international context, where careful direct supervision of police operations is essential, exclusionary rules should at least be a control of last resort. It is unfair to subject a defendant to the burden of proving that evidence was obtained illegally in a foreign jurisdiction after he has been detained and put on trial.

Noteworthy, however, is the irony that the use of deceptive methods in undercover operations has increased in the context of restrictions over the coercive and post-arrest powers of the police in the United States. Executive, legislative, judicial, and internal controls are fewer when it comes to deceptive tactics that may be questionable (Marx 1995).

Observing the standards of host countries

Thus far we have considered the issue of control from the perspective of national law and policy. We have discussed the control of undercover operations to ensure that they conform to the standards of their own national legal and constitutional requirements. A second important issue is the control of the operation under the national law of the country where the operation is to take place. Here a fresh set of questions arise.

What level of control should a country have where part of an international undercover operation is taking place? Should foreign police targeting foreign nationals have to conform to the local law with respect to the collection of evidence? Should the local police or the local judiciary have the ability to veto the operation, even if it does not involve their own nationals and the crime does not harm anyone within their jurisdiction?

The answer to some of these questions turns on the problem of choosing the appropriate substantive criminal law. As criminals move from country to country to commit a major crime, the issue is which country's laws should apply and where should the crime be prosecuted. If a matter is criminal in the country which has started the investigation, but not criminal in the country to which the perpetrator has fled, should the undercover investigation be allowed to proceed? Should a country be allowed to run an operation that is aimed at those committing a cross-border crime when their act is criminal in the country seeking to run the operation but not in the other?

These issues are far from theoretical and will become even less theoretical as time goes on. For example, the United States has a crime described as interstate communication by wire in furtherance of a fraud – commonly known as wire fraud. Criminal confidence men have been operating wire fraud schemes directed against Americans from safe havens in Costa Rica and some island nations in the Caribbean. The countries from which they are working have a crime called fraud which does not have the elements of the use of a telephone or fax machine and the crossing of state lines. Indeed, what the confidence men are doing may not even rise to the level of a crime under local law, because local law does not require disclosures and regular publication of accounts by corporations.

The United States has pressed forward with international police operations in part because it takes an expansive view of its criminal jurisdiction (Nadelmann 1993). If the actions of a criminal have an impact on the United States, federal criminal law asserts that a crime has been committed in the United States. Thus, under the criminal provisions of American antitrust law, two Dutchmen who conspired to fix the price of quinine in the United States at a meeting in the Netherlands, violated American law without setting foot in the country and without being connected to the country by their citizenship.

United States law covering drug smuggling, financial fraud, air piracy, and terrorism directed against United States persons or property outside the United States have a similar extraterritorial reach. Further, the United States federal courts assume jurisdiction over a criminal defendant brought forcibly from overseas without inquiring into the method by which he was brought before the court. Thus, in the Alvarez-Machain case, a Mexican was kidnapped with the connivance of the DEA inside Mexico and brought across the border for trial in the United States. The US Supreme Court, following long established legal precedent, held that the defendant could be tried in the United States for the crimes in the indictment. The court did not question the methods used to bring the criminal defendant within its jurisdiction or examine international law implications.

The Alvarez-Machain decision was widely criticized inside and outside the United States (Glennon 1992; Heymann and Gershengorn 1993; Lowenfeld 1990; Organization of American States Permanent Council 1993; Steinhardt 1993). The government of Mexico was particularly aggrieved and protested vigorously. The justified attack on this assertion of 'extra-territorial' jurisdiction underscores the sensitivity of the issue for international undercover operations.

Handling undercover agents

Working undercover is one of the most difficult jobs in law enforcement. It is fraught with stress and danger and requires support and extraordinary operational security to protect the agents and achieve the case objectives (Girodo 1984; Marx 1988; Miller 1987).

As difficult as the issues are in a domestic investigation, in the international arena they become overwhelming (Passas and Groskin 1995). As long as an agent is working in the United States in an undercover role, he is still an officer of the law. Once he sets foot beyond the borders of the country, he loses his official status and the related immunity and protections. In fact, if the agent operates in a criminal organization in a foreign country, he may become a criminal under the laws of that country.

Even without direct participation in criminal acts, an agent may be violating the criminal laws of foreign jurisdictions by just being there. For example, Switzerland regards foreign investigations of any kind on its soil a violation of its espionage laws. The Swiss routinely threaten investigators who want to go there with arrest unless they have formal official permission.

If an agent is dispatched by his home law enforcement agency to gather information or to observe the citizens of another country, it is possible the agent will be violating both domestic laws and international treaty obligations regarding non-intervention in the internal affairs of other countries.

At the very least, if the undercover agent is to work outside his home country he needs a legal status and some protection. To get that protection it will obviously be necessary for the home country of the agent to inform the country which is the site of the operation. There will have to be some mechanism for coordination of the operation. The mechanism will have to include provisions for tight security to protect the lives of the undercover agents.

Most undercover agents would rather risk being arrested abroad in the course of their work than have their identity disclosed to foreigners they do not know or trust. This attitude should not be surprising. Security of the operation is the single most important concern of an agency running an undercover activity. Each extra person told magnifies the threat of disclosure. If the government of a country which must be informed is corrupt, or has corrupt officials, passing operational information could be fatal to the agent.

Certain relationships which have developed informally among law enforcement agencies are good enough to sustain exchanging information on a voluntary basis. The US Customs Service shared what it was doing in the BCCI case (see below) with the British, the French and the Swiss. None of the information passed on by the American team was compromised. The FBI has developed extraordinary working relationships with the Italian police and have worked very successfully together on cases involving Mafia operations in both countries. The New York County District Attorney's office and the Hong Kong police have developed strong personal relationships which have helped in breaking drug smuggling rings which were shipping heroin from Asia to New York.

But reliance on informal relationships – even ones that are well developed – is an inadequate framework for exchanging information about undercover work. New machinery for dealing with operational security and meeting legal standards for cross border police work has to be developed or invented.

Setting the target

For US federal law enforcement agencies, cross border undercover operations are particularly tempting as a way to make the bosses look good.

From time to time operations they have proposed have had little intrinsic merit. For example, in a number of recent cases, the Customs Service recruited criminals awaiting sentencing to run sting operations. These criminals were induced to help by an offer of reduced sentences and the payment of money based on how successful they were. Several of these stings involved cross border operations. The results of the cases were disastrous. The targets were questionable, the objectives were at best murky, and the guilt of the defendants was unproven (see also Passas and Blum in this volume; Passas and Groskin 1995).

When an international undercover investigation which has started in one country expands across borders and begins to focus on a foreign citizen in a foreign country, the investigation raises profound questions about concepts of sovereignty and individual rights. The basic idea of the 'Law of Nations' is that each citizen is responsible to his or her government. The government is sovereign. The rights of the citizen are determined by the relationship between the citizen and the government.

A recent US Customs case raised these questions in a dramatic way. Customs used an undercover agent to target Ken Walker, a Canadian citizen. The agent encouraged Walker to commit a technical violation of United States export control law from his home in Canada. Despite his repeated attempts to establish the legality of the proposed transaction and the legitimacy of the clients, Walker was arrested and charged when he transited LaGuardia airport on his way to Bermuda to conclude his due diligence work before making the 'deal'. He was released on bail and returned to Canada (Passas and Groskin 1995). Even if every charge against him were true (which is bitterly disputed), he would have violated no Canadian law.

Is this legitimate police work? Do the police of one country have any right to use an undercover sting against foreign nationals who have never set foot on their soil?

The Canadian government responded to these questions with a resounding no and refused to extradite the defendant. The case has strained a police relationship that has been as close and cooperative as that of any two nations on the planet.

The Walker case is one extreme in a continuum of cases and crimes. One can easily posit an undercover case across borders that would evoke sympathy and support. Consider for example, the use of an undercover operation to target an aircraft hijacker or terrorist. In that circumstance the attitudes of the home country of the target might be quite different.

The fundamental questions are: what are the rights of the target and under which law and constitution are they determined? The answer may tell us which sovereign has the responsibility for protecting those rights. Is it the home country of the target? Is it the home country of the investigator? Is it the country where the investigation takes place?

Once these questions are answered the issue then becomes when, where and how the target will be able to assert his or her rights? Are the rights to be asserted in a criminal trial in the country of the investigator? Or should the question of rights be determined in an extradition proceeding? Should the target be able to appeal to the courts of his or her home country?

In one case, a convicted arms dealer working for the Customs Service, lured a group of government officials from Uganda to a meeting in Florida. He told the officials that he wanted to sell them low price blue jeans. The offer was a good one and they were tempted by the opportunity to make money. It was also perfectly legal. After some vague conversation about the blue jeans, the meeting adjourned and the group walked outside to his car where he told them he had a Stinger anti-aircraft missile which he knew they would want to buy. His conversation about the missile was taped and nearby agents jumped out of the bushes to arrest the Ugandans and their American escort.

When the case came before a US District court judge, it was dismissed and the agents and prosecutors were reprimanded for their behaviour. The judge was especially incensed that the 'undercover' who was a criminal looking for time off had been given so much leeway in organizing the sting. The undercover was clearly taking advantage of the Ugandans and their ignorance of the American system.

In another case, an undercover agent for the Customs service arranged for the delivery of weapons in Poland as part of a sting operation. An elaborate set up was arranged so that the delivery could be taped. The problem with the case was that the entire affair was legal under Polish law and the participants could not be arrested.

These cases resulted in personal catastrophes for innocent defendants, well deserved diplomatic protests to the United States and a black eye to the law enforcement agency.

It is apparent that the Customs cases were the result of internal pressure on agents to produce dramatic results against international crime. They were not the result of strategic intelligence, high level planning, or even of careful targeting of suspected organizations. They did not serve the long term objective of deterrence. They could not have served the laudable function of disabling major international criminal organizations.

Thus, it is clear that international sting operations must be subject to careful, high-level control at both the domestic and the international level.

When field level agents propose an international undercover operation, they should be required to establish probable cause. Their information should be correlated with intelligence analysis of other information in law enforcement files. There must be a demonstration that the prospective targets are likely to be engaged in serious criminal activity.

Supervisors ought to consider the value of the target in achieving larger objectives. The successful international undercover operation should be the result of reasoned analysis, not random luck.

The very first decision about an undercover operation – picking the target – is fraught with difficulty. In the United States the presumption of innocence is constitutional and cannot be ignored. An outgrowth of the presumption of innocence is the law prohibiting entrapment (Parry and Hunt 1994; Stavsky 1985). In the United States, the target must be predisposed to criminal activity. The undercover operatives cannot manufacture the crime and entice the target to take part in it. This means that, the instant a target says that he or she does not want to do something because it is illegal, the undercover operation should be over. The police may not persuade the target to commit the crime. Likewise, all international targets should have shown some predisposition to commit a crime before they are targeted.

On the other hand, a *societal* presumption of innocence and regularity is accorded to rich and powerful individuals. Similarly, large organizations and businesses are assumed to be operating within the framework of the law. In general, the larger the organization and the greater its prestige, the greater the societal presumption of innocence. As a result of this presumption, law enforcement agencies may be unduly reluctant to take on well known organizations and individuals. They assume that the mere status of the person or organization is a sign that their behaviour is legal.

The reluctance to take on powerful targets is often manifest at the supervisory level. The bosses know the power and influence of the prospective target and understand that, if the operation fails, their jobs could be at stake.

Thus, the issue of targeting an organization or individual is filled with traps (Marx 1982). Has the target been selected because of commercial rivalry, size, or political unpopularity? Is the target avoiding investigation because of political power, connections, and position? If police at the working level feel sure that they are justified in going after a respected person or organization, should the right of their supervisors to shut them down be subject to further review?

Conversely, police organizations and police at the working level, are tempted to target the weak and vulnerable to make themselves look good. In the United States, many law enforcement agencies award promotions on the basis of arrest and seizure statistics. Agents and supervisors are under pressure to produce cases. In election years they are pressured to produce cases which will look good in the press.

The temptations to base the targeting of an international undercover operation on inappropriate criteria must be controlled before the operation starts.

Operation C-Chase and the BCCI case

The BCCI case – at least the operation C-Chase portion of it – illustrates some of the issues raised by cross border operations. The BCCI Tampa money-laundering case started as a sting operation directed at a Colombian drug gang. The agents running the sting persuaded the drug dealers that they could launder money and provide distribution for cocaine at the American end of the deal.

The undercover operatives manipulated their superiors into targeting the bank by suggesting the bank as the place to open accounts for the sting. The selection was apparently made at random, but in fact the agents suspected that the bank was questionable. They believed that if they voiced their suspicions about the bank, their work would need high level approval before going forward, and that the approval would not have been forthcoming.

In private interviews, these undercover agents said that they were always under pressure to get results quickly and to stay away from making the case too complicated. They understood that further expanding the international scope of the case, would have been too rich an idea to propose to narrow-minded, results-oriented, superiors who were demanding immediate arrests.

When the case began to mushroom, and it became clear that the bank and many of its clients were involved in many other illegal activities, the prosecutors and supervisors cut off further operations. They 'took the case down'. These prosecutors saw the international aspects of the case as a barrier to getting the dramatic short term results they wanted. They were focused on crimes in the Middle District of Florida. They did not want to complicate the case for a jury, they did not want to globalize the case in a way that would have brought senior officials in Washington into the decision making process, and did not want to expand the undercover operation in a way that involved other American jurisdictions (Passas and Groskin 1993).

In fact, had there been a proper management system, the agents should have been able to report their suspicions to superiors who would have appreciated what the agents were trying to do. Top officials would have looked at the evidence that had been gathered and would have correlated it with information from other law enforcement agencies. If they had done that check, they would have found hundreds of other complaints, reports, and references in agency files alleging strikingly similar facts (on BCCI, see Passas 1993, 1995, 1996a, 1996b). Such analysis could have been the basis on which managers would determine that BCCI was an appropriate target in its own right well worth the time and money involved in an expanded and extended operation (Passas and Groskin 1993).

In this light, it is clearly necessary to establish special internal review procedures before an international undercover operation is approved. These should include a survey of existing records to determine whether the target has been the subject of police inquiry in the past, and a weighing of whether the case is serious enough to warrant the use of scarce international resources. Once the decision to move forward is made, the case should receive sophisticated, high level support. Good management has a second benefit. It ensures that standards of probable cause are met and that particular persons should be targeted.

International cooperation and collaboration

In the BCCI Tampa case the undercover agents enlisted the help of a number of foreign government law enforcement agencies. Their objective was the coordination of arrests and the execution of search warrants. There was some coordination which was limited to matters of timing. When the arrests were made, the international coordination was touted at the post-arrest press conferences.

Unfortunately, the coordination which should have taken place never did. That coordination would have included a discussion of the thorny issues which later became apparent. These included:
- Determining the locus and scope of the criminal activity.
- Deciding which law enforcement agencies in which countries were best equipped to handle the issues.
- Deciding which governments should contribute to financing a more complete investigation and bear the burdens associated with it.
- Deciding the best venue or venues for prosecution.

To understand just one example of coordination which missed the point, consider the search warrant executed by UK Customs and Excise at the main office of BCCI on Leadenhall Street in London. Among the records seized by British Customs were a manager's private files on accounts at the bank.

These files contained the records of accounts which did not appear on the regular bank books. Because the case had been confined and because no effort was made at that time to look at the institution as a whole, no one thought to pose the question of how a bank could have 'off the books' accounts and still be a legitimate organization. Even minimal coordination with other law enforcement agencies would have raised red flags about the bank itself.

British Customs put extraordinary restrictions on the seized information, apparently more concerned with protecting the secrecy of bank clients not directly involved in the Tampa case than in understanding the criminal activity of the bank.

Because these larger issues were not raised at the international level, the Tampa prosecutors took charge and directed the foreign police agencies. The result was a limited number of cases in Tampa and in England. The Florida cases were successful, but the end result was far from what it could have been (Kerry Report 1992).

In the United States, with its multi-jurisdictional criminal justice system, the states and federal government frequently cooperate in making the essential decisions about major criminal cases. Federal and local prosecutors meet regularly to decide where an investigation belongs. In complex cases, such as the Unabomber case, representatives of twenty or more jurisdictions met to discuss where and how to charge the defendant.

Similar machinery is essential at the international level, especially in the area of financial fraud. If an investigation points to an important international criminal organization, the reach of the investigators should equal the reach of the criminals. That requires international management of the investigation. Appropriate machinery for that management must be put in place.

Another recent example of an international undercover operation that raised many of the same issues is 'Operation Dinero', a joint venture of the DEA and Atlanta US Attorney's office. In this operation, the American agents actually purchased a dormant bank on the British island of Anguilla. They put the bank into operation and began to launder drug money.

The operation was a smashing success. The bank soon had tens of millions in deposits and the officers running it were able to trace funds from the bank to other offshore accounts controlled by the drug gangs. The agents wanted to keep the operation going, but it was shut down after six months.

The problem was that the operation was too successful. Instead of just attracting drug dealers, it was beginning to attract American tax evaders. Tax evasion in the United States is a criminal felony whereas in Britain, much of the banking industry effectively assists nationals of other countries in avoiding the payment of taxes to their home countries. The British did not want the operation to continue because now it would be used by the United States to trap its own nationals committing an American crime on British soil. The British view was that, since nothing criminal was being done under British law, the British could not let the operation continue. If US agents had continued the operation without British permission, they would violate Anguillan bank secrecy law.

The private sector has provided a model for a type of coordination which makes sense. The security officers of a group of large international banks meet on a regular basis and exchange information on criminals who are attempting to target them in various countries. The security departments then work together to put their adversaries out of business. They set the criminals up by tempting them to pursue their activities in jurisdictions with tough fraud laws and tough prosecutors. When the evidence has been assembled, the security people give it to the police. However, official law enforcement agencies are constrained by international law and custom and a similar arrangement among them requires a more formal framework.

The evidence problem

Police undercover operations should have prosecution as their prime objective, and prosecutions require *admissible* evidence. Making sure that the evidence gathered by police can be used in court is a major problem even when the evidence, the crime and the criminal are all found in the same place as the trial.

As mentioned earlier, the exclusion of evidence is a way of controlling police behaviour. Under American law, evidence gathered improperly (for example without the use of a proper search warrant, evidence which is coerced, and evidence which cannot be properly authenticated) may be excluded from the trial.

When the evidence comes from foreign jurisdictions, questions of admissibility abound. Was the evidence gathered legally under the laws of the place where it was gathered? Which law should apply to determine whether the evidence is admissible? Is it the job of the courts of one country to protect the judicial process of a second country by denying the admissibility of evidence gathered illegally under foreign law but legally under local law?

Even if the methods of gathering evidence pass muster, how can prosecutors ensure that additional supporting foreign evidence can be obtained in an admissible and timely form? For example, if an undercover agent hears a discussion about the use of a bank account or a corporation to launder money, how can the prosecutor ensure that the records of those accounts are received in time for trial?

Defence concerns

So far, the discussion has been from the view of the prosecutor, but the problems faced by the defence need consideration as well. How can defence counsel build a case when the evidence is scattered across the world and is not subject to a simple process by the prosecuting court? Is it fair to try a defendant who cannot bring foreign witnesses to the table, cannot assemble foreign documents and has no way to get access to foreign exculpatory material from foreign police agencies?

Without some tools in the hands of defence attorney, the possibility exists that international police operations can violate human rights, could be misused for political purposes and allow law enforcement agencies to misuse their power.

Both sides of the international criminal evidence issue cry out for a new convention which revises from the ground up existing procedures regarding the delivery of evidence and witnesses. The bilateral system of mutual legal assistance treaties is too cumbersome and too slow. It barely works in simple bilateral situations which are well defined. When the case involves three or more countries and a group of defendants, the machinery grinds to a halt.

Conclusion: an international tribunal

Some of the above problems can be simplified if international undercover operations are properly supervised by judicial authorities as they develop. If the legal and constitutional questions are addressed before the fact, the issue of ex post facto protection is somewhat less acute.

The questions which are raised are classic civil law conflict of laws issues. In the common law system they are resolved by a body of law governing the choice of law which becomes an important threshold issue in a multi-jurisdictional civil case. Choice of law rules frequently split the difference by adopting the procedural rules of the forum and the substantive rules of the locus of the event. The conflict rules provide important intellectual insight for the problems we are discussing. However, they cannot serve to resolve similar issues in the criminal arena. The problem is that the core function of the criminal justice system is adjudicating the rights of the individual. These rights are weighed against the rights of the state. Every question in a criminal case is a potential constitutional issue because a person's liberty is at stake.

From time to time an international criminal court is proposed as a way around this thicket (Ferencz 1992). As attractive as the idea is at first blush, on close analysis, it becomes clear that the present difficulties are so numerous and complex that its materialization is a *long-term* project. Depending on the theory one adopts, criminal law reflects a certain societal consensus or the power balance among various social groups within each society. In either case, criminal cases and prosecutions serve to support the standards of the societies that pursue them. The legitimacy of the courts depends on the standards of the society they judge. Unfortunately an international criminal court, even under United Nations auspices, lacks that political legitimacy.

Furthermore, certainty is an essential aspect of the criminal law. Societies reject ex post facto criminal legislation. Criminal statutes are interpreted much more narrowly than civil statutes. How can an international court operating in an international environment develop and enforce an international criminal law and at the same time meet the certainty test (Schwartzenberger 1950)?

One approach would be to create an international tribunal for the sole purpose of supervising international undercover operations. The tribunal could call upon the services of justices from each country involved in the operation. At the outset the tribunal could be used to determine the appropriateness of an undercover operation by deciding whether probable cause existed. It might also approve, and act as a safe repository for information about, cross border operations which might raise serious questions for the undercover officers.

As the investigation develops, the tribunal would then call on the justices from a particular country to decide issues relating to the rights of their own nationals, under their own law. Similarly judges from the country where evidence is gathered could decide issues of admissibility in a preliminary way, as the evidence is gathered. The judges working together could be given the task of developing a legal road map for the choice of forum, choice of law, and constitutional boundaries.

The kind of tribunal we are proposing would have to be established by international convention and perhaps might best begin on a regional basis. This measure is, of course, neither a panacea nor incompatible with additional control mechanisms. We also recognize that something needs to be done before the international community reaches the necessary consensus for the establishment of such a tribunal. There is a clear need for complementary controls before, during and after the conclusion of a cross-border undercover investigation, some of which may be implemented in the short term (see Passas and Blum, this volume). We emphasize, however, that this proposal has the advantage of not requiring any nation to 'surrender its sovereignty' or giving up the protection of the rights of its citizens. For this reason, it has a reasonable chance of materializing and succeeding.

References

Davies, T. (1983), A Hard Look at What We Know (and Still Need to Learn) about the 'Costs' of the Exclusionary Rule, *American Bar Foundation Research Journal*, pp. 611-690.

Ferencz, B.B. (1992), An International Criminal Code and Court: Where They Stand and Where They're Going, *Columbia Journal of Transnational Law*, *30*, pp. 375-399.

Fijnaut, C., and G.T. Marx (eds.) (1995), *Undercover: Police Surveillance in Comparative Perspective*, The Hague: Kluwer Law International.

Girodo, M. (1984), Entry and Re-entry Strain in Undercover Agents, in: V.N. Allen and E. v.d. Vliert (eds.), *Role Transitions*, New York: Plenum, pp. 169-179.

Glennon, M.J. (1992), State-Sponsored Abduction: A Comment on United States v. Alvarez-Machain, *American Journal of International Law*, *86*, pp. 746-756.

Heymann, P.B., and I.H. Gershengorn (1993), A Missed Opportunity, *Criminal Law Forum*, *4* (1), pp. 155-175.

Kerry Report (1992), *The BCCI Affair*, Washington, DC: GPO.

Lowenfeld, A.F. (1990), Kidnapping by Government Order, *American Journal of International Law*, *84* (3), pp. 712-716.

Marx, G.T. (1982), Who Really Gets Stung? Some Issues Raised by the New Police Undercover Work, *Crime and Delinquency*, (April), pp. 165-193.

Marx, G.T. (1988), *Undercover: Police Surveillance in America*, Berkeley: University of California Press.

Marx, G.T. (1995), The Use of Undercover Methods in Corruption Investigation – The Case of the United States of America, *Collected Works of the Seventh International Anti-Corruption Conference*, Beijing, pp. 598-607.

Miller, G.I. (1987), Observations on Police Undercover Work, *Criminology*, *25* (1), pp. 27-46.

Nadelmann, E.A. (1993), *Cops Across Borders: The Internationalization of U.S. Criminal Law Enforcement*, University Park: Pennsylvania State University Press.

Organization of American States Permanent Council (1993), Legal Opinion on the

Decision of the Supreme Court of the United States of America, *Criminal Law Forum*, *4* (1), pp. 119-134.

Parry, H., and S.S. Hunt (1994), Undercover Operations and White Collar Crime. *Journal of Asset Protection and Financial Crime*, *2* (1), pp. 150-159.

Passas, N. (1993), Structural Sources of International Crime: Policy Lessons from the BCCI Affair, *Crime, Law and Social Change*, *20* (4), pp. 293-305.

Passas, N. (1995), The Mirror of Global Evils: A Review Essay on the BCCI Affair, *Justice Quarterly*, *12* (2), pp. 801-829.

Passas, N. (1996a), The Genesis of the BCCI Scandal, *Journal of Law and Society*, *23* (1), pp. 52-72.

Passas, N. (1996b), Accounting for Fraud: Auditors' Ethical and Legal Dilemmas in the BCCI Affair, in: W.M. Hoffman, J. Kamm, R.E. Frederick, and E. Petry (eds.), *The Ethics of Accounting and Finance*, Newport, CO: Quorum Books, pp. 85-99.

Passas, N., and R.B. Groskin (1993), BCCI and the Federal Authorities: Regulatory Anaesthesia and the Limits of Criminal Law. Presented at the *Society for the Study of Social Problems annual meeting*. Miami Beach.

Passas, N., and R.B. Groskin (1995), International Undercover Operations, in: C. Fijnaut and G.T. Marx (eds.), *Undercover: Police Surveillance in Comparative Perspective*, The Hague: Kluwer Law International, pp. 291-312.

Schwarzenberger, G. (1950), The Problem of an International Criminal Law, *Current Legal Problems*, *3*, pp. 263-296.

Skolnick, J.H., and J.J. Fyfe (1993), *Above the Law: Police and the Excessive Use of Force*. New York: Free Press.

Steinhardt, R.G. (1993), Statement Before the Subcommittee on Civil and Constitutional Rights of the Committee on the Judiciary, U.S. House of Representatives, *Criminal Law Forum*, *4* (1), pp. 135-154.

17 Proactive policing: limiting the role of the defence lawyer

ED CAPE AND TARU SPRONKEN

Introduction

Defence lawyers occupy a potentially ambiguous position in both of the major legal traditions in Europe. The principle of 'equality of arms', implicit in the European Convention on Human Rights (Gomien et al. 1996, p. 190-196), gives rise to the explicit right of a person charged with an offence to the assistance of a lawyer (Article 6.3.c). This has been given a broad interpretation by the European Court of Human Rights, so that the right to legal assistance does not merely arise at the point at which a person is formally charged with a criminal offence but, it would seem, arises at the earlier stage of police interrogation prior to charge.[1] However, whilst the right of access to a lawyer at the interrogation stage has come to be accepted as implicit in the European Convention, the proper role of the lawyer has yet to be explicated. Article 6.3.c refers to the right of a person 'to defend himself in person or through legal assistance', but the precise meaning of 'defend himself' is less than clear, and requires interpretation in the context of other provisions of Article 6 in particular.[2] In any event, a more accurate picture of defence lawyers' actual, as opposed to theoretical, role may be gleaned from analysing the legal context within which lawyers work, and from research into the work that defence lawyers do.

This chapter examines the implications of proactive policing[3] for defence lawyers, and defence lawyering, in the Netherlands and in England and Wales. It seeks to establish those issues that are jurisdiction-specific and, more importantly, those issues that cross jurisdictional boundaries. In circumstances where European states are increasingly seeking harmonization in approaches to policing and crime investigation,[4] and in which proactive methods of police investigation are becoming more commonplace,[5] it considers the effects of proactive police investigation on evidence gathering pre

292 *Ed Cape and Taru Spronken*

and post-charge, and on the use (or non-use) of evidence at trial, and also examines the implications of these developments for the role of defence lawyers.

Whilst there are important, and significant, differences between the legal context of defence lawyers' practice in the Netherlands and in England and Wales, which will be explored in this chapter, it is important to note that a common characteristic of both jurisdictions is that defence lawyers frequently have difficulty in securing access to information in the hands of the police at the investigative stage of the criminal process. This, it will be argued, is crucial in the context of proactive police investigations. Further, whilst the right of a suspect to access to a lawyer during police interrogation does, at present, differ significantly as between the two jurisdictions, the legal consequences of denial of access are not necessarily so divergent.[6]

For the defence lawyer a number of general problems may be identified as arising from, or in connection with, proactive police investigation.

1) Many forms of proactive police investigation are characterized by secrecy, frequently sanctioned by the courts. The involvement of an informer is normally not disclosed to a suspect/defendant; the location of a surveillance post is often kept secret; an undercover police officer may give anonymous evidence. Other problems flow from secrecy, in particular the often intractable problem of establishing relevance, necessary where seeking to persuade a court to order disclosure, or in seeking the exclusion of other evidence.[7]

2) Many forms of proactive investigation are largely unregulated by statute. In England and Wales, only the interception of public postal or telephonic communications is regulated by statute: the use of informers, undercover police, physical and electronic surveillance or bugging is not.[8] This has significant implications for the reception of evidence obtained by such methods. In effect, neither the courts nor government takes responsibility for regulating such activity.[9] In the Netherlands, investigative methods should have an explicit legal basis and police investigations should only take place in the manner laid down by law.[10] However, in the context of the priority which in recent years has been given to countering serious and organized crime, new investigative methods which do not have a legal basis, such as infiltration, front-store operations, various forms of surveillance, and the gathering, registration and processing of data and information, have not been considered by the courts as unlawful. The courts have justified such practices by reference to the general duties of the police and judicial authorities as laid down in

Article 2 (formerly 28) of the 1993 Police Act and Articles 141 and 142 of the Dutch Code of Criminal Procedure.[11] Lack of legal account-ability, when added to secrecy, is an explosive cocktail. The scandal that broke when it was discovered that tonnes of unlawful drugs had been imported into the Netherlands under the supervision of an Inter-regional Crime Squad and the Criminal Intelligence Unit of Kennemerland led to the establishment of the Parliamentary Inquiry conducted by the Van Traa commission.[12] In its final report, the commission advised the Dutch Parliament that it should improve both the standards of competence of and the levels of responsibility for such police activities. The commission stressed that both the examining judge and the trial judge should actively control police investigations. This would require all investigative methods, and their results, to be made known at the trial.[13] The govern-ment accepted most of these recommendations[14] but whether effective regulation and control of investigative methods will be achieved will depend upon the precise form of the new legislation, and the attitude of the courts.

3) In England and Wales the police develop their own law-enforcement priorities for which they are scarcely accountable in a democratic sense. Determining investigative priorities reactively, by relying upon victim or witness reporting, it may be argued, provides only marginally greater accountability. However, when associated with secrecy, proactive policing means that priorities are left entirely to the police to develop and may, in some circumstances, depend upon illegitimate considerations. A person may be targeted, not because of the likelihood of their committing a crime, or because of the significance of crimes that they may be commit-ting, but because they have been identified by an informer who has his or her own motives for placing the police spot-light on them (Cape 1996). Equally, an informer may be given 'permission' by the police to commit crimes.[15] Illegitimate or questionable policing priorities, whilst usually not relevant to the construction of a defence, may be relevant to mitigation, if they could be established.

The general problems outlined above affect the position of the defence lawyer during both the pre-trial stage and the trial stage. Pre-trial the main concern is that of how to advise a client once arrested given the lack of access to information in the hands of the police. This is exacerbated in the Netherlands by the fact that defence lawyers can be, and normally are, denied access to their clients during police interrogation. At the trial stage problems centre on the opportunities for the defence to challenge evidence resulting from proactive police methods. The sanctioning of illegal (or unfair) police activities within the criminal trial, in respect of which the legal traditions of the Netherlands and England and Wales differ significantly in principle, has inevitable consequences for the role of defence lawyers at trial stage.

The pre-trial stage

One of the consequences of proactive police investigations, especially those involving the targeting of people suspected of being involved in crime, is that the police will frequently (although not always) have gathered most of the evidence they need for the purposes of prosecution prior to arrest. Indeed, one of the underlying purposes of proactive policing is to shift the emphasis away from interrogation and evidence of confession.[16] Thus a 'front store' operation will normally have allowed the police to gather electronically recorded evidence of the identity of, and incriminating comments by, the suspect(s), fingerprint evidence, physical evidence of goods stolen, and evidence relating to the source of those goods. A simple undercover drugs operation involving delivery of drugs to a person suspected of dealing in drugs will result in tape-recorded evidence of delivery of a package to the suspect, and of any comments made on delivery, forensic evidence relating to the contents of the package, and possibly electronically recorded evidence of conversations involving the suspect prior to the delivery. Reasonable suspicion for the purpose of justifying an arrest[17] will, therefore, have easily been established.

There are important differences between England and Wales, and the Netherlands, in relation to the position of the suspect and the powers of the police following an arrest. First, the police in England and Wales do not have the power to detain the suspect for interrogation where there is sufficient evidence to charge him or her, but must proceed to make a decision whether to charge.[18] Once the suspect has been charged they may not, in normal circumstances, be questioned about the offence.[19] This is not the case in the Netherlands, where the police are permitted to interrogate a suspect even when there is enough evidence to charge him or her.[20]

Second, a suspect in England and Wales who has been arrested and is detained at a police station has a well established right to legal advice (PACE section 58), which includes a right to have a lawyer present during any police interview (Code of Practice C paragraph 6.8). In the Netherlands the issue of whether the lawyer has a right to be present during the police interrogation of their client is hotly disputed.[21] The common practice of the police is to refuse to allow the lawyer to attend interrogations.[22]

Third, in England and Wales neither the defence lawyer nor the suspect has any right to information from the police at the pre-charge stage, other than the fact of and grounds for arrest (PACE section 28), the reason for detention (PACE section 37(5)), and whatever information is entered on the custody record (Code of Practice C paragraph 2.4).[23] In the Netherlands the suspect and the defence lawyer have, even in the pre-trial stage, the right under Articles 30 and 51 of the Code of Criminal Procedure to all of the information which is included in the file. However, the public prosecutor is responsible for compilation of the file (which should include all relevant information obtained during the police investigation) and is likely to add to the file at this stage only the minimum information necessary to justify pre-trial detention. In any event, during the pre-trial stage, information can be withheld temporarily from the defence in the interests of the investigation (Article 30 sub 2 CCP). The defence can ask the court to order the prosecutor to add all relevant information to the file (Article 31 CCP), but in the initial stage following arrest the courts often agree with the prosecutor that the information should be temporarily withheld from the defence. At the end of the preliminary investigation, and prior to the official charge,[24] the prosecutor has to disclose all material in his or her possession. However, in practice relevant information may be withheld from the suspect at this stage without the defence or the court knowing of it.[25] This is especially likely after a proactive police investigation because the police will frequently want to keep their investigative methods secret. The prosecutor may justify a decision to withhold information by stating that the specific information is not relevant to the question of establishing guilt or innocence, or that it should be kept secret in order not to prejudice future investigations in similar cases.

The crucial point, both in the Netherlands and England and Wales, is that if little or no information about the evidence in the hands of the police has been given to the lawyer, in practice he or she has no (lawful) mechanism for obtaining that information in the period immediately following arrest of the client. If some information is given by the police, the lawyer has no way of knowing whether the information given is complete or, indeed, accurate. In such circumstances, the lawyer may conclude that the safest course of action is for his or her client not to answer police questions. However, the lawyer cannot be sure that failure to answer questions will not ultimately work to the disadvantage of his or her client at a subsequent trial.[26]

In addition to the question of what, and how much, information may be obtained from the police, the question of what evidence the defence lawyer seeks from other sources also arises. Although this is relevant in any type of criminal investigation, it has particular significance with certain forms of proactive police investigation. Where the police have carried out physical surveillance in a city centre, or where a test purchase has been made, the lawyer may wish to discover whether any video cameras contain relevant footage. This may show, for example, that the surveillance record is inaccurate or it may provide alibi evidence. Where the lawyer and/or client suspect the involvement of an informer, which is not admitted by the police, the lawyer may wish to trace the person or at least secure information about him or her. Where the case involves forensic evidence, or other expert evidence, the lawyer may wish to instruct his or her own expert.

At the investigative stage, there are severe impediments in the way of the defence lawyer conducting any but the most rudimentary of investigations prior to interrogation and/or charge. The primary difficulty is that of time. Although the police investigation may have lasted for many months, once an arrest is made, a number of factors come into play. First, the police will be working to their own timescale and may not be willing to delay interrogation for this reason and because of legal constraints on the length of detention.[27] The police do have power to grant bail to a suspect pending further enquiries (PACE section 37(2)), which would have the effect of suspending the detention time limit, but they are likely to be reluctant to do so where the alleged offence is serious. In the Netherlands, the exercise by the suspect of the right to silence will, in most cases, lead to a long period of pre-trial detention. Although bail is possible, it is rarely granted, and never in situations where there are still investigations to be carried out.

Second, defence lawyers do not have the authority of public office or the special powers available to the police to secure access to information or evidence in the hands of third parties. Therefore information or evidence that is outside the immediate possession or control of the client may prove impossible to secure. Third, with regard to physical evidence in the hands of the police, whilst it may be possible at some later stage to gain access to it in order, for example, for forensic examination and tests to be carried out, it would not be possible at this stage.

It may be concluded, therefore, that both in the Netherlands and the UK, the defence lawyer, prior to interrogation or charge, is almost entirely dependent upon the police or prosecutor for information and potential evidence. The police have a wide discretion to decide what information to disclose to the defence, and there is little the defence can do to extract from the police information which they are reluctant to disclose. It is in proactive investigation cases that the police are most reluctant to do so. Yet the suspect is at risk, in terms of the attitude of the court at any trial, if he or she decides (whether or not on legal advice) not to disclose information to the police.[28] Indeed, the question might be asked, what is the lawyer for in such circumstances? Despite the endorsement of the right of access to legal advice by the European Court of Human Rights, in circumstances where there is no right to information from the police, the advantages of such access may be limited.

The trial stage

The proposition that fair trial requires fair pre-trial procedures is fundamental to a due process conception of criminal justice. It is clear that the difficulties of the defence so far considered have implications for the fairness of a subsequent trial. In particular, secrecy and lack of disclosure is a common thread throughout both phases. In this part we examine four issues arising out of proactive policing that are of particular concern to defence lawyers during the trial phase. It is worth noting before proceeding that inquisitorial theory implies that the defence, at trial, will have full knowledge of information gained during the investigation, if only as a by-product of the requirement that the court be appraised of all relevant information. Adversarial theory, on the other hand, enables each party, in principle, to decide what information to disclose to the other, both before and at trial, although in the interests of equality of arms, the prosecution is required to disclose certain information to the defence prior to trial.[29]

The first issue concerns the extent to which the trial provides the defence with the opportunity to effectively challenge irregular or unlawful methods of investigation used by the police in the pre-trial phase. This is, of course, closely related to the question of whether the trial process, besides being a legal construction to establish guilt or innocence by a fair procedure,[30] is also a mechanism for controlling police conduct during the criminal investigation. The second issue concerns the problems for the defence in finding out about any proactive police inquiries that may have been made, and information thus obtained, before the criminal offence occurred or a reasonable suspicion of the defendant arose, which the prosecution may not wish to use or reveal at trial. The third issue concerns the regulatory mechanisms within the criminal trial which preserve the secrecy of proactive investigative methods where such methods produce evidence which can be, and is, presented at trial. One of the primary threats to fair trial is the inherent secrecy of most proactive methods, with the consequence that the resulting evidence cannot be effectively challenged by the defence. The fourth issue is the way in which the European Convention on Human Rights, especially in respect of the procedural guarantees of fair trial (Article 6) and the guarantees protecting privacy (Article 8), can be invoked by the defence in the criminal trial.

Criminal procedure as means of controlling the police

In continental inquisitorial systems the regulation of official action and hierarchical review are basic components of the criminal process (Damaška 1986). In the Netherlands all police activities should be hierarchically supervised, and regulated and monitored by trial judges. This derives from the principle of legality which is laid down in Article 1 of the Code of Criminal Procedure that criminal proceedings must be conducted as provided by law. Articles 140-148 CCP make the prosecutor responsible for criminal investigations by the police, and Articles 152-153 CCP provide that investigating police officers must record all of their activities in official reports which must be added to the file in order to give the judge the opportunity to check whether the prosecution has acted in a lawful way and has had regard to the principles of due process.[31]

The principle that there should be an internally consistent network of rules by which the police, and criminal investigations, are regulated and supervised by the courts, demands that police officers, when requested by the court, must make clear what decisions they have taken and why. This in turn gives the defence an opportunity to play its part in the control of police activities through its participation at trial. The result is that the defence in the Netherlands is not restricted to defending an accused in the classical sense of challenging the inculpatory evidence and putting forward information which could lead to an acquittal or less severe punishment. Besides the defence lawyer's duty to protect the civil rights of defendants, which is seen as part of the common interest in protecting civil rights in general (Corstens 1995, pp. 88-89; De Roos 1991, pp. 14-17), monitoring police and prosecution actions in the pre-trial stage is also useful as a specific defence strategy because unlawful investigation methods may lead a court to order that a trial should not proceed at all, or to decide to exclude the evidence so obtained. As a result the defence lawyer regards it as part of his or her professional duty to check whether the investigating officers – especially during a period of proactive investigation – have exceeded their authority or have breached the rules regarding search, seizure and other investigative methods which, in principle, are regulated by law.

In the adversarial system of England and Wales, where police investigative methods are largely unregulated by statute, the use of proactive methods is lawful unless they involve an activity that is prohibited by the general criminal law.[32] This is the converse of the position in the Netherlands. The traditional common law attitude is that the court's primary concern is that of relevance; it is not for the courts to control police activity. Therefore, not only have the police historically enjoyed freedom of action in the sense that most forms of investigative activity have not been regulated by law and thus the question of illegality does not arise, but even where police investigations have breached the criminal law the courts have taken the view that it is not their concern. As Crompton J. said in the oft-quoted case, *R v Leathem*, 'It matters not how you get it: if you steal it even, it would be admissible in evidence'.[33] However, this stark approach was qualified, even at common law, so that courts have the power to exclude evidence if its probative force is outweighed by its prejudicial value,[34] and an exception has been made in relation to evidence of confession.[35]

The traditional approach must now be seen in the context of a number of statutory and common law developments over the past decade. First, section 76 of PACE provided that evidence of confession by the defendant is not admissible unless (where it is raised by the defence) the prosecution can prove that it was not obtained by oppression or in circumstances likely to render it unreliable. Of more particular relevance to proactive policing is section 78 PACE which grants a discretion to a court to exclude prosecution evidence on the grounds of fairness.[36] In making this decision, the court must have regard to all the circumstances, including the circumstances in which the evidence was obtained. Thus under section 78 a court should not primarily be concerned with issues of illegality, but rather with questions of fairness, which may or may not involve considerations of illegality. This is of particular importance where, as noted above, there is minimal legal regulation of police investigation, so that issues which may in other jurisdictions be issues of legality have to be approached, in England and Wales, by way of the elusive concept of fairness. However, in most cases involving evidence derived from proactive police investigation, the Court of Appeal and the House of Lords have endorsed the view that such evidence, even if involving illegality on the part of the police, should be admitted.[37] Thus in *R v Khan (Sultan)*[38] the House of Lords held that evidence from an electronic listening device placed on a third party's house unlawfully (since it involved civil trespass and possibly criminal damage), but in accordance with Home Office guidelines[39] was admissible.[40] It further held that the judge was entitled to exercise his or her discretion under section 78 not to exclude it even if there had been illegality and even if there was a breach of the right to privacy under Article 8 of the European Convention on Human Rights. Since most proactive police activity is unregulated by law, the question of illegality[41] will not normally arise, the only question for the court being one of fairness of the proceedings. Thus activities which might be unlawful in other jurisdictions, such as the bugging of private conversations (at least without some form of judicial authority), are not illegal and in most cases where the issue has arisen, the courts have not regarded it as adversely affecting the fairness of the proceedings and have, therefore, admitted the evidence.[42]

A further area of development is that in relation to abuse of process, whereby the court is entitled to refuse to allow a prosecution to proceed where to do so would amount to an abuse of the criminal process by reason of oppression or vexatiousness.[43] Whilst this has been used to deal with situations where there has been undue delay in bringing criminal proceedings, it has also been argued by the defence that it should apply where the prosecution have acted unlawfully. For example, in *R v Latif; R v Shahzad*,[44] the defence argued that the prosecution should be stayed where the defendants had been lured to England by means of a trick to receive drugs unlawfully imported by a Customs and Excise officer. However, the House of Lords held that the trial judge was correct, having considered the conflicting considerations of policy and justice, in concluding that there was no abuse of process.[45]

In principle defence lawyers in both jurisdictions must act in the best interests of their clients, which requires them to prepare the most favourable case possible to present to the court.[46] However, unlike their Dutch counterparts, the professional duty of English and Welsh lawyers does not extend to examining the lawfulness of police conduct as such. The English and Welsh lawyer is most definitely not a party to a process of regulating and supervising the police, a role that has, in any case, been largely eschewed by the courts. The concern of the defence lawyer in England and Wales in relation to proactive police investigation is more limited, being confined to the question of whether any police activity in relation to the investigation may find an argument for the exclusion of evidence or, very exceptionally, may enable the lawyer to argue abuse of process.[47] In circumstances where proactive policing is largely unregulated so that most police activity is regarded as lawful, and where the courts are likely to admit evidence obtained by proactive methods even if it has been unlawfully or unfairly obtained,[48] the limits of the role of the defence lawyer in this regard are inevitably severely circumscribed. Even if they do examine the legality of police action, and even if they do discover some unlawful police activity, in most circumstances this is unlikely to benefit their client at trial.[49]

Knowledge of proactive activities

One of the main characteristics of cases involving proactive policing is that the suspect is arrested after the criminal investigation by the police is completed, often caught (apparently) in the act of committing a crime. The arrest is often preceded by long periods of police surveillance, involving a combination of physical and electronic surveillance, telephone tapping, undercover agents, informants or infiltrators. In this context it is important to realise that the line between proactive and reactive policing is rather fluid, and that secretive investigative methods used in the proactive phase such as observation, surveillance and the use of undercover agents or informants, can also be employed in a reactive way. Following arrest the suspect may be confronted with the evidence gathered during the proactive phase of the investigation, although only in so far as the information is likely to be used at trial.[50] However, once caught in the act, there is normally enough evidence to establish guilt at trial without reference to information gathered at the earlier stage, and without reference to the methodologies involved.

The information gathered during the proactive phase, and the methods used in order to gather it, may be important from the defence point of view. It may demonstrate that the police or other investigative agency has acted illegally or unfairly, either because it involved the commission of an offence, or because the police have exceeded their powers.[51] Alternatively, the information may undermine the prosecution evidence that is to be put before the court, or may assist the defence, either by supporting a defence to be put forward or by pointing to another defence not considered. Further, it may include information that may be of assistance to the defence in terms of mitigation, by casting the involvement of the defendant in a different light, perhaps by establishing entrapment or other forms of reduced culpability.

In the Netherlands, proactive methods which have led to such evidence are frequently kept out of the file and thus kept secret from the defendant and his or her lawyer, and also from the trial judge. The initial police record in the dossier usually starts with the announcement that, for instance, the police received information from criminal intelligence sources that at a certain place a drug deal would be made or that in a certain building drugs would be stored. Thus prior to a telephone tapping or surveillance operation the police record may simply state that the subjects of the operation were identified as taking part in a criminal organization. The source of this information is, however, kept secret. According to regular jurisprudence of the Dutch courts the prosecutor is not obliged to disclose the source of such information unless the defence can plausibly argue that the information was gathered in an illegal way or that the information would give the judge serious grounds to suspect that evidence had been gathered illegally.[52] This is, of course, difficult without knowledge of what was going on in the proactive phase. Thus it is often only by accident that the defence discovers that there has been proactive investigation prior to arrest.

In England and Wales, in the absence of an obligation to present all relevant information to the court of trial, the question is whether the prosecution must disclose information relating to or resulting from proactive investigative methods. This involves a two stage process. The prosecution must first decide what evidence it wishes to present to the court of trial in order to seek to establish guilt. Although under a general obligation to act fairly,[53] it is not under an obligation to present evidence that undermines the prosecution or assists the defence. The second stage involves the prosecution in deciding, from the information in its possession that it does not intend to use as evidence, what to disclose to the defence in advance of trial. This has been the subject of rapid jurisprudential development in the past few years. Broadly, the prosecution are under an obligation to disclose information to the defence if it is relevant or possibly relevant to an issue in the case, or raises or possibly raises a new issue that it is not apparent from the evidence that the prosecution intends to use at trial, or which holds out a real prospect of providing a lead on evidence that goes to the former.[54] The purpose is to enable the defence to pursue its own enquiries and to use it as a basis for conducting its own defence at trial. This obligation, of course, entails placing trust in the integrity of both the police and the prosecution since it is only enforceable by the defence if information comes to light that the prosecution has an interest in suppressing.

Even if the trust is justified in most cases, the obligation to disclose is circumscribed by the ability of the prosecution, with the sanction of the court, to withhold relevant information from the defence on the grounds of public interest immunity (PII). Although in some circumstances the prosecution must at least inform the defence of the category of information that they hold, in certain circumstances, the prosecution can withhold even this information.[55] It is well established that most police communications are covered by public interest immunity,[56] as is (normally) information relating to informers and methods of detection such as the identity of a police observation post. The judge, in considering a PII application is, however, under an obligation to balance the competing interests of preserving the integrity of police investigation and fairness to the accused. Thus the judge should not uphold a PII application where disclosure is necessary in order to establish innocence or to avoid a miscarriage of justice, such as where the informer was a participant. What may help to establish innocence, of course, depends in part upon what is regarded as a sufficient reason to exclude evidence. Since proactive policing is largely unregulated, and since even illegal police actions do not necessarily lead to the exclusion of evidence, it will be difficult to persuade a judge that such information, withheld by the prosecution, is necessary to help establish innocence.[57] Further, as in the Netherlands, if the defence are not aware of what was done by way of pro-active policing, it will frequently be difficult if not impossible for them to challenge an application by the prosecution for information to be withheld, a situation exacerbated, of course, if the defence are not even aware of an application to the court. Securing such information may thus depend upon accidental discovery, or on a particularly proactive and persistent defence lawyer.

The problems, and differences in approach between the two jurisdictions are perhaps best illustrated by an example from the Netherlands. In a drugs case, which was dealt with by the Utrecht District Court and the Amsterdam Court of Appeal,[58] the file included several police reports of observations of a shed where drugs were hidden made shortly before arrest, with detailed information about the visitors to the shed and the activities in the shed. At the trial it became clear that the police officers had not been at the scene (as the written records purported to show), but that the observations had been made by a video-camera positioned outside the shed. The police officers who drew up the records were requested by the court to rectify them. In the meantime a feature was published in the newspapers suggesting that the police had broken into the shed and placed a video-camera inside (the press is often better informed than the courts and the defence!). The defence requested that the police officers be questioned in court. It was important to know when the video-camera had been installed, and whether the police had authority to enter the building in order to install the camera, and whether there was reasonable suspicion of a crime at the time that the camera had been installed.[59] The defence also made a request to see the video-tapes, which would demonstrate whether the police officers, who had denied illegally entering the shed during an earlier court session, were telling the truth. It transpired that the videotape had been destroyed, and thus the court stayed the prosecution. It did so on the grounds that it had been wilfully misled by the police and prosecutor – covering up the source of their observations by leaving out of the records the fact that the observations were made by video – and thus giving false information to the court, and by doing so, destroying the evidence (i.e. the video-tapes) necessary for control of the police.

There have been several cases like this, in which important information has been deliberately kept out of the file or where police records were incomplete or contained false information about the source of the information in order to keep the methods and sources secret. In those cases where the information was subsequently given to the court following a request, the courts have decided that the prosecution was admissible (that is, should not be struck out) and the evidence was not excluded.[60] However, in those cases where the courts were left with the impression that the prosecution had frustrated judicial control by withholding information during the trial, evidence was excluded or the prosecution was not permitted to proceed.[61]

How might a court in England and Wales deal with such a case? Assuming that the video film is favourable to the prosecution, since the courts are concerned primarily with factual relevance rather than legality the police and prosecution would almost certainly disclose the video tapes to the defence, and use them as evidence, without risk of exclusion.[62] The defence, having had disclosure, might seek to persuade a court to exclude such evidence on the grounds of unfairness, or might even seek to stop the trial on the ground of abuse of process, but would be highly unlikely to succeed in either tactic. Suppose, however, that the video-camera had been secretly attached to a house opposite the shed. This may have involved illegality on the part of the police officers concerned[63] but, as argued earlier, this is unlikely to act as an impediment to using the evidence so obtained. The primary issue, therefore, would not be whether the video film itself should be disclosed and used as evidence, but whether the location of the video camera should be disclosed. Provided certain guidelines had been followed by the police, it is unlikely that a judge would order the prosecution to disclose the location of the camera, particularly if the occupier of the house feared harrassment as a result of the disclosure.[64]

If the video, in the opinion of the prosecution, tended to undermine the prosecution or assist the defence, they would be under an obligation to disclose the video-tape to the defence prior to trial, although again, not the location of the camera.[65] If the tape would inevitably disclose the location of the camera the prosecution could apply to the court for an order that the tape be withheld on the grounds of PII. The judge would then have to decide whether the prosecution should disclose the tape to the defence in the interests of a fair trial, which would require the judge to decide whether, and to what extent, it undermined the prosecution case or assisted the defence case, but in the absence of detailed knowledge of what the defence case was likely to be.

If the prosecution decided the video-tape was not relevant on the Keane criteria[66] they need not disclose it, either to the defence or to the court. If the defence knew of its existence, it could ask, and if necessary apply to the court, for it to be disclosed. The court would then decide on relevance according to the Keane criteria, subject to any PII claim by the prosecution.[67]

During and after the Dutch parliamentary inquiry of the Van Traa commission into the use of proactive methods, the question of the extent of the prosecution's obligation to add information to the file became an issue, frequently raised in trials. In general the prosecutor is obliged to add to the file all the material evidence for or against the accused.[68] The primary question is whether the prosecution can be effectively obliged to disclose information which in itself is not of direct evidential value, but which may be of importance to establish the (un)lawfulness of the evidence. The District Court of Rotterdam has ruled that all information which could be relevant to the case should be regarded as a record in accordance with Article 30 CCP and must be added to the file.[69] According to the Van Traa commission, all investigative actions, both in terms of relevant information and the methods used to obtain the information, should be reported in the written record,[70] and added to the file, so that it is made known to the judge and defence. However, the commission recommended that when third parties could be threatened, or the public interest could be severely damaged, as a result of the disclosure of such information, the prosecutor should be able to seek permission of the investigating magistrate to withhold the information from the file. If the investigating magistrate refuses to give permission the prosecutor could either add the information to the file or drop the charges. If the examining magistrate gives permission to withhold the information, the defence should be informed that the file is not complete.[71] Until now it has only been at the request of the defence that the courts have ordered the prosecution to disclose information which is relevant to the lawfulness of the evidence. It can hardly be expected that the prosecution will give this kind of information voluntarily, especially when investigative methods will only be effective when they are kept secret. So the dilemma remains. Should the defence be given a full opportunity to control police-activities or should there be exceptions, as suggested by the Van Traa commission, leaving it to the judiciary to decide whether certain information can be kept secret?

In England and Wales, the political impetus toward secrecy has been greater than that reflected by the recommendations of the Van Traa commission's report. The Criminal Procedure and Investigations Act 1996[72] reduces the obligation on the prosecution to disclose unused material, whilst requiring the defence, for the first time,[73] to disclose its defence in advance of trial. Whilst the Act does not directly affect the question of what may be withheld on the grounds of public interest immunity, it does make the prosecution's duty to disclose material which may be of assistance to the defence[74] conditional on the defendant disclosing to the prosecution a defence that shows such information to be relevant. To the extent that the police or prosecution do not wish to disclose material arising from proactive policing, the 1996 Act is likely to make it easier for them to do so.

Anonymous testimony

The previous section was primarily concerned with the question of whether proactive investigation methods, or the product of such methods, should be disclosed to the defence and to the court. We now focus more particularly on the trial process itself and examine the specific issue of anonymous testimony. This concerns, of course, evidence that is put before the court by the prosecution, but in respect of which the prosecution seeks to withhold the identity of the evidence giver, whether or not that person is in court to give their evidence. In the Netherlands the admission of hearsay evidence has opened the way to admitting anonymous written statements as evidence, since once the decision was taken to allow hearsay evidence, there was no legal obstacle to prevent the original source of the evidence from remaining undisclosed.[75] The admission of anonymous testimony has facilitated the use of evidence gathered by proactive policing because in this way statements of informers, infiltrators and undercover police officers can be used as evidence at trial whilst preserving their anonymity and reducing the opportunity for the defence to challenge and question such witnesses. After the *Kostovski* case[76] the use of anonymous testimony as evidence in the Netherlands, which until then had no legal basis, has been regulated by law (Articles 226a-226f CCP, which came into force in February 1994). According to this law anonymity is permitted to threatened witnesses, provided that there is corroborating evidence from a non-anonymous source,[77] and provided that the defendant has had the opportunity to question the witness at some stage (although such questioning can be severely limited by the investigating judge, for example by only permitting written questions). It is still uncertain whether this new regulation is compatible with the requirements of Article 6 of the European Convention. The primary issue is to what extent the rights of the defence to challenge the evidence can be restricted without violating the principles of a fair trial.

Jurisprudence of the European Court requires that normally all evidence must be produced in the presence of the accused at a public hearing with a view to adversarial argument. In certain cases the use of statements obtained in the pre-trial stage is not regarded, in itself, as inconsistent with the paragraphs 3.d and 1 of Article 6, provided that the rights of the defence to question and challenge the witness have been respected.[78] In a recent judgement in the *Doorson* case[79] the European Court ruled that the Convention does not preclude reliance, at the investigation stage, on sources such as anonymous informants, but that the subsequent use of such statements by the trial court to found a conviction is capable of raising issues under the Convention. In the *Doorson* case, because the anonymous witnesses were questioned by an investigating judge in the presence of Doorson's lawyer, who could ask whatever questions he considered to be in the interest of the defence as long as they would not lead to disclosure of the identity of the witness, and since these questions were all answered, the Court was of the opinion that the 'counterbalancing' procedures followed by the judicial authorities were sufficient to have enabled the defence to challenge the anonymous witnesses. Nevertheless the Court considered that even when 'counterbalancing' procedures are found to compensate sufficiently the handicaps under which the defence labours, a conviction should not be based solely, or to a decisive extent, on anonymous statements. In a judgement of 23 April 1997 in the case of *Van Mechelen and Others v Netherlands*, the European Court set out the conditions on which anonymous testimony is admissible.[80] In its report on this case, the European Commission was of the opinion (20 votes to 8) that although the convictions were based to a decisive extent on anonymous statements of police officers Article 6.3.d was not violated because the accused and their lawyers were able to put questions by telephone while the anonymous witnesses were questioned by the investigating judge. The European Court, however, was of a different opinion. According to the Court there had been a violation of Article 6.1 taken together with Article 6.3.d, inter alia because these measures could not be considered a proper substitute for the defence being able to question the witnesses in its presence and to make its own judgment as to their demeanour and reliability.

In the adversarial procedure of the United Kingdom the principle of orality requires that, in general, facts may only be admitted in evidence if they are attested to in court by a witness who perceived those facts. This is reflected by the rule against hearsay. The principle of public justice requires that this process should be carried out in open court. As Lord Diplock stated in *Attorney-General v Leveller Magazine Ltd.*,[81] 'As a general rule the English system of administering justice does require that it be done in public ... in criminal cases at any rate, all evidence communicated to the court is communicated publicly.' This presents particular difficulty for the prosecution where they wish to use evidence that has resulted from proactive policing,[82] since the general principles require that the evidence be presented in a public forum by the percipient witness. There are, however, two mechanisms which may assist the prosecution but, arguably, at the expense of the defence.

The first is provided by sections 23 and 24 of the Criminal Justice Act 1988, which enable first-hand hearsay (in the case of section 23) or first or second hand hearsay (in the case of section 24) to be admitted in evidence at trial in the absence of the witness. In particular, a written statement made by a prosecution witness may be used at trial without the need for the witness to attend provided the prosecution can establish, inter alia, that the witness 'does not give oral evidence through fear or because he is kept out of the way'. In principle this could be used where the witness is, for example, an informer, and even if the evidence forms the major part of the prosecution case. Although such evidence could only be admitted if the court was satisfied that it was in the interests of justice to do so (section 26), and it is less likely to be satisfied where the written evidence does form the major part of the prosecution case, there is no rule that it could not be used in such circumstances.[83]

The second mechanism is by providing for anonymity of a witness who does give oral evidence. This may involve the simple expedient of not requiring them to reveal their identity,[84] or by permitting them to give evidence from behind screens so that they cannot be seen by the defendant or the public.[85] In the past, this has been used to protect the victims of rape and blackmail, and also child witnesses.[86] In *R v Watford Magistrates' Court ex p Lenman*[87] it was used to conceal the identity of witnesses in a case of alleged gang violence, the rationale being that a judge had a duty to see that justice was done. If a judge is satisfied that there is a real risk to the administration of justice because a witness reasonably fears for his or her safety if his or her identity were to become known, the judge has a discretion to take steps to protect the witness and to reassure them so that they would not be deterred from coming forward. However, there is evidence that anonymity is increasingly, if not routinely, being granted to protect the identity of informers or undercover officers (Enright 1996). This is despite the Court of Appeal stating in *R v Taylor*[88] that anonymity should rarely be allowed, and only where there are real grounds to fear the consequences of disclosure and that the evidence must be of sufficient importance to make it unfair to insist on the prosecution proceeding without it.

The problem is that the more important the evidence, the more likely that the defendant will be prejudiced by not knowing the identity of the witness. This is particularly so where the witness is an informer or undercover officer and where, for example, the defendant would wish to show that he or she has been entrapped into committing an offence that s/he would not otherwise have committed, or where the degree of culpability is in issue. In the Netherlands, this is partially alleviated by the requirement that there be corroborative evidence from another source, a requirement that is absent in England and Wales. But in both jurisdictions, the defence may be limited to asking questions (directly, or indirectly in the Netherlands) of a witness whose identity, and therefore credibility, is hidden from the defence and from the court. There is also the problem in England and Wales, as Enright (1996) notes, that 'the mere fact that an officer gives evidence from behind a screen plants the seed of prejudice in the minds of the jury'. The Court of Appeal in the *Taylor* case held that anonymity should only be permitted if no undue prejudice is caused to the accused, but this indicates that the court is willing to permit some prejudice (provided that it does not amount to *undue* prejudice), and since research into juries is severely limited,[89] a judge cannot be sure, in that particular case or in general, that any warning to the jury not to allow the fact of anonymous testimony to affect their judgement, is effective. Again as Enright notes, the options for the defence in such cases are limited.

The European Convention on Human Rights

The European Convention on Human Rights has provided a powerful and effective mechanism for the defence in the Netherlands to challenge the secrecy which surrounds proactive policing. As noted earlier, the European Court has taken a critical approach to the admissibility of anonymous evidence in relation to the concept of fair trial, and also to the implications for fair trial of the right to privacy as laid down in Article 8 of the Convention.[90] In the Netherlands the application of national law can, and must, be set aside by the judiciary when it infringes the rights guaranteed by the Convention. As a consequence Strasbourg case law has become an important source of law that the defence can rely upon. Since the European Court sees it as its task to ascertain whether the proceedings, considered as a whole, are fair as required by Article 6 of the Convention, and since it has stated that the guarantees of Article 6 also apply at the preliminary stages of investigation into an offence by the police,[91] the Convention offers to the defence the opportunity to challenge secretive investigation methods that threaten fair trial or private life as guaranteed in Articles 6 and 8 of the Convention.

The United Kingdom, however, has not incorporated the European Convention into domestic law. Although the government is obliged to take the Convention and the decisions of the European Court into account, it normally takes a minimalist approach, particularly to the latter (Klug et al. 1996, p. 133). The courts, generally, do not see themselves as a suitable forum for adjudication of human rights issues.[92] Use of the Convention, and of decisions by the European Court, is therefore limited. It might be cited by the defence where it is seeking to persuade a court that legislation should be construed in accordance with the Convention,[93] but it was confirmed in *R v Secretary of State for the Home Department ex p Brind*[94] that this is really only relevant where the court is required to construe any provision that is 'ambiguous in the sense that it is capable of a meaning which either conforms to or conflicts with the Convention'.[95] In any event, since most forms of proactive policing are not governed by statute, this form of appeal to the Convention is not normally available.

The defence may argue that evidence obtained by proactive means was secured in contravention of the Convention. However, even if a court accepts that this was the case, it will not necessarily lead to exclusion of the evidence since the basis for exclusion of evidence is fairness rather than illegality. In *R v Khan*[96] the defence argued that in deciding whether evidence from an unlawfully placed listening device should be excluded the court should have regard to the Convention and decisions of the European Court. The House of Lords commented that '[t]he principles reflected in the Convention could hardly be irrelevant to the exercise of the s78 power because they embodied so many of the familiar principles of English law and concept of justice.' However, it went on to hold that since unlawfulness per se was not a reason for excluding evidence, '[t]he fact that the behaviour constituted a breach of the Convention ... could plainly be of no greater significance per se than if it constituted a breach of English law.' Clearly this area of law is developing, but even if the Convention were to be incorporated into English law, its usefulness to the defence will be limited for as long as substantive fairness rather than legality remains the guiding principle for the admission of evidence.

Conclusions

Proactive policing raises in an acute form a number of problems that defendants and defence lawyers experience in both inquisitorial and adversarial systems. It emphasizes the inequalities of power and resources as between the suspect or defendant and the state, whether the suspect/defendant is an object of an inquisitorial investigation or a party to an adversarial process. Under both systems, the police have strong inquisitorial powers and under both the defence lack an effective right to information held by the police, particularly at the investigative stage. At the same time, although the legal systems of the Netherlands, and England and Wales, approach the regulation of police powers in quite different ways, recent experience in the Netherlands has demonstrated that regulatory and supervisory mechanisms characteristic of inquisitorial systems do not necessarily prevent the police from engaging in forms of investigative policing which, although they may be lawful in England and Wales, nevertheless have an adverse effect on the fairness of the trial process.

We have identified one of the major characteristics of proactive policing as being that of secrecy. Secrecy is not a necessary corollary of proactive policing. In England and Wales, given the lack of regulation of investigative methods and the attitude of the courts, the prosecution are often under no particular pressure to withhold information from the defence. However, proactive policing is frequently accompanied by secrecy on the part of the police and prosecution, to protect informers and undercover agents from threat and/or discovery, to protect investigative methodologies, and sometimes to protect against the discovery of police activities that are on the margins of legality.

To the extent that secrecy can be justified, there is a clear need for political, organizational and institutional safeguards. Quite apart from the interests of fair trial, such mechanisms are necessary to ensure democratic accountability of the police, and to prevent a culture of corruption that is likely to develop from a sense of being above the law.[97] That need is all the greater given the likely further development of proactive policing methods in response to the perceived threat of organized and cross-border crime, the political need to be seen to do something about rising crime levels[98] and, as important, developments in available technology. However, it is the impact of secrecy on the possibilities for a fair trial process that is of most concern to defence lawyers, a process that is arguably under threat as a result of the elevation of the public interest in securing convictions, that currently finds public and political favour, above the public interest of fair trial.

It is in this context that regulatory mechanisms in both countries are inadequate. There are two ways in which this is so. First, the law in both jurisdictions facilitates an increasing degree of secrecy, allowing a variety of justifications for withholding information from the defence. Secondly, in so far as the law does not permit the police or prosecution to withhold information, existing mechanisms, whether administrative or judicial, fail to ensure compliance with the law. In both England and Wales, and in the Netherlands, it is ultimately left to the courts to decide what information should be disclosed to the defence. This requires a judge to take into account the interests of the defence without full knowledge of what those interests might be, and often in circumstances where the ability of the defence to argue for disclosure is hampered by the very secrecy which the defence is seeking to expose. Either the defence does not know of the existence of the evidence or it does not have sufficient knowledge of it to persuade the court that it should be disclosed.

The danger in both jurisdictions is that it is increasingly the police who not only decide which members of the population will be targeted for investigation but who, by the selective use and concealment of information, determine who shall be found guilty. In circumstances where secrecy is accompanied by an absence of effective mechanisms to ensure democratic accountability and by a failure of both political and legal institutions to take responsibility, proactive policing presents a danger not only to defendants, but to society as a whole.

Notes

1 In *Murray v United Kingdom* (Case No 41/1994/488/570) (1996) *The Times*, 9 February, the Court held that denial of access to a lawyer during police interrogation, in circumstances where the rights of the defendant might be irretrievably prejudiced, is incompatible with Article 6. The implications for member states of this decision have yet to be fully understood, for it would seem to follow that states must not only introduce (where they do not already exist) provision for legal advice for suspects whilst detained by the police, but must also create provision for the legal advice to be given free of charge where it is in the interests of justice to do so. Note that Principle 7 of the Basic Principles on the Roles of Lawyers, adopted by the Eighth United Nations Congress on the Prevention of Crime and the Treatment of Offenders in Havana, Cuba, on 7 September 1990, provides, somewhat ambiguously, that governments should

ensure that 'persons arrested or detained, with or without criminal charge, shall have prompt access to a lawyer, and in any case not later than 48 hours from the time of arrest or detention'. For the Netherlands see Spronken 1996.

2   The Basic Principles on the Role of Lawyers (see note 1) does set out the duties of defence lawyers (Principles 12-15), but does not cover most of the important questions relating to the role of lawyers being discussed here. This is also true for the Netherlands, where the Code of Conduct (Gedragsregels 1992) contains few specific rules for lawyers in criminal cases.

3   The definition of proactive policing adopted in this chapter is that set out in the introduction.

4   See, for example, the Europol Convention signed by the European Union governments on 26 July 1995.

5   Encouraged in England and Wales by the influential Audit Commission report published in 1993, *Helping with Enquiries: Tackling Crime Effectively*, London: HMSO.

6   In the Netherlands, although a matter of dispute, lawyers do not have a right to be present during the police interview of suspects, and access to clients can be delayed for as long as the interrogation lasts. See for example HR 23 May 1995, DD 95.352 and District Court 's-Hertogenbosch 1 September 1995, NJ 1996, 29. In England and Wales, courts have not necessarily excluded evidence, even where the statutory right to legal advice has been deliberately denied. The mechanism for exclusion is primarily section 78 of the Police and Criminal Evidence Act 1984 (PACE), which requires the court to consider the effect of denial on the fairness of the proceedings. See, for example, *R v Alladice* (1988) 87 Cr App R 380, *R v Walsh* [1989] Crim LR 822, *R v Dunford* [1991] Crim LR 370 and *R v Anderson* [1993] Crim LR 447, and contrast *R v Samuel* [1988] QB 615.

7   For England and Wales, see the Commentary to *R v Smith* (Brian) [1995] Crim LR 658, at p. 660. For the Netherlands see Prakken 1995; Corstens 1995, pp. 228-229.

8   See the Interception of Communications Act 1985. The Police Act 1997, which received royal assent in March 1997, gives the police statutory authority to enter premises and plant bugging devices (although these provisions have not yet been implemented). Similar methods, when used by the security services, are governed by the Intelligence Services Act 1994. The security services were given a criminal investigation role, ostensibly confined to serious crime, by the Security Service Act 1996.

9   For a similar view in the context of the USA, see Marx 1988, esp. p. 48 and 50.

10 Article 1 Dutch Code of Criminal Procedure; Simmelink 1987; Knigge 1990; Naeyé 1995.

11 HR 14 October 1986, NJ 1987, 564; HR 14 October 1986, NJ 1988, 511; HR 8 July 1992, NJ 1993, 29 and HR 19 December 1995, Zwolsman, NJ 1996, 249.

12 Named after the Chairman of the commission.

13 *Inzake opsporing* 1996. However, the commission did suggest that there should be certain exceptions to the principle of full disclosure.

14 (Voorlopig) Regeringsstandpunt Enquête Opsporingsmethoden, TK 1995-1996, 24 072, nr. 26.

15 For a report of recent research, see Dunningham and Norris 1996.

16 In fact, the aim may not be prosecution at all but, for example, the dismantling of a criminal group or organization. Alternatively, proactive investigation may be directed at inflicting economic or fiscal sanctions outside of the criminal process. Nevertheless the Van Traa commission was of the opinion that the aim of exercising powers in relation to criminal offences should always be the imposition of a penal sanction.

17 Generally required for the exercise of powers of arrest. For England and Wales see PACE section 24, and for the Netherlands see Articles 57, 63, 67 and 67a CCP.

18 PACE section 37, although evidence suggests that this is routinely ignored by the police. See McKenzie, Morgan and Reiner 1990 and Bottomley, Coleman, Dixon, Gill and Wall, 1991, esp. p. 88.

19 PACE section 37, and Code of Practice C paragraph 16.5. The PACE Codes of Practice are a form of quasi-legislation issued by the Home Secretary under the authority of PACE section 66.

20 According to Articles 67 and 67a CCP, pre-trial detention is allowed in serious cases (most crimes which can be punished by imprisonment of 4 years and more) and in the interest of the police enquiry.

21 See Fijnaut 1987; Van der Kruijs 1995; Spronken 1997.

22 According to Articles 28 and 50 CCP a suspect is entitled to legal assistance when he or she is arrested, but defence lawyers are usually permitted to speak to their clients only whilst their client is not being interrogated. When a suspect is detained for longer than 6 hours (or 15 hours where night-time is included), he or she has the right to legal assistance paid for out of public funds (Article 40 CCP). Even in these circumstances contact with the lawyer is denied during the course of police interrogation. As a result, only those who can afford to pay for a lawyer can exercise their right to legal advice during the first 6 (or 15) hours, and the right cannot be exercised at any time when the suspect is being interrogated. However, see the brief discussion of the case of *Murray v UK* in note 1.

23 Strictly, Code C paragraph 2.4 only gives the right to sight of the custody record on the lawyer's arrival at the police station, or after release of the suspect, although in practice custody officers will normally allow sight of the custody record on request.

24 Which in the Netherlands can be delayed for as long as three months from the date of the arrest, or even longer in certain circumstances.

25 See the Final Report of the Van Traa commission, p. 387 *et seq.*

26 In England and Wales, failure to answer police questions may lead to adverse inference being drawn at trial by virtue of the Criminal Justice and Public Order Act 1994 sections 34-38. For an examination of the implications of these provisions for the defence lawyer advising at the police station see Cape 1995, esp. chapter 5. See also *R v Condron* [1996] Crim LR 215. In the Netherlands the right to silence is considered absolute in the sense that failure to answer police questions cannot be used as evidence, but as in England and Wales, adverse inferences may be drawn at trial. See HR 12 March 1996, NJ 1996, 539 and HR 19 March 1996, NJ 1996, 540 and Spronken 1997.

27 In England and Wales PACE imposes time limits on detention without charge, initially of 24 hours. Although these may be extended, ultimately up to 96 hours on the authority of a court (or 7 days on the authority of the Home Secretary in terrorism cases), the grounds for doing so relate to the conduct of the police investigation rather than the requirements of the defence.

28 In *R v Condron* [1996] Crim LR 215 the Court of Appeal confirmed that an assertion at trial that the defendant did not answer police questions on the advice of his lawyer was not a sufficient reason to prevent a court from drawing inferences from that failure.

29 For an examination of the extent to which criminal procedure in the two jurisdictions conforms to the two theories, see Brants and Field 1995. As discussed later, in England and Wales the respective duties of defence and prosecution to disclose information to the other prior to trial, having developed rapidly at common law during the late 1980s and early 1990s, are significantly affected by the Criminal Procedure and Investigations Act 1996.

30 A distinction is assumed between establishing guilt or innocence and establishing truth. The trial process and rules of evidence in both jurisdictions enable a factually guilty person to be found not guilty in a legal sense. For a brief discussion, see Ashworth 1996.

31 Corstens 1995, p. 58-69 and 634-642; HR 9 May 1995, NJ 1995, 672; HR 31 May 1994, NJ 1995, 29; Court of Appeal Amsterdam 1 December 1994, NJ 1995, 159; HR 19 December 1995, NJ 1996, 249 (Zwolsman).

32 None of the proactive methods of police investigation considered above is directly governed by statute except the interception of public telephones or post (although see note 8). See Brants and Field 1995, pp. 61-64. See also note 7.

33 (1861) 8 Cox CC 498.

34 *R v Sang* [1980] AC 402.

35 *Ibrahim v R* [1914] AC 599.

36 Section 78 provides that a court may exclude prosecution evidence if it appears that, having regard to all the circumstances, including the circumstances in which the evidence was obtained, the admission of the evidence would have such an adverse effect on the fairness of the proceedings that the court ought not to admit it.

37 See, for example, *R v Latif*; *R v Shahzad* [1996] 1 All ER 353.

38 [1996] 3 All ER 289.

39 Guidelines on the use of Equipment in Police Surveillance Operations (Home Office 1984), which require such operations to be authorized by the Chief Constable.

40 The court confirmed that, despite the European Convention on Human Rights, there is no right to privacy in English and Welsh law and, even if there were, evidence obtained in breach of it was nevertheless admissible (subject to section 78 PACE).

41 In the sense of lack of conformity with regulatory laws as opposed to breach of the general criminal law.

42 See, for example, *R v Ali* (1991), *The Times* 19 February, and *R v Bailey and Smith* [1993] 3 All ER 513.

43 See, for example, *Connelly v DPP* [1964] AC 1254 and *R v Humphrys* [1977] AC 1. In *R v Beckford* [1995] Crim LR 712 the Court of Appeal stated that the two main circumstances where the procedure could be used were (a) cases in which the court concludes that the defendant cannot receive a fair trial, and (b) cases where the court concludes that it would be unfair for the defendant to be tried.

44 [1996] 1 All ER 353; Crim LR 414.

45 Similar conclusions have been drawn in other cases involving proactive policing. Cf. *R v Horseferry Road Magistrates' Court ex p Bennett* [1994] 1 AC 42, where the defendant had been abducted and brought to the UK in contravention of extradition laws.

46 This is a basic rule of professional conduct. For England and Wales, see Practice Rule 1, (1996) *The Guide to the professional Conduct of Solicitors* (Seventh Edition), London: The Law Society, and for the Netherlands see Rule 5 of the Gedragsregels 1992.

47 For criticism of the lack of adversarialism displayed by many defence lawyers, see generally, McConville, Hodgson, Bridges and Pavlovic 1994.

48 The argument here is concerned with proactive policing. It is true that the courts do, with some frequency, exclude evidence under both section 76 and section 78 PACE, particularly where there has been a breach of the PACE Codes of Practice. However, as argued earlier, proactive policing methods do not normally lead to exclusion of evidence except where they are seen as a method of circumventing the protective provisions of PACE, particularly in relation to interrogation. See, for example, *R v Bryce* [1992] Crim LR 728, and the first instance decision in the Colin Stagg case, in which the person suspected of involvement in a particularly gruesome murder was contacted by a female undercover police officer who proceeded to entice him into confessing by pretending that she obtained gratification from acts of sexual violence.

49 The argument here ignores the possible impact of unlawful police activity on sentence. In *R v Sang* [1980] AC 402 the House of Lords did aver that the fact that evidence was obtained by an agent provocateur could be taken into account

in mitigation of sentence, but it is unclear whether the courts do take into account such factors with any consistency.

50 In the Netherlands written documents such as official reports drawn up by the police are admitted as evidence at the trial (Articles 338 and 339 CCP). According to a judgement of the Supreme Court on 20 December 1926, NJ 1927, 85, hearsay evidence may be used to found a conviction. This has had the effect that in practice the importance of the investigation at the trial has dwindled and that the file is the main source of evidence.

51 More likely in the Netherlands for the reasons set out earlier.

52 Corstens 1995, p. 650; Grapperhaus en Nieuwenhuys 1990; HR 25 October 1977, NJ 1978, 137; HR 17 May 1988, NJ 1989, 142; HR 22 September 1992, NJ 1993, 57.

53 See *R v Puddick* (1865) 4 F & F 497 and *R v Banks* [1916] 2 KB 621. See also the Code of Conduct of the Bar of England and Wales, Annex H, paragraph 11, and the Guide to the Professional Conduct of Solicitors (Seventh Edition), Principle 21.19. The Code for Crown Prosecutors paragraph 2.2 states that the duty of the Crown Prosecution Service is to ensure that all relevant facts are given to the court, but in practice this is not interpreted to include evidence that tends to undermine the prosecution case. See also McConville et al. 1991, esp. ch. 8.

54 See Attorney General's Guidelines on the disclosure of information and *R v Keane* [1994] 1 WLR 747. This duty has been significantly weakened, in respect of cases where the investigation started on or after 1 April 1997, by Parts I and II of the Criminal Procedure and Investigations Act 1996.

55 *R v Davis* [1993] 1 WLR 613. See now rules made under section 19 (2) Criminal Procedure and Investigations Act 1996.

56 See, for example, *Taylor v Anderson* (1986) *The Times* October 21. Cf. *R v Horseferry Road Magistrates' Court ex p Bennett* (No 2) [1994] 1 All ER 289.

57 It is clearly established that it is for the defence to satisfy the judge that disclosure is necessary in order to establish his or her innocence. See *R v Hennessy* (1978) 68 Cr App R 419 and *R v Hallett* [1969] Crim LR 462.

58 Court of Appeal Amsterdam 1 December 1994, NJ 1995, 159.

59 The authority to enter a building should be given by an examining magistrate and only if there is a reasonable suspicion of a crime (Article 97 CCP); see also Mols 1996.

60 HR 19 December 1995, NJ 1996, 249 (Zwolsman); Court of Appeal 's-Gravenhage 27 December 1995, NJ 1996, 338; District Court 's-Hertogenbosch 22 December 1994, NJ 1995, 164.

61 Court of Appeal Amsterdam 1 December 1994, NJ 1995, 159; Court of Appeal 's-Gravenhage 29 January 1996, NJ 1996, 413.

62 See *R v Khan* (1996) *The Times* July 5. Note also the implicit endorsement of illegal police action by the Home Office Circular (1984), 'Guidelines on the Use of Equipment in Police Surveillance Operations'.

63 But only in the form of trespass to property, since the use of such methods is unregulated by law and the police are permitted to do anything unless it is prohibited by law. Ironically, when the legislation referred to in note 8 comes into force there will be a stronger argument that actions taken in breach of the new law will, therefore, be unlawful and should be excluded.

64 See *R v Johnson* [1988] 1 WLR 1377, *R v Hewitt* (1992) 95 Cr App R 81, and *Blake v DPP* (1993) 97 Cr App R 169.

65 Failure to do so in these circumstances could be challenged by the defence if it was aware of its existence, and failure to comply with a court order to disclose, as where the tapes had already been destroyed, may result in the case being stayed for abuse of process. For an example, see *R v Birmingham and Others* [1992] Crim LR 117, a Crown Court decision. For investigations commenced since 1 April 1997, the prosecution (if it did not intend to use the evidence at trial) would initially only have to disclose the evidence (subject to PII) if, in the view of the prosecution, it might undermine the prosecution case (section 3 Criminal Procedure and Investigations Act 1996).

66 See note 54.

67 Under the Criminal Procedure and Investigations Act 1996, the defence could only apply to a court for disclosure of the video if it had disclosed the nature of the defence and could satisfy the court that it might assist the defence as disclosed in the defence statement.

68 HR 7 May 1996, NJB 1996, nr. 65; see also ECHR 16 December 1992 (Edwards), Series A, vol. 247-B.

69 District Court Rotterdam, 13 September 1995, NJ 1996, 343. This would include not only information that is relevant to the facts, but also to whether procedural rules have been satisfied, whether the means of securing evidence were lawful, and whether they were in accordance with Article 6 of the European Convention.

70 According to Article 152 of the Dutch Code on Criminal Procedure.

71 *Inzake opsporing* 1996, pp. 458-459.

72 In force, in respect of its disclosure provisions, from Spring 1997.

73 Although it can be argued that the right to silence provisions of the Criminal Justice and Public Order Act 1994 created strong pressure on the defence to disclose the nature of its defence at the interrogation stage in order to avoid adverse inferences from failure to do so.

74 As opposed to information which might undermine the prosecution case, which must be disclosed in any event in serious cases (but only if the defendant pleads not guilty in less serious cases) (Criminal Procedure and Investigations Act 1996 section 3(1)).

75 The admission of hearsay evidence and written statements as evidence at trial in the Netherlands has had the effect, in practice, that the significance of the trial for the assessment of evidence has declined. The records of police investigation, results of proactive policing such as records of observation activities and telephone tapping and statements made by witnesses to the police, are all laid down

in a file, or dossier, which forms the most important source of evidence. The oral procedure of evaluating evidence at the trial mainly consists of the court reading out the written statements in the file and posing additional questions to the accused.

76 ECHR 20 November 1989, Series A, vol. 166.

77 Although the corroborating evidence does not have to corroborate directly the evidence of the anonymous witness, but may be other evidence of guilt.

78 ECHR 24 November 1986, Series A, vol. 110 (Unterpertinger); ECHR 6 December 1988, Series A, vol. 146 (Barberà); ECR 20 November 1989, Series A, vol. 166 (Kostovski); ECHR 27 September 1990, Series A, vol. 186 (Windisch); ECHR 19 December 1990, Series A, vol. 191 (Delta); ECHR 19 February 1991, Series A, vol. 194-A (Isgro); ECHR 26 April 1991, Series A, vol. 203 (Asch); ECHR 15 June 1992, Series A, vol. 238 (Lüdi).

79 ECHR 26 March 1996, 54/1994/501/583, *Doorson v Netherlands*, to be published in Reports of Judgements and Decisions for 1996.

80 ECHR 23 April 1997, nr. 55/1996/674/861-864 to be published in Decisions and Reports 1997.

81 [1979] AC 440.

82 Which, in the light of the earlier discussion, it is clear that they may not have to.

83 See, for example, *R v Setz-Dempsey* (1994) 98 Cr App R 23. The circumstances in which written statement may be adduced in evidence in a crown court trial are also, potentially, considerably widened by section 68 and Schedule 2 of the Criminal Procedure and Investigations Act 1996.

84 As, for example, in the case of *R v Aubrey, Berry and Campbell,* which led to the action against the journal that published the name of the anonymous witness. See *Attorney-General v Leveller Magazine* [1979] AC 440.

85 There is provision for evidence in certain cases to be given by pre-recorded video or by closed-circuit television, but these are confined to cases where the witness is a child or outside the UK. See sections 32 and 32A Criminal Justice Act 1988.

86 See *R v DJX, SCY, GCZ* (1989) 91 Cr pp R 36.

87 [1993] Crim LR 388.

88 (1994) *Times Law Reports* 484.

89 By the Contempt of Court Act 1981 section 8.

90 See i.a. ECHR 24 April 1990, Series A, vol. 176 (Huvig and Kruslin).

91 ECHR 24 November 1993, Series A, vol. 275 (Imbrioscia) and ECHR 8 February 1996 (Murray), to be published in Reports of Judgements and Decisions for 1996.

92 Cf. the contributions of Jacobs 1988 and Jennings 1988.

93 See *Garland v British Rail Engineering Ltd.,* [1983] 2 AC 751.

94 [1991] 1 AC 696.

95 At p. 747. For a discussion of the impact of the ECHR decision of *Murray v United Kingdom*, Case No 41/1994/488/570; (1996) *The Times* 9 February, see Munday 1996.
96 (1996) *The Times* 5 July. See also *R v Morrisey, R v Staines* (1997), *The Times* 1 May.
97 This is so whether the corruption is criminal in intent or what has been termed 'noble cause corruption'. It is interesting to note that the Interim Report of the New South Wales Royal Commission on the Police Service expressly disapproved of the term since process corruption, as it preferred to describe it, 'strikes at the very heart of the administration of the criminal justice system'.
98 The Police Act 1997 which gives statutory authority to the police in England and Wales to search property and place secret listening devices in the investigation of serious crime, defines serious crime to include those well outside the sphere of organized crime.

References

Ashworth, A. (1996), Crime, Community and Creeping Consequentialism, *Criminal Law Review* 220.

Audit Commission (1993), *Helping with Enquiries: Tackling Crime Effectively*, London: HMSO.

Baldwin, J. (1992), *The Conduct of Police Investigations: Records of Interview, the Defence Lawyer's Role and Standards of Supervision*, Research Studies Nos. 2, 3 and 4, The Royal Commission on Criminal Justice, London: HMSO.

Baldwin, J. (1993), Police Interview Techniques: Establishing Truth or Proof?, *The British Journal of Criminology*, (33) 3 Summer.

Bottomley, K., C. Coleman, D. Dixon, M. Gill and D. Wall (1991), *The Impact of PACE*, Hull: University of Hull.

Brants, C. and S. Field (1995), *Participation Rights and Proactive Policing: Convergence and Drift in European Criminal Process*, Deventer: Kluwer.

Cape, E. (1994), Defence Services: What Should Defence Lawyers Do at Police Stations?, in: M. McConville and L. Bridges (eds.), *Criminal Justice in Crisis*, Aldershot: Edward Elgar.

Cape, E. (1995), *Defending Suspects at Police Stations* (Second Edition), London: Legal Action Group.

Cape, E. (1996), Getting to grips with police corruption, *Legal Action* July 8.

Corstens, G.J.M. (1995), *Het Nederlands strafprocesrecht*, Arnhem: Gouda Quint.

Damaška, M.R. (1986), *The Faces of Justice and State Authority*, New Haven and London: Yale University Press.

Dunningham, C. and C. Norris (1996), The nark's game, *New Law Journal* 402 and 456.

Enright, S. (1996), The anonymous witness, *New Law Journal* 1032.

Fijnaut, C. (1987), *De toelating van raadslieden tot het politiële verdachtenverhoor*, Antwerpen: Kluwer, Arnhem: Gouda Quint.

Gomien, D., D. Harris and L. Zwaak (1996), *Law and Practice of the European Convention on Human Rights and the European Social Charter*, Strasbourg: Council of Europe Publishing.

Grapperhaus, M.J. en J. Nieuwenhuys (1990), De gevolgen van onrechtmatige bewijsgaring, *Nederlands Juristenblad*, p. 769.

Inzake opsporing (1996), Eindrapport van de Enquêtecommissie Opsporings-methoden 1 februari 1996, 's-Gravenhage: Sdu.

Jacobs, F.J. (1988), The Convention and the English judge, in: John Matscher and Herbert Petzold (eds.), *Protecting Human Rights: The European Dimension*, Köln: Carl Heymanns Verlag KG, pp. 273-279.

Jennings, Sir Robert (1988), Human Rights and Domestic Law and Courts, in: John Matscher and Herbert Petzold (eds.), *Protecting Human Rights: The European Dimension*, Köln: Carl Heymanns Verlag KG, pp. 295-300.

Klug, F., K. Starmer and S. Weir (1996), *The Three Pillars of Liberty*, London: Routledge.

Knigge, G. (1990), Van opsporing en strafvordering, *Delikt en Delinkwent*, pp. 195-213.

Kruijs, P.M. van der (1995), Kanttekeningen bij de inverzekeringstelling, *Advocaten-blad* 1995, p. 943.

Marx, G.T. (1988), *Undercover: Police Surveillance in America*, Berkeley: University of California Press.

Matscher, J. and H. Petzold (eds.) (1988), *Protecting Human Rights: The European Dimension*, Köln: Carl Heymanns Verlag KG.

McConville, M., A. Sanders and R. Leng (1991), *The Case for the Prosecution*, London: Routledge.

McConville M. and J. Hodgson (1993), *Custodial Legal Advice and the Right to Silence*, Research Study No. 16, The Royal Commission on Criminal Justice, London: HMSO.

McConville, M., J. Hodgson, L. Bridges and A. Pavlovic (1994), *Standing Accused: the organisation and practices of criminal defence lawyers in Britain*, Oxford: Clarendon.

McKenzie, I., R. Morgan and R. Reiner (1990), Helping the Police with Their Inquiries: the Necessity Principle and Voluntary Attendance at the Police Station, *Criminal Law Review* 22.

Mols, G.P.M.F. (1996), Wie niet weg is gezien, Justitieel onderzoek in en rondom de woning, in: C.H. Brants, C. Kelk and M. Moerings, M. (eds.), *Er is meer*, Deventer: Gouda Quint, pp. 191-200.

Munday, R. (1996), Inferences from Silence and European Human Rights Law, *Criminal Law Review* 370.

Naeyé, J. (1995), *Het politieel vooronderzoek in strafzaken*, Arnhem: Gouda Quint.

Prakken, T. (1995), Interne openbaarheid in het strafprocesrecht; een bedreigd goed, *Nederlands Juristenblad*, pp. 1451-1458.

Roberts, P. (1995), Taking the Burden of Proof Seriously, *Criminal Law Review* 783.

Roos, Th.A. de (1991), *Verdediging van belangen: het belang van verdediging*, Arnhem: Gouda Quint.

Simmelink, J.B.H.M. (1987), *De rechtsstaatgedachte achter art. 1 Sv.*, Arnhem: Gouda Quint.

Spronken, T. (1996), Nemo tenetur, zwijgrecht en advocatenbijstand bij het politie-verhoor: de zaak Murray, *Advocatenblad*, pp. 420-424.

Spronken, T. (1997), in: C.P.M. Cleiren and J.F. Nijboer (eds.), *Tekst & Commen-taar Strafvordering,* Deventer: Kluwer.

The Law Society (1996), *The Guide to the Professional Conduct of Solicitors* (Seventh Edition), London: The Law Society.

18 Judicial regulation of covert and proactive policing in the Netherlands and England and Wales

STEWART FIELD AND NICO JÖRG

Introduction

In this chapter we assess the effects of the development of proactive and covert policing on judicial role(s) in England and Wales and the Netherlands. Our choice of countries to compare is in large part pragmatic: these are the two jurisdictions we know best. But there are three reasons for thinking this may be a revealing comparison. First, both these countries are undergoing important reform processes which are being carried out under very different political conditions: in the Netherlands after a fearful scandal over investigative teams out of control, in England and Wales after reforms introduced to enhance the protection given to the secrecy and autonomy of police covert investigations. Thus in this regard the two countries seem to be running off in different directions. Secondly, the two jurisdictions span the two procedural traditions in Europe: the inquisitorial and the adversarial. This is important because the role(s) of the judge and magistrate in criminal cases have traditionally been very differently defined in the two traditions. The adversarial judge has largely been confined to a particular role at trial – that of procedural referee – whereas judges in the inquisitorial tradition have played a more active pre-trial role and fulfilled roles beyond that of procedural referee: they are also supervisors of evidence gathering and also determine legal truth in most cases (for discussion of such contrasts see Jörg, Field and Brants 1995). This means that the traditional resources available to meet the challenges of proactive or covert policing are not the same. Thirdly, the European Convention on Human Rights, with its entrenched rights to privacy under Article 8, is directly applicable in the Netherlands but not so at the moment in England and Wales. This too provides an important contrast in the way judicial regulatory mechanisms operate, something particularly significant for the British reader in trying to assess the impact of the new Labour Government's decision to incorporate the Convention in at least some form into domestic law.[1]

With our comparative choice however comes a problem of terminology. What do we mean by terms like 'judge' and 'judiciary' and 'magistrate' or 'magistracy'? The different traditions have resulted in different terminologies, categories and distinctions. In this chapter we use the term 'judges' to indicate professional judges rather than all those who perform the function of judging within criminal justice systems (thus excluding jurors or lay magistrates). We follow the continental practice of not referring to prosecutors as 'judges' but regarding them as 'magistrates' and as part of the 'judiciary' where they are recruited and trained within the continental career judiciary system.[2] Often this type of prosecutor will be referred to as a 'prosecuting magistrate' to stress the distinction being made. English and Welsh Crown prosecutors and barristers acting as prosecutors, who are trained purely as lawyers and usually recruited from private practice will, of course, be regarded neither as magistrates nor judges and are not included within the concept of 'judiciary' or 'judicial'. However their role – both as it presently exists and as it may be imagined – will be considered at various points as an alternative to judicial monitoring. Again, as in the continental tradition, examining magistrates will be regarded as judges.

Three forms of judicial regulation of proactive and/or covert policing

Given institutional traditions in England and Wales and the Netherlands three forms of judicial regulation of proactive or covert policing are easily imaginable within the criminal process itself.[3] First, judges and/or prosecuting magistrates may act as gatekeepers to particular police techniques, in that the police may have to go to them for prior authorization in the individual case. Secondly, judges might be used to enforce more or less detailed administrative guidelines on *how* proactive methods are to be used. They may do this by exercising discretions to exclude evidence at trial or dismiss the case if those guidelines are breached. This kind of regulation is very limited in current practice in the two jurisdictions but potential for development exists. Thirdly, judges may make decisions in the pre-trial process or preliminary decisions at trial as to the procedural *consequences* of using proactive methods. In particular they may determine defence access to the records of such investigation or other specific details on how the investigation was pursued.[4] All of these forms of regulation can be contrasted with systems where magistrates or judges might actually *lead* proactive or covert investigations themselves. This can sometimes (though rarely) happen in France during an investigation by the examining magistrate (see Field in this volume).[5] However in the Netherlands the investigating magistrate plays a more limited, quasi-judicial role and does not take overall responsibility for directing the police inquiry (Field, Alldridge and Jörg 1995). Further, although the Public Prosecutor is officially charged with directing the police inquiry, in reality control is limited to monitoring and supervision (Swart 1993). In England and Wales neither judges nor prosecutors have led investigations since the demise of the investigating Justice of the Peace in the 19th century (Radzinowicz 1968, p. 192 *et seq.*).

Prior authorization

General considerations

Both jurisdictions already make some use of requirements of prior judicial authorization as a precondition for the exercise of certain coercive powers when used in a reactive context. In England and Wales (normally lay) magistrates perform this function in relation to pre-trial detention and some searches of premises. In the Netherlands, as in other jurisdictions from the inquisitorial tradition, investigating magistrates have historically performed the role, for example in relation to telephone tapping and pre-trial detention. Recent proposals give a greater role to the Public Prosecutor.

As a control over covert or proactive techniques, prior judicial authority has the advantage that judicial regulation cannot be avoided simply by not prosecuting or not using the results in evidence. In the Netherlands in the 1980s, police moves towards using intelligence to destabilize (criminal) organizations by methods other than criminal prosecution and conviction was a factor in enabling some police investigations to step clear of the judicial regulatory framework (primarily the monitoring of prosecutors) in the lead up to the IRT scandal (Brants and Field 1995, especially at p. 46, 51). But if a particular proactive or covert technique *always* requires judicial permission, all such practices are in theory regulated – even if the investigation does not lead to prosecution. It could be argued that, given the civil liberties anxieties, accountability requires that police decision-making in relation to covert and proactive policing should *always* be subject to prior external judicial scrutiny (which would thus include inter alia all contacts with informers who might wish to remain anonymous). But there are principled reasons for thinking that such a routine judicial involvement in covert policing – at least if it involved investigating or trial judges – would lead to too great a confusion between investigating and judging. There is a danger that the more judges have agreed to the use of the more routine proactive methods in an individual case (perhaps granting access to a number of such techniques over a period of time[6]) the more they may be psychologically drawn into a sense of being part of an investigative team. As a result, a necessary distance may be lost if further decisions (perhaps involving more significant intrusions into privacy) are necessary and approval may be given too readily. In other words it is possible to be too involved.[7]

There are thus advantages, in managing the tension between distance and presence in the relationship between judge, prosecutor and police, of a layered system where the more intrusive the technique the more distant the decision-maker. If such controls by judges should be limited to certain proactive or covert methods and not others, we would argue that a key distinction should be built around breach of privacy rights under Article 8 of the European Convention on Human Rights. Not all covert investigative acts involve such violations in the sense accorded to privacy by the European Court of Human Rights. In *Lüdi v Switzerland*, it was decided that the use of an undercover agent in an operation based on 'controlled delivery' was not a violation of privacy because drug-dealers had to expect that the police would use undercover means to detect such forms of crime.[8] No 'reasonable expectation' of privacy had been compromised. But if the policing method does involve such a breach, both procedural fairness and the Convention require that precise legal limits be determined and enforced and that they be based on standards of proportionality (is this case serious enough to warrant this degree of intrusion?) and subsidiarity (can the offence be effectively investigated by some other means?).[9] Such judgements, certainly that on proportionality, depend on the weighing of broad competing social claims: 'immunity [from interference with private life] is almost always qualified, so that privacy claims during criminal investigation are seldom indefeasible' (Alldridge 1996). This balancing of social harms and benefits is surely not appropriately left to police officers where the intrusions are significant – exactly because it is not a technical operational decision.[10] That would leave other covert techniques to be authorized by senior police officers or prosecutors or prosecuting magistrates. We will see that the extent to which these ideas are reflected in practice varies widely as between the two jurisdictions.

The Netherlands

In theory the continental conception of *Rechtsstaat* as well as the direct applicability of Article 8 of the European Convention under the Dutch constitution mean that all police powers that violate an individual's rights under the Article have to have a specific basis in law. In practice however, during the 1970s and 80s most proactive or covert policing methods lacked such an explicit legal basis. The provisions which defined the general functions of the police[11] were regarded by the courts as providing a legally sufficient basis for many such acts without a need for prior authority (telephone taps being one of the exceptions). In the wake of recent scandals (see discussion of the IRT affair in this volume by De Roos and in the introduction) the Supreme Court in the *Zwolsman* case has made a clear distinction between, on the one hand 'limited' violations of privacy – such as taking photos or recording somebody on video in a public place – and, on the other hand, 'serious' violations. The 'legality' requirements of the European Court on Human Rights, with their stress on clear criteria, are said to demand more specific legal authority for serious violations than the general and therefore vague provisions of the Police Act (which defines police functions).[12] This distinction is also at the heart of a recent Bill published in 1997 by the Ministry of Justice[13] which places responsibility for deciding whether specific proactive methods should be used firmly in the hands of the Public Prosecutor. The text allows systematic surveillance of suspects,[14] the covert entry and limited search of non-residential premises,[15] the use of informers (whether or not they are participating)[16] and undercover infiltration by the police[17] and by citizens[18] if authorized in advance by the Public Prosecutor.[19] The interception of communications (including bugging as well as the tapping of phone and fax) will require the Public Prosecutor to get prior permission from the *rechter-commissaris*. Thus the legal basis for a variety of covert investigative techniques will become prior judicial authority, but for the most part that means not a judge but the public prosecutor. Only the most intrusive interventions will require involvement of an examining magistrate.

Of the intrusive investigative methods used by the police, those that raise classical Article 5 issues (arrest and detention) have hitherto been much more closely regulated in the Dutch Code of Criminal Procedure than those that touch upon the more recently developed Article 8 (privacy) matters. The focus on Article 8 in the Bill represents an expansion of the requirement of judicial involvement into the proactive from the reactive phase. But, as with the Supreme Court's reasoning in the *Zwolsman* case, not all proactive investigation will require prior judicial approval. One key distinction is again 'reasonable expectation of privacy' as defined by the European Court of Human Rights in the *Lüdi* case. Those acts regarded as less intrusive, such as limited observation and shadowing of people and taking their photo in a public place,[20] as well as going through their rubbish sacks when placed at the kerbside or intercepting mobile phone calls (provided one does not use sophisticated equipment) will not require such approval. The police will be regarded as acting under the authority of general policing powers contained in Article 2 Police Act 1993. The reasoning is that no-one has a legitimate expectation of not being observed in public places and, in the case of mobile phones, it is well known that these are easily interceptable without complex equipment and so one could not legitimately expect the calls not to be intercepted.

England and Wales

In England and Wales, significant use of prior judicial authority would require profound institutional change. Although it has been pointed out that such prior permission is sometimes required in England and Wales for the exercise of coercive powers, this is not the case with proactive methods. The Diceyan concept of freedom under the rule of law, which states that citizens are entitled to do anything not specifically forbidden, when applied to the police – in accordance with a traditional idea of policeman as citizen in uniform – means that the police can do anything that is not specifically forbidden by law. Given that at the moment the European Convention is not directly applicable and it is not clear that there is a general domestic right to privacy,[21] prima facie new covert investigative techniques require no specific legal authority. Furthermore the absence of a pre-trial investigating magistrate and the limitations of the constitutional function of the Crown Prosecution Service (which has no legal responsibility to control the police or their investigations) mean that suggestions of prior judicial scrutiny always lead to the problem of who is actually going to do the monitoring.[22]

The effect, prior to the 1997 Police Act, was to leave decisions largely to the police. Most such investigative techniques, such as physical surveillance, undercover operations/infiltration by police officers and the use of (even participating) informers, require no prior authority from outside the police service regardless of their intensity or duration. Some, but not all, normally require the authority of the Chief Constable of the relevant force.[23] Thus neither judge nor even the Crown Prosecution Service is required to give permission beforehand. True, condemnation of the United

Kingdom in the *Malone* case[24] has meant that tapping a public telecom-munications system requires the authority of the Home Secretary. But there is no prior *judicial* involvement.[25] Bugging other than via such a public telephone system requires the consent of the Home Secretary if it is carried out by MI5 in pursuit of its new mandate under the Security Service Act 1996 to investigate 'serious crime'. Before the 1997 Police Act the only prior authority for electronic surveillance required in police investigation was that of the Chief Constable[26] and the then Conservative Government had intended to put this position on a statutory footing. However a rebellion in the Lords led by Lord Browne-Wilkinson and widespread media dissent led to the introduction of a system whereby some bugging will require prior authorization by a Commissioner who will be a serving or former high court judge. This will be necessary where the device is to be placed in a dwelling, hotel bedroom or an office or where the device is likely to pick up matters subject to legal privilege (e.g. client/lawyer discussions) or material held in confidence and acquired or created in a professional context (which specifi-cally includes journalism).[27] In other cases the authorization of a senior police officer[28] will be sufficient. There are some anxieties about the detail of the system. The power of senior police officers to authorize even intrusive surveillance where they believe that the case is an urgent one might be abused (but given that this is subject to the power of the Commissioner to subsequently quash the authorization it may be that independent minded Commissioners might forestall this). The criteria for 'serious crime' are too broad, including any conduct by a large number of persons in pursuit of a common purpose even where there is no violence involved or substantial financial gain likely.[29] But the main problem may remain one of personnel: fears have been expressed that the Commissioners (who may well still be holding high judicial office) may be London based and therefore less acces-sible outside the capital and less familiar with local conditions (and particu-lar officers) (Ewing and Gearty 1997). There will only be five or six of them and presumably those who remain High Court judges will have other responsibilities. Hence the call of the Liberal Democrats during the debates for Circuit judges (of whom there are over 550) to be given the responsibil-ity (for the Liberal Democrat position see Lester 1997).

The absence of professional magistrates with direct responsibility for monitoring police investigations in England and Wales (and perhaps that of a structured two-phase conception of pre-trial proceedings) has meant that the existing requirements of prior authorization have come to be seen as isolated decisions requiring particular scrutiny rather than steps in a struc-tured judicial monitoring process. This may be one reason why 'inquisitorial jurisdictions'[30] such as Belgium, Germany and the Netherlands have more easily adopted the technique of prior judicial authority to structure access to the use of covert or proactive methods.

Enforcing guidelines: judicial control by exclusion of evidence or dismissing the case

England and Wales

Judicial control of the detailed routine practice of proactive policing – of how it is done – cannot realistically be done by prior authority in the individual case: it is too time consuming and confuses management and regulatory functions. Furthermore, as guidance to officers, administrative codes or rules of practice have an advantage over both legislation and case law in that they can be detailed and precise, use language that police officers can easily understand, and can be adapted periodically to reflect new needs and problems after consultation with relevant parties, but without the time-lag required for full-scale legislation. One danger however is that they may be ignored by police-officers if there is no effective sanction for breach.[31] It is here that judicial influence can be felt via enforcement at trial. The model in England and Wales here might be the 1984 Police and Criminal Evidence Act where evidence obtained in breach of the Code of Practice C on Interrogation is excluded where there are 'serious and substantial' breaches of the key sections – those that bear most centrally on suspects' rights.[32] This has significantly affected interrogation practice.[33] Home Office guidelines do already exist in relation to the use of informers, and restrict the conditions under which 'participating informers' may be used. These demand that the permission of a senior police officer be obtained and that cases involve 'complex crimes' or 'sophisticated and ruthless criminals' where the use of participating informers is the 'only realistic means to identify offenders, frustrate their illegal intentions and secure the evidence necessary to sustain a prosecution'.[34] Guidelines also existed prior to the new Police Act in relation to the use of electronic surveillance which entrenched proportionality and subsidiarity.[35] They have in part been superseded by the Code of Practice on Intrusive Surveillance issued by the Home Office under the new Act.[36] However the courts have not used these guidelines to control police practice by stating that breach (or even 'significant breach' or 'breach that prejudices the defendant's interests') will require exclusion. The House of Lords in the recent *Khan* case made much of the existence of guidelines on

electronic surveillance to indicate that such methods were subject to requirements of legality, but stressed the traditional view that illegality (and a priori
breach of guidelines) would not normally lead to exclusion of relevant
evidence.[37] It was not the function of the discretion to exclude evidence
under section 78 PACE to police the police. Generally in covert policing
cases judicial criteria for excluding evidence under section 78[38] are multiple, may point in different directions in the same case and therefore have
to be weighed against each other. Furthermore, the cases show no very clear
criteria for the balancing.[39] Evidence will only be definitely excluded where
police officers have incited an offence that would not otherwise have taken
place[40] or have sought to sidestep controls on interrogation by questioning
suspects while undercover.[41] Thus judges in England and Wales have not,
as they did with PACE and interrogation methods, developed the apparatus
for a detailed control of the limits of proactive policing.

The Netherlands

Numerous guidelines for the police are issued by the Ministry of Justice via
the Public Prosecution Service or by the Service itself. They may deal with
particular investigative techniques or how to handle specific crimes. If a
guideline has been published and is regarded as creating rights for individuals, citizens are regarded as having a legitimate expectation that the execu-
tive/administration will obey them. Breach of such rules will have consequences. For example, if there is a breach of the prosecution guideline that
social security fraud below a certain amount should not be charged, the
prosecution would be struck down. But normally guidelines are regarded as
'instruction-norms' not 'warranty-norms', which means they do not confer
rights and a citizen may not base his or her case upon them. Only if breach
of an 'instruction-norm' violates the principle of fairness in criminal
proceedings or makes investigation results unreliable[42] will breach have
consequences, and this will depend on the defect. If breach of the rules
seriously violates fundamental rights (like Article 5 or 8 ECHR), evidence
gained as a result will almost always be excluded, provided that there is a
direct causal link between the breach and the obtaining of the evidence and
the violated norm was intended specifically to protect that defendant. That
would not be the case if a letter addressed to X were illegally intercepted,
opened and read by the police and they found evidence against Y. Furthermore, if the police are still in the proactive phase (and the suspect does not
yet realize he is under investigation) and they expect evidence to be
excluded, they may then try to repair the weaknesses by further investiga-

tion. As a result the likelihood of breach losing the officers their case seems quite remote. On the other hand, the consequences of not giving an accurate account of all investigative acts – illegal as well as legal – are quite disastrous, as the *Coral Sea II* case shows.[43] If it can be established that judges have been misled by the withholding of relevant information (which is contrary to guidelines issued by the Procurators-General governing written reports by the police)[44] the case will be dismissed – even long after a final verdict, via a 'revision procedure' if the deception is crucial to the defendant's guilt. Apart from this, officers may be – and are – disciplined or prosecuted for violations. In the above *Coral Sea* case two officers were dismissed, two others transferred to less important posts. The officers were also prosecuted and received the maximum sentence possible: community service and a six month suspended prison sentence.

Procedural consequences of proactive policing: determining the limits of defence access to information[45]

The third type of judicial intervention is when decisions are taken about the record and results of covert or proactive policing. Typically this will take place after the investigation has 'gone reactive' – that is to say somebody has usually been arrested because the proactive policing has generated a reasonable suspicion that an offence has been, is being or will be committed. Then the accused or his or her lawyer will usually start to seek information about the case. They may want to know whether the accused has been denounced by somebody and, if so, by whom. They may want to see police surveillance records or to know the positioning of surveillance posts.[46] This leads to perhaps the most difficult role for magistrates in proactive or covert policing cases, where they are still determining procedural rights but not as a gatekeeper controlling police penetration of individual privacy but rather as one who limits defence access to the state world of prosecution and police files. It is not state coercion or intrusion into private life that is the issue but party access to information.

The problem posed by proactive policing in both jurisdictions is that the ideal – from the police point of view – is not just that the key investigative acts should take place before suspects are aware of them. The key demand of covert policing – that of secrecy – often leads to more than simply postponing access to information: it is a demand that suspects should *never* be allowed to know who has informed against them or where surveillance posts have been set up. Clearly this will limit (or eliminate) the capacity of the defence to challenge those aspects of the police case. But without this limitation of knowledge, it is doubtful whether proactive policing methods can be used at all. The traditional ethics of the legal profession mean that one cannot (normally) disclose information to the defendant's lawyers without disclosing that information to the defendant because there can be no secrets between lawyer and client. And defendants (especially those involved in sophisticated organized crime) do sometimes make illegitimate use of that information. Informers could not be extensively used, especially against organized crime, if their identities were routinely disclosed to defence lawyers because they would quickly come under threat or worse. The public in certain areas would be reluctant to allow the police to set up surveillance posts on their property if that would become known to the target of surveillance.

This leaves judges with difficult decisions to make. Sometimes these issues may be determined by applying precise rules: at the moment, more often they involve in both jurisdictions the exercise of broad discretion in individual cases by the balancing of competing social values: on the one hand, the need of society for effective policing; on the other, the need to enable the defence to challenge the prosecution case as both a method of promoting truth-finding and as part of the participation rights expected by citizens within modern democracies (Brants and Field 1995, pp. 72-73).

In deciding these questions, the fundamental starting point should surely be 'could the information legitimately reinforce the claim that the defendant is not guilty?' If so it must be disclosed or the prosecution abandoned. Brants and Field have argued that this is an inherently difficult judgement because normally the issues in a case are only fully defined through debate between parties and the decision has to be made before that happens (Brants and Field 1995, p. 73). The extent and nature of the problem this poses often varies depending on whether covert methods are being used *reactively* (after the offence has been committed but almost always before arrest) or proactively (before the offence takes place). Often the effect of covert policing *when used proactively* is that the police are able to intervene at the very moment of the offence, being forewarned that it will take place by the proactive work. In this situation, the evidence the police wish to advance at trial is the evidence obtained at the point of the offence and often it may be very strong evidence. In some of these cases, if the evidence is overwhelming, the argument that the identity of the informer or the position of the video-camera should be revealed will be weak. But where there are problems with the evidence obtained at the moment of the crime that need to be assessed in the light of what has gone before, access to the detail of the police operations may bear strongly on the question of truth.

Some examples may bring out these distinctions. Police officers video the defendant(s) entering a bank putting on masks and producing weapons; or the police film the defendant(s) handing a packet to another person and receiving money in exchange; or perhaps the police or relevant environmental authority record a company truck discharging chemicals into a river while other agents are taking samples. In each case the police reveal themselves and arrest the defendant on site. In such a situation, provided the video pictures are clear, or the packet or the river sample appropriately analysed, the argument from the defence for access to details of the proactive work (the name of the informer who told the police of the time and place of the offence, the location of the video-camera) is not usually about whether their client 'did it' in a crude sense. Suppose that, in the pollution example, the police have been tipped off by one of the company's ex-workers, does it make a difference, provided that the video and the sample is good, if the worker has just been fired and therefore has a grudge, or now works for a competitor or simply has a disinterested commitment to ecological matters? In the Netherlands the defence primarily want the records of proactive or covert investigations in such cases because it might lead to the discovery of police illegality and thus exclusion of admittedly probative evidence. This has been a bitter part of the argument in the 'mega-cases' on proactive policing in the Netherlands because illegally obtained evidence and its fruits are almost always excluded (provided always that there is a direct causal link between the illegality and the obtaining of evidence and the rule violated was intended to benefit that particular defendant). Given that such methods have often been targeted at those suspected of involvement in organized crime the stakes have been high on both sides. In England and Wales, given the more restrictive interpretations of section 78 PACE, even if access to details of the methods were to disclose illegality, this is not likely to impact on the trial result. On the other hand, what might cut some ice is a claim of entrapment. If the informant has persuaded or tricked the defendant(s) into committing an offence he or she would not otherwise have committed, though in one sense that cannot change the fact that the defendant, crudely speaking, 'did it', it will probably change legal assessment of guilt (i.e. of the 'legal truth' of the matter).[47] In such a situation – and this applies equally to the Netherlands – the identity of the informers and their role may well be crucial.

The claims of the defence are likely to be stronger where covert methods are used *reactively* (after the offence has been committed) exactly because the quality of the evidence obtained at the point of the offence may be much less convincing. The case of Colin Stagg[48] is a good example: he was targeted after a brutal murder for largely circumstantial reasons. His home was nearby, he had no alibi, he showed physical similarities with somebody seen near the scene, he had a previous conviction for indecent exposure and he fitted the psychological profile of the killer drawn up by a psychologist. But the key evidence that the police sought to rely on – his allegedly detailed knowledge of the victim's injuries – was generated directly by the covert methods (an undercover police operation). Clearly the details of this, who he spoke to, exactly what he said and under what conditions would be crucial to assessing the truth of the matter. Sometimes, as in the *Stagg* case, such difficulties may be resolved by having the undercover officer testify as a disguised witness under controlled circumstances but on other occasions the identity of the informer may be obvious or one may wish not to reveal the very existence of an undercover operation. Surveillance cases sometimes raise the same problems: several of the key cases in England and Wales on revealing the location of surveillance points were in cases where there was no video-camera evidence and the police officers were simply asserting that they recognized the accused.[49] Then the location of the surveillance point might well be crucial given that distance may affect the reliability of the officers' observations.

The difficulty is in distinguishing between those cases where the evidence obtained at the scene at the moment of the offence is sufficiently strong to be taken at face value and those where defence questioning may open up legitimate doubts about guilt. It is important to recognize the role that this may ultimately give to the judicial decision-maker in that sometimes particular hypotheses about truth will be effectively eliminated without giving the defence full opportunity to explore them. Suppose an informer denounces a suspect. He or she wishes to remain anonymous for fear of reprisal. There is at least a general possibility that he or she has an ulterior motive for denouncing the suspect (his or her own culpability, revenge, money?). The defence, on the basis of pre-trial disclosure (in England and Wales) or access to the official file (in the Netherlands) ask to know who the informer is, suggesting that such motives may be in play. Is this relevant to the defendant's guilt? If proactive or covert policing is to be effective at least sometimes somebody is going to have to take the decision that this is not relevant and so the defence do not need to know the informer's identity. And the only appropriate candidate is surely a judge, whether the trial judge, or possibly a magistrate preparing the case pre-trial – somebody upon whom the responsibility of determining truth or balancing public interest is routinely and legitimately vested and yet someone who can be trusted to keep a professional secret (he or she can know who the informer is). We typically think of the determining of truth as a formal, definitive and positive declaration at the end of the trial process. Earlier determination of truth appears illegitimate exactly because the full process of party presentation of, and challenge to, evidence has not yet occurred.[50] But here judges may end up making preliminary decisions about truth without full defence participation in the decision-making process. In some cases the decisions will be easy: for example a jealous neighbour of a person on social security with an improbably expensive lifestyle tells the police and they start an investigation. The defence would have to raise more than motive to know the details. But it is a decision nevertheless that eliminates one possible story explaining events. Where and how are these decisions taken in the two jurisdictions?

The Netherlands

In the Netherlands these issues are posed in terms of access to the official dossier and how much detail of the investigation the dossier should contain. The Supreme Court decision in *Zwolsman* is now the leading case on what the police must record, what must be placed in the dossier and the conditions under which information may be withheld. It was decided in an atmosphere of concern for greater openness that followed the IRT scandal and its revelations of how little was known by defence, judges or even prosecutors about some police covert operations. Article 152 Code of Criminal Procedure requires police officers to make a *proces-verbaal* (written report) of every investigative act conducted in a criminal inquiry in the reactive phase (i.e. in this case after reasonable suspicion has arisen that a criminal act has occurred).[51] This would include the use of covert police methods. In *Zwolsman*, the Supreme Court stated that a reasonable exception could be made if the officer comes to the conclusion – which is reviewable by the public prosecutor on the basis of police reports – that what he or she has done cannot reasonably be of any value for any decision made by the trial judge. But in such a case the officer has to record his findings so that he or she can, if necessary, justify that part of the investigation to the trial judge. The personal interests of third parties do not justify a failure to record an investigative act: rather their interests may be taken into account in the way in which the report is drafted (e.g. by omitting names or addresses of informers or those in whose house surveillance posts have been set up).

However these requirements do not apply to the proactive phase of investigation (i.e. before reasonable suspicion has arisen). But the Supreme

Court stated that police activity must be recorded because if a reactive investigation later starts a *proces-verbaal* will need to be drawn up summarizing those proactive acts. Furthermore the trial judge may ask to be informed about the information gathered: the requirements of a fair trial demand that he or she be able to check the legality of the investigative acts and the reliability of the information produced.[52] The sanction at trial for breach may be the dismissal of the case, the exclusion of the relevant evidence or nothing at all depending on the trial judge's assessment of the violation of principles of fair trial. If the *aim* of the failure was to prevent the judge from assessing the relevant act or evidence the sanction should be dismissal of the case. But this rarely happens: more often minor or even major rule-breaking is dealt with as in the *Coral Sea* case.

The recent Government Bill follows the line of the *Zwolsman* case in its definition of the recording duties of police officers. It stresses that only such an extensive duty can enable the prosecutor to control and supervise investigative acts (even in the proactive phase) and the trial judge to check the reliability and legality of the information. It confirms the settled case law that there is no obligation to insert into the dossier *processen-verbaal* which contain no relevant information.[53] A declaration by the Public Prosecutor that the file is complete is sufficient legal basis for the judge to reject a defence request to add material to the file which might be of interest to the defence.[54] Nevertheless an index should be placed in the dossier of all special investigation methods to enable the trial judge, whether or not the defence requests it, to check the legality of the investigation by demanding further information if necessary. This confirms the ending of the special practice that had developed and which lead to the IRT scandal, of certain proactive investigations (those involving the importation and sale of cannabis under controlled circumstances) being conducted but concealed from Prosecutor and *rechter-commissaris* (examining magistrate). (The practice had been stopped after criticism in the Parliamentary Inquiry into the IRT affair.)

Nevertheless, the defence will still have no absolute right to discuss all the collected information (i.e. the information on which initial suspicion was based as well as evidence presented at trial), just as there is no absolute right to confront a witness. The *rechter-commissaris* (if there is a judicial investigation) or the Prosecutor may decide under Article 50 Code of Criminal Procedure that evidence be temporarily excluded from the dossier in the 'interests of the investigation'.[55] In such cases they will have to submit their decision immediately to the court which will accept or reject this after defence submissions. The identity of threatened witnesses may be concealed and defence rights to question witnesses limited under legislation that flowed from the *Kostovski* case (even though their testimony remains part of the official dossier used as a basis of decision-making at trial).[56] Personal information about a witness interviewed by the *rechter-commissaris* may be withheld if there is a serious suspicion that the witness may experience personal annoyance or adverse consequences for his professional life. (This rule is not governed by the procedure under Article 50.[57]) A trial judge may refuse to allow particular questions to be answered at trial.[58] Case law suggests that this is done if investigative methods or names of informers may be revealed where these methods or informers are not being put forward by the prosecution as evidence.[59] More recent case law shows that the detail of certain *processen-verbaal* or reports may be limited to protect witnesses or informers or keep their identity secret: this is justified in the general interests of crime investigation.[60]

In some of these cases it may be difficult for the defence to show on a reasoned basis that there are justifiable doubts about the legality or reliability of the evidence collected. But nevertheless it is normally not sufficient for the defence simply to make the claim: some basis for it must be shown. On the one hand, the Bill – with its demand that all investigative methods used be listed in the files – will give defence lawyers more of an opportunity to demand further details of investigative acts of possibly challengeable legality. On the other hand, the Bill itself confirms that there are a broad range of legal reasons for denying the defence information: the desire not to jeopardize informers, to protect ongoing investigations or an investigative technique one may want to use again, the readiness of citizens to assist the police in the investigation of serious crime, the desire to use the same undercover agent in different operations. And this may go further: the Minister of Justice has argued that the right under Article 190 Code of Criminal Procedure to withhold information about witnesses should be extended to situations where this is necessary to protect a strong investigative interest.

Where the defence is excluded from information about the detail of policing methods then the need for dialogue between prosecutor, police and a judicial authority with more distance from the inquiry seems essential. Here, the Bill sets out innovative new powers to allow the *rechter-commissaris*, on his or her own initiative, or at the request of defence, prosecutor or trial judge, to investigate the legality of some police activities during the inquiry. These will not be activities that have led directly to the production of evidence that is to be presented in court – that will continue to be part of the assessment by the trial judge of that evidence at trial. These are likely to be inquiries into the reliability and legality of the proactive methods which generated initial suspicions: information that will not be presented in court. Thus the examining magistrate, if a question arises about the running of an informer but where that informer's testimony will not be presented at court, may interview the police-officers running the informer and, in exceptional cases, the informer him or herself.

It is by these means – essentially reaffirming the traditionally active truth-finding role of the investigating magistrate and the trial judge, that the Bill seeks to reconcile the need to keep secret certain aspects of the proactive investigative methods used with the demands of the European Court on Human Rights. The principle of a fair trial and the right to put questions about the whole of the police investigation can be abridged only because the search for information helpful to the defence can be entrusted to the *rechter-commissaris* and only if the defence is allowed to trigger this kind of involvement by the investigating magistrate. This is regarded as compatible with the terms of the European Court as laid down in *Doorson v Netherlands*[61] and *Lüdi v Switzerland*. In the former the safety of witnesses and, in the latter, the interests of the investigation, were regarded as legitimately necessitating the limiting of defence rights (though both cases stressed that defence rights to interrogate witnesses and cast doubt on their credibility should be limited as little as possible). In the balance between these rights and the protection of witnesses one important element is the amount and strength of other evidence. The proposed Dutch reforms require at the end of the process that the trial judge decides whether there is enough information available to take an appropriate decision. He or she may require prosecutor or police to provide more information. If this is still not available, and the interests of the defence have been prejudiced, the case should be dismissed or (more frequently) the defendant acquitted.[62]

Thus the limitation of defence rights to information that proactive policing is perceived as requiring entails in turn implications for the role of the judge. In order to decide that a hypothesis suggesting that the defendant is innocent (or is being incriminated by illegally obtained evidence) can be safely discounted, judges are being encouraged to adopt a more active role exactly to compensate for the lack of debate between parties. This is the reassertion of traditional roles within the inquisitorial tradition (whether one is talking about the role of the examining magistrate or the trial judge): the judge as truth-finder and supervisor of the collecting of evidence. But these kinds of role are much more startling and alien within the adversarial tradition.

England and Wales

In England and Wales, since the 1980s, duties have been imposed on the prosecution to disclose to the defence information uncovered during the police investigation but which the prosecution do not propose to use ('unused material'). But the system was discredited by the miscarriages of justice revealed in the 1990s: the rules were applied in the individual case by the prosecution and as one might expect in a system built on contest and without real pre-trial judicial control, police and prosecution defined their duties of disclosure restrictively. The judicial response, developed through case law in the early 1990s, was to develop very extensive duties of prosecution disclosure with determination of the key issues by *judges*.[63] This has had profound implications for proactive and covert policing in England and Wales.

Prior to the 1990s judges might be asked *at trial* whether the defence might pose questions that revealed detail of proactive methods (such as the identity of an informer or the location of a surveillance post). The case law suggested that the judge could forbid such questions if it was in the public interest but that if posing the questions could help to show the defendant's innocence, the balance of the public interest fell on disclosure.[64] The case law of the 1990s transferred to the trial judge the same decisions in relation to all the materials the prosecution was not going to present as evidence at trial. The system that developed was that the prosecution supplied a schedule of unused material (which involved more or less the whole of the information accumulated during the investigation) to the defence which was invited to inspect material listed: in theory records of investigation, including proactive and covert methods, had become available to both sides. Only if a judge on application by the prosecution ruled that the public interest in concealing sensitive material outweighed defence rights to information could the material be withheld.

Immediately the police complained that defence lawyers were beginning inter alia to force the state to drop cases by demanding disclosure of the role of informants and their identity (Rose 1995). The Metropolitan Police Commissioner claimed that 100 cases were dropped in 1994 to avoid disclosing confidential information or surveillance techniques (Gibb 1994). The Association of Chief Police Officers, in evidence to the House of Commons Home Affairs Select Committee inquiry into organized crime, claimed 72 cases had been withdrawn in the 18 months between January 1992 and June 1993.[65] The Director of Public Prosecutions felt this was a consequence of not getting the 'balance right' in determining applications for disclosure

(Gibb 1994). A Home Office Consultation Paper supported these views though without any systematic empirical evidence on the extent of the problem.[66] It did however cite three examples where prosecution had been immediately withdrawn once the judge ordered disclosure. All concerned access to classic aspects of proactive methods (records of undercover operations, the identity of informers and the location of surveillance posts). In the first, three members of the Animal Liberation Front had been charged with arson and applied for police intelligence files on the organization to be disclosed. When this was granted the prosecution was dropped because to comply would 'compromise future investigations' (presumably surveillance or undercover operations or activities of informants). In the second, disclosure of video tape of undercover police buying drugs with marked money was ordered; the prosecution was dropped because it enabled the location of the surveillance post to be identified (in a nearby flat). In the last, an informer reported that defendants were trying to sell forged bank-notes. After an undercover operation lead to their arrest in possession of large quantities of such notes with their fingerprints on them, the prosecution was dropped after a judge ordered disclosure of the informer's identity. Citing these cases, the Consultation Paper concluded that the courts were obliged to order disclosure in cases where the actual relevance of sensitive material may be 'marginal at best, and which in any event does not have to be adequately justified by the defence'. We would argue that the disclosure *rules* at the time could not be said to compel judges to make these decisions. Most of the case law simply reiterates the point that judges must weigh the public interest in non-disclosure against the private and public interest in disclosure – which leaves a broad discretion with the judges. The Government was, in effect, covertly objecting to the way judges were balancing the respective values. It seemed to think that judges were being hoodwinked by defence lawyers who were seeking 'to obscure the real issues or even on occasions to come forward with a plausible but fictitious defence.'[67]

It may be that one difficulty was that judges would sometimes need to engage in extensive consideration of the case materials. Without that, and without a structured dossier, it is difficult to rule out the possibility that the defence might discover something that supports a legitimate defence. In the currency forgery case above, the identity of the informer could only be relevant to an issue bearing on culpability if he or she played an active role in persuading the defendants to commit the offence (which might even require an acquittal if they would not have committed the offence without his intervention). Did the trial judge inquire himself or herself into the credibility of this hypothesis or was the fact that it was an abstract possibility enough to prompt the requirement of disclosure? Did the judge view the video of the surveillance in the drugs case to determine whether there were plausible doubts about authenticity or interpretation that required the revealing of the intelligence post? Did he or she look at the records of the undercover operation in the Animal Liberation Front case to see whether legitimate doubts could be cast on the nature of the undercover involvement (did somebody incite offences for example?) Without answers to these questions it is impossible to offer definitive judgement but it may be that trial judges – brought up in the adversarial tradition with its model of the passive trial referee – were uneasy about adopting the kind of active 'truth-finding' role that would be required to discount such possibilities. If this is so, against a background of repeated manifestation of the dangers of non-disclosure in reactive cases, it may not be surprising if judges read the criteria to be applied cautiously.[68]

The Government response was to take some of the key initial decisions on disclosure away from the trial judge. The Criminal Procedure and Investigations Act 1996, based on the Consultation Paper, restricts prosecution duties of disclosure, creates extensive duties of defence disclosure and introduces a more elaborate pre-trial preparation regime built around a new power for judges to determine legal issues before trial and a new system of preparatory hearings in complex cases. These changes have the potential to shift the English and Welsh system some way away from the traditional adversarial model of the passive trial judge who comes to the opening of the full case at trial with little knowledge of its detail (having played no role in its preparation). True, in some ways judges will play a more restricted role than in the early 1990s because the prosecution is made again the initial judge of relevance of material held by the police. But given that defence lawyers now have extensive experience of what can be found in prosecution files and that, under the Act, challenges to prosecution views of relevance can be made before a judge, and that a decision to restrict access to relevant but sensitive material remains a judicial decision, the new power to make binding rulings and the new preparatory hearings may still develop into a new and significant pre-trial role.

The starting point is what the police must record. The Act creates a police disclosure officer who must disclose to the prosecutor any material that might undermine the prosecution case or might reasonably be thought to support the line of argument the defence is advancing. Beyond that he or she has to produce two separate schedules of material gathered during the investigation. The first relates to sensitive material which, as defined by Paragraph 6.12 of the Code of Practice,[69] includes details of informers, surveillance and undercover operations. The second contains a list of non-sensitive material. The prosecution will then disclose information that it considers might undermine the prosecution case and the schedule of non-sensitive material.[70] The defence will thus not see the schedule of sensitive material. Then the defence must, if it wants further disclosure, set out its case in general terms and why it disagrees with the terms of the prosecution case.[71] Once the defence do so the prosecution must ordinarily disclose any further information that 'might reasonably be expected to assist the accused's defence' as disclosed by the defence statement. Thus far the Act envisages no judicial involvement. A judge becomes involved when (a) the defence wish to challenge the prosecution claim that it holds no (further) relevant material or (b) the prosecution wish to avoid disclosing material that it considers relevant but 'sensitive' and where it considers disclosure would not be in the public interest. Trial judges may then decide in preliminary proceedings that information is not relevant or sufficiently central to guilt or innocence to justify defence access: again this means that aspects of the truth will be effectively, if provisionally, determined pre-trial.[72]

The problem with the system is that the judicial role in defining relevance is only engaged by the initiative of the defence who by definition are acting in the dark as regards proactive or covert methods.[73] Given that police officers like to avoid disclosing details of such methods,[74] any traces will usually be in the schedule of sensitive material that the defence will not see. And without a reasoned basis for application linked to a defence already disclosed there is no obligation on the prosecution for further disclosure. A hunch would not seem to be enough.

The second point at which judges will intervene is where prosecution makes an application not to disclose sensitive but relevant material and the court must decide whether it is in the public interest that it be disclosed. In some circumstances this can be done ex parte without the defence being present.[75] Justice in its recent Consultation Paper on disclosure suggested that such ex parte applications have become very frequent, being used in relation to almost all informer cases.

It is not clear how judges will determine these disputes over relevance and sensitive material. There are two principal sources on which to base decisions. First, there is material in the possession of police or prosecution, which may be voluminous. Simply reading what the prosecution wanted not to disclose after the *Ward* decision was said to put significant strains on the workload of Crown Court judges, so much so that one barrister has suggested that independent counsel be instructed to do it (Glynn 1993). The second source on which to base decision-making is defence submission which might help to define the issues but will be based on limited information and thus may not go much beyond a preliminary outline of the defence's case and what it suspects about information it has not got. (In ex parte applications there will not even be that.) Will the judges demand that the defence demonstrate that there is relevant material and where it may be found? The danger is that defence lawyers will be asked to demonstrate the relevance to their defence of information they do not yet know.

The only other way for the judge to find out whether the location of the observation post or the identity of the informer is relevant is to find out himself or herself. If the defence suspects relevant information has been concealed or simply not appreciated will the judges trawl through *all* the investigation papers? No doubt sometimes defence requests in organized crime cases may be prompted by client desire to delay or get information on police investigation for reasons other than the promotion of the search for the truth. Trial judges will sometimes understandably be sceptical and not anxious to spend the time reading the materials themselves without some concrete reason. But if they are not simply to take prosecution case-papers on face value a conscientious judge might often have to hear police officers in private to determine disclosure issues in covert or proactive policing cases. This is what seems to be envisaged under the proposed Dutch system (under that system, the trial judge could also commission the *rechter-commissaris* to do the necessary research but, in the absence of an investigating judge, that option is not open in England and Wales). Whether judges will do this is another question. In the absence of a strong tradition of pre-trial judicial decision-making it would be surprising if practice was not variable. One of the reasons for the limited effectiveness of preparatory hearings in fraud cases has been that judges, for a variety of reasons, have not been able or willing to be very interventionist (Levi 1993).

Judicial case management?

Justice has made the point that the acceptability of the disclosure and pre-trial regimes varies because there are effectively two separate regimes. Full-scale preparatory hearings, where there will be continuity of judge, will be restricted to a small percentage of Crown Court cases. Where a preparatory hearing will not take place, a judge who will know that he or she will probably not be the trial judge, will have to master the relevant material and decide (usually in a Plea and Directions Hearing).[76] Either this will, as Justice comments, mean long and burdensome PDHs or judges will have to limit the amount of examination of materials they conduct, leading to a tendency to take prosecution case-papers for granted. When defence participation is limited this is exactly what is dangerous. A serious monitoring role for the judiciary requires real judicial case management which requires continuity: judges being allocated a case-load they alone control or prepare for trial. A Bar working party (the Seabrook Committee) on pre-trial issues thought judicial case-management impossible for logistical reasons: heavy reliance on part-time judiciary, lack of available judicial time, a tradition of circuits so that judges are on the move and a lack of staff and information technology available to them.[77]

This suggests British systems of selection and recruitment of judiciary – built around a very small prestigious full-time judiciary which in turn reflects the very absence of a pre-trial role – have or will become major impediments to any system of active judicial preliminary decision-making on the kind of issues that proactive policing poses. If this were solved – and it would probably require a radical change in recruitment systems – one would be left with the problem of culture. As Mike Redmayne has recently put it, if the Criminal Procedure and Investigations Act really leads where it has the potential to lead, one would have to trust the judges not to abuse their managerial powers (Redmayne 1997, p. 93). This is particularly important in proactive policing cases. Will the culture applied be that of managers or magistrates? It is possible to be pessimistic but the judges' work in policing Code C PACE (Canale) and in developing duties of prosecution disclosure (Ward, Maguire) does suggest that when attempts by police officers to sidestep regulatory regimes are clearly linked to miscarriages of justice the judiciary can be stirred to action.

Conclusion

This chapter suggests that there are means available for a calibrated judicial control of covert and proactive policing. This might involve a combination of methods known in other areas such as prior authorization, enforcement of administrative Codes of Practice and interventions aimed at regulating the trial consequences of the secrecy necessary to such policing. Criteria for prior authority could be based on the widely accepted criteria of proportionality, subsidiarity, a prohibition on entrapment, and a limitation to those suspected of serious[78] or organized crime. For the more significant intrusions on privacy judicial decision-making is a necessary precaution because the weighing of social values required should not be left to the police alone.

How far this produces a balance that is satisfactory depends of course on the cultural values in play.[79] But other forms of judicial scrutiny, such as at trial itself, are insufficient because they extend only to cases that are prosecuted. It is also possible for judicial controls to support indirectly detailed administrative controls on the organization and recording of the results of proactive policing. What is needed are guidelines enforced by the use of exclusion of evidence if there are significant and substantial breaches which entail prejudice to the defendant's interests.

So far what we are discussing is simply a matter of adapting known regulatory techniques to the 'new' policing methods. Dealing with the secrecy implications of covert policing may require greater structural change. Here we have argued that, where defence access to material is limited there is a need for an active pre-trial judicial presence to check what the defence cannot. In the Netherlands this is being taken more seriously because the problems have been most spectacularly demonstrated there. However the implications for judicial roles may be more radical for adversarial systems.

Judges within inquisitorial jurisdictions have traditionally played three different roles: they adjudicate on procedural matters, collect evidence and/or supervise or commission its collection, and actually determine legal truth themselves. The role of the *professional* judge in criminal cases is more restricted within most adversarial jurisdictions and certainly in England and Wales. There is traditionally a focus, amongst the three roles, upon the determining of procedural rights rather than judicial truth-finding or the collection (or supervision of the collection) of evidence. Since the rise of the organized police force and the end of the tradition of the Anglo-Saxon examining magistrate, the role of judges in collecting and supervising collection of evidence in the pre-trial process has almost disappeared. The main function of the professional judge in criminal cases is thus that of trial referee at the Crown Court. This chapter suggests that this is one of the things that will have to change if criminal procedure in adversarial jurisdictions is to square the secrecy necessary for covert policing with demands of procedural fairness and protection of the innocent. Judges would need to begin to play a more active (albeit preliminary) role in eliminating certain hypotheses about truth in situations where the defence is excluded from access to possibly relevant information. Unfortunately the Criminal Procedure and Investigations Act 1996 seems to provide neither the procedural framework nor the institutional supports to make this possible.

Notes

1 For discussion of Labour plans see 'In the News: A Bill of Rights for the UK?' (1997) 147 (6800) *New Law Journal* 1018 and Wadham 1997. It appears domestic courts will not be given the power to strike down domestic legislation that is in breach of the Convention but that the Government thinks that its incorporation will obviate the need for domestic privacy legislation: Kampfner and Rice 1997.

2 For consideration of the Dutch Prosecutor as Magistrate see Van de Bunt 1985. The Dutch act governing the organization of the judiciary includes the Public Prosecution Service but contains a number of provisions guaranteeing the independence of 'judges' which do not apply to Public Prosecutors: Swart 1993.

3 One can imagine others outside the criminal process but we leave these aside in the analysis which follows.

4 In adversarial jurisdictions judges may decide that information relating to the proactive operation need not be disclosed to the defence and in jurisdictions within the inquisitorial tradition, they may decide material need not be placed in the official dossier to which the parties have access.

5 Even there the *juges d'instruction* would not lead genuinely *proactive* investigation because an offence has to have been already committed before the prosecutor refers the case to them. Covert policing might then be used (especially if nobody has been arrested and the inquiry has been opened against X rather than a named person). Generally see Field in this volume.

6 Or indeed, in the case of French examining magistrates, commissioning their use.

7 A criticism voiced of the French examining magistrates is that their dual functions of leading an investigation and controlling access to the coercive powers used in that investigation lead to abuse because of these psychological effects. See M. Delmas-Marty 1991, especially at p. 125-132.

8 ECHR 15 June 1992, Series A, vol. 238, *Lüdi v Switzerland.*

9 ECHR 24 April 1990, Series A, vol. 176-A, *Kruslin v France.*

10 Though note that until the Police Act 1997 Home Office guidelines on bugging required Chief Constables to make just such judgements on proportionality and subsidiarity. See *R v Khan* [1996] 3 All ER 289 at 294b-d. Under the provisions of the Act, they will now be made by one of half a dozen judicial commissioners (retired or serving High Court judges).

11 Articles 141, 142 of the Code of Criminal Procedure and the former Article 26, now Article 2, Police Act 1993.

12 HR 19 December 1995, NJ 1996, 249. See De Roos in this volume for discussion of the distinction between 'serious' and 'non-serious'.

13 TK 1996-1997, 25403 nrs. A, B, 1-3.

14 Article 126g.

15 A superficial looking around is permitted (which might include placing a bug on an object) but not an intensive search of drawers etc. The search of homes is not permitted: Article 126k.

16 Articles 126j, 126v.
17 Article 126h.
18 Article 126w.
19 In some of these cases permission must come from the Procurators-General advised by a Central Review Committee.
20 On which see HR 19 February 1991, NJ 1992, 50.
21 In *R v Khan, op. cit.,* Lord Nolan, who gave the main speech stated that 'under English law, there is, in general, nothing unlawful about a breach of privacy'. But three of the other Law Lords, Lords Browne-Wilkinson, Slynn and Nicholls stressed that it was not necessary to decide this issue and (explicitly or implicitly) reserved their position.
22 During the passage of the 1997 Police Bill, the then opposition parties differed profoundly in their demands that police bugging be made subject to prior scrutiny. The Liberal Democrats wanted circuit judges to do it, whereas Labour wanted specially appointed Commissioners (current or retired High Court judges). Eventually amendments agreed by Labour were introduced. See Travis 1997.
23 For example the use of technical bugging devices (see Bevan and Lidstone 1991, p. 210-214 for a summary of the rules) and participating informers (see Greer and South in this volume).
24 ECHR 2 August 1984, Series A, vol. 82 (*Malone v UK*).
25 However it should be noted that England and Wales is, for the moment at least, in the unusual position of not allowing the results of such taps to be used in evidence at trial. For the police, telephone taps simply provide the information upon which evidence-gathering may proceed. Of course, given the lack of judicial involvement in controlling the use of taps, one might well conclude that the inability to use the results of taps is only appropriate.
26 And this does not affect the formal legality of the procedures.
27 Police Act 1997, section 99.
28 Normally a chief constable or an assistant chief constable.
29 Police Act 1997, section 93(4)a.
30 More accurately mixed jurisdictions with an inquisitorial tradition.
31 Recent research evidence suggests the internal guidelines on informers are often broken by investigating officers in the British police. Dunnighan and Norris 1995.
32 *R v Keenan* (1990) 90 Cr. App. R. 1
33 Contrast the portrait of pre-PACE interrogation practice in Irving and Hilgendorf 1980 with that in Baldwin 1993.
34 Home Office Circular 97/1969 'Informants who take part in crime' and now see ACPO (1990) Guidelines on the Use and Management of Informants.
35 Guidelines on the Use of Equipment in Police Surveillance Operations 1984.
36 See Home Office 'Intrusive Surveillance: Draft Code of Practice' (August 1997).
37 *R v Khan, op. cit.*

38 The courts have a discretion to exclude under this section where not to do so 'would unduly prejudice the fairness of proceedings.'

39 See especially *R v Smurthwaite and Gill* [1994] 1 All ER 898 at 903.

40 *R v Gill and Ranuana* [1989] CrimLR 358.

41 *R v Smurthwaite and Gill* [1994] 1 All ER 898.

42 An example would be an incorrectly performed confrontation.

43 HR 10 February 1997, nr 104.194.

44 Ned. Staatscourant 1997, 68, p. 8.

45 The first part of the following section is a development of the argument in Brants and Field 1995, p. 44 *et seq.* and conclusion.

46 See Cape and Spronken in this volume for a fuller discussion of the perspective and problems of the defence lawyer.

47 See *R v Gill and Ranuana, op. cit.*

48 See the introduction to this volume for more details and Ames 1994, Doherty 1994.

49 *R v Brown and Daley* [1988] 87 Cr App R 52 and *R v Agar* [1990] 2 All ER 442.

50 Hence the suspicion, especially from the inquisitorial tradition, of pleabargaining.

51 *Zwolsman* case, *op. cit.* at para. 11.2.1

52 *Op. cit.* at para. 11.2.2

53 For a recent case see HR 29 June 1993, NJ 1993, 692.

54 HR 21 January 1997, DD 97.142.

55 Article 50, section 2, CCP.

56 Article 226a-f CCP. For discussion of the *Kostovski* case see Beijer, Cobley and Klip 1995.

57 Article 190 CCP.

58 Article 288 CCP.

59 Case law also suggests that the contents of dossiers may be restricted by reference to perceived relevance for reasons of efficiency: not all the interviews conducted during a house to house operation in the neighbourhood have to be added to the dossier – only those which produce relevant results.

60 HR 5 December 1995, NJ 1996, 422.

61 ECHR 26 March 1996, NJ 1996, 741.

62 Cases are dismissed (regardless of the strength of evidence against the accused) when an unlawful act by the prosecutor or police deliberately violates principles of fair procedure or demonstrates gross neglect of the defendant's interest in a fair trial. More usually the doubts about the evidence generated might lead to acquittal.

63 See *R v Ward* [1993] 2 All ER 577, *R v Saunders* (Unreported, CCC), *R v Keane* [1994] 2 All ER 478

64 *R v Brown and Daley* [1988] 87 Cr App R 52 and *R v Agar* [1990] 2 All ER 442.

65 Quoted in Justice 1995, p. 6.

66 Home Office Cm 2864, Disclosure: A Consultation Document, 1995 at para. 14.

67 *Ibid.* at paras. 14 and 17.

68 It has been noted that little attention was drawn to cases where prosecution disclosure of informers' identities enabled the defence to show that they had an unsavoury past or dubious motives for wanting to inform on the defendant. See M. Redmayne (1997), 60 MLR 79 at 81, citing Rose 1996, pp. 192-207.

69 Home Office 1997.

70 Section 3(1). It is apparently not enough to require disclosure that material 'may be relevant to' the defence case.

71 Section 5(4).

72 Provisionally because the trial judge might decide during the course of the trial that the information had to be revealed after all. Note that preparatory hearings are defined as part of the trial so technically decisions there are not part of the pre-trial process.

73 Justice described this as a game of blind man's bluff (1995, p. 12).

74 British police officers routinely exclude all trace of the existence of an informer from files if the informer is not going to testify exactly so as to prevent prosecutors from deciding that such information should be disclosed. Indeed many admit to being prepared to lie to a court to protect an informer's anonymity. Dunnighan and Norris 1995.

75 Rules of Court have been introduced under the Criminal Procedure and Investigations Act 1996 which put on a statutory basis the procedures established by the Court of Appeal in *R v Davis, Johnson and Rowe* [1993] 2 All ER 643: see now Rule 2, The Crown Court (Criminal Procedure and Investigations Act 1996) (Disclosures) Rules 1997. Rowe and Davis are challenging the disclosure procedure introduced in that case before the European Court of Human Rights, the European Commission having ruled that there is a case to answer. The case concerns inter alia the withholding from the defence of the fact that payments were made to informers, Gibb 1997.

76 The Crown Court survey conducted for the Runciman Commission in 1993 showed that, when there was a pre-trial review, in over 80 per cent of cases the eventual trial judge did not preside. Zander and Henderson 1993.

77 Seabrook Report (General Council of the Bar, 1992) *The Efficient Disposal of Business in the Crown Court.*

78 Which needs to be more narrowly defined than under section 93(4) Police Act 1997.

79 For the argument that British state culture, in its disregard for fundamental freedoms, may be too strong to be much changed by prior judicial approval see Young 1997.

References

Alldridge, P. (1996), *'They spreade their poison in secrete ...': Privacy in Substantive and Adjectival English Criminal Law*, Unpublished paper given to Faculty of Law, University of Uppsala, Sweden.

Ames, J. (1994), Nickel case acquittal 'good news for justice', 91 (34) *Law Society Gazette* 4.

Baldwin, J. (1993), Police Interviewing Techniques: Establishing Truth or Proof?, 33 *British Journal of Criminology* 325.

Beijer, A., C. Cobley and A. Klip (1995), Witness Evidence, Article 6 ECHR and the Principle of Open Justice, in: P. Fennell et al. (eds.), *Criminal Justice in Europe: A Comparative Study*, Oxford: Clarendon Press, pp. 283-300.

Bevan, V. and K. Lidstone (1991), *The Investigation of Crime: A Guide to Police Powers*, London: Butterworths.

Brants, C. and S. Field (1995), *Participation Rights and Proactive Policing: Convergence and Drift in European Criminal Process*, Deventer: Kluwer.

Bunt, H.G. van de (1985), *Officieren van Justitie: verslag van een participerend observatie-onderzoek* (Doctoral Thesis, University of Utrecht), Zwolle: Tjeenk Willink.

Delmas-Marty, M., *Commission Justice pénale et droits de l'homme* (1991) *La Mise en état des affaires pénales,* Paris: Documentation Française.

Doherty, M. (1994), Watching the Detectives, 144 (6670) *New Law Journal* 1525-6.

Dunnighan, C. and C. Norris (1995), *Practice, Problems and Policy: Management Issues in the Police Use of Informers*, Paper to British Criminology Conference, July.

Ewing, K. and C. Gearty (1997), Check mission control, *The Guardian* 12 February.

Field, S., P. Alldridge and N. Jörg (1995), Prosecutors, Examining Judges and Control of Police Investigations, in: P. Fennell et al. (eds.), *Criminal Justice in Europe: A Comparative Study*, Oxford: Clarendon Press, pp. 227-249.

Gibb, Frances (1994), DPP blames law on disclosure for guilty going free, *The Times* 29 November, p. 5.

Gibb, F. (1997), Men convicted of M25 murder win ruling on human rights, *The Times* 2 October.

Glynn, J. (1993), The Royal Commission on Criminal Justice: (4) Disclosure, *Criminal Law Review* 841.

Home Office (1997), *Criminal Procedure and Investigations Act 1996, Code of Practice*, London: Stationery Office.

Irving, B. and L. Hilgendorf (1980), *Police Interrogation: the Psychological Approach*, Royal Commission on Criminal Procedure Research Paper No 1, London: HMSO.

Jörg, N., S. Field and C. Brants (1995), Are Inquisitorial and Adversarial Systems Converging?, in: P. Fennell et al. (eds.), *Criminal Justice in Europe: A Comparative Study*, Oxford: Clarendon Press, pp. 41-56.

Justice (1995), *Disclosure: A Consultation Paper, the JUSTICE response*, London: Justice.

Kampfner, J. and R. Rice (1997), 'Government decides against privacy law', *Financial Times*, 17 September.

Lester, A. (1997), A Question of Balance, *The Observer*, 19 January.

Levi, M. (1993), *The Investigation, Prosecution and Trial of Serious Fraud*, London: HMSO.

Radzinowicz, L. (1968), *A History of English Criminal Law, vol 4, Grappling for Control*, London: Stevens.

Rose, D. (1995), On the dangerous road to a police state, *Observer* 21 May, p. 21.

Rose, D. (1996), *In the Name of the Law: The Collapse of Criminal Justice*, London: Jonathan Cape.

Swart, B. (1993), The Netherlands, in: C. van den Wyngaert (ed.), *Criminal Procedure Systems in the European Community*, pp. 279-316.

Travis, A. (1997), Straw U-turn on 'spy bill', *The Guardian*, 17 January.

Wadham, J. (1997), A Model Bill, 147 (6798) *New Law Journal* 950.

Young, H. (1997), The Police Bill fiasco is worse than I thought, *The Guardian*, 23 January.

Zander, M. and M. Henderson (1993), *Crown Court Survey*, London: HMSO.

19 Proactive policing and the principles of immediacy and orality

JOHN R. SPENCER[1]

Introduction

The principles of orality and immediacy[2] are subjects which writers on criminal procedure in Germany and Holland have analysed earnestly and at length.[3] A glance at this literature reveals that these two principles mean different things to different people. The writers discuss at length what the principle of immediacy includes, and how it relates to the principle of orality, before going on discuss why these two related notions are important, and whether the legal system they are writing about sufficiently protects them. This theoretical discussion about orality and immediacy does not have any exact counterpart in the legal literature of England and Wales. However, every common lawyer is well aware of the rule that criminal cases must normally be heard in public, and they are equally aware that the most basic rules of criminal evidence in their jurisdictions include the rule that witnesses in contested cases must testify orally and in open court, and the rule that they must avoid hearsay when they do so – i.e. must not repeat what other people told them. In the English-speaking world there has been plenty of theoretical discussion of these particular rules,[4] even if there has been none, as such, about the principles of immediacy and orality.

In the first part of this chapter I do not propose to analyse the Dutch and German literature on immediacy and orality, or the English language literature on hearsay and public justice. Instead I intend to take a deconstructionist approach. I propose to analyse the contents of the packages to which the labels 'orality' and 'immediacy' are variously applied, examine the broad lines of the English rules on hearsay and public justice, and to present in concrete terms and at a fairly low level of abstraction a list of guiding principles about this general part of criminal procedure and evidence which are widely agreed to be important (although in neither Holland nor the United

Kingdom are they absolutely protected). In the second part of this chapter I shall examine how these five principles relate to proactive and secret police methods.

Orality and immediacy: five guiding principles

The first of these principles is the principle that criminal courts should sit in public.

In England and Wales this important principle, like a number of others, has no statutory basis. It was stated in emphatic terms, however, by the House of Lords in a leading case in 1913.[5] In England and Wales, as elsewhere, it exists subject to a certain number of exceptions, the most important of which concern young offenders, from whose trials the public are usually excluded; there are also more limited exceptions where national security is at stake, and where juveniles have to give evidence in sex cases (Emmins 1997, pp. 294-297). In the Netherlands, by contrast, the rule that trials must take place in public is laid down in the Constitution (*Grondwet*), Article 121 of which proclaims that 'Except in cases where statute otherwise provides, court hearings shall take place in public'. In criminal proceedings the main case where statute otherwise provides is Article 273 of the Code of Criminal Procedure (*Wetboek van Strafvordering*) which, adopting the phraseology of the European Convention on Human Rights, permits the court to sit in camera in the interests of morality, public order or state security, or to protect juveniles, or to respect the private life of the accused or of other persons connected with the case (Corstens 1995, pp. 516-520).

The usual reason why it is said to be important for criminal courts to sit in public is that public scrutiny makes sure that the judges carry out their job fairly and properly. As Bentham put it, 'Publicity is the very soul of justice. It is the keenest spur to execution, and the surest of all guards against impropriety. It keeps the judge himself, while trying under trial' (Bentham 1793, p. 316). The principle is also sometimes justified by saying that the public, for whose benefit the State makes laws and tries to catch and prosecute those who break them, has a legitimate interest seeing and hearing with its own eyes and ears that this is properly done. And it is also said that doing criminal justice in public has an important educative role, because it shows the public that criminals are punished and (we hope) punished fairly, thereby reinforcing respect for the law.[6] There is also the point that in countries like Holland and the United Kingdom, where judges are nominated by the Government, 'the judge operates in a democratic vacuum' (Corstens

1995, p. 56). Enabling the public to watch them do their job ensures at least some degree of democratic responsibility.

The second principle is that the trial court must decide the case only on evidence that has been publicly debated. Like the principle of public justice previously discussed, this principle is (at least in theory) fully recognized in both Dutch and English criminal procedure. In the Netherlands it is laid down by Article 338 of the Code of Criminal Procedure, which provides that 'A finding that the accused has committed the act of which he stands accused can be made by the judge, provided he has been convinced *at the trial* by the contents of legally recognized forms of evidence'; a provision similar in spirit to Article 247 (2) of the French Code of Criminal Procedure, which provides that 'The judge may not base his decision on anything except evidence which has been put before him at the hearing and discussed in his presence.' In England and Wales, where of course there is no code of criminal procedure,[7] we look again in vain for any overt statement of this principle in legislation. But it is tacitly present nonetheless, and is important. It underlies two important bodies of case law. The first are decisions requiring judges and jurors to decide the case on evidence heard in court and not on their own personal knowledge of the facts of the case, if they happen to have any.[8] The second are decisions declaring it improper for magistrates or jurors to receive further information about the case after they have gone to the retiring-room to consider their verdict.[9] The main reason for this rule is that it is essential in order to give the defendant a fair chance to answer the case against him, but it is also related to the principle of public justice: as part of seeing justice done, the public needs to be able to discover what the evidence is and to hear what the parties have to say about it.

The third principle, closely connected with the previous one, is that all the evidence must be presented orally in court. In England and Wales this principle is usually put forward as part and parcel of the hearsay rule: witnesses must testify *orally to the court* on the basis of their own first-hand knowledge. This means, of course, that what common lawyers elipically refer to as the hearsay rule is really not one rule but two: a rule forbidding witnesses to give indirect testimony, and a rule requiring them to testify orally to the court of trial. But in England and Wales the rule that evidence must be given orally extends beyond the limits of the hearsay rule, because even where some exception to the hearsay rule makes the statement of an absent witness admissible in evidence, this statement must usually be read aloud so that everyone in court can hear it, and not just handed over in written form to the magistrates or jurors so that only they can tell what it contains.[10] Equally, evidence must in principle be presented orally in the

Netherlands. Although in Dutch law there is no direct equivalent of the hearsay rule and statements made out of court are admissible in evidence, whether made by defendants or by absent witnesses, Article 297 of the Code of Criminal Procedure requires written statements either to be read aloud at trial, or summarized orally. By Article 297(5) 'On objection by the defence, no weight shall be given, on pain of nullity, to any document which has not been read aloud or summarized in conformity with the provisions above.' This principle can be justified on the same grounds as the principle that all evidence must be publicly debated: first, we need to make absolutely sure that the defendant knows what the evidence against him is in order to enable him to answer it, and secondly, the public needs to know the evidential basis on which he or she is eventually convicted or acquitted.

The fourth principle is that the court of trial must hear evidence directly from the original source of the information, not second-hand through the mouth of an intermediary; and this means, furthermore, that the original source of the information must come to court in order to be examined orally.[11]

Unlike the previous three principles, the 'direct evidence' principle is not universally respected, and those legal systems which do respect it afford it different levels of protection.

In German criminal procedure it is protected in two ways. The first is the rule that the judge at trial is under a general duty to take whatever steps are necessary in order to discover the truth. Article 244 II of the German Code of Criminal Procedure provides that 'In order to search out the truth the court shall on its own motion extend the taking of evidence to all facts and means of proof that are important for the decision'.[12] This is interpreted as requiring the trial judge to make sure that the original source of information, if available, is brought before the court for oral examination. The second is the principle contained in Article 250 of the German Code of Criminal Procedure, which provides that 'If the evidence of a fact is based upon a person's observation, this person shall be examined at the trial. The examination may not be replaced by reading the record of an earlier examination, or by reading a written statement'.[13] The rule that emerges from these provisions is positive, not negative: that the German court *must* hear direct evidence if available, and not (as in England) that the court must not receive any hearsay. In Germany, indeed, hearsay evidence is generally admissible – although German case law limits the extent to which the courts are permitted to base convictions on it.[14]

In England and Wales the 'direct evidence' principle is upheld by the celebrated hearsay rule (Choo 1996; Cross and Tapper 1995), which is negative in form: in contested criminal proceedings hearsay is inadmissible. 'Hearsay' is defined to include not only repetition to the court by witness X of what non-witness Y told him, but even any direct communication emanating from Y himself, like a letter or even a tape-recording, which falls short of oral testimony at trial. The consequence is that if the parties wish to put in evidence the fact that Y heard or saw or experienced something, they have no alternative, usually, to bringing Y to court to 'tell his tale'. In England and Wales, however, the support the hearsay rule provides for the directness principle has been whittled away as Parliament has proceeded to enact wider and wider exceptions to it. In 1988 Parliament rendered potentially admissible as evidence the out-of-court statements of people who absent themselves from trial for various specified reasons,[15] including those who fail to testify 'through fear', and more radically – and rather alarmingly – a further statutory change in 1996 makes potentially admissible at a Crown Court trial the written statement that virtually any missing prosecution witness has earlier made to the police, whatever the reason for his non-appearance at the trial.[16] This new statutory exception, like the one in 1988, gives the presiding judge a wide discretionary power to exclude the evidence that it makes potentially admissible; how big this dent in the directness principle proves to be will obviously depend on how trial judges choose to exercise their new discretion.

In Dutch law the 'direct evidence' principle is barely recognized at all. A preliminary glance at the Dutch Code of Criminal Procedure suggests that it does in fact form part of the Dutch law of evidence, because Article 338 requires convictions to be based on 'legal forms of evidence', Article 339 lists these as including the 'declaration of a witness', and Article 342(1) then defines the 'declaration of a witness' as 'the report, during the enquiry at trial, of facts or circumstances of which he has personal knowledge or experience'. In a famous decision in 1926, however, the *Hoge Raad* drove a coach and horses through any support which these provisions might have provided for the principle of direct evidence. In a famous ruling,[17] the court held that if a witness previously heard a third person describe an event, the third party's act of describing the event to the witness counts as 'a fact or circumstance' of which the witness then 'has personal knowledge or experience', and hence can testify about (Corstens 1995, p. 615 *et seq.*; Nijboer 1995, p. 105 *et seq.*; Garé 1994, p. 88 *et seq.*). To some limited extent, however, Dutch law is now moving in the direction of requiring witnesses to give evidence directly to the court of trial as an incidental result of its having to accept the need, imposed on it by the European Court of Human Rights, to give the defence the opportunity to confront their accusers (see below). '*Verhoor getuigen AH-overval doet rechtbank zelf*', proclaimed a headline in the *NRC Handelsblad* on 8 September 1993 – thereby communicating a fact sufficiently unusual to be newsworthy in Holland, namely that a trial court proposed to examine the key witnesses to a major robbery itself, instead of reading the deposition they had made before a *rechter-commissaris* (the approximate Dutch equivalent of a *juge d'instruction*).

For the 'direct evidence' principle a number of different reasons have been put forward. One is the theory that making witnesses testify directly, openly and publicly encourages them to tell the truth. As Sir Matthew Hale put it in his *History of the Common Law of England*

'... The excellency of this OPEN course of evidence to the jury in the presence of the judge, jury, parties and counsel, and even of the adverse witnesses, appears in these particulars:– First, that it is open, and not in private before a commissioner or two, and a couple of clerks; where oftentimes witnesses will deliver that which they will be ashamed to testify publicly' (p. 290).

Whilst there may be truth in this, the other side of this coin, of course, is that the experience also terrifies some vulnerable witnesses into total silence (Spencer and Flin 1993). Another argument, frequently heard in England and Wales, is that where evidence is given orally and directly the court can observe the 'demeanour' of the witness as an aid to discovering whether or not he or she is telling lies: a notion that is probably misguided, because 'demeanour' is in truth a very uncertain guide to truthfulness.[18] It is also said that a person who gives evidence other than directly does not do so on oath, and so evades one of the normal safeguards of truthfulness that are applied to witnesses in legal proceedings; which may be generally the case, but is not necessarily so, because (for example) indirect evidence may take the form of a written statement that an absent witness swore on oath.[19] It is also said that indirect evidence is potentially subject to transmission errors: which it often is, of course, but is not always, because indirect evidence can (for example) take the form of the statement from an absent witness that has been recorded on audiotape or videotape, which is free from transmission errors (Law Commission 1997, pp. 24-25). A more convincing argument on principle against indirect evidence is that it is only where the court hears evidence directly from the original source of the information that it can be meaningfully tested by asking the witness further questions. Where a witness is merely recounting what another person told him, he can always reply 'Well that's what he said to me'; and the same is true if he is reading the deposition of an absent witness, or playing a tape-recording of an interview with him (Wigmore 1940, vol. V, para. 1362; Garé 1994; Crombag et al. 1992; Law Commission 1997).

The fifth principle, closely related to the last one, is what I shall call the principle of confrontation. This is that the defendant must be given an opportunity to challenge the truthfulness of the witnesses called against him by confronting them with his version of events, and asking them questions designed to test the accuracy of their recollections and to expose any motivation they may have to lie.

In England and Wales this principle is an ancient one, although typically it is nowhere stated in any statutory provision. In practice it is safeguarded by the hearsay rule which ensures that witnesses normally come to court and give their evidence orally, because in the common law world, testifying at trial for the prosecution carries with it the obligation to submit to being cross-examined by or on behalf of the defence. In England and Wales, too, legal debate about the principle of confrontation is usually conducted in terms of the hearsay rule. The importance of maintaining the defendant's right to cross-examine his accusers is usually put forward as the main justification for retaining the hearsay rule, or the main objection to creating some new exception to it. With this in mind, when enacting new exceptions to the hearsay rule rendering admissible as evidence written depositions made by witnesses out of court, Parliament has traditionally provided some sort of safeguard for the defendant's right of cross-examination[20] – although in recent years it has sometimes strikingly neglected to do so.[21]

In Dutch law, by contrast, the confrontation principle is less well protected. The questioning of witnesses is principally in the hands of the presiding judge.[22] And, more fundamentally, all sorts of statements made by absent witnesses, which would normally be rejected under the hearsay rule in England, are admissible in Dutch criminal proceedings, as we have seen. In principle, this obviously greatly limits the ability of the defence to probe the prosecution evidence, because in the nature of things it is not possible to cross-examine (for example) a written deposition as it would have been possible to cross-examine the maker of it had he been present live in court.

At one time, indeed, the absence of any confrontation principle in Dutch law even led to a situation in which the Dutch courts felt able to convict defendants on the basis of written statements provided by anonymous informants, whose denunciations the defence had had virtually no opportunity to test or challenge (Beijer et al. 1995; Beijer 1997). Under the influence of the European Convention on Human Rights, however, which in the Netherlands has direct effect, the position of the defendant in this respect has been improved. Under Article 6.3.d of the Convention, one of the minimum guarantees for defendants in criminal cases is the right 'to examine or have examined the witnesses against him ...' In a series of important decisions, one of which was *Kostovski v The Netherlands*,[23] the European Court of Human Rights has declared this article to mean that the defence must in principle be given the opportunity to confront their main accusers – if not at the trial itself, then on some earlier occasion. This has led to the Dutch enacting special legislation which attempts to deal with the problem of threatened witnesses by providing the defence with certain limited rights to put questions to them indirectly via a *rechter-commissaris*.[24]

As with the 'direct evidence' principle, a number of different reasons have been given to support the principle of confrontation. One, which seems implausible to me, is that making an accuser give his evidence in the presence of the person he accuses makes it harder for him to lie and more likely to tell the truth (Spencer and Flin 1993, ch. 10). Other writers have justified the confrontation principle by saying that wider issues are involved. Truthfulness apart, they say, it is an essential ingredient in general fairness that the person who is accused of doing something dreadful should have the opportunity to call his accuser a liar to his face (Weinstein 1966). Or that it exists less to promote truthfulness in witnesses than public confidence in the decisions of the courts, because it prevents key witnesses undermining verdicts by claiming afterwards that what they said – or are said to have said – was false. A witness who has gone through the ordeal of giving direct evidence and being cross-examined, so this argument goes, is unlikely to retract his evidence afterwards – and if he does, the public will believe his courtroom evidence in preference to his retraction (Nesson 1985).

Once again, the most convincing justification for the 'confrontation' principle seems to be that it enables the validity of the prosecution evidence to be tested by questions designed to probe the accuracy of the prosecution witnesses' recollections and to tease out any motive they may have to conceal, exaggerate or lie (Wigmore 1940, vol. V, para. 1362; Garé 1994; Crombag et al. 1992; Law Commission 1997).

The five principles in relation to proactive and secret policing

In the second part of this chapter I shall try to examine how far these five principles are in conflict with the practices of secret and proactive policing. Viewing the problem from one end, do secret and proactive police methods potentially threaten these five principles by tending to undermine them?

Looking at it from the other, does a proper respect for these five principles provide the means by which proactive and secret policing could be kept properly in check?

At first sight, the answer appears to be 'Plainly not!' The five principles explained above relate in general to how trials are conducted, and in particular to how evidence is heard and tested at them. Proactive and secret policing are largely about gathering background information, not evidence for use at trial. Not being needed as evidence at trial – or even admissible as evidence at trial – the material these practices produce never gets heard at trial, and the questions posed in the previous paragraph simply do not arise. To take a simple example, suppose the police obtain by bugging, infiltrators or informers the information that a bank-robbery is planned for a given place and time. Thanks to this advance information the police, instead of turning up at the bank after the robbers have gone, catch them when they arrive, complete with guns, gloves and balaclava helmets. At trial the eye-witness evidence of the police is all that is needed to secure conviction, and this evidence obviously creates no problems with the five principles at all. In other words, secret and proactive policing and the principles of orality and immediacy largely operate in different spheres. The general truth of this is vividly demonstrated by the current legislation in England and Wales which regulates telephone-tapping. Astonishingly, in the view of Continental lawyers, this actually limits the use of telephone-tapping to the investigative phase, and even provides that the content of conversations lawfully intercepted under the designated procedure may not be used in evidence at trial.[25]

Furthermore, insofar as secret and proactive policing does produce evidence rather than mere background information it is often evidence that is usable without creating any possible conflict with the principles of orality and directness. For example, as in one famous English case, undercover police officers set up an apparently louche antique-shop, so luring the local burglars to try and 'fence' the fruits of their dishonest labours, only to have their dishonest possession and attempted sales indelibly recorded on concealed video-cameras.[26] The use of these video-recordings as evidence at trial may be contentious on the grounds that the evidence was obtained illegally or unfairly (Scheer 1992). But there is no question of its contravening any aspect of the rules about orality or directness.

However, the matter is a little more complicated than this.

First, secret and proactive policing methods do sometimes produce evidence which as a practical matter can only be used if the principles of orality and directness are in some way bent or circumvented. The obvious case is where an informer or an undercover police officer actually sees or hears the defendant committing an offence, or hears the defendant confessing to it, and his life – or at any rate, his continued usefulness as an informer or infiltrator – would be in jeopardy if his identity were revealed. In these circumstances, pressure builds up from the police and the prosecution for the creation of some means by which his evidence can be put before the court in the form of a written statement from an anonymous informant, whilst allowing the informer himself to stay at home. This, of course, is exactly what happened in the Netherlands with anonymous witnesses, and at first the courts gave in to the pressure, as we have seen. It was the assertion of one of five principles discussed in the first part of this chapter, the 'confrontation principle', by the European Court of Human Rights in the *Kostovski* case[27] that caused the Dutch to abandon the practice of simply allowing the statement of the anonymous informant to be put in evidence, and to devise the scheme described in the first section of this chapter, under which the defence are given their chance to put questions to the threatened witness indirectly through a *rechter-commissaris*, who puts them to the witness in the absence of the defence at a special hearing ahead of the final trial.

Similar pressures exist at present in the United Kingdom, and have already caused the principles of orality and directness to be bent to some small extent. Recent case law, following case law from Northern Ireland,[28] allows the judge to permit a witness who is frightened of reprisals to testify at trial anonymously, with his identity withheld not only from the public but also from the defence, provided the judge is satisfied that the witness's credibility is not materially affected by who and what he is.[29] As we have seen, the provisions of the Criminal Justice Act of 1988 now also give the trial judge a discretion to admit in evidence a written statement earlier taken by the police from a witness who then fails to give evidence at trial through fear, and, remarkably, these provisions could on the face of them even allow the court to hear in evidence such a statement taken from a witness who remains anonymous – although it seems unlikely that a judge in England and Wales would in practice admit such a statement in such circumstances. In the light of the current trend in England and Wales to make exceptions to the hearsay rule that simply allow transcripts of police interviews with witnesses to replace their live evidence at trial, it might even be said that the English could now learn a lesson in this area from the Dutch. The new Dutch procedure for dealing with threatened witnesses[30] does at least allow the defence some chance to put their questions to the accuser, albeit only indirectly – a possibility denied to them completely where an exception to the English hearsay rule simply allows the prosecution to put the absent accuser's evidence before the court in the form of a police witness-statement. The second way in which secret and proactive policing can in fact come into conflict with the principles about immediacy and orality is when the police investigation ultimately gives rise to some further piece of evidence which is capable of being delivered in open court by way of oral evidence, but which can only properly be countered if the defence can prize out of the police and prosecution some further information they are anxious to conceal about the way the evidence was obtained. A defendant, for example, is prosecuted for illegal possession of drugs, a policeman giving oral evidence that he raided the defendant's home and discovered the drugs under the defendant's bed. The police obviously raided him 'acting on information received', and the plausibility of defendant's claim that the drugs were planted on him while he was out may be crucially affected by the identity of their informer, because if he was someone who had access to defendant's house, the defendant's story is more likely to be true. The quesion therefore arises as to whether, as the price of being able to call their evidence, the prosecution should be obliged to reveal to the defence how they came to have it.

In England and Wales, the current position is 'Yes, within limits'. At trial, police witnesses are in principle privileged to refuse to answer defence questions which reveal the identity of informers or other secret details about how the police go about their job,[31] but the judge may override this privilege and require such questions to be answered if he or she believes, in the light of the other evidence in the case, that the information may be genuinely necessary in order to enable a possibly innocent person to make out a plausible defence.[32] Similar principles now also govern how far the police and prosecution must make such information available to the defence before trial; in principle they can keep quiet about it, but if it might plausibly be helpful to the defendant in the light of the defence that he intends to run at trial, they must either reveal it, or apply to a judge ex parte for a ruling as to whether it should be revealed.[33]

In the Netherlands, on the other hand, the position is not so favourable to the defence. Central to a criminal case in the Netherlands is the *dossier* or case file, which the public prosecutor (or *rechter-commissaris* where one of these is involved) compiles as the case progresses. To this the defence have limited but generous rights of access in the pre-trial phase, and the right to inspect it in its entirety before the final trial (Prakken 1995). The question, however, is how much (if any) background information, as against hard evidence of the offence being committed, the prosecutor is obliged to record in this *dossier*. According to the *Hoge Raad*, it is only matters which bear directly on the guilt or innocence of the accused which have to be included; background information does not necessarily have to be included.[34] So, unlike in England and Wales today, the prosecutor is not obliged to take the initiative in disclosing background material which might undermine the prosecution case or be helpful to the defence. It remains possible, of course, for the Dutch defendant to ask the prosecutor specific questions about this, either in the pre-trial phase or at the trial itself. The prosecutor's refusal to answer them can be challenged in court, and in deciding whether or not to require the prosecutor to answer, the Dutch courts apply broadly similar principles to the English courts when faced with a refusal by the police to reveal the name of an informant. But even so the Dutch defendant is in a weaker position than his English counterpart, because if he wants to discover the details of the police investigation he must start the ball rolling by asking specific questions. In the Netherlands it is not the case, as it now is in England, that the prosecution has to take the initiative in disclosing material which it should know would help the defendant make out the defence that he intends to run. This is important, because as Cape and Spronken point out in their chapter, the defence usually have an uphill struggle to persuade a court that a piece of tangentially relevant information is of genuine importance to them if they only have a vague idea of what it is – and no chance at all if they are completely unaware of its existence.

This state of affairs is heavily criticized by various Dutch writers, one of whom writes

'In the last fifteen years a noticeable tendency has emerged for large parts of the preliminary enquiries (for example CID information) to be kept out of sight. Such an "inquisitorial" tendency is to be criticized and deplored. It is not just the abandonment or neglect of procedural safeguards that can be disadvantageous. Behind these safeguards lie the methods of a fact-finding process that is not only proper, but also reliable and accurate – something which disregarding these safeguards undervalues' (Nijboer 1995, p. 134).

Here, perhaps, it is the English who can teach a lesson to the Dutch.

By now, English readers may be feeling that this chapter has strayed away from its supposed topic. To English lawyers, the matters we have been discussing are usually categorized as 'privilege' and 'advance disclosure', which are thought of as something separate from orality and immediacy. To the Dutch lawyer, however, these matters are connected. In Dutch legal discourse it is said that an essential ingredient of properly-conducted criminal proceedings is 'openness' (*openbaarheid*). This quality is said to consist of two elements. The first is 'external openness' (*externe openbaarheid*), which means the various rules about trials taking place in public, and evidence being given orally and publicly debated. The second is 'internal openness' (*interne openbaarheid*), which means what English lawyers call the rules about public interest immunity and disclosure, and French ones *accès au dossier* (Corstens 1995, pp. 516-521).

This leads to a final and perhaps rather more abstract point.

It could be said that part of the reason why the rules about orality and immediacy exist is to enable the legality of the proceedings to be subject to the check of public examination; that by this we mean a public check not only on what goes on at trial itself, but of the proceedings leading up to it, including the police enquiry; and that it follows from this that the principles of orality and immediacy require enough of the pre-trial phase to be disclosed for its legality to be checked (Garé 1994, pp. 70-78).

This notion perhaps sounds strange to lawyers from England and Wales, who may now think this chapter is straying even further off its supposed subject, which is orality and immediacy. If we keep within the usual categories in which lawyers from the common law world think about these matters, the idea just put forward confuses the issue by bringing in two notions which are separate and distinct from orality and immediacy – namely the rules about excluding improperly obtained evidence and the concept of 'abuse of process'. Traditionally, common-lawyers have taken a very trial-centred view of criminal procedure. Until recently, what happened before the trial in England and Wales was little regulated – so little, in fact, that it barely occurred to many legal writers that criminal procedure was in fact a two-stage process, text-book writers generally starting with the trial and relegating any discussion of what happens pre-trial to a section at the end entitled 'miscellaneous matters'. In so far as the gathering of evidence was subject to rules and regulations, trial courts were little interested in whether or not these had been followed. The traditional common law approach is summed up in the famous statement from a nineteenth-century English case: 'It matters not how you get it; if you steal it even it would be admissible in evidence'.[35] The notion that the trial exists in part to check the legality of the pre-trial phase is foreign to traditional English legal thinking.

In the Netherlands, as elsewhere in Continental Europe, things have traditionally been viewed differently – as Cape and Spronken also explain in chapter 17. In Continental Europe, criminal procedure has customarily been viewed as a two-stage process: a preliminary and private phase during which the evidence is gathered, followed by a second and public phase at which the evidence so collected is publicly examined and debated and a decision reached as to guilt or innocence (and if appropriate, sentence). In principle, the Dutch courts have always taken an intense interest in the legality of what went on during the preliminary phase – to the point where, in recent years, they have been publicly criticized for being too pernickity, and legislation has been enacted with the aim of reducing the number of prosecutions which ultimately fail because some procedural rule has not been respected. Until recently, a Dutch court could sanction a breach of the rules by the prosecutor of the police in one of the two following ways: (i) forcing the prosecutor to drop the prosecution, (ii) ruling inadmissible the evidence he had improperly obtained. To these possibilities the new Article 359a of the Code of Criminal Procedure now adds a third: letting the proceedings stand, admitting the evidence, but compensating the defendant for the failure to respect his rights by giving him a lighter sentence.[36]

In recent years, criminal procedure in England and Wales has been moving in the same direction as Continental Europe. Detailed rules have now been made to regulate the gathering of evidence, to the point where writers have even begun to talk about criminal procedure as being a two-stage process. And trial courts have begun to take a serious interest in whether the rules regulating the pre-trial phase were followed. Thus in England and Wales, breaches of the rules regulating the pre-trial phase can potentially result in improperly obtained evidence being ruled inadmissible, or in extreme cases, the entire prosecution being quashed as an abuse of process (although no one has so far suggested that as a compromise it might be a ground for reducing the sentence[37]). So perhaps it is not now so strange to suggest to readers in England and Wales that one of the incidental functions of a public trial in England and Wales is to enable the propriety of the pre-trial phase to be publicly examined.

As a practical matter, it seems obvious that if the excesses of secret and proactive policing are to be effectively controlled, this can only be done by setting legislative limits to what the police can do, and trial courts taking notice of whether the rules so made have been obeyed or broken. If this is so, and the rules the courts apply when examining the legality of the pre-trial phase are properly considered as part of the principles of orality and immediacy, then obviously immediacy and orality (in this broad sense) are central to the control of secret and proactive policing, and not just incidentally relevant to it.

Notes

1 I would like to thank Taco van der Zwaag, who provided some of the ideas and materials contained in this chapter. I am also grateful to Heleen Scheer for providing me with some of the materials (and, more fundamentally, for teaching me to read Dutch). My thanks are also due to Caroline Pelser for her useful comments on my text.

2 The *onmiddellijkheidsbeginsel* in Dutch; the *Grundsatz der Unmittelbarkeit* in German.

3 In German the classic discussions from the nineteenth century are by Von Feuerbach and by Mittermaier. A more recent German study is by Geppert 1979. The position in the Netherlands is fully discussed by Garé 1994, in whose book the earlier Dutch and German literature is reviewed; the present author found Garé's study particularly helpful.

4 Jeremy Bentham discussed at length the merits of oral versus testimony, and the merits of public justice, in his *Rationale of Judicial Evidence*. The reasons underlying the hearsay rule were discussed at length by Wigmore 1940. The hearsay rule has been discussed at a theoretical level by various other writers, including most recently Choo 1996. See also the Law Commission's Consultation Paper on hearsay 1995, and its Report 1997.

5 *Scott v Scott* [1913] AC 415.

6 'As a general rule the English system of administering justice does require that it be done in public. If the way the courts behave cannot be hidden from the public ear and eye this provides a safeguard against judicial arbitrariness and idiosyncracy and maintains the public confidence in the administration of justice'; per Lord Diplock in *AG v Leveller Magazine* [1980] AC 440.

7 Although surprisingly Scotland in effect has one in the Criminal Procedure (Scotland) Act 1995.

8 *Rosser* (1836) 7 C & P 648, 173 ER 284.

9 As in *R v Tiverton JJ ex pte Smith* [1981] RTR 280, where a conviction for driving a car with bald tyres was quashed because the magistrates had conducted their own tests on the tyres with a tyre-gauge in the privacy of their retiring room.

10 A number of the provisions making written statements admissible in evidence in England and Wales expressly require them to be read aloud, or if not, to be orally summarized; see for example Criminal Justice Act 1967 section 9(6); cf. Criminal Procedure and Investigations Act 1997 section 68 and Schedule 2.

11 Older writers on the Anglo-American law of evidence sometimes talk about a 'best evidence rule', to the effect that a party who wishes to establish a fact must always use the strongest evidence available in preference to any weaker form; see e.g. Cross 1967, p. 11 *et seq*. The notion stems from Gilbert's treatise on evidence which first appeared in 1754; see Twining 1990. The principle stated in the text could be seen as an application of this rule.

12 An important principle of German criminal procedure which has acquired a list of formidable names: *Inquisitionsmaxime, Instruktionsmaxime, Ermittlungs-grundsatz, Wahrheitsermittlungspflicht* and *Auflkärungspflicht*; see Schroeder 1993, p. 144.

13 To this there are a number of important exceptions. For a brief account in English, see the Law Commission's Consultation Paper (note 3 above), pp. 268-272.

14 In particular, a case law prohibition on convicting on the strength of hearsay evidence alone: BGH 08. 01; StV 1991, 197.

15 Criminal Justice Act 1988 sections 23 and 24.

16 Criminal Procedure and Investigations Act 1996 section 68 and Schedule 2; Emmins 1997, p. 277.

17 HR 20 December 1926, NJ 1927, 85.

18 'At the risk of oversimplification, the conclusions of a large body of psychological research may be summed up as follows. In tests designed to discover how good people are at telling whether another person is lying, subjects rarely manage a success rate that is much above chance level, or what they would achieve by shutting their eyes and ears and making a guess', Spencer and Flin 1993, p. 280; Crombag et al. 1992, pp. 248-249.

19 The early writers on the common law of evidence seem to have regarded the absence of an oath as the most important objection to hearsay evidence: see Gallanis 1997, IV-39 *et seq.*

20 Magistrates' Courts Act 1980 section 105 making admissible in evidence certain depositions taken by magistrates from sick witnesses who later die; sections 42 and 43 Children and Young Persons Act 1933, enabling a written deposition to replace the live testimony of a child witness for whom a court appearance would involve serious danger to life or health.

21 In particular, no such safeguard attaches to the important new exceptions created by sections 23 and 24 of the Criminal Justice Act 1988 and by section 68 and Schedule 2 of the Criminal Procedure and Investigations Act 1996 (see notes 14 and 15 above).

22 Article 285 CCP. 'After the witness has given his statement the judges, and after them the public prosecutor and the defence (or if the witness has been called ... by the defendant, the defendant and the public prosecutor), can ask him questions ...'

23 Series A vol. 166; (1990) 12 EHRR 434.

24 Beijer 1997. The 'threatened witness provisions' were enacted by the Law of 11 November 1993, and they work by adding (among other things) new Articles 226a-226f to the Code of Criminal Procedure which set out the procedure for hearing threatened witnesses, and a new Article 344a prohibiting the courts from basing convictions on anonymous witness evidence alone. The new provisions withstood a challenge in the European Court of Human Rights in *Doorson v the Netherlands* (1996) 22 EHRR 330, but fared less well in *Van Mechelen v the*

Netherlands 23 April 1997 (see Cape and Spronken's chapter in this book).
25 Interception of Communications Act 1985 section 9; see *Preston* [1994] 2 AC
 310, *Effick* [1995] 1 AC 309.
26 *Christou* [1992] QB 979.
27 Note 22 above.
28 *Murphy* [1990] NI 306.
29 *Taylor* [1995] CrimLR 253.
30 Note 23 above.
31 *Hardy* (1794) 24 St Tr 199; *Blackstone's Criminal Practice* F9.5.
32 *Turner* [1995] 1 WLR 264.
33 Criminal Procedure and Investigations Act 1996 sections 3(6), 7(5), 8(5), 9(8)
 and 14 and 15 – provisions largely reproducing the effect of pre-existing case
 law.
34 HR 7 May 1996, NJ 1996, 687.
35 Per Crompton J. in *Leathem* (1861) 8 Cox C.C. 498.
36 For criticism of this provision, see Mevis 1995.
37 Although in *Sang* [1980] AC 402, 446, Lord Fraser did suggest that if a person
 had committed an offence as a result of entrapment, that factor might operate in
 mitigation of sentence.

References

Beijer, A. (1997), *Bedreigde getuigen in het strafproces*, Deventer: Gouda Quint.
Beijer, A., C. Cobley and A. Klip (1995), Witness evidence, Article 6 of the
 European Convention on Human Rights and the Principle of Open Justice, in: P.
 Fennell, C. Harding, N. Jörg and B. Swart (eds.), *Criminal Justice in Europe:
 A Comparative Study*, Oxford: Clarendon Press, pp. 283-300.
Bentham, Jeremy (1793), *Draught for the Organisation of Judicial Establishments,
 compared with that of the National Assembly, with a Commentary on the same.
 Works*, ed. John Bowring, Edinburgh: William Tait.
Bentham, Jeremy, (1827), *Rationale of Judicial Evidence*, London: Hunt and Clarke.
Blackstone's Criminal Practice, 1997 edition, London: Blackstone Press.
Choo, A.T. (1996), *Hearsay and Confrontation in Criminal Trials*, Oxford: Oxford
 University Press.
Corstens, G.J.M. (1995), *Het Nederlands strafprocesrecht* (2nd ed.), Arnhem: Gouda
 Quint.
Crombag, H.F.M., P.J. van Koppen and W.A. Wagenaar (1992), *Dubieuze Zaken –
 de Psychologie van Strafrechtelijk Bewijs*, Amsterdam/Antwerpen: Contact.
Cross, *Evidence*, 3d edition (1967), London: Butterworths.
Cross and Tapper on Evidence, 8th ed. (1995), London: Butterworths.
Emmins on Criminal Procedure (1997) (ed. J. Sprack), London: Blackstone Press.

Feuerbach, A.R. von (1821 and 1825), *Betrachtungen über die Oeffentlichtkeit und Mündlichkeit der Gerechtigkeitspflege*, Gießen.

Gallanis, T.P., *Aspects of the Common Law of Evidence, 1754-1824, with special reference to the rule against hearsay*. Ph.D. thesis, Cambridge, 18 April 1997.

Garé, Dorothé (1994), *Het onmiddellijkheidsbeginsel in het Nederlandse strafproces*, Arnhem: Gouda Quint.

Geppert, K. (1979), *Der Grundsatz der Unmittelbarkeit im deutschen Strafverfahren*, Berlin: Walter de Gruyter.

Hale, M. (ed. Runnington, C.) (1779), *History of the Common Law of England*.

Law Commission (1995), Consultation Paper No. 138, Report (No. 245, 1997), *Evidence in Criminal Proceedings: Hearsay and Related Topics*.

Law Commission (1997) Report No. 245, *Evidence in Criminal Proceedings: Hearsay and Related Topics*.

Mevis, P.A.M. (1995), De rechtsgevolgen van onrechtmatigheden in het vooronderzoek, in: J.P. Balkema, M. Barels, J.A.W. Lensing, A.J.M. Machielse and H.J.B. Sackers, *Dynamisch strafrecht*, Arnhem: Gouda Quint.

Mittermaier, C.J.A. (1845), *Die Mündlichkeit, das Anklageprinzip, die Oeffentlichkeit und das Geschworenengericht*, Stuttgart and Tübingen.

Nesson, C.R. (1985), The Evidence or the Event? On judicial proof and the acceptability of verdicts, *Harvard Law Review* 1357.

Nijboer, J.F. (1995), *Strafrechtelijk bewijsrecht*, Nijmegen: Ars Aequi Libri.

Prakken, Ties (1995), Interne openbaarheid in het strafproces: een bedreigd goed, *Nederlands Juristenblad*, pp. 1451-1458.

Scheer, H.P., (1993), Evidence from an undercover agent, 157 *JP* 22.

Schroeder, F-C. (1993), *Strafprozeßrecht*, Munich: Beck.

Spencer, J.R. and R. Flin (1993), *The Evidence of Children – the Law and the Psychology*, London: Blackstone Press.

Twining, William (1990), The Rationalist Tradition in Evidence Scholarship, in: Twining, *Rethinking Evidence*, originally published by Basil Blackwell Ltd in 1990, reprinted by Northwestern University Press, Illinois, 1994.

Weinstein, Jack B. (1966), Some difficulties in devising rules for determining truth in judicial trials, 66 *Columbia Law Review* 223.

Wigmore, J.H. (1940), *Treatise on the Anglo-American System of Evidence in trials at Common Law* (3d ed.), Boston: Little, Brown & Co.

20 Invading the private?
Towards conclusions

STEWART FIELD

Introduction

Bob Hoogenboom comments in this volume that almost all the developments we are chronicling are 'designed to thrill'. They thrill those who seek what appear fast solutions to crime problems which require neither substantial change to social structures nor in 'ways of seeing'. He argues that the accelerating globalization of economies has reinforced an existing tendency to try to marginalize politically those who are already marginal to the economic system. In recent years, rather than trying to integrate such minorities, modern states have defined their potential threat as a problem of crime that requires a 'technological fix'.

This can be interpreted in at least two ways. David Garland, in an important recent article, has outlined a series of modern state adaptations – some of them contradictory – to the apparent incapacity of government agencies to control crime in insecure post-modern cities (Garland 1996). Amongst these is 'denial', a sometimes hysterical response at the political level that simply reaffirms, in the face of the evidence, that state punishment, if harsher and more certain, can deal with the problem. Another response in clear tension with this operates at the administrative level: it seeks to lower citizens' expectations of the state's capacity to control crime by redefining success and failure. The rise of covert and proactive policing on the one hand, and the technologically sophisticated systems of information gathering and sorting that this volume considers, could be seen as part of both of these contradictory responses. On a political level it provides some answer to the presentational need of modern governments to show that 'something is being done'; something to deny the message written in generally rising crime rates of the state's incapacity to deliver security. That it can be packaged as new and technological is helpful; that one can take journalists along on raids timed and coordinated to maximize publicity makes it all the more so. On the other hand it can also be seen as part of an attempt to redefine success and failure. Garland suggests that the British police are now seeking to claim success in detecting serious crime or serious criminals while diminishing public expectations that routine, opportunist crime can be controlled by the police. Covert or proactive policing provides a technique specifically adapted to the targeting of particular crime problems and the focusing of resources on them. It is a technique that requires a rather particular demon. The nature of the demon may vary from society to society and over time and its reality may be uncertain but such resource intensive policing forms are ill-adapted as a generalized response to crime. In Germany and the Netherlands, where levels of anxiety over street crime seem less acute than in the United Kingdom, the demon has been at various times, organized crime and commercial fraud. In the United Kingdom it has been the football hooligan and the persistent burglar and car thief. By socially constructing a particular crime problem, on which scarce resources may be focused, policing solutions can be seen to have a new credibility.

Effectiveness: the problems of measurement

How far covert and proactive policing can actually deliver this, and how far they will come to be seen as merely new presentational devices, cannot be determined definitively now. Of the Dutch situation, Klerks has complained of the 'near-total absence of any public accountability over the credit balance of covert policing, i.e. over the revenues of special teams and methods and their effects on serious crime' (Klerks 1995, p. 136). Similarly Van Outrive and Cappelle comment that in Belgium 'real analysis of the cost-effectiveness of these tactics has not been done' (Van Outrive and Cappelle 1995, p. 153).

Some analysis has been done in the United Kingdom but its credibility is doubtful. Stockdale and Gresham (1995) did an analysis of Operation Bumblebee in London, Operation Gemini in Gloucester and a series of organizational changes made in the Hampshire Constabulary, all of which aimed to facilitate proactive, intelligence-led policing. Their conclusion was that in all three cases performance in controlling burglary was seen to benefit from the greater use of intelligence and targeting of offenders. However the conclusion is problematic because it requires one to ignore long-recognized anxieties about the measures of effectiveness used: principally clear-up rates and police-recorded crime statistics.

Stockdale and Gresham report that recorded burglary statistics fell by 12.8 per cent in the seven months after the introduction of Operation Bumblebee throughout the Metropolitan area in 1993. They report similar falls in the other two areas where covert and proactive policing of burglary was being developed. Yet during the 12 months to June 1994, 35 out of the 43 police forces in England and Wales show percentage decreases, seventeen of more than 10 per cent and nine with percentages higher than those of the studied forces with their high-profile proactive strategies. Furthermore evidence from sweeps of the victim-based British Crime Survey suggest that changes in recorded burglary offences during this period were in part the product of falls in reporting and recording. From 1991-1995 reporting of all burglaries fell by nearly 6 per cent and recording fell by 7 per cent. Thus the figures hardly seem conclusive.

The report authors also stress that the clear-up rate in the area covered by the Metropolitan Police rose from 10.9 per cent in 1992 to 15 per cent in 1993. Yet there was only a very small increase in primary clear-up rates whereas secondary clear-up rates showed dramatic increases.[1] This was because the police were putting more resources into post-sentence visits to encourage offenders to confess to offences for which they would probably not then be punished. The increase is very unlikely to be the direct result of adopting proactive or covert policing. In the two other forces, where post-sentence visits were not part of the strategy, clear-up rates actually fell.

The researchers also attribute these falls in police recorded statistics to the new investigative methods when they may well be due to other causes: all three operations involved a number of elements and not all of these can be termed proactive or covert *investigative* tactics.[2] For example resources were put into rather traditional crime prevention tactics with security advice being given to recent victims; work in developing Neighbourhood Watch schemes; property identification initiatives; and loudspeaker warnings if a burglary took place in a particular location. Lastly it is not possible to exclude the possibility that any benefits are the result of a resources effect since the additional expenditure of Bumblebee proved impossible to quantify.

Similarly some approaches in the United Kingdom to the use of informers have lacked some necessary scepticism. The Audit Commission, basing itself on police figures on monies paid to informers, concluded that it was highly cost-effective.[3] But work by Dunnighan and Norris has challenged the basis of these conclusions, arguing that they fail to take into account many of the other costs of running informers.[4]

This is not to argue that we can dismiss the possibility of some gains in the control of particular forms of crime through such techniques. But before we can make definitive statements we need more convincing measures of effectiveness. The Officers interviewed by Maguire and John argued that clear-up rates were a very poor measure of covert and proactive policing because the logic of such strategies was to focus on 'quality' of offences cleared-up or offenders convicted (Maguire and John 1995, p. 48). The danger of clear-up rates is that its focus on numbers encourages the police to prioritise high volume, 'easy' arrests: in drugs terms that might mean processing a large number of offenders for small-scale possession with intent offences when it might make more sense to concentrate on larger scale commercial suppliers.

More generally Maguire and John raise questions as to the extent to which the logic of covert or proactive policing has fully been embraced in the United Kingdom. They argue that in the main there have been merely piecemeal attempts to introduce proactivity often with little impact in practice: it is difficult to adapt organizational structures geared to reactive policing, such operations are very resource-intensive, and there are problems in getting precise intelligence to make reasonable decisions on whom to target for surveillance (Maguire and John 1995, p. 6). For the use of proactivity to become more generalized there is a need to assess properly its cost-effectiveness. For that there is a need to address the broader and intractable problem of assessing the 'quality' of police work.

Accountability: the challenge of the 'new' policing to adversarial and inquisitorial traditions

We are far from finding answers to the procedural challenges posed by covert and proactive investigations and policing based on new information technologies. In this volume and in other recent surveys by Gropp and Joubert as well as by Fijnaut and Marx, consistently the tension has been stressed between the traditional mechanisms of accountability in criminal process – whether they be adversarial or inquisitorial – and the new techniques (Gropp 1993; Joubert 1994; Fijnaut and Marx 1995). Within the inquisitorial tradition, the capacity of the prosecuting and examining magistrates to monitor and supervise the police investigation through the institution of the official *dossier* has been frequently compromised. To protect the secrecy considered essential for such policing, the police systematically resist the presentation of details in the official file. Overloaded prosecutors and examining magistrates may find it hard to look below the surface of apparently straightforward *dossiers*. Very often they cannot be prompted to do so by defence counsel because the lawyers do not themselves know what has happened. The upsetting of the relationship between judicial supervision and defence participation has been the cause of failures of accountability in several European jurisdictions, notably Holland and Belgium.[5] But limited access to information and its impact on participation rights is equally problematic for defence lawyers within the adversarial tradition where it is their responsibility autonomously to seek out and present exculpatory evidence. Most covert, proactive investigation is completed before the lawyer enters the case. If the police resist disclosure of the details of the investigation, arguing they must protect informers, surveillance posts or undercover officers, the defence may know little of how the operation was conducted or the relations between police and (participating) informers. Given that defence resources do not stretch to extensive independent investigation, the consequent shift in the balance of arms in the gathering of information threatens the very basis of adversarial claims to find truth through the presentation of competing accounts (See Field and Jörg in this volume).

The more diverse range of new information gathering techniques that are outlined in Part 2 add a further element to this potential disequilibrium. Hoogenboom's chapter points to the rise of systems of investigation that are invisible and untraceable without complete command of rapidly changing and advancing technologies. Can private lawyers ever expect to have the resources and knowledge to trace such investigation? Admittedly, not all clients are defenceless. There are claims that organized criminals themselves operate professional surveillance teams against the police (Klerks 1995, p. 128). There have also been reports that drug traffickers in Mexico had themselves successfully infiltrated police services.[6] But this is a very long way from the typical case of the legally aided lawyer defending marginal clients which have formed the majority of recent miscarriage of justice cases in Europe. Here tracing and challenging the basis of prosecution information is likely to become highly problematic.

Changes in the operation of systems of judicial supervision, in the balance of arms and in defence participation are only part of the way 'new information gathering' can shift the traditional balance between suspect and state. The traditional protections of due process such as the privilege against self-incrimination are sometimes being directly restricted but as often simply sidestepped. If, instead of openly accumulating information against somebody with the status of suspect, we start to use expanding technological capacities to accumulate and sort information gathered outside the criminal process, later making it available to the criminal justice authorities, much of the significance of the privilege as regulator of state/suspect relations is lost.[7]

Regulatory responses

Legal and administrative regulations

Legal regulation of such techniques may take many forms: it may set out the criteria for their use, who should determine whether they may be used in the individual case, and the precise procedures the investigators are to follow when using them. At the moment there is great variation in the form and extent of regulation even across the Northern European jurisdictions that we have examined. Joubert points out that some countries continue to regard covert or proactive policing as matters of state security which cannot be regulated by public statutes, while others regard methods as matters of police technique which simply do not require regulations (Joubert 1994, p. 22).

Nevertheless several countries in Northern Europe have moved in recent years to more regulated systems. Monjardet and Lévy suggest that the regulatory life of innovative investigative techniques has three phases (Monjardet and Lévy 1995). In the first, there is a complete absence of either internal administrative or formal legal rules regulating the practice, then gradually a regime of internal rules develops (phase 2) until finally systematic formal legal regulation is introduced (phase 3). But this volume suggests that the process is historically contingent on a wide range of variables, with political scandal (and its precise manifestation), the external pressures of constitutions[8] and a bureaucratic desire to 'rationalize' use of the technique all playing a part. Germany is perhaps the only European country to have fully reached the third stage with detailed legislation at both Länder and Federal level in the 1990s (Gropp 1993). As both De Roos and Field and Jörg explain in this volume, the Netherlands is moving in the same direction. As a result of the recommendations of the Van Traa commission, regulations are to be laid down in the Code of Criminal Procedure setting out criteria for, and constraints upon, the use of covert or proactive methods where these involve 'serious' intrusions into the privacy of the citizen. From a position in which the legal authority for covert and proactive policing rested merely in the general criminal procedure provisions governing policing functions and control was exercised by prosecutorial guidelines, legal regulation will become general. In Belgium the unregulated 1970s and 1980s gave way to (secret) prosecutorial guidelines in the 1990s but the move to more formal legal regulation has been more limited, to situations where Treaty obligations or ECHR decisions have demanded it (in relation to telephone tapping and datastorage: see Fijnaut and Verbruggen in this volume). In both countries, scandals which have exposed lack of accountability, have been the driving force for reform and yet the Netherlands has gone further toward phase 3 than Belgium. In France, scandal has, as yet, produced less developed internal regulations from the Prosecution Service: there is greater reliance on more traditional judicial supervision (especially by the *juge d'instruction*). Yet scandal in drug smuggling and trafficking cases has produced a particular statutory regime confined to the context of illegal narcotics. Otherwise in France the general criminal offence of 'interference with the intimacy of private life' may have had a constraining effect on police electronic surveillance. In England and Wales, despite evidence of problems in handling informers, scandals have not brought clear messages, with the result that generally regulation remains by internal administrative guidelines (with the exception of intrusive surveillance based on what would otherwise be trespass, which is given a statutory basis by the 1997 Police Act). However it seems likely that increasing Europeanization will lead to some kind of rapprochement of this highly variable pattern of regulatory systems.

It is possible to overemphasize the importance of having precise criteria and constraints laid down in formal legislation. In the context of interrogation, the Police and Criminal Evidence Act 1984 has demonstrated the advantage of detailed administrative Codes of Practice: they can set out procedural requirements in language (reasonably) accessible to police officers which may nevertheless entail external scrutiny. This is through sanction for breach through exclusion of evidence at trial. Not every technical violation leads to exclusion but 'serious and substantial' breach of key provisions will: arguably a mature approach to enforcement.[9] But few European jurisdictions appear to have applied this regulatory approach to covert and proactive policing.[10] No doubt if they did there would be some move to reshape behaviour towards new unregulated uses (by for example using the intelligence obtained in ways not aimed at prosecution but rather extra-legal sanctions). However, the evidence of PACE is that the room for discretionary manoeuvre and abuse can be reduced by legal change (contrast on this the position of Dixon 1992, with McConville, Sanders and Leng 1991). A possible alternative, particularly for those jurisdictions like France where there is a reluctance to exclude relevant evidence, might be an external disciplinary system controlled by judges or prosecuting magistrates in which breach of Prosecutor Guidelines could be sanctioned.

Due process and privacy: towards prior judicial authority

It is clear that regulation of proactive and covert policing requires a different focus to that of reactive policing with guarantees of privacy becoming central rather than due process (a point made by Alldridge 1996). Full conceptions of due process guarantees are incompatible with many covert and proactive policing techniques. They can often be sidestepped where intelligence accumulation is not geared toward prosecution: the police do not need to adhere to procedural constraints which are to be enforced at a criminal trial that will not take place. Further, even where evidence-gathering and prosecution is the ultimate goal, the capacity to assert due process rights such as the right to silence or to access to a lawyer or disclosure of evidence will, in practice, necessarily be seriously weakened because they rely on conscious defence strategies. The police will be seeking to secure evidence secretly against the suspects: they may not yet have committed the offence and will very probably have no notion that they are subject to investigation and need to assert defensive rights. Even later in the process, when the target acquires the official status of suspect due process rights are likely to be attenuated to protect the secrecy of the new methods. The absolutist line would be to require reasonable suspicion of a specific offence before the use of covert methods and that once the target is arrested the defence should always be given early access to a dossier containing full details of the methods used and their results (Brants and Field 1995a, p. 72). But, as we have seen, this would significantly reduce the crime investigation potential of such techniques. Given the uncertainties about the empirical evidence as to their effectiveness, that might be thought to be an acceptable cost for preserving defence participation rights and the due process guarantees that rely on that participation. But the political choices being made about the new policing of Europe seem unlikely to run in that direction.

If, to make possible covert policing, one permits *some* erosion of traditional due process guarantees built around strong defence rights, the regulatory focus must turn toward privacy rights. Covert or proactive techniques that entail significant intrusions of privacy should always require prior judicial authority (an argument made in detail in Field and Jörg in this volume). But there is no European consensus as to whether such authority is required before interference with such rights, even amongst the limited number of Northern European jurisdictions studied in this volume. In Belgium, internal guidelines require prosecuting magistrates generally to supervise the use of informers; prosecuting or investigating magistrates must be informed as soon as possible of surveillance operations and they need to approve some operations in advance – where infiltration by the police is proposed or where a criminal offence is to be permitted. Metering or tapping of phones requires approval by examining magistrates or, in urgent cases, prosecuting magistrates (see Fijnaut and Verbruggen). The new Act in the Netherlands will require prior approval by prosecuting magistrates of techniques that require serious intrusion of privacy. Thus systematic surveillance of suspects, the covert entry and limited search of non-residential premises, the use of informers (whether or not they are participating) and undercover infiltration by the police and by citizens will need to be authorized in advance by the Public Prosecutor.The interception of communications (including bugging as well as the tapping of phone and fax) will require the Public Prosecutor to get prior permission from the rechter-commissaris (see De Roos and Field and Jörg for discussion). In Germany the Code of Criminal Procedure requires that monitoring and recording private conversations be authorized beforehand by a judge or, in urgent cases, by a prosecuting magistrate (Gropp 1993, p. 29). Federal law on control of organized crime requires that generally undercover operations be authorized by prosecuting magistrates and in some cases, a judge (though outside the context of organized crime state legislation varies on the need for such prior judicial authority (Gropp 1993, p. 32; Joubert 1994, pp. 32-34). In France, prior authority for infiltration and sponsoring of participating informers is required from prosecutors but only in the context of drugs cases. However prosecutors or examining magistrates would normally expect to be consulted about surveillance and undercover work in other street-crime contexts (see Field in this volume). Telephone taps require permission from examining magistrates. Political surveillance and monitoring is a different – and much less regulated – matter (contrast Journès in this volume). In England and Wales police autonomy, the lack of prosecuting or examining magistrates and a pre-trial supervisory relationship between police and judiciary, restricts prior judicial authority to intrusive surveillance as defined by the 1997 Police Act (see John and Maguire). The adversarial reliance on due process guarantees based on extensive defence rights, and probably traditional views of judicial function as based on the model of trial referee, seems to have cut across extensive pre-trial involvement of judges (see Field and Jörg).

Seeing privacy rights as the key to the regulation of the 'new' policing means that the European Convention on Human Rights may play a vital role in establishing a European standard. Article 8 establishes individuals' rights to respect for private or family life, their home or correspondence. Article 8.2 permits interference with these rights only if 'in accordance with the law' and where 'necessary in a democratic society' inter alia for the 'prevention of disorder or crime'. The *Kruslin and Huvig* case explained the meaning of the requirement that infringement of privacy rights under the Convention was permissible only if 'in accordance with law'.[11] Not only does the interference have to be proportionate to the needs of policing in a democratic society, but there must be a legal basis for intrusive surveillance the provisions of which are reasonably clear and precise and accessible to the individual. Further the Court approved its earlier comments in *Klass v Federal Republic of Germany*[12] that a system of telephone tapping (and presumably by implication other covert or proactive techniques that interfere with privacy), must contain 'adequate and effective guarantees against abuse'. In that case the Court had emphasized that the then West Germany's system of accountability involved scrutiny by bodies other than those carrying out the surveillance and with sufficient powers to exercise an effective and continuous control. This clearly does not *require* prior judicial authority: the German system approved in that case had no such requirement.[13] Further in *Esbester v UK*[14] the Commission stressed that in determining whether there were effective and adequate guarantees against abuse reference to other national systems was of limited relevance. The task of the Commission was to determine whether the system under examination in the concrete case passed the threshold of acceptability imposed by the Convention. Normally diversity of systems of regulation in Europe counts against precise and demanding requirements (Harris et al. 1995, pp. 9-11). Prior judicial authority would have to become more generalized at a domestic level to become a standard enforced at the European level.

The situations to which these requirements apply – infringements of the rights in Article 8.1 – cannot be very clearly stated. The European Court of Human Rights has not always clearly defined the notion of private life, nor separated the scope of a state's obligation to respect private life and the kind of claims that might justify interference (Harris et al. 1995, p. 305). However, the Court has adopted a broad view of the right to private life so that it is not confined to the idea of the sanctity of one's home or other physical places in relation to which one has exclusive rights of access.[15] There is also protection of one's right to lead one's life and establish personal relationships without outside interference – a concept clearly pertinent to covert policing by surveillance or undercover operations. This may even extend to relations in a business context where there is a reasonable expectation of privacy. But the precise scope of the idea of one's psychological 'private space' is not yet clear. Case law suggests that slight or foreseeable intrusions on one's right to be left alone and not to be interfered with in places to which others have legal access, may well not constitute infringement of one's right to respect for private life. Thus much 'shadowing', use of long-range mikes and photographing, where suspects are in public places, may not require legal justification (Harris et al. 1995, p. 309).[16] Further the use of the limiting concept of a 'legitimate expectation of privacy' in *Lüdi v Switzerland*,[17] and the notion that those involved in crime must expect the police to interfere with their activities, may mean that most undercover work – perhaps even when intensive and long-term – will not constitute interference.[18] (Unless of course it turns out the 'suspect' is not in fact committing offences when presumably he or she has a reasonable expectation of privacy). On the other hand, respect for 'correspondence' would extend to interception of letters, metering or tapping telephones and other forms of communications where there is an expectation of confidentiality (Harris et al. 1995, p. 320). Similarly the collection and storage of data about an individual without his consent may interfere with rights to respect for private life (Harris et al. 1995, pp. 309-310).

Due process and participation rights: the right to know

If states accept that some limitations must be placed on defence rights to information (the right to know) to protect the secrecy necessary to covert or proactive policing (Brants and Field 1995a, p. 72), the least that must be demanded is balanced determination of defence claims to information and participation, and active and early judicial involvement to determine those rights and claims. Restrictions may take two forms in relation to covert or proactive policing: of defence rights to pose questions directly to undercover officers or informers and of defence rights to information on the detail of the methods used. Such restrictions should be decided by judicial figures who themselves know enough of the detail of the case – necessarily prior to the prosecution opening statement at trial – to determine whether non-disclosure or limitation of rights to pose questions might compromise a legitimately conducted defence. If the relevant judicial figure is to be in a position to decide this, it may well require in some cases, that questions be posed in the pre-trial process by judges to those who may or may not then testify at trial. This will require more radical procedural innovation for adversarial jurisdictions than for those from the inquisitorial tradition.

The extent to which the Convention provides criteria for such procedures varies. Articles 6.1 and 6.3.d have been repeatedly invoked to place constraints on the use of the testimony of anonymous witnesses. Domestic law in several European jurisdictions has had to be modified.[19] However more general questions of disclosure are regulated only by very vague standards. Article 6.1 of the Convention states the general principle that individuals have a right to a fair trial and Article 6.3.d that those charged with criminal offences have the 'right to examine or have examined witnesses against

[them] and to obtain the attendance and examination or witnesses on his behalf under the same conditions as witnesses against him.' The practice of basing convictions mainly or exclusively on the written evidence of anonymous informers or undercover officers and not giving the defence the right to pose questions to the witness was declared contrary to these rights.[20] The principles are not entirely clear in their detail nor, in some expositions by the Strasbourg court, terribly demanding.[21]

The broader question of the range of information about the detail and results of covert or proactive policing that must be disclosed to the defence is even less clearly regulated. Article 6.3.b declares that those charged with criminal offences have the right, inter alia, to adequate 'facilities' for the preparation of their defence. In *Jespers v Belgium*, the European Commission argued that rights under Article 6.3.b were an aspect of 'equality of arms' (a well established requirement under the Convention) because such defence rights were the counterbalance to the superior investigative resources of the prosecution. This included the right to any facilities 'which assist or may assist [the accused] in the preparation of his defence' and access to all 'relevant elements that have been or could be collected by the competent authorities.'[22] In *Edwards v UK* the European Court clearly stated that it was a requirement of fairness under Article 6.1 that the prosecution disclose to the defence all 'material evidence for or against the accused'.[23] In *Bendenoun v France* the European Court accepted that the right to a fair trial might extend to a requirement to disclose documents upon which the prosecution did not seek to rely.[24] This is also implicit in the *Jespers* case.

Nevertheless, in accordance with its normal cautious practice of limiting decisions to the facts of the case, the Court has not considered the extent of any possible exception to the disclosure principle on public interest grounds such as protecting police investigation techniques. One judge in the *Edwards* case did comment that public interest immunity could never justify non-disclosure of relevant evidence in criminal cases but it is not clear whether such a trenchant view will find general favour.[25] Some views have been expressed as to the required precision of defence requests for information – a characteristic difficulty in covert policing cases. In *Jespers*, the Commission stressed that the applicant could not be expected to specify which undisclosed documents should be made available because the very lack of access complained of made this impossible to do. However, in *Bendenoun* the Court argued that it was 'necessary, at least, that the person concerned should have given, even if only briefly, specific reasons for his request'.[26] Because the applicant had never put forward any precise argument as to why he needed to obtain copies of the full file on him to conduct his defence the

Court decided there was no breach of the Convention.[27] In the wake of the Criminal Procedure and Investigations Act 1996, which has restricted prosecution duties of disclosure exactly to protect covert and proactive methods, civil rights organizations in Britain are urging lawyers to go to Strasbourg to establish whether the Act breaches the Convention (Wadham 1997). Only active (pre-trial) judicial decision-making, based on a thorough reading of the file and in some cases pre-trial interview of witnesses can possibly reconcile the needs of policing with the claims of defendants to know relevant information about the investigation (see Field and Jörg). The requirements of the European Court have not as yet been anywhere near as precise or demanding as this.

Enough has been said to indicate that the European Court is not suddenly going to resolve the problems of accountability posed by the 'new policing'. The nature of an interference with privacy, the procedural constraints required to regulate interference, the exceptions permitted to principles of defence rights to information, are still answered, if at all, at very high levels of abstraction. More concrete questions have not even been posed. What are the legitimate criteria for suspicion that might ground use of invasive techniques in the individual case? Should it be enough that there are reasonable grounds to suspect the target of serious crime or should a narrower criterion be required? Should police officers and civilians be permitted to commit criminal offences? If so, should immunities be at the level of substantive law or granted on the basis of the 'opportunity principle' in prosecution? In relation to some of these questions, Strasbourg may prompt a generalizing of common standards but given the current lack of a European consensus, most will inevitably need to be addressed at the level of domestic law.

Final remarks: Beyond criminal process?

The rise of the new police information-gathering techniques charted in this book permit no simple response: its relationship to individual or collective freedoms is a highly contingent one. Many people travelling home at night on public transport systems with manned surveillance cameras on the stations or trains may experience this as increased freedom rather than an invasion of privacy. But the extent to which these technologies produce social freedoms rather than constraints and how one judges this depends on clear-eyed assessment of their real effectiveness, sensible restraint on their use, and clear and effective mechanisms of accountability. Some combination of prior judicial authority, detailed Codes of Practice (with exclusion of evidence where significant breach takes place) and closer judicial supervision of rights to information might address these problems. Given the recent past in a number of European jurisdictions it is easy to be pessimistic even on this score (which one might argue simply requires these jurisdictions to make good on their general promises about the rule of law and rational policy-making).

However, there are even more problematic issues about the 'reach' of traditional rule of law notions of accountability in criminal process: we have stressed that perhaps the key decision in the use of the new intelligence and information gathering techniques is the decision to target someone. Like all selective enforcement decisions, such questions of targeting are not merely technical matters of professional judgement but are questions of weighing competing social harms. What is the kind of serious offender who might merit such attention? At an individual level that must remain a technical decision for investigators, but at the level of general priorities in principle systems for defining targets should involve some democratic influence that nevertheless respects the legitimate expectations of marginalized minorities (for a perceptive general analysis of the problem of democratic control of the police see Lustgarten 1986). This is a more radical and problematic demand because mechanisms of accountability for these value-judgements on social harm are notoriously rudimentary at policy level even for the more 'visible' decisions on prosecution.[28]

Perhaps the most intractable problem is control on the use of the techniques where their purpose is not predominantly to support evidence-gathering in preparation for criminal trial but rather disruption of the lives of the targets. The potential is general. One can oppose the granting or renewal of licences necessary or useful for the targets' businesses, one can pass information to the Revenue or Social Security or their landlord, one can let the targets know they are under surveillance or that all their associates are systematically being offered money to inform on them, one pass distorted, but apparently informed information about them within the circles of professional or career criminals. The capacity to mess with peoples' lives is almost limitless if one knows enough about them. And the arrival of national security services – for whom criminal prosecution is not the first option for 'neutralizing' threats – onto the traditional policing terrains in the last ten years is likely to accelerate the tendency.

Systems of accountability within the criminal process simply cannot routinely reach these activities. Organizations that are geared to work that is purely or predominantly intelligence-gathering need mechanisms of accountability outside the criminal process. An effective oversight system outside ordinary criminal procedure is required that would play a role analogous to – but more substantial than – the oversight systems existing in relation to security intelligence work (Klerks 1995, p. 105 and passim). But a critical culture towards 'the technological fix' to crime control within the mass media, human rights organizations, political parties, and the academic community may be as crucial. Put like this, it is easy to be pessimistic about the future.

Notes

1 Secondary clear-ups are where a suspect who has been arrested and admitted a principal offence (the primary clear-up) then admits to further offences, usually on the understanding that no additional punishment will accrue. Comparing the year 1992-3 with 1993-4, the number of primary clear-ups for burglary in the Metropolitan Police area decreased by 5 per cent but the number of secondary clear-ups increased by 103.8 per cent.
2 Though some of them are proactive in a broader crime preventive sense.
3 Audit Commission 1993.
4 Dunnighan and Norris 1996. See also Dunnighan 1994.
5 See Van Outrive and Cappelle 1995, pp. 148-153, and Fijnaut and Verbruggen in this volume for Belgium; see Klerks 1995, pp. 110-114, 122, 128-129, Brants and Field 1995a, pp. 51-61 and De Roos in this volume on the Netherlands.
6 Several members of the anti-drug unit (INCD) had been arrested, among them the head of the unit for protecting (by tipping off) key members of Mexico's drug cartels: *Le Monde*, 14 and 20 February 1997.
7 In this volume, see Lamp, Levi and Kerver on powers to extract information from financial bodies, Costigan and Brants on powers to do so from journalists, as well as Alldridge and Swart on the erosion of the privilege against self-incrimination generally.
8 The regulatory regime in Germany owes its origin to a 1983 judgement of the Federal Constitutional Court. See Gropp 1993, p. 21.
9 *R v Keenan* (1990) 90 Cr. App. R. 1.
10 A Code of Practice on Intrusive Surveillance has been issued under section 101 of the Police Act 1997. As yet the courts' approach to breach has not been tested.
11 ECHR 24 April 1990, Series A, vol. 176-A and 176-B, (1990) 12 EHRR 528.
12 ECHR 6 September 1978, Series A, vol. 28, (1979/80) 2 EHRR 214.
13 See Churchill and Young 1991, pp. 321-326.
14 (1993) 18 EHRR CD 72.

15 See *Niemietz v Germany* ECHR 16 December 1992, Series A, vol. 251-B. Confirmed in *Halford v United Kingdom*, ECHR 25 June 1997, not yet officially reported.
16 The point made in recent Dutch case law: see De Roos and Field and Jörg in this volume.
17 ECHR 15 June 1992, Series A, vol. 238, 12 EHRR 173.
18 See the critique offered by Joubert 1994, p. 21 on the basis that all individuals should have a right to privacy, interference with which should require justification and regulation.
19 Generally see Harris et al 1995, pp. 211-212. For France see the cases in (1991) *Revue de Science Criminelle et Droit Pénal, Chronique de Jurisprudence*, for Italy see Chiaviario, p. 25 and for the Netherlands see Beijer, Cobley and Klip 1995, p. 283.
20 *Kostovski v Netherlands* ECHR 20 November 1989, Series A, vol. 166, (1990) 12 EHRR 434.
21 See discussion in Harris et al. 1995, pp. 211-212 and *Doorson v Netherlands*, (1996) 22 EHRR 330, *Van Mechelen a.o. v Netherlands*, 23 April 1997 (discussed in the chapter by Cape and Spronken).
22 27 DR 61 (1981) at 87-8.
23 (1992) 15 EHRR 417; see Field and Young 1994.
24 (1994) 18 EHRR 54 at 77.
25 (1992) 15 EHRR 417, at 433.
26 (1994) 18 EHRR 54, at 77-8.
27 Though the fact that the applicant had at certain stages actually had access to full file weighed in this decision.
28 For a comparative analysis see Brants and Field 1995b. For an example of the kind of arguments for greater democratic control of policing policy that became prominent on the left in the 1980s see Jefferson and Grimshaw 1984.

References

Alldridge, P. (1996), *'They spread their poison in secrete...', Privacy in Substantive and Adjectival English Criminal Law*, unpublished paper given to Law Faculty in Uppsala, Sweden.

Audit Commission (1993), *Helping Police with their Enquiries: Tackling Crime Effectively*, London: HMSO.

Beijer, A., C. Cobley and A. Klip (1995), Witness Evidence, Article 6 of the European Convention on Human Rights and the Principle of Open Justice, in: in: P. Fennell, C. Harding, N. Jörg and B. Swart (eds.), *Criminal Justice in Europe: A Comparative Study*, Oxford: Clarendon Press, pp. 283-300.

Brants, C. and S. Field (1995a), *Proactive Policing and Participation Rights: Convergence and Drift in European Criminal Process*, Deventer: Kluwer.

Brants, C. and S. Field (1995b), Discretion and Accountability in Prosecution: A Comparative Perspective on Keeping Crime out of Court, in: P. Fennell et al. (eds.) *Criminal Justice in Europe: A Comparative Study*, Oxford: Clarendon Press, pp. 127-148.

Chiaviario, M., *La Riforma del Processo Penale*, p. 25.

Churchill, R. and J. Young (1991), Compliance with Judgements of the European Court of Human Rights and Decisions of the Committee of Ministers: the Experience of the United Kingdom 1975-1987, *British Yearbook of International Law* 283.

Dixon, D. (1992), Legal Regulation and Policing Practice, 1 *Social and Legal Studies* 515.

Dunnighan, C. (1994), Helping with Enquiries?, 17 *Criminal Justice Matters* 12.

Dunnighan, C. and C. Norris (1996), The Role of the Informer in the Criminal Justice System, summarised by D. Campbell, Police are using more informers than ever but are they delivering value for money?, *The Guardian* 30 April.

Field, S. and J. Young (1994), Disclosure, Appeals and Procedural Traditions: Edwards v United Kingdom, *Criminal Law Review* 264.

Fijnaut, C. and G.T. Marx (eds.) (1995), *Undercover: Police Surveillance in Comparative Perspective*, The Hague: Kluwer Law International.

Garland, D. (1996), The Limits of the Sovereign State. 36(4) *British Journal of Criminology*, 445.

Gropp, W. (1993), Special Methods of Investigation for Combatting Organized Crime, 1 *European Journal of Crime, Criminal Law and Criminal Justice*, pp. 20-36.

Harris, D., M. O'Boyle and C. Warbrick (1995), *Law of the European Convention on Human Rights*, London: Butterworths.

Jefferson, T. and R. Grimshaw (1984), *Controlling the Constable*, London: Frederick Muller.

Joubert, C. (1994), Undercover Policing - A Comparative Study, 2 *European Journal of Crime, Criminal Law and Criminal Justice*, pp. 18-38.

Klerks, P. (1995), Covert Policing in the Netherlands, in: C. Fijnaut and G.T. Marx, *Undercover: Police Surveillance in Comparative Perspective*, The Hague: Kluwer Law International, pp. 103-140.

Lustgarten, L. (1986), *The Governance of Police*, London: Sweet and Maxwell.

Maguire, M. and T. John (1995), *Intelligence, Surveillance and Informants: Integrated Approaches*, Crime Detection and Prevention Series: Paper No 64, London: Home Office Police Research Group.

McConville, M., A. Sanders and R. Leng (1991), *The Case for the Prosecution*, London: Routledge.

Monjardet, D. and R. Lévy (1995), Undercover Policing in France: Elements for Description and Analysis, in: C. Fijnaut and G.T. Marx, *Undercover: Police*

Surveillance in Comparative Perspective, The Hague: Kluwer Law International, pp. 29-53.

Outrive, L. van and J. Cappelle (1995), Twenty years of Undercover Policing in Belgium: The Regulation of a Risky Police Practice, in: C. Fijnaut and G.T. Marx (eds.), *Undercover: Police Surveillance in Comparative Perspective*, The Hague: Kluwer Law International, pp. 141-153.

Stockdale, J. and P. Gresham (1995), *Combating Burglary: an Evaluation of Three Strategies*, Police Research Group Crime Detection and Prevention Series: Paper No 59, London: Home Office.

Wadham, J. (1997), Prosecution disclosure, crime and human rights, 147(6791) *New Law Journal* 697.